TOWARD SAFER FOOD

Perspectives on Risk and Priority Setting

EDITED BY

SANDRA A. HOFFMANN
MICHAEL R. TAYLOR

RESOURCES FOR THE FUTURE
WASHINGTON, DC, USA

An RFF Press book
Published by Resources for the Future
1616 P Street NW
Washington, DC 20036–1400
USA
www.rffpress.org

Library of Congress Cataloging-in-Publication Data

Toward safer food : perspectives on risk and priority setting / Sandra Hoffmann and Michael R. Taylor, editors.
    p.   cm.
  An RFF Press book
  Includes index.
  ISBN 1-891853-89-9 (cloth : alk. paper)—ISBN 1-891853-90-2 (pbk. : alk. paper)
  1. Food—Safety measures.   2. Food adulteration and inspection.
I. Hoffmann, Sandra.   II. Taylor, Michael R.
  TX531.T85   2004
  363.19′2—dc22   2004014237

The paper in this book meets the guidelines for permanence and durability of the Committee on Production Guidelines for Book Longevity of the Council on Library Resources.

This book was designed and typeset in Minion by Agnew's, Inc. It was copyedited by Chernow Editorial Services, Inc. The cover was designed by Maggie Powell. Cover photo © CORBIS.

ISBN 1-891853-89-9 (cloth)   1-891853-90-2 ISBN (paper)

About Resources for the Future *and* RFF Press

Resources for the Future (RFF) improves environmental and natural resource policymaking worldwide through independent social science research of the highest caliber. Founded in 1952, RFF pioneered the application of economics as a tool for developing more effective policy about the use and conservation of natural resources. Its scholars continue to employ social science methods to analyze critical issues concerning pollution control, energy policy, land and water use, hazardous waste, climate change, biodiversity, and the environmental challenges of developing countries.

RFF Press supports the mission of RFF by publishing book-length works that present a broad range of approaches to the study of natural resources and the environment. Its authors and editors include RFF staff, researchers from the larger academic and policy communities, and journalists. Audiences for publications by RFF Press include all of the participants in the policymaking process—scholars, the media, advocacy groups, NGOs, professionals in business and government, and the public.

Resources for the Future

Directors

Contents

PART III
Tools for Risk-Based Assessment of Food Safety Policy Priorities

PART IV
Identifying Lessons

Preface

The century-old food safety system in the United States has changed dramatically over the years in response to technological, economic, and social change, and resulting change in the nature of both real and perceived food safety problems. The government and the food industry recognize the importance of food safety to the success of the food system at home and internationally, and U.S. regulatory programs for food safety are among the strongest in the world. The decade of the 1990s saw food safety emerge, however, as a recognized public health issue, with highly visible outbreaks of illness associated with pathogens such as *E. coli* O157:H7, *Listeria monocytogenes,* and *Salmonella,* and with much-improved surveillance of foodborne illness by the Centers for Disease Control and Prevention. The focus of regulatory oversight shifted during the 1990s toward prevention of illness through adoption of Hazard Analysis and Critical Control Points (HACCP) approaches to preventive process control for food safety.

During this period, two seminal reports from the National Academy of Sciences (NAS) pointed the way toward further progress on food safety. The 1998 report *Ensuring Safe Food From Production to Consumption* called for a more integrated science- and risk-based approach to food safety, including more attention to risk-based priority setting and resource allocation. The 2003 NAS report *Scientific Criteria to Ensure Safe Food* called for use of risk-based performance standards in food safety regulation and better linking of proposed food safety standards and interventions with health outcomes, measured in terms of reduced risk of foodborne illness. These reports recognize and build on the recent progress in CDC's illness surveillance programs, the efforts of the federal food safety regulatory agencies to assess and target preventively the risks posed by specific microbial hazards in food, and the food industry's implementation of technological and process control interventions to reduce risk.

The widely desired direction of change to improve food safety is clear, but much remains to be done to move in that direction and to achieve significant improvement in how society's resources are used to reduce foodborne illness. As outlined in the NAS reports, there are statutory and institutional obstacles to optimal risk-based resource allocation across the food safety regulatory system as a whole. Regardless of the statutory or institutional structure for food safety, however, there is a need for new analytical and decision tools to compare and rank food safety risks, to prioritize opportunities to reduce risk (taking into account feasibility, effectiveness, and cost of possible interventions), and to allocate efforts and resources accordingly. In short, there is a need for a risk analysis framework and priority-setting tool kit for food safety that does not currently exist.

The need for such a framework and tool kit has captured the attention of scientists, policy analysts and policymakers in government and the research community, and work to develop the framework and tools is underway. *Toward Safer Food* is an effort to present in one place, at this critical early stage in the development of a new food safety framework, an overview of the subject of risk-based food safety priority setting. By its nature, this is a multidisciplinary effort. The book thus brings together leading food safety scientists, risk analysts, and economists, as well as highly experienced food safety regulators and policy analysts, to survey what is known about the data and tools available to construct the new risk analysis and priority setting framework, and to point the way forward. It provides a multidisciplinary introduction to existing data, research, and methodological and conceptual approaches that are being drawn on in this effort. It also provides an overview of the institutional context in which this effort is taking place. An effort has been made to make this introduction accessible to people from a wide variety of backgrounds, while not compromising the core conceptual sophistication needed to understand the challenges involved in developing the analytical framework and tools for integrated and risk-based food safety priority setting. The purpose of the book is to provide a common resource on which this multidisciplinary effort can draw. The editors hope that this book will help the U.S. move beyond calls for an integrated, risk-based food safety system toward its actual construction.

SANDRA A. HOFFMANN
MICHAEL R. TAYLOR

Contributors

ROBERT BUCHANAN currently serves as senior science advisor at the U.S. Food and Drug Administration Center for Food Safety and Applied Nutrition. He has also served as deputy administrator for science with the U.S. Department of Agriculture Food Safety and Inspection Service. He was a member of the National Academy of Sciences Institute of Medicine Committee on Emerging Microbiological Threats and is widely published in the food safety field.

JEAN BUZBY is an economist at the U.S. Department of Agriculture's Economic Research Service (ERS). For the past decade, she has researched the economics of food safety, including foodborne illness costs, product liability for food poisoning cases, and the intersection between food safety and international trade. Other research interests include school nutrition programs and food consumption.

JULIE A. CASWELL is a professor in the Department of Resource Economics at the University of Massachusetts. She has studied the operation of domestic and international food systems, with particular emphasis on the economics of food quality, especially safety and nutrition, and international trade. Her book publications include *Economics of Food Safety, Valuing Food Safety and Nutrition,* and *Global Food Trade and Consumer Demand for Quality.*

STEPHEN CRUTCHFIELD is the staff analysis coordinator for the U.S. Department of Agriculture's Economic Research Service (ERS) and the deputy director for Staff Analysis and Communications in ERS's Food and Rural Economics Division. At ERS he has directed and conducted research on the costs and benefits of private and public policies relating to nutrition, food consumption, food demand, and food safety in the U.S.

MICHAEL L. DEKAY is an associate professor in the Department of Engineering and Public Policy and the Heinz School of Public Policy and Management at Carnegie Mellon University. His recent research has focused on judgment and decision making, including risk perception, risk ranking, precautionary reasoning, and repeated decisions. He is currently a member of the National Research Council's Panel on Public Participation in Environmental Assessment and Decision Making. He has authored or coauthored numerous articles, including several in Risk Analysis and Medical Decision Making.

LAWRENCE J. DYCKMAN, director for Natural Resources and Environment at the U.S. General Accounting Office (GAO), is responsible for GAO's work on food and agricultural issues. He previously managed Superfund program reviews at the U.S. Environmental Protection Agency and served as associate director in EPA's Housing and Community Development issue area.

PENELOPE A. FENNER-CRISP is executive director of the Risk Science Institute of the International Life Sciences Institute (ILSI). She formerly served as a senior science advisor and director of the U.S. Environmental Protection Agency's Office of Pesticide Programs (OPP). She has written extensively on scientific and regulatory issues related to drinking water contaminants, toxic substances and pesticides, including endocrine disruptors.

PAUL S. FISCHBECK is a professor in the Department of Social and Decision Sciences and the Department of Engineering and Public Policy at Carnegie Mellon University. He is also director of the University's Center for the Study and Improvement of Regulation and coeditor with Scott Farrow of *Improving Regulation: Cases in Environment, Health, and Safety.* He has completed risk assessments on the space shuttle, off-shore oil platforms, school buses, oil tankers, and fire sprinklers.

BARUCH FISCHHOFF is Howard Heinz University Professor in the Department of Social and Decision Sciences and Department of Engineering and Public Policy at Carnegie Mellon University. He is a member of the Institute of Medicine of the National Academy of Sciences and has served on more than two dozen of its committees. His research includes risk perception and communication, risk management, adolescent decisionmaking, medical informed consent, and environmental protection.

H. KEITH FLORIG is a senior research engineer in the Department of Engineering and Public Policy at Carnegie Mellon University. His recent research explores risk and economic development in China, public preferences for home-land security interventions, and processes for managing risks of ionizing and nonionizing radiation.

PAUL D. FRENZEN is a demographer with U.S. Department of Agriculture's Economic Research Service (ERS). His research interests include measuring the burden of illness due to known and unknown foodborne pathogens, and con-sumer acceptance of safer food products and technologies.

ELISE GOLAN is an economist at the U.S. Department of Agriculture's Eco-nomic Research Service (ERS). She served as a senior staff economist on the President's Council of Economic Advisers from 1998-99. At ERS, she focused on the distributional consequences of food policy, the economics of product differentiation, and domestic and international food safety policy.

JAMES K. HAMMITT is an associate professor and director of the Harvard Cen-ter for Risk Analysis. His research includes investigation and comparison of methods for valuing health risk, such as willingness to pay and health-adjusted life years. His current focus includes the management of long-term environ-mental issues with important scientific uncertainties, such as global climate change and stratospheric-ozone depletion and the characterization of social preferences over health and environmental risks.

SANDRA A. HOFFMANN is a fellow at Resources for the Future with research interests in food safety and the environmental impacts of agriculture. She is developing a comparative risk ranking to inform priority setting for U.S. food safety policy. She has authored publications on water quality management, for-est resources, and the regional economic impacts of environmental and natu-ral resource policy.

KAREN E. JENNI is a principal decision analyst in the Denver Office of Geomatrix Consultants, Inc. Her current areas of interest include using deci-sion analysis methods to support large-scale environmental policy decisions and working with large companies to develop consistent and cost-effective corporate-wide strategies for dealing with specific environmental issues.

HELEN H. JENSEN is professor of Economics and leader of the Food and Nutri-tion Policy Research Division in the Center for Agricultural and Rural Devel-opment at Iowa State University. Her research focuses on food demand, the economics of food safety and food hazard control, food assistance and nutri-tion policies, and issues related to food security. She has published extensively in the areas of food policy and food safety, and has contributed as both editor of and contributor to numerous proceedings and books, including *Food Security: New Solutions for the 21st Century.*

ALAN J. KRUPNICK is a senior fellow at Resources for the Future. His research focuses on the benefits, costs, and design of air pollution policies, as well as climate policy and urban transportation and development issues. He cochaired an advisory committee that counseled the U.S. Environmental Protection Agency on new ozone and particulate standards and served as senior economist on the President's Council of Economic Advisers, advising the Clinton administration on environmental and natural resource policy issues.

FRED KUCHLER has worked at the U.S. Department of Agriculture's Economic Research Service (ERS) since 1981. His current projects include food labeling and connections between knowledge and weight status. His past work covered foodborne illness, dietary exposure to agricultural pesticides, and impacts of biotechnology.

RICHARD A. MERRILL is the Daniel Caplin Professor of Law and Sullivan and Cromwell Research Professor of Law at the University of Virginia School of Law. He served as chief counsel to the U.S. Food and Drug Administration in 1975 and on several Institute of Medicine committees of the National Academy of Sciences that explored risk assessment in environmental decision-making, pesticide regulation, and food addition reform. Merrill has been a consultant to the Office of Technology Assessment of the U.S. Congress, the White House Office of Science and Technology Policy, and the Environmental Protection Agency.

KARA M. MORGAN is a senior advisor for Risk Analysis at the U.S. Food and Drug Administration. Her research interests focus on developing communication methods and process tools to improve decision making. She recently assisted in the development of a process that used quality principles to prioritize data gathering efforts for the residual risk program at U.S. EPA.

M. GRANGER MORGAN is professor and head of the Department of Engineering and Public Policy at Carnegie Mellon University, where he is also University Professor and Lord Chair Professor in Engineering; he is also a professor in the Department of Electrical and Computer Engineering and in the H. John Heinz III School of Public Policy and Management. He is a coauthor with Max Henrion of *Uncertainty: A Guide to Dealing with Uncertainty in Quantitative Risk and Policy Analysis* and coauthor with Baruch Fischhoff, Ann Bostrom, and Cynthia J. Atman of *Risk Communication: A Mental Models Approach.*

J. GLENN MORRIS, JR., is currently professor and chair of the Department of Epidemiology and Preventive Medicine at the University of Maryland School of Medicine. An epidemiologist with an extensive research and publication record in the field of foodborne and emerging pathogens, Morris worked at the U.S. Department of Agriculture Food Safety and Inspection Service from 1994–96, where he played a key role in development of the new Pathogen Reduction/HACCP regulations and in creation of a strong public health focus in the agency.

PETER NELSON is a research associate at Resources for the Future. His research interests include the accuracy of regulatory costs estimates and the linkages between transportation planning and air quality policy. Before joining RFF he was editor-in-chief of Greenwire, a daily environmental news briefing service.

KATHERINE RALSTON conducts research and analysis at the U.S. Department of Agriculture's Economic Research Service (ERS) on the economics of food safety and nutrition. Before coming to ERS, she worked in Indonesia, researching intrahousehold food distribution and timely warning systems to prevent food crises.

TANYA ROBERTS is an economist at the at the U.S. Department of Agriculture's Economic Research Service (ERS). She pioneered ERS' estimates of the social costs of bacterial and parasitic foodborne diseases, and testified before Congress in 1987. Her current research interests include the public and private economic incentives for food safety innovations, the economics of new rapid tests for pathogens, and integrating risk assessment into benefit–cost analyses of control options.

BERNARD A. SCHWETZ is the acting principal deputy commissioner of the U.S. Food and Drug Administration (FDA) and an adjunct professor in the Department of Pharmacology and Toxicology/Division of Interdisciplinary Toxicology, at the University of Arkansas for Medical Sciences. He has served as director of FDA's National Center for Toxicological Research and as editor of *Fundamental and Applied Toxicology.*

STUART SESSIONS is an economist with over 25 years of experience in supervising and performing analyses of environmental, energy, and natural resource policy issues. He has researched government priority-setting techniques, particularly comparative risk analysis in environmental planning. At the U.S. Environmental Protection Agency, he managed the division responsible for analyzing regulatory issues associated with air and water pollution, and solid and hazardous waste disposal.

FRANCIS (BART) SUHRE is a residue chemist in the Office of Pesticide Programs Health Effects Division. During his 30-year tenure at USDA and EPA, he has been involved in a wide range of research in pesticide chemistry and dietary risk assessment.

ROBERT V. TAUXE is chief of the Foodborne and Diarrheal Diseases Branch Division of Bacterial and Mycotic Diseases at the National Center for Infectious Diseases at the Centers for Disease Control and Prevention. He also serves as an adjunct faculty member in the Division of International Health at Emory University's School of Public Health.

MICHAEL R. TAYLOR, senior fellow at Resources for the Future, was a former administrator of the U.S. Department of Agriculture's Food Safety and Inspection Service. After practicing food and drug law for ten years, he served as deputy commissioner for policy at the Food and Drug Administration from 1991–1994. He is an adjunct professor of law at Georgetown University Law Center.

LAURIAN J. UNNEVEHR is a professor in the Department of Agricultural and Consumer Economics, University of Illinois at Urbana-Champaign. Her research explores the social welfare implications of food safety, looking at diet and health linkages, including new products and new regulations. Her edited books include *New Approaches to Food Safety Economics* and *Economics of HACCP*.

MILTON C. WEINSTEIN is the Henry J. Kaiser Professor of Health Policy and Management and Director of the Program on Economic Evaluation of Medical Technology at the Center for Risk Analysis in the Harvard School of Public Health, and Professor of Medicine at the Harvard Medical School. His research concerns the use of decision analysis and modeling in the economic evaluation of medical technologies and public health programs. He is coauthor of four books, including *Cost-Effectiveness in Health and Medicine* (with M. Gold, J. Siegel, and L. Russell) and *Decision Making in Health and Medicine: Integrating Evidence and Values* (with M. Hunink, P. Glasziou and others).

TOWARD
SAFER FOOD

PART I

Framing the Design Problem

1

Getting to Risk-Based Food Safety Regulatory Management: Lessons from Federal Environmental Policy

SANDRA A. HOFFMANN*

For the past 20 to 30 years the central theme in federal food safety policy has been a call for modernization. This call comes despite an impressive record of achievement. It reflects the fact that changes in food production, processing, and distribution, as well as in consumption patterns, have raised new challenges that existing policy appears ill equipped to meet. Coupled with this is the recognition that new technological developments, particularly in information technology and microbiology, provide new policy opportunities that have yet to be fully exploited.

This call for modernization has coalesced around demands for development of a more integrated, system-wide approach to managing food safety risk that uses science-based standards and decision criteria. Policy makers in such a system would rely on risk analysis and the supporting development of scientific data it requires to inform their decisions. Authors in this book at times use both the terms science-based and risk-based to talk about aspects of this approach to food safety regulation.

Advances have been made in response to this call for modernization. Over the past 20 years, significant improvements have been made in food safety data collection systems, particularly for pathogen hazards. A new science of microbial risk assessment is being developed by federal food safety agencies based in

*The author owes a note of appreciation to Terry Davies for sharing his extensive experience with the use of risk analysis in federal environmental regulation. This allowed me to correct several of my misinterpretations of the documents and literature on this topic. Remaining mistakes are solely my responsibility. I am also very grateful to Maggie Glavin, Pete Nelson, and Mike Taylor for their helpful comments and suggestions.

part on these data. Along with this has grown the recognition of the need for a means of integrating this new information in ways that can guide more effective resource use. This book is an effort to assess where we are in this process of better data collection, analysis, and integration of knowledge and management and to identify next steps toward a system of science-based decision analysis that can use this information to guide more effective use of federal food safety regulatory resources.

Since the early 1970s, federal agencies have demonstrated an ongoing interest in the use of quantitative risk analysis to inform more effective management of health and environmental risks (Andrews 1984; McGarity 1991; Anderson 1996). Food safety policy has been part of this reorientation of federal regulatory efforts around a risk paradigm. Comparative risk assessment and comparative risk rankings are an intuitively appealing model for thinking about use of risk information in regulatory decision analysis. In recent years, there has been increasing interest in use of comparative risk assessment among professionals concerned about food safety policy. Under circumstances very similar to those faced by food safety regulatory decision makers, environmental policy makers pursued this approach during the 1980s and 1990s. Those concerned about food safety should be interested in what this experience teaches about what comparative risk assessment has and has not been able to provide by way of assistance to regulatory decision makers.

A reasonable conclusion to draw from experience with the use of comparative risk assessment in the environmental policy arena is that although comparative risk assessment provides a first cut of information for effective resource allocation, it is only a first step. As one prominent group of risk analysis researchers noted, "Ranking risk does not solve the management problem and . . . may not translate directly into budgetary priorities" (Morgan et al. 1996). In this chapter, I argue that scientists, managers, and policy makers working on food safety during the past 30 years have developed risk analysis tools that provide an important complement to comparative risk assessment. These tools have been used primarily at the firm level in the private sector. I contend that they can also be drawn on to develop a framework for providing a sound scientific basis for future food safety resource allocation within government.

This chapter begins by providing a historical background on the current interest in risk-based priority setting in the food safety arena. It looks briefly at the development of microbial risk assessment, efforts to improve data collection to support it, and interest in comparative risk assessment as a framework to inform regulatory priority setting. It then examines EPA's experience with use of comparative risk assessment in the 1980s and 1990s as a means of informing and shaping regulatory priorities. Finally, it examines development of risk-based process control, particularly Hazard Analysis Critical Control Point (HACCP), for use by firms in ensuring food safety. It then suggests how the concepts behind HACCP might provide the basis for strengthening the contributions that comparative risk assessment can make to better food safety resource allocation. The chapter ends with an overview of the book and the contributions each chapter makes to an assessment of where we are and where we need to go in developing a sound scientific basis for food safety regulatory decisions.

Toward More Effective Food Safety Regulation

In 1998, the National Academy of Sciences (NAS) committee, in drafting "Ensuring Safe Food from Production to Consumption," defined the mission of an effective food safety system as protecting and improving public health "by ensuring that foods meet science-based safety standards through the integrated activities of the public and private sectors." The committee focused on risk as an organizing principle for an effective food safety regulatory system. The committee noted that system should be "science-based," with "a strong emphasis on risk analysis and prevention." "Risk analysis provides a science-based approach to address food safety issues" (NAS 1998, 5). According to the NAS report, use of regulatory resources should be prioritized on the basis of actual impact on public health risk rather than public perception of risk. Similar risks should receive similar levels of effort. Legal standards and regulatory mechanisms should be based on scientific evidence and should be responsive to risk rather than determined by fixed, non–risk based protocols. Such a system would be preventive and anticipatory, rather than reactive, in nature. Most fundamentally, such a system is supported by "a reliable and accurate system of data collection, processing, evaluation and transfer."

Developments in management of pathogen-related foodborne hazards provide a clearer understanding of the motivation behind food safety policy makers' interest in such a risk-based system. Concerns about pathogen-related food safety hazards have focused on modernization of the federal meat inspection system. The basic structure of U.S. meat safety regulation has remained largely unchanged since adoption of its original enabling legislation in 1906. The 1906 Meat Inspection Act focused on critical risks of the time: zoonotic diseases such as tuberculosis, trichinosis, and brucellosis; grossly unsanitary slaughter and processing conditions; and purposeful adulteration of processed foods. The antemortem examination of animals, postmortem examination of carcasses and vital organs, and continuous inspection of slaughter and processing facilities were effective methods of detecting many of these zoonotic diseases and reflected control methods available before development of modern statistical quality control methods and modern microbial testing.

By the early 1970s, animal disease eradication programs and improved animal husbandry practices had effectively controlled many of these zoonotic hazards on-farm. Other foodborne pathogen hazards such as *E. coli* O157:H7, which were not necessarily animal health problems and were not detectable by sensory inspection, had emerged as significant human health hazards (Alte-kruse et al. 1997). At the same time, a tightening federal budget in the wake of the first oil embargo and slowing of the post–World War II economic expansion increased pressure to improve the cost-effectiveness of meat inspection programs. The result was a push for modernization of federal meat and poultry regulatory programs. Modernization ultimately meant refocusing on current risks and using new scientific and analytical methods of detecting, evaluating, and controlling hazards.

In the 1970s and 1980s, a series of government studies, culminating in the 1985 NAS report, *An Evaluation of the Role of Microbiological Criteria for Foods and Food Ingredients,* developed the theme that modernization of federal food safety programs—in particular meat, poultry, egg, and seafood safety—should involve movement toward risk-based performance standards, flexible allocation of both private and public resources in accordance with public health risk, and development of the scientific knowledge base for doing this. In 1976, USDA's Food Safety Inspection Service (FSIS) commissioned a study of cost-effectiveness in meat inspection (Booz, Allen and Hamilton 1976). The report reiterated the recommendation to move toward risk-based performance standards, as well as to shift primary responsibility for food safety assurance to the private sector, to transform the role of inspector to that of verifier; and to recognize that food safety is jointly produced by actors from farm to consumer. In the early 1980s, FSIS adopted a total quality control (TQC) approach to federal meat inspection in response to U.S. General Accounting Office (U.S. GAO) recommendations (U.S. GAO 1977). Although TQC was later criticized by NAS (1985) as being improperly focused on non-risk (marketability) concerns, it marked a movement toward adoption of modern statistical approaches to quality control. In 1985, the NAS committee on microbiological criteria recommended that federal agencies ultimately adopt the HACCP approach to controlling microbial hazards in foods, which the World Health Organization had been advocating since the mid-1970s (WHO 1976; WHO/ICMSF 1982). But the committee found its evaluation of the scientific basis for HACCP programs frustrated by a lack of comprehensive quantitative risk analysis of foodborne human health hazards (NAS 1985, *154*). The NAS emphasized use of quantitative risk assessment and formal risk analysis as the principal tools for managing federal food safety programs.

The recommendations of the 1985 NAS report were picked up by GAO. In a long series of reports, GAO has attempted to draw Congressional attention to the need to reform federal food safety programs to make them more able to respond to changing health risks. GAO pointed out inconsistencies in the frequency of inspections of similar establishments under Food and Drug Administration (FDA), U.S. Department of Agriculture (USDA), and Department of Commerce (DoC) jurisdiction and lack of relationship between inspection frequency and risk (U.S. GAO 1992). (A description of the federal agencies' major food safety responsibilities is provided in Appendix A.) GAO argued that the intensity and type of inspection of food processing establishments should be based on the health risk posed by specific foods and production processes and establishments' histories of compliance (U.S. GAO 1992, 1993). It highlighted the need for better data collection on foodborne illness (U.S. GAO 1996a, 2001). GAO recognized the value of using statistical quality control procedures and microbial testing and the value of comprehensive risk assessment in guiding agency policy (U.S. GAO 1996b, 1997). Although GAO's analysis has focused on the ways legislatively created agency structure and mandates could be reformed to promote a more risk-based system, the underlying understanding is that an effective, modern food safety system operates on a factual foundation of sound scientific assessment of the human health risks posed by food products and on analysis of how those risks enter the food chain.

Together, the policy debates and recommendations of the past 20 years outline the basic components of a modern, science-based food safety system. Such a system is responsive to changing risk profiles, bases regulatory requirements and administrative resource allocation on risk, and is preventive rather than reactive in orientation. Implementation of such a system requires effective data collection, scientific methods for assessing risks, risk responsive regulatory mechanisms, and the analytical and administrative capacity to use risk information in program management.

Risk-Based Decision Analysis in the Federal Government

Efforts to modernize food safety regulation organized around the concept of risk reduction were not taking place in a vacuum. The 1985 NAS committee on microbial criteria was well aware of the increasing use of risk analysis in the management of other federal administrative programs. The committee was operating in an environment in which the science of risk assessment and the management tools of risk analysis were gaining prominent use in federal regulatory agencies.

In the early 1970s, the federal government was taking on increasing responsibility for environmental quality. Federal environmental legislation governing toxic chemical hazards was adopted in the early 1970s (FIFRA Amendments Pub. L. 91-601 Dec. 30, 1970; TSCA 15 U.S.C. secs. 2601 *et seq.* (1976); RCRA 42 U.S.C. secs. 6901 *et seq.* (1976)). These statutes implicitly or explicitly relied on risk criteria. Implementation of these statutes fostered development of scientific methods and administrative capacity, both in the government and in industry, to base regulatory decisions on risk criteria (Hornstein 1993, note 10). Explicit use of quantitative risk assessment to support regulatory decisions expanded significantly.

During the 1980s, the role of risk in federal environmental and public health regulation developed in two directions. First, the methodology of risk assessment and of risk management was improved and institutionalized within EPA, OSHA, and the Consumer Products Safety Commission (CPSC). Second, by the end of the decade the concept of comparative risk assessment and the goal of risk reduction had taken a prominent place in debates about environmental policy priority setting. Throughout the decade, risk pervaded the discussion and administration of environmental policy. As one observer noted, "By the end of the 1980s, risk assessment was established as the primary language of analysis and management at EPA" (Andrews 1994, *217*). Both external and internal forces drove this policy innovation.

In 1980, the Supreme Court ruled that OSHA could not regulate the occupational exposure to benzene without showing that exposures posed "a significant risk of harm" (*Industrial Union Dept., AFL-CIO v. American Petroleum Institute* 448 U.S. 607 (1980)). Other agencies took the case as a signal that they might also be required to provide courts with quantitative justification of their risk reduction regulations (NAS 1994; Anderson 1996). The "benzene" case led to rapid expansion of the use of quantitative risk assessment by federal agencies with responsibility over toxic substances. In 1981, in response to the benzene case, Congress commissioned a National Academy of Sciences assessment of federal agency capacity to conduct quantitative risk assessment.

If the benzene case was a watershed in the conceptual framework for environmental law, the 1983 NAS report *Risk Assessment in the Federal Government: Managing the Process* was a watershed in its administration. The report defined a four-step framework for health risk assessment: (1) hazard identification; (2) dose–response assessment; (3) exposure assessment; and 4) risk characterization. The structure of risk assessment and the relationship between risk assessment and risk management set out in the report have guided development of environmental and public health regulation, both in the United States and internationally, ever since.

Throughout the 1980s, quantitative risk assessment provided EPA with a means of justifying its programs to OMB, Congress, and other federal agencies (Landy et al. 1994). In 1983, EPA Administrator William Ruckelshaus relied on the use of risk assessment and NAS recommended administrative separation of risk assessment from risk management in rebuilding the Agency's credibility in the wake of charges that EPA had manipulated science for political purposes under his predecessor, Ann Gorsuch (Goldstein 1993). Ruckelshaus' goal was to reestablish public confidence that EPA decisions were based on "sound science" rather than politics (Ruckelshaus 1983). Ruckelshaus and his successors saw risk analysis as giving EPA a way to shift the language of policy evaluation and oversight from OMB's cost–benefit analysis to a science-based, outcome-focused analysis (Andrews 1984). To build scientific capacity and enhance analytical consistency, EPA began ongoing development of a series of risk assessment guidelines (U.S. EPA 1986a–d, 1987a, 1988, 1991, 1992). The developments in risk assessment methodology that resulted from development of these guidelines enhanced the capacity of all federal agencies to conduct risk assessments.

Under Ruckelshaus' successor, Administrator Lee M. Thomas' leadership, EPA launched an effort to develop new risk analysis tools that could guide the Agency's strategic planning (Andrews 1999). One of the most notable efforts was development of an expert judgment-based approach to comparative risk assessment, "Unfinished Business." The objective of the "Unfinished Business" project was "to develop a ranking of the relative risks associated with major environmental problems that could be used as one of several important bases on which EPA could set priorities" (U.S. EPA 1987b). The underlying premise was that agency resources are most effectively allocated by addressing the worst problems first (Finkel and Golding 1994).

In conducting this risk-ranking project, the agency formed four task forces of senior agency management staff and scientists. Each group focused on one of four risk types: cancer risks, non-cancer health risks, ecological risks, and "welfare" risks (risk of damage to property, goods, and services to which monetary value is often assigned). Each task force identified ranking criteria, collected existing risk data, and on the basis of that data and expert judgment ranked 31 problems regulated by EPA by severity of risk (U.S. EPA 1987b). No attempt was made to create a common metric combining the four types of risk. Instead, a risk profile was created showing a separate ranking of the 31 problems for cancer, non-cancer, ecological, and welfare risk. A survey of public perception of the risks posed by these problems revealed that agency priorities were more consistent with public perception than with the expert judgment found in this comparative risk ranking exercise (U.S. EPA 1987b). In conducting this ranking, the project explicitly set aside consideration of: availability and cost-effectiveness of regulatory interventions, risk characteristics such as familiarity or dread, social benefits associated with the hazardous activity, and statutory mandates (U.S. EPA 1987b).

The final report, *Unfinished Business: A Comparative Assessment of Environmental Problems,* concluded that comparative risk assessment could be a "useful tool" in helping to set priorities within EPA programs, nationally and regionally (U.S. EPA 1987b; Morgenstern and Sessions 1998). EPA's Science Advisory Board endorsed CRA as an approach to setting policy and budgetary priorities (U.S. EPA 1990b). In 1991, Thomas' successor, Administrator William Reilly, announced that EPA would use risk comparisons to set internal program priorities and directed regional EPA offices to conduct comparative risk assessment to prioritize their activities based on an objective of risk reduction (Hornstein 1993, note 29; Landy et al. 1994). The state and regional comparative risk assessments generally involved significant public participation. Evaluations of these projects suggest that one of their primary benefits has been improved risk communication and enhanced public engagement in environmental policy priority setting (Minard 1996).

OMB embraced EPA's movement toward risk-based priority setting and its commitment to "focusing the Agency's limited resources on cases of greatest risk" (U.S. OMB 1991; Applegate 1992). In the early 1990s, both OMB and GAO recommended that other agencies use comparative risk assessment coupled with the goal of risk reduction to set budget priorities for environmental and public health programs (Hornstein 1993, note 30; Andrews 1994, *223*), OMB released plans to require use of "risk management budgeting" for health and safety programs in six federal agencies (21 Env't Rep. (BNA) No. 41 at 1796 (February 8, 1991)). At roughly the same time, Senators Moynihan and McClusky asked EPA to provide a risk-based agency budget. In the end, EPA found that available risk information was simply too coarse to meet the need for detail required for administrative budgeting (private communication with Terry Davies November 18, 2003). Ultimately, however, the larger impediment to use of comparative risk assessment to guide agency level environmental priority setting was the fact that, as is the case with food safety, EPA effort and budget are largely dictated by enabling legislation. Only a small proportion of the EPA budget could be affected by risk-based priority setting. Activities in the largest programs, air and water, are largely dictated by the technical standards of their respective enabling acts.

This is not to say that the comparative risk assessment and risk-based budgeting efforts were without effect. Around the margins, hazards ranked high by "Unfinished Business," such as radon in homes, may have received more attention than they would have without these efforts. But low-ranked activities, such as solid waste, did not receive less effort (private communication with Terry Davies November 18, 2003). In the view of one long-time observer of EPA administration, perhaps the greatest legacy of these efforts has been introduction of risk information into more traditional administrative management and budgeting processes/tools in a more sophisticated and effective way (private communication with Stewart Sessions October 20, 2003).

The push both within EPA and at OMB for risk-based priority setting has not been without its critics. Criticisms have focused on the political function of decision analysis, the appropriateness of risk reduction as an organizing focus for environmental policy, and technical issues related to the application of comparative risk analysis. One set of concerns has to do with the role of risk-based priority setting in a democratic society. It may be appropriate, some argue, that EPA priorities were more in line with public perceptions and concerns than expert judgment. In a democracy, the public has the right to set priorities (Hornstein 1992). Some saw the push for "rational planning" in the 1980s as political cover for deregulation (Finkel 1994). The political strength of this perspective was so strong that a Democratic bill to elevate EPA to cabinet status was defeated by a Democrat-controlled House after an amendment requiring risk analysis was attached (*Washington Post* 1994). There is also a growing debate about the adequacy of risk reduction as an organizing principle for environmental and health policy. Some argue sustainable development and pollution prevention are more appropriate long-term goals (Andrews 1994, 1999). A related concern continues to be that quantitative risk analysis may mask qualitative attributes of risk, such as dread or familiarity (Dwyer 1990; Hornstein 1992). From a practical perspective, students of public administration note that comparative risk assessment provides only part of the information needed for priority setting (Davies 1996). Most prominently missing is analysis of alternative mitigation strategies, costs, and public evaluation of relative risk reduction benefits.

Several government agencies, NGOs, and academic reports have recommended refinements in regulatory use of risk analysis. A 1990 National Academy committee noted considerable debate "about appropriate ways to make comparisons across time and among illnesses, disabilities, and economic or social groups (NAS 1990, *11*). The NAS committee drafting Science and Judgment in Risk Assessment (NAS 1994) urged that OMB's case-by-case approach of regulatory oversight be deemphasized in favor of "forward-looking" guidance. This same committee insisted that a focus on average population risk was ill placed given differences in risk factors across a population and noted a need for development of assessments that take account of individual variability and population heterogeneity (NAS 1994). The Food Quality Protection Act (1996) and the Clean Air Act Amendments of 1990 addressed this concern by requiring consideration of impacts on sensitive populations, including children, the elderly, and asthmatic individuals. The Presidential and Congressional Commission on Risk Assessment and Risk Managment (1997) focused on the need to look at multiple hazards in an integrated manner, rather than risk by risk. Finally, concern has been expressed about the lack of explicit links between risk analysis and decisionmaking processes and a concern that risk ranking could degenerate into analysis for the sake of analysis (Finkel 1994). Minard (1996) observed that although the EPA state projects plans include a phase for setting goals and developing strategies to achieve those goals, the risk ranking process itself required so much effort and energy that this stage was rarely reached.

The U.S. Food Safety System as Risk-Based

Risk-based regulatory priority setting is one pillar of a science-based food safety system, but it is not the only one. A major structural challenge in designing risk-based public health policy is the need for regulatory mechanisms that have a degree of flexibility to respond as risk profiles change. Experience with the 1906 Meat Inspection Act shows what can happen to policy that originally has a strong risk basis when such flexibility is not provided. This is not an easy challenge to meet. A tradeoff inevitably exists between the benefits of being able to commit to a course of action and maintaining the ability to adapt to changing circumstances.

One of the major innovations in food safety has been the development of a Hazard Analysis and Critical Control Point (HACCP) approach to preventive process control and its adoption as an approach to food safety regulation. HACCP process control systems were first developed by the Pillsbury Company in conjunction with NASA in the 1960s as a means of helping meet elevated safety requirements of food for space flights (www.fao.org/docrep/W8088E/w8088e05.htm). HACCP gradually gained adherence in industry and public health circles as a rational, structured way of managing food safety within a production process. FDA adopted HACCP principles in its 1974 low-acid canned food regulations. In 1982, the WHO and the International Commission on Microbiological Specification of Foods (ICMSF) endorsed the approach (WHO/ICMSF 1982). The Codex Alimentarius Commission adopted guidelines for application of the HACCP system in 1993 and included the HACCP system and guidelines as an annex to its Recommended International Code of Practice—General Principles of Food Hygiene (CAC/RCP 1-1969, Rev 3 (1997)). The Sanitary and Phytosanitary (SPS) Agreement and the Agreement on Technical Barriers to Trade of the Uruguay Round of trade negotiations place special emphasis on international standards (http://www.fao.org/docrep/w9114e/W9114e06.htm accessed November 20, 2003). Codex standards are specifically identified as a baseline for safe food production in the SPS agreement.

HACCP provides a systematic approach to identification, assessment, and control of health risks in a food production system. The first steps in developing such a system are describing the food and its distribution, identifying the intended use and consumers of the food, and developing and verifying a flow diagram of the process used to produce and distribute the food (NACMCF 1998). The foundation of the system is a HACCP plan that involves seven elements: (1) a hazard analysis; (2) identification of critical control points; (3) establishment of critical limits; (4) monitoring the implementation of control procedures for each control point; (5) establishment of a plan of corrective actions to be taken in the event the critical limit is exceeded; (6) establishment of procedures to verify the adequacy of the HACCP system; and (7) record keeping and documentation of monitoring, corrective action, and verification (NACMCF 1998).

Following on the NRC recommendation that HACCP be used as a way of modernizing meat and poultry safety regulation, the National Advisory Committee on Microbiological Criteria for Foods (NACMCF) developed a series of guidance documents aimed at facilitating adoption of a HACCP system approach to food safety management (NACMCF 1989, 1992, 1993, 1994). Starting in the early 1990s, FDA and USDA began a shift to mandated use of HACCP systems as a basic approach to meeting their regulatory responsibilities (seafood 60 FR 65096–65202, December 18, 1995; meat and poultry 61 FR 38806, July 25, 1996; fresh juice 66 FR 6137–6202, January 19, 2001; pork sausage (proposed) 63 FR 1800–1802, January 12, 1998; milk (proposed) 63 FR 1800–1802, January 12, 1998, NCIMS 1970). HACCP regulations require affected plants to analyze their own production process and identify points where hazards that can potentially affect food safety can be controlled. The plants must develop a written HACCP plan to ensure that these hazards stay within "critical limits" at each control point and maintain records to allow federal inspectors to verify control.

The new HACCP approach to regulation met with mixed reactions. For many in industry, it represented a rational way to ensure product quality and provided firms with flexibility to respond to changing technology and market structure in meeting food safety requirements (personal communication with M. Glavin 1994). Consumer groups supported the HACCP concept, but voiced concern that without enforceable performance standards a HACCP approach to food safety regulation could not hold industry accountable for producing safe food (Jacobson 2000).

In recognition of this concern, the proposed and final meat and poultry HACCP rules included pathogen reduction performance standards. The final rule required microbial testing for *Salmonella* in finished meat and poultry. By defining *E. coli* O157:H7 contaminated ground meat as adulterated, FSIS also established a de facto performance standard for *E. coli* O157:H7 contamination. Under the *Salmonella* rules, USDA could suspend inspection of plants whose product repeatedly exceeded the *Salmonella* performance standard, effectively shutting the plant down. Supreme Beef Processors, Inc. successfully challenged this provision as applied to *Salmonella* in ground beef (*Supreme Beef Processors, Inc. v. United States Dep't of Agric.* 275 F.3d 432 (5th Cir. 2001)). Although USDA continues to use the *Salmonella* performance standard as a way of evaluating the effectiveness of a plant's HACCP plan, the enforceability of pathogen reduction performance standards remains an unsettled legal question.

CRA: Only a First Step

A basic criticism of EPA's use of comparative risk analysis in the 1980s and 1990s has been its lack of practical integration with strategic planning, identification of regulatory control options, and enforcement. Without this, there is danger that, as regional EPA offices and state governments experienced, comparative risk analysis of food safety hazards could remain a "stand-alone" exercise that does not meet the demands placed on it to help guide regulatory priority setting.

There are several reasons to hope that, in the food safety arena, more effective forms of analysis may in the end be available to assist decision makers. Food safety policy makers deal with a narrower, more homogeneous set of risks and hazard-generating processes than environmental policy makers. EPA is faced with setting priorities between programs governing health risks, ecological risks, hazards to current populations, and hazards to generations who live decades and even thousands of years in the future. Food safety agencies are charged with preventing human illness in people currently eating food and, in some cases, their offspring. The food production system and the hazards that can enter it are complex, but not as diverse or complex as the wide range of industrial and agricultural production, consumption activities, and ecological processes that determine the impact of toxics in the environment. Finally, as the HACCP regulations show, existing food safety statutory and regulatory frameworks do provide some scope for risk-based targeting of governmental and industry precautionary efforts, despite the inflexibility of the anti- and postmortem examination requirements of the meat and poultry inspection acts.

At a public briefing on the recent NAS report on microbial performance standards, committee co-chair Claude Earl Fox commented that, in order to establish clear links between food safety regulatory criteria and public health objectives:

> It is first necessary to be able to connect food borne illnesses to the foods that are the sources of the disease-causing agents. To optimize food safety, the responsible regulatory agencies need a clearer vision of which points along the food production continuum to regulate, and they need a way to measure the effectiveness of regulations once they are in place. To develop effective standards, agencies must monitor the levels of pathogen contamination of specific foods at various stages in the food system. . . . Knowing this, it will be possible to optimize interventions to control the hazards associated with each food and to confirm that specific interventions achieve their public health objectives once applied. (Fox 2003).

In other words, something analogous to HACCP analysis is needed at a food system level.

As the 2003 NRC report urges, there is a fundamental need to improve the collection and analysis of risk data throughout the food production process. It is fundamental to any risk analysis to know where hazards are likely to enter a system. While comparative risk assessment makes a first cut at providing insight into risk reduction priorities, what is needed is a way to integrate risk information into a picture of the overall food production, distribution, and consumption process so that government (and private) decision makers can analyze the hazard generation process and the effectiveness of interventions. One way to think about this is a "farm to fork" risk assessment. But what is needed is an analysis that also integrates analysis of possible points for regulatory intervention. HACCP may ultimately provide a useful model for thinking about how to link risk analysis forward into strategic planning, budgetary priority setting and implementation, and enforcement of food safety regulation.

Federal food safety policy appears to be moving toward use of performance standards with microbial testing as a way of ensuring that HACCP plans protect public health. HACCP, coupled with performance standards and microbial testing, has the dual benefit of assuring public health and at the same time harnessing market incentives meeting this goal cost-effectively. It may be worth considering whether the data needed for system-wide, HACCP-like analysis could be designed to provide monitoring data that would allow enforcement of performance standards. By looking beyond comparative risk assessment to HACCP as a rough model for system-wide analysis to support risk-based regulatory priority setting, it may be possible for agencies to integrate data collection and analysis needed both for priority setting and for actual regulation and enforcement. The whole process of risk-based priority setting could help build the scientific and institutional capacity to create and enforce a flexible approach to food safety regulation. Such an approach could take advantage of the cost-saving features of market forces to assure that public health is protected. This is only one possible avenue for advancement. Nelson and Krupnick suggest other approaches to solutions-based priority setting in their chapter of this book.

As the chapters of this book make evident, at this point in the development of regulatory analysis capacity it may not be possible to move on to the integrated use of data collection for analysis of risks, interventions, and possibly enforcement. But as food safety agencies in the United States and elsewhere move forward with improved data collection and comparative risk rankings, as they are likely to do, they may do well to keep in mind that this analysis is not an end in itself. Data collection efforts and development of decision analysis frameworks such as risk comparisons should be designed with the recognition that they can also be tied into strategic planning, design of regulatory mechanisms, and, ultimately, enforcement of food safety regulation. This in itself is a way of avoiding a new type of dysfunctional "lock-in"—development of data collection and analysis capacity that is well designed for priority setting but ill designed for actual implementation of those priorities.

Overview of Chapters

In 1998, NAS outlined the basic features of a risk-based food safety system (NAS 1998). To the extent possible, a risk-based system effectively reduces actual risk rather than assuaging public perception of risk. While being able to commit to a policy path, it maintains the flexibility to respond to changes in the risk profile presented by changing food production, processing, marketing, and consumption patterns. Agency priorities are set in accordance with risk. From the perspective of day-to-day implementation, it means developing approaches to regulation and enforcement that help focus agency resources on the basis of risk rather than on the basis of fixed non–risk-based protocols. For example, a risk-based meat inspection rule might be to base inspection frequency on past pathogen counts rather than mandating continuous inspection of all establishments. To the extent politically possible, rather than being driven by the latest outbreak or crisis, a risk-based system is based on systematic analysis of risks. It relies on the best available scientific methods and data and pushes to improve these. NAS explicitly saw such a system as involving decisions based on quantitative risk assessment and use of formal risk analysis as a framework for decisions.

This book addresses the question of what we know and what we need to know to guide regulatory priority setting in a risk-based food safety system. In Chapter 2 Richard Merrill creates an institutional context for examination of this question by providing a historical overview of the legal authority governing federal food safety regulation.

Risk-based resource allocation would suggest that food safety regulatory resources should be allocated on the basis of risk or on the basis of risk reduction opportunity. Resources should be used to reduce risk as effectively as possible. The chapters in Part I of this book address basic questions that must be answered to evaluate the effectiveness of the food safety system in using limited resources to protect public health. What do we know about the magnitude and distribution of risks in the food supply? What do we know about current intervention efforts, their costs, and their benefits? How do these align with the hazards?

Chapters 3 and 4 focus on what is known about the magnitude and distribution of risks in the food supply. In Chapter 3, Robert Tauxe of the Centers for Disease Control examines what is known about microbial hazards in the U.S. food supply. He proposes an approach to using available epidemiological data that can be used to construct a risk profile for the U.S. food supply. This method complements individual risk assessments by providing a framework for the complex task of mapping microbial hazards through the U.S. system of food production, distribution, and consumption.

Although past assessments of microbial hazards have tended to focus on ex post analysis using epidemiological data, assessments of chemical hazards have used ex ante analysis based on laboratory testing and the 1984 NRC four-step risk assessment. In Chapter 4, Penny Fenner-Crisp provides a synthesis of what has been learned through this approach about risk to U.S. consumers' health from exposure to chemicals in food. The challenge to assessing microbial risk has been the difficulty of applying risk assessment principles where the hazard is a population of living organisms. The challenge faced in chemical risk assessment is the absence of epidemiological data due to long latency periods and interaction with other chemicals. As a result, Fenner-Crisp's analysis focuses on what can be gained from collecting better exposure data. She reviews current federal monitoring programs, results, and analyzes how this can be used to build a national aggregate exposure profile.

Chapters 5 and 6 focus on public and private efforts to reduce foodborne health hazards, their cost, and how they relate to the occurrence of hazards in the nation's food supply. In Chapter 5, Lawrence Dyckman of GAO examines

FSIS and FDA expenditure of the $1 billion annual federal food safety regulatory budget. This chapter draws on a decade and a half of GAO reports on food safety and reaches many of the same conclusions as past GAO reports. Moving to a risk-based inspection system would provide more effective use of FSIS resources. FDA regulation leaves open food safety concerns that could be addressed with additional funding. Increased frequency of risk-based FDA inspection of U.S. food-processing plants and heightened oversight of imported foods and antibiotic use in animals could provide greater assurance of safe foods in the United States.

In Chapter 6, Helen Jensen and Laurian Unnevehr look at what is currently known about private industry and consumer costs of complying with existing food safety regulation. They both look at methods for estimating these costs and summarize existing studies to give a picture of what is known about these costs. In particular, they focus on what is known about the structure of costs and market incentives to improve food safety. Assignment of costs and changes in the nature of costs depends on an understanding of how the food production system is integrated. They conclude that: (1) the distribution of costs is likely more important than market price effects in assessing the impacts of food safety regulation; (2) regulation affects the long-term incentives to invest in new technologies or inputs and likely will bias the nature of productivity growth; (3) market incentives can reduce the cost of and therefore increase the level of mitigation; and (4) a risk-based systems approach may be the best way to understand the costs, incentives, and risk outcomes resulting from alternative interventions.

Evaluation of the contribution of food safety programs to public health involves comparison of outcomes as different as prevention of developmental disorders and acute gastroenteritis. In Chapter 7, Elise Golan of the USDA Economic Research Service presents federal estimates of the benefits of food safety programs. The usefulness of these estimates is affected by the comparability of methods federal agencies use to measure the outcomes of food safety programs. Golan discusses how adoption of coordinated approaches to measuring benefits would facilitate an understanding of program outcomes. She concludes by arguing that a risk ranking that is restricted to direct health impacts would exclude one of the most important benefits of food safety programs: maintaining confidence in the food supply system.

The chapters in Part II of this book focus on methodological tools necessary for quantitative analysis of risk management decisions. Risk assessment forms the cornerstone of risk-based management of food safety hazards. In Chapter 8, Robert Buchanan, Bart Suhre, and I summarize the state of the art of chemical and microbial risk assessment. We focus on refinements in chemical risk assessment motivated by the 1996 Food Quality Protection Act and on recent development of quantitative microbial risk assessment.

In the past, risk-based priority setting has focused on addressing "worst-things first." In Chapter 9, Peter Nelson and Alan Krupnick examine in more detail available priority-setting models and their usefulness for food safety policy. They argue for a solutions-based approach to risk-based priority setting. Decision makers should focus on actions that produce the greatest or most cost-effective risk reductions rather than on allowing decisions to be driven by raw risk rankings.

Traditionally risks are evaluated separately, even sequentially, often in response to crises. In 1993, the Carnegie Commission on Science, Technology and Government recommended that federal agencies make wider use of risk ranking as an input to risk-management decisionmaking. Chapter 10 provides a brief summary of past government risk ranking efforts outside the food safety arena. In response to the Carnegie Commission recommendations, the Office of Science and Technology Policy asked several research groups to develop methods that allow risk ranking exercises within or across agencies. In Chapter 10, Paul Fischbeck and other researchers at Carnegie Mellon describe how the approach they developed, which involves elicitation of multiattribute risk preferences from lay groups, could be used in ranking the importance the public places on reducing different food safety risks.

Another approach to ranking risks is to value each using a common metric that then allows comparison across risks. One class of metrics commonly used in public health policy is quality-adjusted life years (QALYs) indices and their variants. QALYs index the severity of a health outcome using various psychometric scales. If information is available on the probability of the outcome as well as on the cost of reducing these probabilities, it is possible to rank the relative value of applying resources to reducing alternative risks. In Chapter 11, Milton Weinstein examines the potential role of QALYs in informing food safety regulatory decision making and research that would help make QALY assessment a practical tool for food safety priority setting.

A competing class of metrics is economic valuation metrics. These measures estimate individual or public willingness to pay to reduce risks. Because they assign a monetary value to the importance of reducing a risk, they can be compared directly with the cost of reducing the risk. Having a common metric for both the costs and benefits of reducing food safety risks would allow for absolute rather than only relative ranking of risks. This means that not only could an agency see that it is more cost effective to reduce one risk rather than another but it could also see how much more worthwhile it is. In Chapter 12, Jim Hammitt examines how willingness to pay measures could be used to inform food-system–wide food safety priority setting and evaluates their strengths and weaknesses relative to other measures.

The authors of the last two chapters of the book evaluate the lessons that can be drawn from this book about food safety risks and opportunities to reduce risk. They point to directions for development of tools and data that will allow a more system-wide, risk-based approach to priority setting in federal food safety programs.

Glenn Morris focuses on advances that have been made over the past decade or more in collecting data needed to understand the epidemiology of foodborne illness. He asseses data collection and modeling needed to provide a sound, scientific basis for a risk-based systematic approach to preventing foodborne illness.

Julie Caswell, a food safety economist, argues that information to make *better* decisions on effective use of food safety regulatory resources is available. The impediments to better management of the overall risk portfolio are organizational and political rather than technical. Caswell argues for comprehensive, even if crude, rather than narrowly focused, but very high quality, risk analysis. In Caswell's view, what is needed for priority setting is an adequate picture of the whole risk portfolio rather than a detailed understanding of only parts of it. She recommends a two-tiered approach to generating better information for effective regulation: first, organization of broad, comprehensive information on risks, health outcomes, incentives, benefits, and costs; and then, based on analysis of this information, development of narrow and in-depth information on risks that appear to be of high priority.

Mike Taylor, former FSIS Administrator and former Deputy Commissioner for Policy at FDA, concludes the book with a call for development of new quantitative decision analysis tools that could help food safety regulation to move toward the goals outlined in recent NAS reports. He describes three types of models that are needed to provide input into a system of food safety risk management: risk ranking models, models of the effectiveness of current and proposed interventions, and resource allocation models that integrate information about severity of risk and effectiveness and cost of interventions. He argues that these tools need to be used in "an ongoing, dynamic process that makes data collection, risk analysis, and program evaluation 'build-in' features of how society addresses foodborne illness, with continuous feedback as risk patterns change and progress occurs over time."

References

Altekruse, S.F., M.L. Cohen, and D.L. Swerdlow. 1997. Emerging Foodborne Diseases. *Emerging Infectious Disease* 3(3): 285–293. http://www.cdc.gov/ncidod/eid/vol3no3/cohen.htm (accessed November 24, 2003).

Anderson, F.R. 1996. CRA and Its Stakeholders: Advice to the Executive Office. In *Comparing Environmental Risks,* edited by J. Clarence Davies. Washington, DC: Resources for the Future.

Andrews, R.N.L. 1984. Economics and Environmental Decisions, Past and Present. In *Environmental Policy under Reagan's Executive Order: The Roles of Benefit-Cost Analysis,* edited by V. Kerry Smith. Chapel Hill, NC: University of North Carolina Press.

———. 1994. Risk-Based Decisionmaking. In *Environmental Policy in the 1990s,* edited by Norman J. Vig and Michael E. Kraft. Washington, DC: Congressional Quarterly Press.

————. 1999. *Managing the Environment, Managing Ourselves.* New Haven, CT: Yale University Press.

Applegate, J.S. 1992. Worst Things First: Risk, Information, and Regulatory Structure in Toxic Substances Control. *Yale Journal of Regulation* 277: 320–346.

Booz, Allen, and Hamilton, Inc. Study of the Federal Meat and Poultry Inspection Program, Volume 1—Description of the Meat and Poultry Inspection Program, June 1977, Volume II—Opportunities for Change—An Evaluation of Specific Alternatives, June 1977, Volume III—Executive Summary, July 1977.

Codex Alimentarius Commission. 1997. Recommended International Code of Practice —General Principles of Food Hygiene. CAC/RCP 1–1969, Rev 3 (1997).

Davies, J.C. (ed.). 1996. Comparative Risk Analysis in the 1990s: The State of the Art. In *Comparing Environmental Risks: Tools for Setting Government Priorities.* Washington, DC: Resources for the Future.

Dwyer, J. 1990. Limits of Environmental Risk Assessment. *Journal of Energy Engineering* 116: 231–246.

Finkel, A.M. 1994. Should We—and Can We—Reduce the Worst Risks First? In *Worst Things First? The Debate over Risk-Based National Environmental Priorities,* edited by Adam M. Finkel and Dominic Golding. Washington, DC: Resources for the Future.

Finkel, A.M. and D. Golding. 1994. Worst Things First? The Debate over Risk-based National Environmental Priorities. Washington, DC: Resources for the Future.

Fox, C.E. 2003. Opening Statement at Public Briefing on Institute of Medicine National Research Council, Scientific Criteria to Ensure Safe Food http://www4.nationalacademies.org/news.nsf/isbn/s030908928X?OpenDocument (accessed November 20, 2003).

Goldstein, B.D. 1993. If Risk Management Is Broke, Why Fix Risk Assessment? *EPA Journal* 9(Jan./Feb./March): 37–38.

Hornstein, D.T. 1992. Reclaiming Environmental Law: A Normative Critique of Comparative Risk Analysis. *Columbia Law Review* 92: 562–633.

————. 1993. Lessons from Federal Pesticide Regulation on the Paradigm and Politics of Environmental Law Reform. *Yale Journal of Regulation* 92: 562–633.

Jacobson, M.F. Comments before the FDA Commissioner's Consumer Roundtable. Washington, DC, Dec. 13, 2000 www.cspinet.org/reports/mjcomments_cfsan.html (accessed October 10, 2003).

Landy, M.K., M.J. Roberts, and S.R. Thomas. 1994. *The Environmental Protection Agency: Asking the Wrong Questions from Nixon to Clinton.* New York: Oxford University Press.

McGarity, T. 1991. *Reinventing Rationality: The Role of Regulatory Analysis in the Federal Bureaucracy.* New York: Cambridge University Press.

Minard, R.A. Jr. 1996. CRA and the States: History, Politics, and Results. In *Comparing Environmental Risks,* edited by J.C. Davies. Washington, DC: Resources for the Future.

Morgan, M.G., B. Fishoff, L. Lave, and P. Fischbeck. 1996. A Proposal for Ranking Risk within Federal Agencies. In *Comparing Environmental Risks: Tools for Setting Government Priorities,* edited by J.C. Davies. Washington, DC: Resources for the Future.

Morgenstern, R., and S. Sessions. 1988. Weighing Environmental Risks: EPA's Unfinished Business. *Environment* 30 (July/Aug.): 14–17.

National Academy of Sciences. 1983. *Risk Assessment in the Federal Government: Managing the Process.* Washington, DC: National Academy Press.

———. 1985. *An Evaluation of the Role of Microbiological Criteria for Foods and Food Ingredients.* Washington, DC: National Academy Press.

———. 1990. *Cattle Inspection, Committee on Evaluation of USDA Streamlined Inspection System for Cattle (SIS-C).* Washington, DC: National Academy Press.

———. 1994. *Science and Judgment in Risk Assessment.* Washington, DC: National Academy Press.

———. 1998. *Ensuring Safe Food From Production to Consumption.* Washington, DC: National Academy Press.

———. 2003. *An Evaluation of the Role of Microbiological Criteria for Foods and Food Ingredients.* Washington, DC: National Academy Press.

NACMCF (National Advisory Committee on Microbiological Criteria for Foods). 1989. Hazard Analysis and Critical Control Point System. Obtained by the author from the NACMCF Executive Secretariat, USDA, FSIS, Washington DC (September 2004).

———. 1992. Hazard Analysis and Critical Control Point System. *International Journal of Food Microbiology* 16: 1–23.

———. 1993. Generic HACCP for Raw Beef. *Food Microbiology* 10: 449–488.

———. 1994. The Role of Regulatory Agencies and Industry in HACCP. *International Journal of Food Microbiology* 21: 187–195.

———. 1998. Hazard Analysis and Critical Control Point Principles and Application Guidelines. *Journal of Food Protection* 61:1246–1259.

National Conference on Interstate Milk Shipments (NCIMS). 1997. Proposed Milk HAACP.

Presidential and Congressional Commission on Risk Assessment and Risk Management. 1997. *Risk Assessment and Risk Management in Regulatory Decision Making* [S.L.]: U.S. GPO. http://www.riskworld.com (accessed Sept. 23, 2004).

Ruckelshaus, W.D. 1983. Science, Risk and Public Policy. Speech delivered at the National Academy of Sciences, Washington, DC, June 22, 1983. Reprinted in *Vital Speeches of the Day* August 1, 1983.

USDA (U.S. Department of Agriculture) Food Safety Inspection Service, National Advisory Committee on Microbiological Criteria for Foods. 1989. HACCP Principles for Food Production. http://www.fsis.usda.gov/OPHS/nacmcf/reports.htm (accessed October10, 2003).

———. 1992. HACCP System. http://www.fsis.usda.gov/OPHS/nacmcf/reports.htm (accessed October 10, 2003).

———. 1993a. The Role of Regulatory Agencies and Industry in HACCP. http://www.fsis.usda.gov/OPHS/nacmcf/reports.htm (accessed October 10, 2003).

———. 1993b. Generic HACCP for Raw Beef. http://www.fsis.usda.gov/OPHS/ nacmcf/reports.htm (accessed October 10, 2003).

———. 1997. Hazard Analysis and Critical Control Point Principles and Application Guidelines. http://www.fsis.usda.gov/OPHS/nacmcf/reports.htm (accessed October 10, 2003).

U.S. Department of Defense. OSD Comptroller Center. The Planning, Programming and Budgeting System. www.dod.mil/comptroller/icenter/budget/ppbsint.htm (accessed October 10, 2003).

U.S. EPA (Environmental Protection Agency). 1986a. Guidelines for Carcinogen Risk Assessment. *Federal Register* 51: 33992–34003.

———. 1986b. Guidelines for Mutagenicity Risk Assessment. *Federal Register* 51 (185): 34006–34012.

———. 1986c. Guidelines for the Health Risk Assessment of Chemical Mixtures. *Federal Register* 51 (185): 34014–34025.

———. 1986d. Guidelines for the Health Assessment of Suspect Developmental Toxicants. *Federal Register* 51 (185): 34028–34040.

———. 1987a. *Risk Assessment Guidelines of 1986.* EPA-600/8-87/045. Washington, DC: National Technical Information Service (NTIS).

———. 1987b. *Unfinished Business: A Comparative Assessment of Environmental Problems.* Washington, DC: NTIS.

———. Office of Research and Development. 1988. *Technical Support Document on Risk Assessment of Chemical Mixtures.* EPA-600/8-90/064. Washington, DC: NTIS.

———. 1990a. *Environmental Investments: The Cost of a Clean Environment.* Washington, DC: NTIS.

———. 1990b. *Reducing Risk: Setting Priorities and Strategies for Environmental Protection.* Washington, DC: NTIS.

———. 1991. Guidelines for the Developmental Toxicity Risk Assessment. *Federal Register* 56(Dec. 5): 63798–63826.

———. 1992. Guidelines for Exposure Assessment. *Federal Register* 57(May 29): 22,888–22,938.

U.S. GAO (General Accounting Office). 1977. *A Better Way for the Department of Agriculture to Inspect Meat and Poultry Processing Plants.* RCED 78-11. Washington, DC: U.S. GAO.

———. 1992. Food Safety and Quality. *Uniform, Risk-based Inspection System Needed to Ensure Safe Food Supply.* RCED 92–152. Washington, DC: U.S. GAO.

———. 1993. *Food Safety: Building a Scientific, Risk-Based Meat and Poultry Inspection System.* RCED 93–22. Washington, DC: U.S. GAO.

———. 1996a. *Food Safety: Information on Foodborne Illnesses.* RCED 96–96. Washington, DC: U.S. GAO.

———. 1996b. *Food Safety: Reducing the Threat of Foodborne Illnesses.* RCED 96–815. Washington, DC: U.S. GAO.

———. 1997. *Food Safety: Fundamental Changes Needed to Improve Food Safety.* RCED 97–57. Washington, DC: U.S. GAO.

———. 2001. *Food Safety: CDC Is Working to Address Limitations in Several of Its Foodborne Disease Surveillance Systems.* GAO 01-973. Washington, DC: U.S. GAO.

U.S. Office of Management and Budget. 1991. Regulatory Program of the U.S. Government. April 1, 1990–March 31–1991, p. 441.

Washington Post. 1994. Analyzing Risk Assessment at EPA; Some See It as Management Tool; Others Call It Unreasonable, by Gary Lee. March 8, A17.

WHO. 1976. Report of the thirteenth session of the Codex Committee on Food Hygiene, Rome, May 10–13. Food and Agriculture Organization of the United Nations.

———. 1982. International Commission on Microbiological Specifications for Food. Report of the WHO/ICMSF Meeting in Hazard Analysis, Critical Control Point System in Food Hygiene. Geneva: World Health Organization, VHP/82.37.

2

The Centennial of U.S. Food Safety Law: A Legal and Administrative History

RICHARD A. MERRILL

The importance of safe food is obvious. Although estimates of the incidence of foodborne illness are imprecise, most people are in agreement that it is significant and possibly growing (NAS 1998). However, most foodborne illnesses are transitory, or difficult to trace to their source (Lassiter 1997). As a result, neither markets nor tort claims can be relied on to force suppliers to internalize their costs. Consumers can guard against many hazards through careful handling of food, but other dangers cannot be controlled at the site of preparation.

Most observers agree, therefore, that government has important roles to play, that federal authorities are critical in fulfilling those roles, and that significant federal resources should be devoted to food safety regulation. The focus of this chapter is on the organization of these governmental activities, and how resources are allocated within the federal food safety system. Highly publicized food poisoning episodes have rekindled criticisms of the regulatory process. The critics' central claim is that the organization of federal food protection functions is seriously flawed. To state it frankly, their claim is that no "organization" worthy of the name exists. Instead, responsibility is dispersed among several agencies that lack central direction and administer diverse, not always consistent, statutes (NAS 1998). (See Appendix A on p. 304 for a breakdown of specific agency responsibilities.) The primary "reform" implied by this critique is consolidation of federal food safety functions in one organization, under the direction of a single leader and advocate.

This, in substance, is the message of a recent report from the National Academy of Sciences (NAS). The report, *Ensuring Safe Food From Production to Consumption,* described the federal programs that share responsibility for food safety and highlighted the puzzling allocation of federal resources among them (NAS 1998). It recommended:

Congress should establish, by statute, a unified and central framework for managing federal food safety programs, one that is headed by a single official and which has the responsibility and control of resources for all federal food safety activities, including outbreak management, standard-setting, inspection, monitoring, surveillance, risk assessment, enforcement, research, and education. (NAS 1998, *12*)

This is not the first time that a respected body has endorsed reorganization. In the last 50 years, more than a dozen expert panels inside and outside government have called for the consolidation of the federal agencies that share food safety responsibilities (NAS 1998). Repetition of these proposals, however, has so far proved ineffective. The current federal food safety structure closely resembles the one described a generation ago by the Senate Governmental Affairs Committee Study on Federal Regulation (U.S. Senate 1977).

Origins of the Federal Food Safety Bureaucracy

Although nearly a century old, today's balkanized food safety bureaucracy originated in a single cabinet department, the U.S. Department of Agriculture (USDA). The formal dispersal of functions began in 1940 when the Food and Drug Administration (FDA) was removed from the Department. From the beginning in 1906, however, administrative separation was encouraged by statute. Congress created separate legal regimes for regulating meat products and non-meat foods, and responsibility for administering the two newly divided laws fell to separate units in USDA.

Foundations of Federal Food Safety Regulation

Congress passed the first statute prohibiting the adulteration of domestic food in 1886 (Wilson 1942). This statute taxed margarine and sought to regulate butter and cheese imitations. Three years later, Congress appropriated funds for a "Chemical Division," whose purpose was to enable the Secretary of Agriculture to extend and continue the investigation of "the adulteration of foods, drugs, and liquors" (Wilson 1942, *12*). The Bureau of Chemistry, the precursor of today's FDA, thus was based in a department, USDA, whose primary mission at the time was to assist American food producers.

Passage of the Pure Food and Drug Act (PFDA) and the Meat Inspection Act (MIA). While Congress prohibited food adulteration in the District of Columbia in 1879, it took nearly 30 more years and the defeat of 190 bills before legislation was passed to prohibit the marketing of adulterated food in interstate commerce (Wilson 1942). A coalition including the American Medical Association, the American Public Health Association, labor unions, and consumer groups formed to support the legislation, and to overcome the opposition of food producers (Wiley 1929). Publication of Upton Sinclair's *The Jungle* helped persuade President Theodore Roosevelt to support, and Congress to pass, the PFDA and the MIA in 1906, on the same day (MIA 1907; PFDA 1906; Wilson 1942). The PFDA made it a misdemeanor to introduce adulterated food into interstate commerce and it granted the Secretary of Agriculture authority to examine food samples for possible adulteration and report potential violations to the Department of Justice (PFDA 1906). The MIA established the program of continuous examination by resident federal inspectors in meat processing facilities that persists to this day (MIA 1906). Implementation of the PFDA was assigned to the new Bureau of Chemistry; the Department's Bureau of Animal Industry assumed responsibility for administering the MIA (Herrick 1944).

Friction Within USDA. From 1906 to 1940, relations within USDA were often turbulent. Dr. Harvey Wiley, Chief of the Bureau of Chemistry until 1912, had long been an advocate for the federal government's responsibility for food safety (Wiley 1929). According to several accounts, agriculture secretaries often attempted to dampen Wiley's vigorous approach to regulation. Between 1907 and 1911, the Department declined to publish at least a dozen of the Bureau's scientific reports on such topics as the use of sulfur dioxide in fruits, corn syrup as a synonym for glucose, the use of glycerin in meat preparation, and the bacterial content of shell eggs (Wiley 1929). Only a year after PFDA was signed, the Secretary created a new Board of Food and Drug Inspection, whose official role was to advise the secretary on issues of food and drug enforcement but whose real objective, Wiley believed, was to dilute the influence of the Bureau of Chemistry (Wiley 1929).[1]

The Bureau of Chemistry suffered an important defeat in 1908. President Roosevelt, who on the advice of his doctor took saccharin every day, became enraged when he learned that the Bureau was considering banning the sweetener (Merrill and Taylor 1985). Roosevelt had previously appointed Dr. Ira Remsen, the discoverer of saccharin, to chair a new Board of Consulting Scientific Experts to help resolve issues of food and drug safety.[2] After the Board advised that saccharin was safe, Secretary of Agriculture James Wilson kept the

---

[1]The effect of this Board was to dilute the power of Dr. Wiley. Prior to the establishment of the Board of Food and Drug Inspection, the Bureau of Chemistry alone advised the Secretary on enforcement matters, as the Bureau was the only USDA agency mentioned in the PFDA. When the Secretary of Agriculture placed two of his allies in positions on the new three-person Board with Dr. Wiley, the chief of the Bureau of Chemistry called the situation "a complete paralysis of the law."

[2]According to another account, Roosevelt had appointed the Remsen Board to help the Bureau address the controversial issue of the safety of food preservatives, such as

product on the market (Merrill and Taylor 1985).[3] A critical House committee later charged: "Thus the administration of the [PFDA] began with a policy of compromise between the Secretary and the purveyors of our national food supplies" (quoted in Wiley 1929, *180*).

Because of the perceived conflict between the Bureau of Chemistry's research duties and its enforcement responsibilities, pressure grew to separate its two functions (NAS 1998). Dr. Walter Campbell, who succeeded Wiley, proposed this split, suggesting that the Bureau's enforcement responsibilities be assigned to a new Food, Drug, and Insecticide Administration (FDIA) still within USDA. In 1927, Congress created FDIA and three years later deleted the "I" from the agency's name, leaving the title that we use today (NAS 1998).

1938 Federal Food, Drug, and Cosmetic Act (FDCA). The next major federal food safety legislation was FDCA (FDCA 1938). The FDCA's most significant innovation was the requirement that new drugs be shown to be safe before marketing (21 U.S.C. 355 (1994)), but it also strengthened FDA's food authority (Wilson 1942).[4] The Act authorized the agency to inspect factories, establish safety tolerances for unavoidable poisons, and create identity and quality standards. It also required manufacturers to label food ingredients (21 U.S.C. 341-374 (1994)).

Passage of the 1938 Act was protracted (Hutt and Merrill 1991). One of the battles in the struggle to enact FDCA revolved around which agency should have authority to regulate the advertising of foods, drugs, and cosmetics. Although many in the food and advertising industries favored FDA, based on the agency's presumed scientific expertise, the Proprietary Association and the Institute of Medicine Manufacturers argued that jurisdiction should rest with Federal Trade Commission (FTC), which they saw as less threatening (Jackson 1970). In the end, FTC was given exclusive jurisdiction to regulate the advertising of food, drugs, medical devices, and cosmetics (FTCA 1938; Jackson 1970). Only much later was FDA given limited authority over the advertising of prescription drugs and later still, restricted medical devices.

FDA's Removal from USDA

FDA was moved out of USDA in 1940. While the agency had never represented a significant financial responsibility for the Department, many saw a conflict

---

benzoate of soda. Choppin, Clayton A., and Jack High. 1999. *The Politics of Purity.* Ann Arbor, MI: The University of Michigan Press.

[3]Seventy years later, the Bureau of Chemistry's successor agency, the FDA, would once again be rebuffed—this time by Congress—in an attempt to ban saccharin as a carcinogenic food additive.

[4]For a brief comparison of the 1906 PFDA to the 1938 FDCA see also (Jackson 1970, 195–96).

between its food safety mission and USDA's primary goals (Kallet and Schlink 1933). Advocates for removal envisioned a new agency that "would be staffed with men disposed to take as prompt and effective steps in a food and drug and health emergency as the Department of Agriculture now does on the Mexican bean beetle, the corn-borer, a grasshopper plague, or an epidemic of hog cholera" (Kallet and Schlink 1933, *277*).

USDA fought to retain FDA and, surprisingly, offered instead to surrender its meat inspection responsibilities. Arguing that FDA would fit better in the new Federal Security Agency (FSA), however, the Bureau of the Budget advised President Franklin Roosevelt:

> It is true that most food traces back to the soil, and hence to agriculture, but it is not to be believed that the activities of the Department of Agriculture in tomato culture, for example, vests it with any legitimate interest in canned tomatoes where the problem becomes one of toxicity, under measure, adulteration, or deceptive labeling. (quoted in U.S. Senate 1977)

On April 11, 1940, Roosevelt proposed to transfer FDA into FSA (Wilson 1942). At the time, the Federal Security Administrator oversaw a diverse group of agencies including the Public Health Service, the Civilian Conservation Corps, the Office of Education, and the Social Security Administration (NAS 1998). A decade after World War II, these and additional functions were assembled in a new cabinet Department of Health, Education, and Welfare (HEW) (Hutt and Merrill 1991). Even with FDA's relocation, however, the separation of regulation from promotion was not complete. Meat and poultry inspection remained the responsibilities of USDA's Bureau of Animal Husbandry, later renamed Food Safety and Inspection Service (FSIS).

Sources of Administrative Fragmentation

The jurisdictional boundaries that divide federal food safety functions are anchored in the statutory framework that Congress created in 1906. In addition to enacting separate laws for meat and other foods, Congress subdivided authority for implementing PFDA. The 1906 Act provided that "the Secretary of the Treasury, the Secretary of Agriculture and the Secretary of Commerce . . . shall make uniform rules and regulations" for implementing the statute (PFDA 1906). This dispersal of authority set the pattern that continues today. By 1949, FDA regulated food labeling while FTC oversaw food advertising; FDA set limits for and monitored pesticide residues on food while USDA was responsible for approving the marketing of pest control agents used by farmers; FSA regulated human drugs while USDA monitored drugs used in livestock; and the Department of the Treasury administered the tax on margarine and imitation cheeses and regulated the labeling of alcoholic beverages.

Two generations later, the food safety "organization chart" had become even more complex. In 1970, President Nixon reassigned responsibility for pesticide registration from USDA to the new Environmental Protection Agency (EPA), which also inherited FDA's responsibility (and personnel) for setting pesticide tolerances on food. Research on food, nutrition, and health became divided among several units within USDA and shared with the CDC and the National Institutes of Health (NAS 1998). The Commerce Department has a program for overseeing the harvesting, processing, and shipment of seafood.

The Birth of EPA

Since World War II, the federal government has administered companion regimes for regulating the marketing of agricultural pesticides and protecting consumers from unsafe residues on food. These programs are governed by two separate statutes, both currently administered by EPA. In 1910 Congress passed the first federal pesticide law, the Insecticide Act, to regulate the labeling of pesticides (Insecticide Act 1910). USDA's Bureau of Chemistry performed the testing necessary to set allowable levels for pesticide residues on food. During the early part of the century, one third of its staff was involved in pesticide regulation (Kallet and Schlink 1933; Wilson 1942). This role sharpened the tension implicitly caused by the Bureau's location within USDA. Despite claims that industry had "captured" the pesticide program, however, when FDA was later removed, responsibility for administering the Insecticide Act remained with USDA.

In 1947, Congress passed the Federal Insecticide, Fungicide, and Rodenticide Act (FIFRA), replacing the outdated Insecticide Act (FIFRA 1947). FIFRA required pesticide manufacturers to obtain USDA approval before shipping any pesticide for use on food crops (7 U.S.C. 136a (1994)). Responsibility for setting permissible residue levels on food remained with FDA (21 U.SC. 346a (1994)). Congress amended FDCA in 1954 and again in 1958 to confirm FDA's authority to set safe "tolerances" for pesticides on food and place on industry the responsibility of conducting the tests necessary to set such limits (21 U.S.C. 346a (2001)).

In 1970, President Nixon transferred the responsibility for administering FIFRA to the newly created EPA. At the same time, he also gave EPA the tolerance-setting function that FDA had been performing (Reorganization Plan 1970).

Geographic Dispersal

The fragmentation of federal food safety programs is not only statutory and organizational, it is physical as well. The major participants—USDA, FDA, and EPA—are based in several different locations in and around the nation's capitol. FDA occupies some 40 buildings in nearly 20 locations around Washington, DC. (U.S. FDA 2000). The FDA Center for Food Safety and Applied Nutrition (CFSAN) has field personnel in 5 regional offices, 21 district offices, 16 laboratories, and 120 resident posts that serve as bases for its investigators (U.S. FDA 1999b). USDA's several programs with food safety-related functions are equally widely distributed. FSIS alone has 18 district offices and a technical center (9 C.F.R. 200.3(c) (1999)).

This snapshot of the bureaucratic landscape does not reflect the even more obvious dispersal of personnel and facilities that is the inevitable result of a system that relies on physical examination of facilities and of products. USDA's meat and poultry inspectors are based in approximately 6,000 establishments (USDA 1999). FDA's field inspection force is situated in fewer locations but is responsible for monitoring nearly 10 times as many business establishments. In FY 2002, FDA performed 11,236 direct inspections on food establishments and contracted to the states for an additional 7,517 inspections (U.S. FDA 2004). This summary does not account for other governmental bodies, most notably the numerous state and local agencies that have important roles in assuring safe food and investigating outbreaks of foodborne disease.

A Closer Look at the Contemporary Structure of Food Safety Regulation

Overview

Four federal agencies now share primary responsibility for federal food safety. The largest of these, USDA's FSIS, regulates meat and poultry through the continuous inspection of processing operations and review of product labels (21 U.S.C. 451-471, 601-695 (1994)). FSIS also regulates the safety and labeling of egg products and enforces EPA pesticide tolerances in meat, poultry, and egg products. FDA, through CFSAN, monitors the safety and labeling of most non-meat and processed foods, and licenses food-use chemicals other than pesticides (21 U.S.C. 301-397 (1994)). EPA Office of Pesticide Programs (OPP) registers pesticides and sets pesticide tolerances that are enforced by FDA or FSIS (7 U.S.C. 135-136y (1994); 21 U.S.C. 342(a)(2)(B) (1994)). A fourth agency, Centers for Disease Control and Prevention (CDC), within the Department of Health and Human Services (HHS), is the federal government's primary clearinghouse for disease surveillance data, and its chief resource for epidemiological investigations (U.S. CDC 2000a).

In addition to these four principal units, at least a dozen other federal agencies play supporting roles in the government's regulatory efforts. They include USDA's Agricultural Marketing Service (AMS); USDA's Grain Inspection, Packers and Stockyards Administration (GIPSA); USDA's Office of Risk Assessment and Cost–Benefit Analysis; Commerce Department's National Marine

Fisheries Service (NMFS); USDA's Agricultural Research Service (ARS); USDA's Animal and Plant Inspection Service (APHIS); USDA's Cooperative State Research, Education, and Extension Service (CSREES); USDA's Economic Research Service (ERS); Treasury Department's Bureau of Alcohol, Tobacco and Firearms (ATF); Federal Trade Commission (FTC); and U.S. Customs Service (U.S. GAO 1990a; U.S. FDA 1998).

Several categories of food are subject to regulation by more than one agency. For example, identity standards for grain are established and enforced by GIPSA (7 C.R.F.2.81 (1998)), pesticide residues on grains are regulated by EPA (7 U.S.C. 136(a) (1994)) and enforced by FDA (7 U.S.C. 342(a)(2) (1994)), while grains or their derivatives that become ingredients in processed food are potentially subject to FDA regulation as food additives (7 U.S.C. 321(s) (1994)). Seafood and eggs are both subject to regulation by two agencies. In addition, although USDA traditionally inspects meat processors, the FDA shares with USDA authority to carry out surveillance and enforcement of meat adulteration standards once products have left USDA-regulated processing plants (12 U.S.C. 679(b) (1994)). Further overlap is occasioned by FDA's responsibility for approving additives to meat and poultry products (9 C.F.R. 318.7 (1999)).

Food and Drug Administration

FDA's Food Safety Responsibilities. FDA has responsibility for the safety and wholesomeness of all food sold in interstate commerce, other than meat, poultry, and processed egg products (CFSAN 1998). However, both its budget and workforce are much smaller than those available to FSIS. Moreover, food safety is not FDA's only, or indeed its major, responsibility. The agency devotes the majority of its resources to assuring the safety and effectiveness of all drugs and medical devices. In addition, it regulates cosmetics, blood products, radiation-emitting products, veterinary drugs, and a host of exotic medical technologies, such as gene therapy, tissue transplants, and xenografts (21 U.S.C. 393(b)(2) (1999)).

FDA uses several means to protect the safety of food. The agency performs premarket safety reviews of food and color additives (21 U.S.C. 348 (2001)). It periodically inspects food processing and storage operations (21 U.S.C. 374 (1999)). It establishes and enforces regulations governing food labels (21 U.S.C. 331(b) (1994)). FDA also has formal authority to police sanitation in supermarkets and restaurants but it relies on state and local officials to inspect such establishments (21 U.S.C. 342(a)(4) 1994). Finally, FDA conducts research—although on a smaller scale than USDA—into the health risks posed by foodborne chemicals and microbiological contaminants (U.S. FDA 1997).

FDA's main food safety functions are divided between its headquarters-based CFSAN and a sizable force of field inspectors and laboratories. Roughly speaking, the Center establishes the standards, and field personnel are largely responsible for ensuring that they are met. Together these units oversee a vast industry that includes more than 60,000 domestic establishments that process, store, or distribute food (U.S. FDA 2004). Another facet of FDA's food safety activity is its regulation of animal drugs and feeds. Some animal drugs may leave harmful residues that could enter the human food supply. The Center for Veterinary Medicine (CVM) in FDA is responsible for premarket approval of new animal drugs and, in cooperation with field inspectors (and USDA), for surveillance of animal drug use (Friedman 1996a).

FDA's Approach to Food Safety. FDA's food safety functions fall under two broad headings. The agency is concerned with threats of acute poisoning caused by harmful microorganisms that may contaminate or grow in food. It is also responsible for controlling potentially toxic materials that get into food through human activity.

In confronting the first challenge, FDA's primary instruments are the establishment and enforcement of standards for the selection, preparation, storage, and handling of ingredients and finished foods. Several categories of food within FDA's jurisdiction present significant risks of microbial contamination. One is seafood, for which FDA shares responsibility with the Department of Commerce through the NMFS (50 C.F.R. 260 (1999); Friedman 1996b). In 1995, FDA promulgated regulations that mandate Hazard Analysis and Critical Control Points (HACCP) regulation of seafood products (U.S. FDA 1995). HACCP is a quality assurance strategy that requires producers and transporters to: (1) identify significant food risks (e.g., bacterial contamination) that can occur at every stage of production, transport, and storage; (2) specify validated processes to control such risks (e.g., refrigeration); and (3) establish record-keeping and monitoring procedures to verify effectiveness and detect errors (U.S. FDA 1995; Jaykus 1996).

Other potentially high-risk food categories under FDA's jurisdiction include fresh produce (*E. coli* O157:H7 and *Salmonella*), cheese and other dairy products (*Listeria monocytogenes*), and shell eggs (*Salmonella enteriditis*). FDA has not established HACCP requirements for these foods but relies on the general adulteration provisions of FDCA, which prohibit foods produced under unsanitary conditions or that contain potentially harmful bacteria.

Even though monitoring compliance with processing standards such as HACCP or FDCA's adulteration provisions is labor intensive, FDA lacks the resources to inspect more than a small percentage of food processors in any year (NAS 1998). FDA's approach thus differs significantly from that employed by FSIS for meat and poultry. Rather than attempting regularly to inspect all producers, FDA relies heavily on prescribed operating standards or FDCA's statutory prohibitions and the good faith of processors to implement them. Firms have significant incentives to self-monitor for quality and cleanliness, but the fact remains that FDA's overburdened inspection resources have declined in relation to the number of firms subject to its jurisdiction.

Licensure of Food Use Chemicals. The second major focus of FDA's food safety efforts is reflected in its regulation of chemicals that are likely to appear in food. The agency is responsible for evaluating the safety of ingredients added to processed foods, including products subject to USDA inspection (Hutt and Merrill 1991). This responsibility is imposed by the 1958 Food Additives Amendment, which requires that any "food additive" be found by FDA to be safe (21 U.S.C. 348 (1994)). The 1960 Color Additive Amendments establish a similar requirement for colors added to food (or drugs or cosmetics) (21 U.S.C. 379e (1994)). FDA devotes significant resources to these licensing programs because the law not only mandates that it review new ingredients, but also obligates it to act within a prescribed time limit, an obligation the agency often struggles and fails to meet (21 U.S.C. 348(c)(2) (1994)).

CFSAN's Office of Premarket Approval also has responsibility for monitoring the safety of two classes of ingredients that do not meet the technical definition of a "food additive": (1) substances sanctioned by FDA or USDA before 1958 and (2) substances that are "generally recognized as safe." In addition, the statutory definition of "food additive" includes food-contact materials (21 U.S.C. 321 (1994)). FDA's responsibility for reviewing the latter class of chemicals has been a major drain on the Center's resources. The same agency scientists are also responsible for the FDA program to control environmental contaminants of food. Substances such mercury, PCBs, and aflatoxin contaminate several foods, and can pose serious potential health risks.

FDA's Food Safety Budget. With a fiscal 2002 budget exceeding $1.3 billion and more than 10,000 full-time-equivalent employees (FTEs), FDA has grown dramatically since 1940, but so have its responsibilities (U.S. FDA 2003). During the 1990s, resources for drug regulation grew fairly rapidly owing to the enactment of user fee legislation to support the new drug approval program, but resources for food regulation lagged. In the last few years, however, FDA's budget for food regulation, which includes labeling and nutrition programs but is devoted predominately to food safety and hygiene, has grown in response to heightened concerns about food safety and bioterrorism. In 2002, FDA's food regulation budget was $393.3 million or 29% of FDA's total budget of more than $1.3 billion. Of this, $143.2 million went to CFSAN headquarters activities, and $250.1 million was devoted to field activities, including inspections, laboratory analysis, and enforcement. In addition, Congress appropriated $85.6 million for FDA's animal drug and feed regulatory program, overseen by the Center for Veterinary Medicine. This program affects food safety, as well as animal health, because it covers the safety of animal drug and feed additive residues in animal-derived food products and such issues as bovine spongiform encephalopathy (BSE). These resources are split between CVM headquarters function ($55.7 million) and field activities ($29.9 million).

Department of Agriculture

USDA's Food Safety Programs. The USDA food safety budget was $704 million in 2002 (USDA 2003). Because the Department's mission has grown to include helping fund land-grant colleges, rural development projects, the nationwide Extension Service, support for and regulation of agricultural marketing arrangements, and provision of farm loans, however, this amount represents less than 1% of USDA's total 2002 budget of more than $71.3 billion (USDA 2003).

More than a half dozen different USDA units have food safety responsibilities. Many of these activities are overseen by the Under Secretary for Food Safety, a position created in 1994 to address claims that USDA's agricultural promotion activities inevitably dominate food safety efforts (7 C.F.R. 2.18 (1998)).[5] The most important of these units, FSIS, is responsible for inspecting on a continuous basis each plant that processes meat or poultry, and food containing meat or poultry intended for interstate distribution (7 C.F.R. 2.53 (1998)). Agricultural Marketing Service (AMS) operates a large voluntary inspection system for the grading of eggs, and Animal and Plant Health Inspection Service (APHIS) oversees programs to prevent animal and plant disease (7 C.F.R. 2.79-2.80 (1998)). APHIS is also responsible for the USDA's regulation of agricultural biotechnology products.[6] The Grain Inspection, Packers and Stockyards Administration (GIPSA) inspects grains for safety as well as quality (7 C.F.R. 2.81 (1998)). The Agricultural Research Service (ARS); Cooperative State Research, Education, and Extension Service (CSREES); and Economic Research Service (ERS) each undertakes or funds research, including some food safety-related research (7 C.F.R. 2.65-2.67 (1998)). USDA units expended more than $60 million in 1998 on food safety research—far more than the rest of the government (NAS 1998).

---

[5]In 1994, then-Congressman Robert Torricelli had proposed moving the USDA's meat and poultry inspection responsibilities to FDA. While the democratic leadership of the House Agriculture Committee opposed this move, Congress created the USDA's Under Secretary for Food Safety as a means of "elevating and keeping completely separate all food safety activities within the Department." Representatives Torricelli and Stenholm. *Congressional Record.* 1994. 140: H9967, September 28.

[6]Under its authority to protect crops and animals from disease, APHIS issues permits that govern the release of genetically modified pesticides. Both EPA and FDA also regulate genetically modified organisms under their traditional statutes. See Animal and Plant Health Inspection Service, U.S. Department of Agriculture. United States Regulatory Oversight in Biotechnology. http://www.aphis.usda.gov/biotech/OECD/usregs.htm (accessed November 11, 2000).

Food Safety and Inspection Service

In contrast to FDA's undirected authority to police commerce for adulterated food, the Secretary of Agriculture is under statutory obligations to examine every meat and poultry carcass intended for food sold in interstate commerce (21 U.S.C. 331(a) and 604 (1994)). These continuous inspection programs claim a larger share of federal food safety resources than any other activity, with FSIS 2002 budget of $704 million being by far the largest budget of any federal food safety agency. In 1998, FSIS devoted approximately 88% of its personnel budget to in-plant inspection (U.S. GAO 1994; U.S. OMB 1998), a ratio that has remained relatively constant. The law's continuous inspection mandates have thus become "resource anchors" for the USDA. While FDA relies on approximately 250 field inspectors to oversee some 60,000 food establishments (U.S. FDA 2002), FSIS employs 7,600 full-time residential inspectors (USDA 2003) in approximately 6,000 meat and poultry plants.

FSIS' primary reliance on organoleptic (sight, touch, and smell) examination of each carcass or bird has long been controversial (U.S. GAO 1992). The MIA and the Poultry Products Inspection Act (PPIA) mandates appear strict (PPIA). For example, the law states:

> The Secretary shall cause to be made by inspectors appointed for that purpose a post mortem examination and inspection of the carcasses and parts thereof of all cattle, sheep, swine, goats, horses, mules, and other equines to be prepared at any slaughtering, meat-canning, salting, packing, rendering, or similar establishment in any State, Territory, or the District of Columbia as articles of commerce which are capable of use as human food . . . (21 U.S.C. 604 (1994))

PPIA similarly obligates the secretary to conduct a "post mortem inspection of the carcass of each bird processed" (21 U.S.C. 455(b) (1994)). This is resource-intensive work, and as other methods have been developed to monitor product safety, the FSIS has come under pressure to modernize its approach (NAS 1987).

FSIS admitted that "inspection methods have . . . not been modified sufficiently to address the microbial causes of foodborne illness" (FSIS 1997). The agency has responded to the NAS' criticism in several ways. While continuing sight and smell inspection of each carcass and bird, it has also adopted requirements for bacterial testing of products. Further, it has mandated HACCP protocols in meat and poultry processing plants (FSIS 1996). The agency's endorsement of HACCP has been controversial in some quarters. Its unionized inspectors have opposed any USDA move away from carcass-by-carcass inspection (Beers 1999). With strong support from the Clinton administration, however, USDA embraced implementation of HACCP as a major priority (U.S. OMB 1999).

Defenders of carcass-by-carcass inspections say they are mandated by law (U.S. GAO 1998b). The official Department position is more nuanced. In response to a recent GAO report questioning the allocation of resources, USDA Under Secretary for Food Safety stated:

> Neither statute states how these inspections are to be conducted. There is no statutory requirement that the inspections be accomplished as currently conducted under the FSIS' inspection program and regulations. (Woteki 1998)

MIA and PPIA may not mandate the form of organoleptic inspection of meat and poultry products that is currently practiced, but they do seem to require more than a sampling of carcasses (21 U.S.C. 455(b), 604 (1994)).

Environmental Protection Agency

EPA's primary food safety responsibilities involve establishing tolerance levels for pesticide residues on food through the registration process for new pesticides and the retrospective review of previously registered pesticides, many of which were first approved for use under less stringent safety standards than exist today. These functions are performed by the agency's Office of Pesticide Programs (OPP) pursuant to FIFRA and FDCA, respectively. In 2002, EPA's total budget for its food safety activities was $109 million, of which about $47 million was for regulation of new pesticides and $62 million was for the retrospective review and regulation of old ones (U.S. EPA 2003c).

The statutory scheme for controlling dietary pesticide risks is complex. Under FIFRA, a pesticide may not be sold in the United States unless it has been registered by EPA (7 U.S.C. 136a(a) (1994)). FIFRA requires the manufacturer of a new pesticide to conduct tests and report the results, which EPA uses to evaluate its risks and benefits (7 U.S.C. 136d (1994)). To control dietary exposure to pesticides, EPA also establishes binding upper limits, or tolerances, for residues left on food. This function is governed by FDCA (21 U.S.C. 346a (2001)). Pesticide tolerances are approved under a recently revised health-based safety standard that specifically requires EPA to consider aggregate pesticide exposure and the special vulnerabilities of children (21 U.S.C. 346b (2001); U.S. EPA 2003b).

If consolidation of federal food safety functions were seriously contemplated, EPA's pesticide residue program seems a strong candidate for inclusion. It is the largest federal unit responsible for evaluating the safety of chemicals added to food, with a current workforce of 680.

While EPA establishes allowable limits for pesticides, FDA and FSIS are responsible for monitoring food to ensure compliance with those limits. Responsibility for investigating on-farm compliance with EPA-prescribed limitations on pesticide use rests with the states under agreements with EPA (U.S. EPA 2003a).

Centers for Disease Control and Prevention

FDA, FSIS, and EPA variously seek to control foodborne risks through inspection, production surveillance, and product approval, but none of them systematically investigates the prevalence or causes of foodborne disease. At the federal level, this task falls to CDC, which surveys morbidity and mortality by cause and undertakes epidemiological investigations of diseases including foodborne illnesses (U.S. GAO 1990b). CDC's spending in the latter area has risen from $2.9 million in fiscal year 1995 to $14.5 million in fiscal year 1998 (NAS 1998), a rise partially attributable to the FoodNet program that CDC established in collaboration with FSIS and FDA (Binder et al. 1998). CDC's food safety budget has continued to grow, with the total reaching $36 million in 2002 (U.S. CDC 2003b).

CDC obtains most of its data on disease incidence through the reporting of physicians nationwide (U.S. CDC 2000a).[7] CDC's National Center for Infectious Diseases (NCID) maintains a list of "nationally notifiable" illnesses for which the agency maintains detailed records. NCID analyzes data on specific diseases from state health agencies, laboratories, physician networks, hospitals, and national databases (U.S. CDC 2000b).

In 1996 CDC established FoodNet, an active foodborne illness surveillance network, in several locations around the country. Today FoodNet monitors clinical laboratories for specific foodborne pathogens in Connecticut, Georgia, Maryland, Minnesota, Oregon, and selected counties in California, Colorado, New York, and Tennessee—a total population of 37.6 million. CDC hopes to include surveillance data from New Mexico in 2004. FoodNet targets nine common foodborne pathogens that pose the greatest risks to public health: *Campylobacter, E. coli* 0157:H7, *Salmonella, Listeria monocytogenes, Shigella, Vibrio, Yersinia enterocolitica, Cryptosporidium,* and *Cyclospora* (U.S. CDC 2003a). CDC also conducts focused epidemiological investigations to determine the causes of morbidity and mortality in medical emergencies (U.S. CDC 2000a). Between 400 and 500 disease outbreaks are reported to CDC each year, accounting for upwards of 10,000 individual cases of food-related illness (Satcher 1996).

---

[7]In an example of the federalist patchwork of the U.S. health structure, the CDC is required by Congress to collect morbidity and mortality information on specific diseases; however, the states are not required to provide these data to the CDC.

Other Agencies with Food Safety Responsibilities

The Commerce Department's National Marine Fisheries Service (NMFS) has, for many years, operated a fee-based voluntary seafood inspection and surveillance service, which had a total budget of $18.5 million in 1998 (U.S. GAO 1990b; NAS 1998). Although the Clinton Administration proposed reassigning this program to FDA, a shift that would have centralized federal seafood regulation, it remains part of the Commerce Department (Murphy 1999).

Two units of the Treasury Department, the U.S. Customs Service and the Bureau of Alcohol, Tobacco, and Firearms (ATF), play important roles. Customs collaborates with several regulatory agencies, including FDA and USDA, to enforce federal laws at borders and ports (U.S. FDA 1998). ATF oversees the production and marketing of alcoholic beverages and investigates cases of possible adulteration of domestic and foreign spirits (U.S. GAO 1990b).[8]

Finally, FDA and FSIS share with Federal Trade Commission (FTC) overlapping authorities to police food marketing practices. To express in oversimplified terms, FTC has jurisdiction to respond to false or misleading advertising practices, while FDA and FSIS retain authority to prescribe the contents of labels and labeling (21 U.S.C. 378 (1994)).

No description of the country's food safety "system" would be complete without mention of the state and local agencies that play important, and in some instances growing, roles in preventing or responding to foodborne illness. State and local officials, based in public health units or agriculture departments, or sometimes both, play the lead role in regulating retail food service establishments, including grocery stores. While federal officials focus on major production facilities, hundreds of state and local agencies are the primary overseers of the approximately 750,000 restaurants, supermarkets, and other retail establishments nominally subject to FDA jurisdiction (Taylor 1997). USDA's jurisdiction over meat and poultry products does not extend to retail establishments such as meat markets, grocery stores, and restaurants (U.S. Justice Department 1972). Thus, USDA depends on state inspection resources and the much more limited efforts of FDA to monitor such establishments. FDA contracts with state and local agencies to conduct milk and seafood inspection under federal oversight, and commissions state and local officials to conduct inspections and collect samples in other food handling facilities (U.S. FDA 1999a; 21 U.S.C. 372(a) (1994)).

State regulatory structures exhibit as much fragmentation as the federal apparatus. For example, a 1999 Illinois Food Safety Task Force reported that more

[8]In yet another example of the patchwork organizational structure of the federal food safety agencies, FDA regulates wine coolers, while ATF retains jurisdiction over all other alcoholic beverages (U.S. GAO 1990b).

than 90 local health departments and 135 municipalities in Illinois alone provide food safety services by inspecting restaurants, schools, food stores, and caterers. The Illinois Department of Agriculture functions like a local USDA—preventing animal disease, monitoring slaughter, inspecting meat and poultry processing, and overseeing egg grading. The Illinois State Department of Public Health mimics FDA—inspecting food processing and warehousing of all non-meat and poultry products, monitoring milk safety, and inspecting food retailers and restaurants (Illinois 1999). Some states, such as Texas and New York, combine the regulation of meat, non-meat, processed food, and retail operations in a single agency, but this is by no means the universal pattern (New York 2000; Texas 2000).

The Challenge of Food Imports

In addition to monitoring the domestic products and suppliers of food, U.S. regulators must meet the even greater challenge of assuring the safety of food produced beyond the country's borders. American demand for imported agricultural products has risen dramatically. To illustrate, in 1980, U.S. food manufacturers imported only 9% of their broccoli for use in processed foods. By 1995, 85% of broccoli for processing was imported. By 1995 more than half of all fish and shellfish consumed in the United States was imported, as was one third of all fresh fruit (U.S. GAO 1998a). In 1997, FDA inspectors physically examined just 1.7% of imported products under its jurisdiction; by contrast, FSIS inspectors visually inspected all of the products under its jurisdiction and performed physical inspections on 20% of them (U.S. GAO 1998c).

The lack of inspectional resources particularly hampers the FDA efforts to control the risks of imported food but it is not the only constraint that the agency faces. The USDA is required by law to verify that any country from which the United States imports meat or poultry maintains an inspection system that is functionally equivalent to the U.S. system (21 U.S.C. 466(d) (2001)). FSIS requires exporting countries to apply for meat and poultry importation eligibility, and USDA personnel regularly visit these countries to verify the effectiveness of their respective regimes. FDA has no similar statutory authority to require that exporting countries maintain controls comparable to those it enforces domestically. Although it has authority to negotiate voluntary "equivalency" agreements with foreign countries, it lacks the resources to verify the effectiveness of their regulatory systems (U.S. GAO 1998c).

The interdependence of FDA, USDA, and U.S. Customs Service presents another challenge. Because Customs has the power to refuse entry of a product, coordination at ports is essential. A recent GAO report charges that due to lack of communication, Customs has been unaware of the FDA's refusal to accept certain shipments of food. Consequently, food that FDA had refused entry may have been allowed into commerce by the Customs Service (U.S. GAO 1998a).

Conclusion: Implications for Resource Allocation

This summary makes clear that the United States in no sense operates an "integrated food safety system." Rather, Congress has allocated tasks and resources among several agencies with discrete, although sometimes interrelated authorities and responsibilities. These boundaries and connections are largely the result of legislative decisions made decades ago, when food production was almost exclusively domestic and the distinctions among producer sectors were much easier to discern. These decisions nevertheless have important implications for how resources are allocated in today's food safety program, and we can draw lessons from several decades experience under the program's current structure.

First, if Congress mandates a particular, resource-intensive method of food safety regulation, such as FSIS's carcass-by-carcass inspection in slaughter plants and daily inspection in processing plants, that activity will tend to draw more resources than discretionary functions, such as FDA's inspection and policing activities. Under the inspection laws, meat and poultry products cannot leave the production plant unless they have been inspected and passed by FSIS. Congress and the regulated industry thus collaborate to ensure that FSIS has the resources it needs to carry out this function. There is no similar "resource anchor" for FDA's inspection and compliance programs.

Second, premarket approval programs, such as those Congress has established for pesticides and food additives, require significant resources that must be provided if new technologies are to enter the market. Market-driven pressures to innovate create an external impetus for Congress to maintain the resource base needed by EPA and FDA to manage these programs, which inevitably compete for resources with discretionary functions.

Third, as a result of these past legislative choices about the mode of regulation for particular categories of food products and substances, a substantial portion of the total federal food safety budget is spoken for. The current allocation of resources has a history and rationale of its own and certainly reflects, at least to some extent, perceptions of risk at the time the legislative mandates were established. The current allocation derives, however, from a time when certain preferred means of regulation and matters of agency jurisdiction were more important than risk as drivers of food safety legislative policy. It is fair to say that the current congressional allocation of food safety resources is not calibrated to current assessments of risk or to any analysis of most cost-effective ways of reducing risk.

Finally, resource allocation is not primarily an organizational issue. The many calls for organizational unification of the food safety system are premised in large part on the belief that this would facilitate better allocation of resources across the system, and there is no doubt that putting one official in charge of the system could make an important difference for system-wide planning and priority setting. Organizational change and unified leadership by themselves, however, would not alter the legislative choices and mandates that Congress has built into the food safety system through nearly a century of enactments and mandates. In the U.S. system of government, resource allocation is controlled largely by Congress, and any substantial change in the allocation of food safety resources— whether toward a more risk-based allocation or in any other new direction—will require change by Congress in its legislative mandates to the food safety agencies.

References

Beers, A. 1999. Inspectors Lobby Lawmakers to Support Continuous Inspection. *Food Chemical News* 40(49): 14–16.

Binder, S., R. Khabbaz, B. Swaminathan, R. Tauxe, and M. Potter. 1998. The National Food Safety Initiative. *Emerging Infectious Diseases* 4(2): 347–49.

CFSAN (Center for Food Safety and Applied Nutrition), U.S. Food and Drug Administration.

1998. FDA Almanac. http://www.cfsan.fda.gov/~lrd/almcfsan.html (accessed November 9, 2000).

FIFRA (Federal Insecticide, Fungicide, and Rodenticide Act). 1947. Act of October 30, 1947, ch. 125, 61 Stat. 163.

Friedman, M. 1996a. Statement on Protecting the U.S. Consumer from Food Borne Illnesses before the Subcommittee on Human Resources and Intergovernmental Relations, Committee on Governmental Reform and Oversight, U.S. House of Representatives. 104th Cong., May 10.

———. 1996b. Statement on Inspection of Seafood Products before the Subcommittee on Livestock, Dairy, and Poultry, Committee on Agriculture, U.S. House of Representatives. http://www.fda.gov/ola/1996/cfood.html (accessed November 11, 2000). 104th Congress, May 22.

FSIS (Food Safety and Inspection Service), U.S. Department of Agriculture. 1997. HACCP-Based Meat and Poultry Inspection Concepts. *Federal Register* 62(June 10): 31553–556.

———. 1996. Pathogen Reduction; Hazard Analysis and Critical Control Point (HACCP) Systems. *Federal Register* 61(July 25): 38,806–989.

FTCA (Federal Trade Commission Act). 1938. Act of March 21, 1938, ch. 49, 52 Stat. 111.

Herrick, A.D. 1944. *Food Regulation and Compliance.* New York: Revere.

Hutt, P.B., and R.A. Merrill. 1991. *Food and Drug Law,* 2nd edit. New York: Foundation Press.

Illinois Department of Agriculture and Illinois Department of Public Health. 1999. *Final Report of the Illinois Food Safety Task Force.* http://www.idph.state.il.us/about/fdd/foodsafetytaskforce1.pdf (accessed April 3, 2003).

Insecticide Act. 1910. Act of April 26, 1910, ch. 191, 36 Stat.331.

Jackson, C.O. 1970. *Food and Drug Legislation in the New Deal.* Princeton: Princeton University Press.

Jaykus, L-A. 1996. The Application of Quantitative Risk Assessment to Microbial Food Safety Risks. *Critical Reviews in Microbiology* 22: 279–93.

Kallet, A., and F.J. Schlink. 1933. *100,000,000 Guinea Pigs – Dangers in Everyday Foods, Drugs, and Cosmetics.* New York: Vanguard Press.

Lassiter, S. W. 1997. From Hoof to Hamburger: The Fiction of a Safe Meat Supply. *Williamette Law Review* 33: 411, 417–44.

Merrill, R.A., and M.R. Taylor. 1985. Saccharin: A Case Study of Government Regulation of Environmental Carcinogens. *Virginia Journal of Natural Resources Law* 5(1):1–84.

MIA (Meat Inspection Act). 1907. 21 U.S.C. 601-695 (1907), Public Law 59-242, 34 Stat. 1260, amended by Wholesome Meat Act Public Law 90-201, 81 Stat. 584 (1967), Meat Inspection (1994).

Murphy, J. 1999. NMFS, FDA Plan to Move Ahead with Seafood Inspection Consolidation. *Food Chemical News* 40(47): 7.

NAS (National Academy of Sciences). 1987. *Poultry Inspection: The Basis for a Risk Assessment Approach.* Washington, DC: National Academy Press.

———. 1998. *Ensuring Safe Food: From Production to Consumption.* Washington, DC: National Academy Press.

New York State Department of Agriculture and Markets. Food Safety and Labeling. http://www.agmkt.state.ny.us/Fsi/FSI1.html (accessed Nov. 11, 2000).

PDFA (Pure Food and Drug Act). 1906. 21 U.S.C. 11 (1906), repealed by 21 U.S.C. 392(a), Federal Food, Drug, and Cosmetic Act, Public Law No. 75-717, 52 Stat. 1040 (1938).

PPIA (Poultry Products Inspection Act). Reorganization Plan No.3 of 1970. 1970. *Federal Register* 35: 15623.

Satcher, D. 1996. Statement on Foodborne Diseases before the Subcommittee on Human Resources and Intergovernmental Relations, Committee on Government Reform and Oversight, U.S. House of Representatives. 104th Congress, May 23.

Taylor, M.R. 1997. Preparing America's Food Safety System for the Twenty-First Century – Who Is Responsible for What When It Comes to Meeting the Food Safety Challenges of the Consumer-Driven Global Economy? *Food and Drug Law Journal* 52(1): 13–30.

Texas Department of Health. Associateship of Consumer Health Protection: Bureau of Food and Drug Safety. http://www.tdh.state.tx.us/bfds/ (accessed April 3, 2003).

U.S. CDC (Centers for Disease Control and Prevention). 2000a. National Center for Infectious Diseases Surveillance Activities http://www.cdc.gov/ncidod/ncidsurv.htm (accessed November 9, 2000).

———. 2000b. National Notifiable Disease Surveillance System http://www.cdc.gov/epo/dphsi/nndsshis.htm (accessed April 7, 2003).

———. 2003a. What is FoodNet? http://www.cdc.gov/foodnet/what_is.htm (accessed April 7, 2003).

———. 2003b. CDC Budget Request Summary 2004 (February 2003). http://www.cdc.gov/fmo/budgetrequestsummary.pdf.

USDA (U.S. Department of Agriculture). 1999. USDA 2000 Budget Summary. http://www.usda.gov/agency/obpa/BudgetSummary/2000/text.html#fs (accessed November 10, 2000).

———. 2003. USDA 2004 Budget Summary. http://www.usda.gov/agency/obpa/Budget-Summary/2004/master2004.pdf (accessed April 3, 2003).

http://www.usda.gov/agency/obpa/Budget-Summary/2004/09.FSIS.htm.

U.S. EPA (Environmental Protection Agency). 2003a. Pesticides: Compliance and Enforcement. http://www.epa.gov/pesticides/enforcement/monitoring.htm (accessed April 7, 2003).

———. 2003b. Summary of FQPA Amendments to FIFRA and FFDCA. http://www.epa.gov/oppfead1/fqpa/fqpa-iss.htm (accessed April 3, 2003).

———. 2003c. Summary of the EPA's Budget (accessed October 7, 2004). http://www.epa.gov/ocfopage/budget/2003/2003bib.pdf.

U.S. FDA (Food and Drug Administration). 1995. Procedures for the Safe and Sanitary Processing and Importing of Fish and Fishery Products Final Rule. *Federal Register* 60 (Dec. 18): 65095.

———. 1997. Statement of Organization, Functions, and Delegations of Authority. *Federal Register* 62: 2674, October 10.

———. 1998. Food Safety: A Team Approach. http://www.fda.gov/opacom/backgrounders/foodteam.html (accessed November 9, 2000).

———. 1999a. 1999 FDA Food Code. http://www.cfsan.fda.gov/~dms/fc99-toc.html (accessed April 3, 2003).

———. 1999b. Description of Field Activities, in FY 2000 Budget Request. http://www.fda.gov/oc/oms/ofm/budget/2000/fieldfoods.htm (accessed April 2, 2003).

———. 2000. Buildings and Facilities. http://www.fda.gov/oc/oms/budget/faclegres.htm (accessed November 9, 2000).

———. 2002. FDA's FY 2002 Annual Financial Report Management Discussion & Analysis. http://www.fda.gov/oc/oms/ofm/accounting/cfo/2002/CFSAN.htm (accessed April 7, 2003).

———. 2003. Food and Drug Administration. http://www.fda.gov/oc/oms/ofm/Budget/2004/TOC.htm (accessed April 5, 2003).

———. 2004. Justification of Estimates for Appropriations Committees. http://www.fda.gov/oc/oms/ofm/budget/2004/1Foods.htm).

U.S. GAO (General Accounting Office). 1990a. *Food Safety and Quality: Who Does What in the Federal Government.* GAO/RECD-91-19A.

———. 1990b. *Food Safety and Quality: Who Does What in the Federal Government.* GAO/RECD-91-19B.

———. 1992. *Food Safety: Uniform, Risk-Based Inspection System needed to Ensure Safe Food Supply.* GAO/RCED-92-152.

———. 1994. *Food Safety: Risk-Based Inspections and Microbial Monitoring Needed for Meat and Poultry.* GAO/T-RCED-94-110.

———. 1998a. *Food Safety: Federal Efforts to Ensure the Safety of Imported Foods Are Inconsistent and Unreliable.* GAO/RCED-98-103.

———. 1998b. *Food Safety: Opportunities to Redirect Federal Resources and Funds Can Enhance Effectiveness.* GAO/RCED-98-224.

———. 1998c. *Food Safety: Weak and Inconsistently Applied Controls Allow Unsafe Imported Food to Enter U.S. Commerce.* GAO/TRCED-98-271.

U.S. Justice Department. 1972. Applicability of the Federal Meat Inspection Act to Retail Establishments Opinion of the Attorney General 42 (462).

U.S. OMB (Office of Management and Budget). 1998. Fiscal Year 1999 Budget of the United States, Appendix.

———. 1999. Fiscal Year 2000 Budget of the United States.

U.S. Senate. Committee on Governmental Affairs. 1977. *Study on Federal Regulation: Regulatory Organization 113.* 95th Congress Committee Print.

Wiley, H. 1929. *The History of a Crime Against the Food Law.* Washington, DC: Harvey Wiley.

Wilson, S. 1942. *Food & Drug Regulation.* Washington, DC: American Council on Public Affairs.

Woteki, C.E. 1998. Letter to Mr. Lawrence J. Dyckman, U.S. General Accounting Office, July 7. Reprint in U.S. General Accounting Office. 1998. *Food Safety: Opportunities to Redirect Federal Resources and Funds Can Enhance Effectiveness.* GAO/RCED-98-224, 36–37.

PART II

Risks and Resources to Reduce Them

3

Linking Illnesses to Foods: A Conceptual Framework

ROBERT V. TAUXE

Foodborne infections are a substantial public health burden. In the United States, an estimated 76 million cases occur each year, affecting one in four individuals (Mead et al. 1999). These infections are associated with 325,000 hospitalizations, or approximately 1 in every 1,000. Patient-related costs have been estimated at up to $6.7 billion, for the principal bacterial foodborne infections alone (Buzby and Roberts 1996). Preventing foodborne diseases depends in part on reducing contamination and preventing recontamination of food with chemicals, as well as with pathogens and their toxins. How best to focus prevention efforts in a rational allocation is a complex issue that depends on our knowledge and our best estimates of where risk enters and propagates. The issue is complex: there are many chemical and biological hazards, many foods, and many points from farm to table at which microbes or other hazards can enter foods, and where microbes can multiply or be eliminated. The issue is complicated further by the fact that, while a body of experience has been built up with chemical risk assessment and comparative risk assessment, the science of microbiological risk assessment is new. Virtually no formal work has been done in comparative risk assessment of foodborne pathogens. The discussion in this chapter presents a preliminary "Lewis and Clark" exploration of the complex terrain of charting microbial hazards through the food supply. It provides a conceptual framework for mapping risks across the food production system, rather than a final answer on how to prevent or minimize risk.

In any such assessment of the current situation, it is important to remember that the spectrum of foodborne diseases has changed substantially over time. Past efforts led to development of the successful control programs now in place that have made many formerly common foodborne diseases rare. For example, universal pasteurization of milk prevented typhoid fever and septic streptococcal infections and now continues to protect the public from *Salmonella, E. coli* O157:H7, and *Campylobacter* infections, which otherwise would frequently be transmitted by raw milk. It is difficult to estimate the disease burden that is prevented by pasteurization, but it is undoubtedly very large. Similarly, although brucellosis and tuberculosis from cattle and trichinosis from pork have virtually disappeared, they could return if current control measures were dropped. Resource decisions need to include the successful programs that are critical to sustained disease prevention.

The allocation of the public health burden across the food system must include several specific considerations, outlined in the following paragraphs. The proposed framework develops a risk profile for each of 28 known major foodborne pathogens, using available information combined with informed expert judgment, to map the general groups of foods that are contaminated with that pathogen, and the general location in the chain of production where the contamination occurs. This simple risk profile reflects preliminary thinking on a conceptual framework for more formal, quantitative comparative risk assessments of foodborne pathogens. One challenge is that microbial hazards are different from chemical hazards, for which this sort of analysis is more routinely attempted. For microbial hazards, we have reasonably good data on the burden of acute illness itself, and these data have improved since the mid-1990s with enhancements of public health surveillance such as FoodNet (Angulo and FoodNet Working Group 1997). However, data are sparse on where in the chain of food production microbes contaminate food, where they multiply, and what the level of contamination is at any point. For chemical hazards, the situation is reversed. Few data are available on the direct health impacts, but better information has been gathered on where these hazards enter the food chain.

Fundamental Considerations

The framework proposed in this chapter is organized around six fundamental considerations that influence our understanding of the health impact of foodborne pathogens: diversity, growth, routes of transmission, cross-contamination and recycling, data availability, and epidemiological information.

Diversity

One general consideration is the tremendous diversity of microbes and foods. Each microbe has a different natural habitat, or reservoir, where it persists, with a life cycle that ultimately can bring it into contact with human food. The culinary complexity of our food supply itself is remarkable; the process of food production and preparation is one of the most complex and diverse of human endeavors (Mintz 1997).

The recent estimate of the public health burden of foodborne infections compiled by Mead et al. (1999) included the 28 principal foodborne infectious pathogens (Table 3.1). Some of the 28 pathogens have only recently emerged

TABLE 3.1. Principal Foodborne Infections, as Estimated for 1997, Ranked by Estimated Number of Cases Caused by Foodborne Transmission Each Year in the United States

Pathogen	Number of Cases
Norwalk-like viruses*	9,200,000
Campylobacter*	1,963,000
Salmonella (nontyphoid)	1,342,000
Clostridium perfringens	249,000
Giardia lamblia	200,000
Staphylococcus food poisoning	185,000
Toxoplasma gondii	112,000
E. coli O157:H7 and other Shiga-toxin producing E. coli*	92,000
Shigella	90,000
Yersinia enterocolitica*	87,000
Enterotoxigenic E. coli*	56,000
Streptococci	51,000
Astrovirus*	39,000
Rotavirus*	39,000
Cryptosporidium parvum*	30,000
Bacillus cereus	27,000
Other E. coli	23,000
Cyclospora cayetanensis*	14,000
Vibrio (noncholera)*	5,000
Hepatitis A	4,000
Listeria monocytogenes*	2,000
Brucella	777
Salmonella typhi (typhoid fever)	659
Botulism	56
Trichinella	52
Vibrio cholerae, toxigenic*	49
Vibrio vulnificus*	47

Values greater than 1,000 are rounded to the nearest 1,000. Organisms that have emerged as recognized foodborne pathogens since 1970 are indicated with an asterisk.

Data from Mead et al. (1999).

as being of significant public concern; either they are newly discovered or the important association with food is newly discovered (Tauxe 1997). Even this list leaves out many described illnesses associated with the 28 major pathogens. In 1982, Bryan indexed an exhaustive list of 250 foodborne infections and intoxications (Bryan 1982).

The diversity of pathogens can be accounted for by constructing an allocation for each of the principal pathogens, with some subdivision, such as for common *Salmonella* serotypes or common *Vibrio* species. To illustrate the logical framework, three pathogens, for which some data exist, serve as examples. Similarly the diversity of foods can be consolidated into three general groups: foods derived from land animals, from plants, and those obtained from the sea.

Microbial Growth

Many bacterial microbes multiply rapidly, given favorable conditions. This means a simple threshold level, or tolerance, such as is set for a chemical contaminant, is less appropriate for pathogens. For example, 10 *Vibrio parahaemolyticus* organisms on a plate of cooked seafood are unlikely to cause illness. This organism multiplies rapidly, however, doubling in 12 to 18 minutes in seafood held at warm ambient temperatures (Oliver and Kaper 1997). With a doubling time of 15 minutes, after 2 hours the 10 microbes become 2,560 microbes, and after 6 hours, 167 billion, a substantial dose. Given the subsequent growth, even 10 pathogenic organisms were too many in the initial food. Depending on the nature of the food and the pathogens, once a food becomes contaminated with a pathogen capable of multiplying, the hazard continues, and may increase through the chain of production, unless the pathogen dies off in the food, or there is a definitive pathogen reduction step. The framework should account both for the initial contamination and for subsequent conditions or treatments.

Routes of Transmission

Transmission through food is just one in the spectrum of routes of contamination that affect the public health. Although some pathogens have a single route of transmission, and may even be restricted to a single food group, many foodborne pathogens are also transmitted through several different routes in addition to food, including direct exposure to ill persons, consumption of contaminated water, contact with pets or other animals, or even contact with contaminated inanimate objects.

It may be difficult to determine the route of spread that led to any given individual case, unless other people develop the same illness following a shared exposure. For example, a person infected with *E. coli* O157:H7 may report several possible exposures within the incubation period, such as eating an undercooked hamburger, swimming in a shallow and crowded lake, having contact with a child in a daycare center, or visiting a county fair stock pavilion. Without further information, it may be difficult to decide which had been the most likely route. Similarly, even if no likely nonfood source is identified, and it appears that the infection was foodborne, the person may have consumed several potentially contaminated foods during the probable incubation period. If the pathogen is one that is often transmitted through a variety of foods, the interview by itself will not clearly determine which was most likely. An individual *E. coli* O157:H7 infection could plausibly be related to an undercooked hamburger, raw apple cider, lettuce, or alfalfa sprouts, as all have been documented as vehicles of this infection. Again, without further information, it is often not possible to determine which of these is the true source.

Several kinds of scientific data can shed light on the likelihood of each of the various exposures as the source of infection. In epidemiological case-control studies, interviews are conducted with a series of individuals representing sporadic cases, and their responses are compared to those of other persons who remained healthy. This comparison can identify specific exposures that are statistically more frequently reported by the individuals, indicating that the exposures are associated with disease. Such studies may indicate that several different exposures are independently associated with illness. For rare or distinctive exposures, such studies may provide a reasonable measure of the proportion of cases that are attributable to the exposure. For very common exposures, the studies may identify the risk, without providing as accurate a measure of fraction of cases attributable to the exposure; for universal exposures, the studies will miss the risk altogether (Rose 2001). As the sources of the foods that cause sporadic cases are likely to have been a variety of separate lots, batches, or meals, prepared in a variety of locations that are difficult to identify, it is unusual for a sporadic case-control study to provide information on how the food was contaminated.

Investigations conducted in the outbreak setting are often the way in which new food hazards are identified. When everyone in a group of persons is infected with the same pathogen at the same time, the likelihood that a single source accounts for the illnesses is greatly increased. When the outbreak investigation identifies a single batch or lot of food as the source, further detailed investigation may reveal how it became contaminated. This investigative review of production is typically undertaken when convincing evidence exists that a particular food item was the source, and requires multidisciplinary expert traceback and assessment of production, processing, and preparation.

Additional information is increasingly becoming available as advanced molecular subtyping ("DNA fingerprinting") techniques are applied to pathogens identified in people, foods, and animals. It may be possible to link specific subtypes of a pathogen to specific animal reservoirs, or even to specific production or processing locations. For example, with intensive sampling for *Salmonella* in healthy animals, foods, and people, combined with extensive characterization and subtyping of the strains isolated, public health authorities in Denmark can estimate the proportion of salmonellosis attributable to each of the major food animal groups (Anon. 2002).

Considerations of the routes of transmission can be addressed by making judicious use of the epidemiological and microbiological data available on sources of infections, including outbreak investigations, case-control studies, and detailed case investigations, as well as surveys of pathogens in commodities.

Cross-Contamination and Recycling

Some pathogens can move from one food group to another, perhaps more easily than do chemical contaminants. Two situations allow pathogens to move from one food to another: cross-contamination and recycling. In cross-contamination, the pathogen is transferred from one food to another nearby food by contact with an unwashed hand or piece of equipment. It can happen at the level of production, when, for example, the same farm wagon is used to haul both calves and cabbages. It can happen in a processing plant, when contaminated processing water or equipment contaminate animals or vegetables that were clean when they entered the plant. It can happen in food preparation when hands are not washed or when unwashed utensils are used in the kitchen. For example, *Yersinia entercolitica* infection in infants has been associated with consumption of formula prepared by someone who is simultaneously handling raw pork intestine (Lee et al. 1990). It is particularly important in the case of pathogens with a low infectious dose, as the transfer of minimal numbers of pathogens may be sufficient to cause illness. The result is that contamination, and the risk of illness, spreads across food categories, obscuring the original source and making allocation more complex.

Recycling is the use of processing byproducts or rejected parts of animals or plants to feed or fertilize other animals or plants. This is routine general practice, supported by the rendering industry. During production, contamination can occur when uncomposted manure is used on produce, transferring pathogens from animal reservoirs to plants. It has been documented that *E. coli* O157:H7 can survive in manure for many months, and thus could contaminate produce (Wang et al. 1996; Solomon et al. 2001) Contamination can also occur when byproducts of one animal group are fed to another, such as when chicken litter or other byproducts contaminated with *Salmonella* are fed to cattle. For some pathogens the allocation process should explicitly include cross-contamination and recycling, where it has been identified.

Limited Data

Many common foodborne microbes have been recognized or have emerged as foodborne problems relatively recently (Tauxe 1997). When a pathogen is first recognized as foodborne or a microbe is first recognized as pathogenic, very few data exist about its reservoirs, its identification in foods, or even which foods it is likely to contaminate (Holmberg and Feldman 1984). With time, more information accumulates about a pathogen, and control measures are devised and improved. If reasonable prevention measures are successful, even if they are based on less than perfect knowledge, the disease may become rare. Of the 28 principal pathogens listed by Mead et al., 13 pathogens have emerged as foodborne in the last 35 years (Table 3.1). These 13 account for 11,527,000 cases in the Mead et al. estimate, or 83% of the 13,815,000 cases attributed to known pathogens (Mead et al. 1999). Formal risk assessment depends on the availability of much information, which is the result of years of research, and thus it may not realistically be performed soon after a pathogen is recognized. Nonetheless, we must use the best available information to make decisions about how to protect the public health.

As an example of how information accumulates, *E. coli* O157 was first identified as a human pathogen in 1982. As of 1985, three years after this bacterium was first recognized as a human pathogen, the model of what was known about the transmission of this pathogen was extremely simple: consumption of undercooked beef that contained *E. coli* O157 (Ryan et al. 1986). It was not known how the meat became contaminated, whether there was an animal reservoir, or whether any other food vehicles or routes of transmission existed. However, this information was sufficient to target the first control recommendations on cooking ground beef (Riley et al. 1983; Ryan et al. 1986). By 2001, after hundreds of outbreak investigations and other studies, it became clear that the routes and vehicles of transmission of this organism are much more complicated (Griffin et al. 2002). Cows are the chief gateways to humans, via meat, raw milk, or direct contact at the petting farm (Figure 3.1). Cattle manure may contaminate vegetables or water. Deer, sheep, or even caribou or other ungulates may also be involved. Children can spread it to other children in a daycare center or in a swimming pool. Other pathways are yet to be identified.

Given the limited data available for many pathogens, estimates of the allocation of illness burden across different food categories are not likely to be precise, particularly for the more recently recognized foodborne pathogens. It is not realistic to expect quantitative estimates; semiquantitative methods that include uncertainty ranges are more appropriate.

Available Epidemiological Information

For each principal foodborne pathogen, Mead et al. included an estimate of the proportion of infections that were food related (Mead et al. 1999). The epidemiological information available to divide this burden further into separate components includes outbreak investigations, case-control studies of sporadic

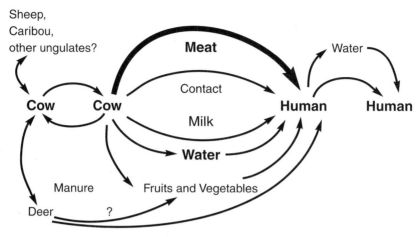

FIGURE 3.1. Routes of Transmission for *Escherichia coli* O157:H7

cases, and for a few pathogens with very restricted sources, detailed case interviews. As noted earlier, outbreak investigations often provide an opportunity to obtain detailed information about a particular food source. A series of outbreaks implicating a range of foods is primary and useful information about the sources of the infection. For a few pathogens, data are available from epidemiological case-control studies of sporadic cases, which determine how frequently persons with that particular infection report a certain host characteristic or exposure in comparison with healthy neighbors or the general population. For pathogens with a restricted range of food vehicles, a series of detailed case interviews that include exposure information can be helpful.

Allocating the burden of foodborne illness by the second dimension, the stages of food production, depends on what is known about the biology of the organism and its reservoir. A food is first produced on a farm or in a fishery, then processed in a slaughterhouse or packing plant, and finally prepared in a kitchen. These three simple stages provide a general outline of the dimension. The information available to allocate the burden to the stage of production is limited. In outbreak investigations, and occasionally in individual case investigations, it is possible to trace and evaluate the source. For a few pathogens, data are available from sampling of foods and food sources. Microbiological surveys of the prevalence of pathogens in specific foods or animals are also helpful, although comprehensive surveys are time intensive and expensive, as well as uncommon. For some pathogens, detection methods are simply not available. It may be necessary to estimate and account for the proportion of cases related to foreign travel as well, as food exposures occurring in other countries are presumably less amenable to control measures taken in the United States.

The available epidemiological information can be combined in a semiquantitative approach. If sufficient data are available for a single pathogen–food combination, it will then be possible to conduct a formal risk assessment model.

Three Illustrative Pathogens

The six considerations discussed in the preceding section form the dimensions around which a comparative burden allocation can be organized. In this section I suggest a structure for organizing the information about the risks posed by foodborne pathogens in a framework that allows comparison of risks across the food production consumption system. To illustrate the conceptual framework, I sketch a preliminary allocation of the illness burden of three foodborne pathogens for which some information is available. This exercise is intended as a preliminary illustration of how a comparative risk framework might be developed for microbial pathogens. The qualitative rankings and quantitative allocations developed here are for illustrative purposes only.

Vibrio parahaemolyticus

Vibrio parahaemolyticus was first identified as a cause of human illness in Asia and by 1972 emerged as a foodborne problem in the United States (Daniels et al. 2000). By 1974, its natural habitat in association with shellfish was well described. The burden for this pathogen can be estimated as 48% of the burden represented by "other *Vibrio*" in the 1999 Mead et al. estimates, since *Vibrio parahaemolyticus* represented 48% of the *Vibrio* infections reported to the CDC *Vibrio* surveillance between 1988 and 2000, after exclusion of toxicogenic *Vibrio cholerae* and *Vibrio vulnificus* (U.S. CDC unpublished data). This indicates that this pathogen causes an estimated 3,800 cases each year in the country, and 48 hospitalizations. The typical routes of transmission are food and direct contact with seawater leading to wound infections. Available epidemiological information for *Vibrio* comes from surveillance conducted in Gulf Coast states for more than a decade yielding a case series and an outbreak series (Daniels et al. 2000) and from monitoring of shellfish and surveys of seafood.

Information on *Vibrio parahaemolyticus* from the surveillance case series indicates that about 35% of cases are wound infections, caused by direct contact with water. The balance (65%) of *Vibrio parahaemolyticus* cases can be presumed to be foodborne. Information from the foodborne outbreak series is useful to allocate the foodborne illnesses among the three broad food categories: all of the outbreaks are related to consumption of seafood. This means that the foodborne portion of the total burden of 3,800 cases a year and 48 deaths, or 2,470 cases and 31 deaths, can be allocated to seafood.

Knowledge of the biology of the organism helps allocate this disease burden along the second dimension, stages of food production. *Vibrio parahaemolyticus* has a natural reservoir in warm marine waters (Oliver and Kaper 1997). Filter-feeding shellfish efficiently take up the organism and retain it in their intestinal tracts. It is generally killed by cooking, although it can survive light steaming (Oliver and Kaper 1997). If vibrios are present in cooked shellfish, they may grow rapidly if the holding temperature is warm. It was reported that seafood had been eaten raw in 38% of seafood *Vibrio parahaemolyticus* outbreaks (Daniels et al. 2000). Undercooking or recontamination after cooking was presumably a factor in the others. Thus contamination of the seafood involved in these outbreaks typically occurs during production (Figure 3-2A). The organism is present in the water in which the shellfish are growing and therefore in the shellfish beginning at the point of harvest. The organism remains there as the food is processed and prepared, during which time warm temperature, cooking, or other processes may lead to an increase or decrease in the number of organisms.

The two dimensions thus far examined, food type and stage of food production, can be diagrammed as three rows of three squares, with an arrow that starts in production and flows down through to preparation and to the consumer. Because contamination likely occurs early in the production stage, events that happen subsequently are also important. This could be indicated by a plus sign in each of the three boxes in the seafood column, indicating that the pathogens are present at that stage, and that the number of pathogens may be affected by events at each stage. If a particularly critical determinant of risk is observed at some stage, this can be indicated by adding an additional plus sign (Figure 3.2). For *Vibrio parahaemolyticus,* the events around production and harvest would appear to be such a point, as the water temperature is a critical determinant of contamination, and as rapid cooling on the oyster boat will prevent further growth (Oliver and Kaper 1997). Therefore, a second plus sign is added to the first stage of production.

With four pluses in the seafood column, the burden of the 65% of *Vibrio parahaemolyticus* infections that are foodborne can be allocated following the weights indicated by the plus signs. One half, or 33%, falls into the top right box, for the production stage of seafood, as two of the four pluses are there, and one quarter, or 16% of the overall burden, falls into the box for processing and the box for preparation (Figure 3.3). This illustrates a conceptual distribution of the burden of *Vibrio parahaemolyticus* infections across the entire foodborne system: it is concentrated in the seafood columns, and starts at the level of harvest. Investment in surveillance and research would be needed to provide reliable estimates of these weights. A formal risk assessment of *Vibrio parahaemolyticus* in shellfish would be necessary to evaluate the potential effectiveness of control measures.

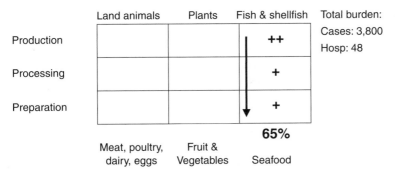

FIGURE 3.2. Schematic for Hypothetical Allocation of Public Health Hazard for *Vibrio parahaemolyticus.*

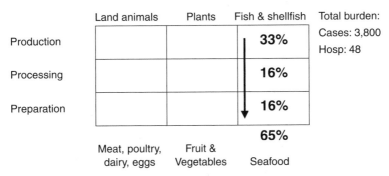

FIGURE 3.3. Schematic for Hypothetical Allocation of Public Health Burden for *Vibrio parahaemolyticus.*

Campylobacter jejuni

Campylobacter jejuni is the most common cause of bacterial diarrhea in many industrialized nations (Friedman et al. 2000). It was first identified as a cause of human illness in 1957, at a time when its source was unknown. By 1981 the foodborne route via raw milk was established, and soon thereafter the poultry route. A reservoir in poultry and cattle, and contamination of food derived from them, has been well documented (Jacobs-Rietsma 2000). It has been estimated to cause 2.4 million cases of illness annually in the United States, most of which are mild and undiagnosed, and 13,000 hospitalizations (Mead et al. 1999). The incidence has been declining in recent years (U.S. CDC 2002). The organism is transmitted through food, water, or animal contact, and rarely from one ill human to another.

Available information for *Campylobacter* comes from active surveillance for human illness in FoodNet, beginning in 1996 (U.S. CDC 2002). A series of outbreaks has been reported, although few occur relative to the frequency of the infection (Friedman et al. 2000). Other data include case-control studies conducted at various times, and some data of the frequency in meat and poultry. Systematic comparisons of strains from poultry and humans indicate they are similar in many respects (Friedman et al. 2000). Mead et al. estimated that 80% of *Campylobacter jejuni* infections are foodborne (Mead et al. 1999).

Outbreaks and sporadic cases of *Campylobacter* infection appear to have different specific sources, as outbreaks are more likely to be attributable to consumption of raw milk than to any other source, while poultry is the most frequently identified source of sporadic cases (Friedman et al. 2000). However, since both of these are land animal sources, for the purposes of this illustration, we may attribute approximately 75% of the total burden to the column of foods derived from land animals, that is, meat, poultry, milk, and eggs. As some outbreaks have been attributed to produce, a small portion may move from the land animals to contaminate fruit and vegetables via cross-contamination, and a similar small proportion may cross over at some stage to contaminate seafood. In this example, it is hypothesized that perhaps 2.5% is related to fruits and vegetables, and a similar small proportion to seafood. Again, actual implementation of this framework would require empirical research to provide reliable estimates of the rate of cross-contamination.

The ecology of *Campylobacter jejuni* can be used to allocate the burden by stage of production. One major natural habitat for this organism is the gastrointestinal tract of birds, where it causes no symptoms. It is also present in cattle. Poultry meat becomes contaminated during slaughter. Contamination can be spread among the chicken carcasses by water baths in processing, a major multiplier event, and it is present in most raw poultry at retail. The organism is killed by drying and atmospheric oxygen, so *Campylobacter* that contaminates surfaces tends to die rather than multiply over time (Nachamkin 1997).

The allocation of *Campylobacter* infections by stage of production can be indicated starting with the reservoirs in the animals at production and then continuing through processing and preparation. Although arguments can be made for an additional importance at each step, none is overwhelming, and so for illustrative purposes the burden can be viewed as distributed equally across stages of production (Figure 3.4). As *Campylobacter* on the surface of food tends to die off, it seems likely that cross-contamination occurs largely in the final stage of kitchen preparation. The 2.5% attributable to fruits, vegetables, and seafood is allocated to the preparation stage. Thus the 75% associated with land animal foods can be allocated in equal portions across production, processing, and preparation, and the burden of fruits, vegetables, and seafood can

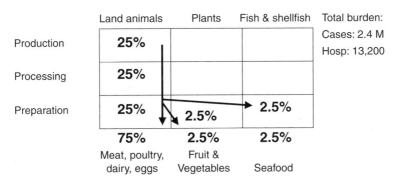

FIGURE 3.4. Schematic for Hypothetical Allocation of Public Health Burden for *Campylobacter jejuni.*

be allocated in each case to the preparation stage in those columns. Again, these figures are primarily for the purposes of illustration, and represent a hypothetical allocation only.

Escherichia coli O157:H7

Escherichia coli O157:H7 was first identified as a cause of illness in 1982 (Riley et al. 1983); the foodborne route was apparent from the first outbreaks, and the natural habitat in cattle was identified in 1987 (Griffin and Tauxe 1991). The burden of illness in the United States was estimated at 73,000 cases of illness annually, with slightly more than 2,000 hospitalizations (Mead et al. 1999). Several typical routes of transmission exist: food, water, animal contact, and person-to-person transmission. Mead et al. estimated that 85% was foodborne (Mead et al. 1999).

Available epidemiological information includes public health surveillance for *E. coli* O157 in some states beginning in 1988, active surveillance in Food-Net beginning in 1996, an outbreak series that is in preparation for publication, and several case-control studies. Within the food-related category, information from outbreaks and from case-control studies in combination suggests that most of the burden is associated with foods derived from land animals, estimated at 75% of the total burden. However, outbreaks have also been related to lettuce, other fruits and vegetables, apple cider, and alfalfa sprouts (Griffin et al. 2002). For the purpose of this illustration, it is hypothesized that 10% of the total can be allocated to fruits and vegetables. To date, no outbreaks have been linked to seafood, nor have sporadic case-control studies suggested seafood as a risk factor; therefore none of the burden is allocated to that sector.

It is well established that this organism is often found in the intestinal tracts of cows and other ruminants, but causes no symptoms there (Dean-Nystrom et al. 1998). Meat becomes contaminated with animal feces and rumen contents during slaughter. The contamination is amplified further when the meat of many animals is ground together. The pathogen is occasionally present in raw ground beef, where it can be killed by thorough cooking or can survive if cooking is less thorough. Fresh produce itself can be contaminated during production, as in the contamination of apples that fall to the ground in orchards or alfalfa seeds at harvest; during processing, such as when lettuce is contaminated by contaminated hydrocooler water; or during final preparation in the kitchen via cross-contamination from raw meat.

The allocation of the health burden of this infection across the stages of production begins with the land animals that serve as the principal gateways through to the meat and milk derived from these animals (Figure 3.5). The pathogen appears during animal production and continues through processing and preparation. Because of the great potential for amplifying the risk at the production stage by grinding and mixing of beef, and because of the critical prevention step of milk pasteurization, the land animal processing box may merit an additional weight. As the plant-derived foods can be cross-contaminated at each stage, each receives an equal weighting. Half of the 75% of the burden that is allocated to the land animal column goes into animal product processing and a quarter each into production and preparation; the 10% of the burden that was allocated to produce can be divided evenly across the three boxes in that column. These figures are primarily for the purposes of illustration and represent a hypothetical allocation only.

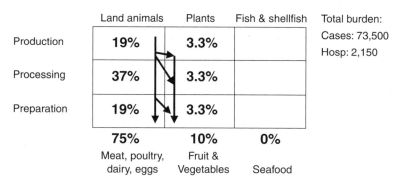

FIGURE 3.5. Schematic for Hypothetical Allocation of Public Health Burden for *Escherichia coli* O157:H7.

Working toward an Integrated Matrix

Having estimated an allocation of the health burden for individual pathogens, it is conceptually possible to sum the burden across pathogens. The summation could be done for the burden of cases, of hospitalizations or of deaths, by calculating the weighted distribution matrix of that burden for each pathogen, and then summing the burdens in each matrix. The result will allocate some burden to each box, as the farm-to-table issue spreads across different food categories.

These crude conceptual estimates may be refined by further dividing the food categories—fish and shellfish; fruits, vegetables, and nuts; and meat, poultry, eggs, or dairy foods—and estimating from limited available data, with some level of uncertainty. It may also be possible to specify the production stages in more detail. For example, it might be appropriate to model contamination during transport and in holding pens (lairage) as a separate stage for land animals. However, the data with which to do so are limited, and the more detailed the model of that dimension is, the more appropriate it is to carry out a formal pathogen-food risk assessment.

Other pathogens pose a greater challenge than the three chosen here, because of either the complexity of their transmission or the limited data available, or both. *Salmonella* is a challenge because of its sheer complexity. Several hundred serotypes, all capable of causing disease to varying degrees, have been detected in the United States (U.S. CDC 2001). Recycling and cross-contamination events are likely to be common for *Salmonella*. Systematic comparisons of strains from animals, foods, and people such as have been done in Denmark routinely would be likely to improve our understanding, but have been performed only to a limited extent in the United States.

Listeria is also a particular challenge, both because of its complexity and because information is limited. Only a small number of outbreak and case-control studies are available (Slutsker et al. 2000). Interpretation of food surveys is complex, as some strains may be more pathogenic than others, although we lack markers to distinguish them, except for identification of the strains associated with human illness.

To improve the burden allocation process and the entire risk assessment process in the future, more detailed investigations of the entire chain of production are needed in outbreak settings. More case-control studies of sporadic cases would be helpful in considering some foodborne pathogens. More systematic surveys of different stages of the food chain for prevalence of specific pathogens are likely to be particularly useful. Comparison of molecular subtypes of strains isolated in those surveys with those from people is likely to provide better estimates for specific food sources in the case of some pathogens. It is likely that more new foodborne pathogens have emerged, and the known pathogens are likely to find their way into new food vehicles. Any systematic allocation of burden will be a snapshot in time.

Conclusions

A conceptual framework has been outlined for allocating the public health burden of identified foodborne infections across the major food groups and pathogens. Three pathogens are used to illustrate the conceptual model. Multiple epidemiological data sources can be integrated into broad categories, and the burden of specific pathogens can be roughly allocated by food group by stage of production from farm to table. Cross-contamination and recycling are important vehicles of transmission of some pathogens. Precise numeric allocation may not be realistic for many pathogens at this point. Although not accounted for in this model, it is important to be cognizant of past disease control successes, and to expect food safety challenges from new directions in the future.

References

Angulo, F. and the FoodNet Working Group. 1997. Foodborne Diseases Active Surveillance Network (FoodNet). *Emerging Infectious Diseases* 3(4): 581–83.

Anon. 2002. *Annual Report on Zoonoses in Denmark, 2001.* Copenhagen: Ministry of Food, Agriculture and Fisheries.

Bryan, F. 1982. *Disease Transmitted by Foods (A Classification and Summary),* 2nd edit. Atlanta: Centers for Disease Control, HHS Publication No. (CDC) 83-8237.

Buzby, J., and T. Roberts 1996. ERS Updates U. S. Foodborne Disease Costs for Seven Pathogens. *Food Review* 19(3): 20–25.

Daniels, N., L. MacKinnon, et al. 2000. *Vibrio parahaemolyticus* Infections in the United States, 1973–1998. *The Journal of Infectious Diseases* 181: 1661–66.

Dean-Nystrom, E., B. Bosworth, et al. 1998. Bovine Infection with Shiga Toxin-Producing *Escherichia coli.* In Escherichia coli *O157:H7 and Other Shiga-Toxin Producing* E. coli *Strains,* edited by J. Kaper and A. O'Brien. Washington, DC: American Society for Microbiology Press, 261–67.

Friedman, C.R., J. Neimann, et al. 2000. Epidemiology of *Campylobacter jejuni* Infections in the United States and Other Industrialized Nations. In *Campylobacter,* 2nd ed. Washington, DC: American Society for Microbiology Press, 121–38.

Griffin, P.M., and R.V. Tauxe 1991. The Epidemiology of Infections Caused by *Escherichia coli* O157:H7, Other Enterohemorrhagic *E. coli,* and the Associated Hemolytic Uremic Syndrome. *Epidemiologic Reviews* 13: 60–98

Griffin, P., P. Mead, et al. 2002. *Escherichia coli* O157:H7 and Other Enterohemorrhagic *E. coli.* In *Infections of the Gastrointestinal Tract,* 2nd edit., edited by M. Blaser, P. Smith, H. Greenberg, J. Ravdin, and R. Guerrant. Philadelphia: Lippincott Williams & Wilkins, 627–42.

Holmberg, S., and R. Feldman 1984. New and Newer Enteric Pathogens: Stages in Our Knowledge. *American Journal of Public Health* 74: 205–7.

Jacobs-Rietsma, W. 2000. *Campylobacter* in the Food Supply. In Campylobacter, 2nd edit., edited by I. Nachamkin and M. Blaser. Washington, DC: American Society for Microbiology Press, 467–81.

Lee, L.A., Gerber, R.A., et al. 1990. *Yersinia enterocolitica* O:3 Infections in Infants and Children, Associated with the Household Preparation of Chitterlings. *New England Journal of Medicine* 322:984–87.

Mead, P., L. Slutsker, et al. 1999. Food-Related Illness and Death in the United States. *Emerging Infectious Diseases* 5(5): 607–25.

Mintz, S. 1997. *Tasting Food, Tasting Freedom; Excursions into Eating, Culture, and the Past.* Boston: Beacon Press.

Nachamkin, I. 1997. *Campylobacter jejuni.* In *Food Microbiology: Fundamentals and Frontiers,* edited by M. Doyle, L. Beuchat, and T. Montville. Washington DC: American Society for Microbiology Press, 159–70.

Oliver, J., and J. Kaper 1997. *Vibrio* Species. In *Food microbiology; Fundamentals and Frontiers,* edited by M. Doyle, L. Beuchat, and T. Montville. Washington DC: American Society for Microbiology Press, 228–64.

Riley, L. W., R. Remis, et al. 1983. Hemorrhagic Colitis Associated with a Rare *Escherichia coli* Serotype. *New England Journal of Medicine* 308: 681–85.

Rose, G. 2001. Sick Individuals and Sick Populations. *International Journal of Epidemiology* 30: 427–32.

Ryan, C.A., R. Tauxe, et al. 1986. *Escherichia coli* O157:H7 diarrhea in a Nursing Home: Clinical, Epidemiological, and Pathological Findings. *Journal of Infectious Diseases* 154: 631–38.

Slutsker, L., M.C. Evans, et al. 2000. Listeriosis. In *Emerging Infections,* Volume 4, edited by W. Scheld, W. Craig, and J. Hughes. Washington, DC: American Society for Microbiology Press, 83–106.

Solomon, E., S. Yaron, et al. 2001. T 31 Transmission and Internalization of *Escherichia coli* O157:H7 from Contaminated Cow Manure into Lettuce Tissue as Monitored by Laser Scanning Confocal Microscopy. Paper presented at International Association for Food Protection 88th Annual Meeting, Minneapolis, MN, IAFP, Des Moines, IA.

Tauxe, R.V. 1997. Emerging Foodborne Diseases: An Evolving Public Health Challenge. *Emerging Infectious Diseases* 3(4): 425–34.

U.S. CDC (U.S. Centers for Disease Control). 2001. Salmonella *Surveillance: Annual Summary, 2000.* Atlanta: U.S. Department of Health and Human Services, CDC.

———. 2002. Preliminary FoodNet Data on the Incidence of Foodborne Illnesses – Selected Sites, United States, 2001. *Morbidity Mortality Weekly Report* 51: 325–29.

Wang, G., T. Zhao, et al. 1996. Fate of Enterohemorrhagic *Escherichia coli* O157:H7 in Bovine Feces. *Applied and Environmental Microbiology* 62: 2567–70.

4

Where Are Potential Chemical Hazards in the U.S. Food Supply?

Penelope A. Fenner-Crisp

The food that humans eat is a variable and complex mixture of chemicals. Most of these chemicals are naturally occurring, while the others are man-made. For centuries, we have manipulated the naturally occurring constituents of agricultural commodities to improve their hardiness, for example, their ability to resist pests and tolerate extremes of weather; to minimize or eliminate components that may be deleterious to human health, for example, solenaceous substances in potatoes; and to enhance their flavor and nutritive value. In more recent times, as science has revealed the risks and benefits of too little, too much, or the right amount of those chemicals needed to achieve and sustain good health—vitamins and minerals, fats, proteins, and carbohydrates—we have continued to modify the form and quantity of these naturally occurring substances. We also are using many additional chemicals, both natural and synthetic, to further improve yield, nutritive content, flavor, and texture appeal. Chemicals are combined with basic foodstuffs in creative ways to provide a wide selection of processed foods, making it possible to offer consumers thousands of choices.

In theory, one might conclude that all of the substances in food, whether natural or synthetic, intentionally or unintentionally present, might warrant continuous and active attention in a formal, structured food safety program. After all, people have the potential to be "exposed" to all of them, simply by virtue of eating to sustain life. However, we long ago abandoned such an approach in the United States, if, in fact, it was ever considered in the first place. Instead, a food safety system has evolved, informed by science, that focuses on a much smaller universe of chemicals, a system developed in bits and pieces, supported by a variety of legislative mandates, managed by multiple authorities. Many aspects of the existing system are prospective in nature;

that is, before the pesticide, direct or indirect food additive, color additive, or veterinary drug product can be used in or on food, it must be evaluated for potential hazard and risk. In other cases, no premarket approval process may be in place, but monitoring may be conducted for substances with particular toxicological risk in foods, including water used for drinking and food preparation. Depending on the category into which the monitoring falls, if the findings suggest a need for concern or are in violation of the applicable regulations, steps may be taken to reduce or prevent contact with consumers. Among the possibilities are that the food may be withheld from distribution in commerce or advisories may be issued to potential consumers, recommending that they place limits on their consumption of those foods. Finally, many substances used in foods receive little if any regulatory oversight by virtue of their anticipated magnitude of exposure or hazard potential, or their actual lack thereof.

Over time, we have settled into implementing a food safety system that focuses on a relatively small number of all substances that are or could be components of food. In recent years, for a number of reasons, significant questions have been raised as to whether the current system is adequate, is focusing on the right sets and uses of food chemicals, is expending the right amount of resources in the right places, and so forth. Widespread, but not unanimous, support exists for evolution to a more unified food safety system, but one that continues to be science based. To do this wisely and with the most efficient expenditure of resources, both monetary and human, while still ensuring safety, one must understand, to the extent possible, where and how risk currently is distributed.

Focus on Six Categories/Residue Types

This chapter reflects an attempt to begin the synthesis of information on the potential for risk to consumers from exposure to constituents in food. This initial analysis along with significant additional work is requisite to achieving the longer term objective of understanding the distribution of risk across population groups and sources to (1) determine where any disproportionate or unacceptable risks may be occurring at present; (2) identify opportunities for risk reduction in the short term, under the current regulatory scheme; and (3) posit and critically evaluate options for modification or reinvention of the current state, in accordance with a science-based scheme that ensures maximum effectiveness in protecting the public health as well as wise and efficient allocation of resources.

A shorthand definition of risk (R) describes it as the multiple of two factors: exposure (E) and hazard/toxicity (H/T), that is, $R = E \times H/T$. Because of time and resource constraints, this chapter is focused solely on the collection and partial integration and analysis of data on exposure to residues in food, representing six categories of chemicals or other substances. As an experiment to test whether the average consumer could determine his or her personal exposure as well as that of family members or others to substances in these groups, all information used in this preliminary analysis is publicly available. Much of it was gathered from the websites of the three key federal agencies with regulatory responsibilities for food safety: U.S. Environmental Protection Agency (EPA), U.S. Food and Drug Administration (FDA), and U.S. Department of Agriculture (USDA).

The obvious follow-on tasks required to develop a more robust understanding of potential risk would include the completion of the exposure analysis. This more robust exposure analysis also would need to incorporate data on inhalation and dermal absorption rates, drinking water, and food consumption patterns. This analysis may even need to describe exposures not only for the general population, but also for subpopulations as defined by age, ethnicity, or geography. The other side of the risk equation also would require analysis—integration of information on the hazard and toxicity characteristics of the constituents falling into each of the six categories. Hazard and toxicity data that are developed to support premarket approval are housed with EPA and FDA, the two agencies responsible for establishing enforceable residue limits, or exemptions thereto. Additional hazard and toxicity data on preapproved substances and on those not subject to a preapproval process are scattered widely across many government and nongovernment databases and in the publicly available scientific literature.

The six categories of substances, or residue types, that are the focus of this preliminary analysis include pesticides of conventional chemistry; biopesticides; direct, indirect ("food contact") food and color additives; environmental contaminants; veterinary drugs; and naturally occurring toxins. Some examples of "conventional" pesticides include the organophosphorus and carbamate insecticides, the triazine herbicides, and the ethylenebis-dithio-carbamate (EBDC) fungicides. Biopesticides are certain types of pesticides derived from such natural materials as animals, plants, bacteria, and certain minerals. This group is made up of microbial pesticides consisting of a microorganism—a bacterium, fungus, virus, or protozoan—as the active ingredient; biochemical pesticides that are naturally occurring substances that control pests by nontoxic mechanisms, for example, pheromones; and plant-incorporated-protectants (PIPs), which are pesticidal substances that plants produce from genetic material that has been added to the plant, for example *Bacillus thuringiensis* (Bt) endotoxin in corn, cotton, or potatoes.

Food and Color Additives

In the past, FDA has informally characterized a food additive as being a "direct additive" if it was intended to have a technical effect in food, a "secondary direct additive" if it was intended to have a technical effect on food during food processing but not in the finished food as consumed, or an "indirect additive" if it was intended to have a technical effect in a food contact material. Indirect additives are now more commonly referred to as "food contact additives." Subsection 201(t) of the Federal Food, Drug, and Cosmetic Act defines color additive to mean:

> a material which . . . is a dye, pigment, or other substance made by a process of synthesis or similar artifice, or extracted, isolated, or otherwise derived, with or without intermediate or final change of identity, from a vegetable, animal, mineral, or other source, and . . . [that] when added or applied to a food, drug, or cosmetic, or to the human body or any part thereof, is capable (alone or through reaction with [an]other substance) of imparting color thereto . . . The term 'color' includes black, white, and intermediate grays.

Environmental contaminants of particular interest and concern in food include metals such as lead, cadmium, and mercury; persistent organic substances such as dioxins, polychlorinated biphenyls (PCBs); and organochlorine pesticides such as dichlorodiphenyltrichloroethane (DDT), aldrin/dieldrin, and chlordane, among others. Veterinary drugs used as growth promoters or to prevent or remedy disease in domestic animals used for human food present a potential source of exposure if residues remain in the meat, milk, poultry, or eggs at the time of consumption. Naturally occurring toxins such as aflatoxin, fumonisin, patulin, or paralysis-inducing shellfish toxin may be present in foods as consumed, at levels reflective of the growing, harvesting, storage, and handling conditions for the commodities on which they can be found, for example, corn and other grains, peanuts, apple, and shellfish.

It should be noted that the six categories evaluated in this preliminary analysis are not fully inclusive of all food constituents. For several reasons, natural food constituents, including both macro- and micronutrients; prions, for example, from bovine spongiform encephalopathy (BSE); and dietary supplements are not being examined at this time. Discussion is warranted as to whether this exclusion was appropriate and whether one or more of these groups should be included in any subsequent analyses. Other categories also might be considered in later efforts. All of the categories covered in this preliminary analysis are currently the subject of some sort of regulatory control, under one or more federal statutes, to a greater or lesser degree. For some of these categories, where formal, binding regulations may not exist, informal guidance or advisories may have been issued. In either case, the desired result is that an "acceptable" upper limit on exposure is identified, consistent with our current understanding of the potential for risk.

Sources and Magnitude of Exposure

Many factors influence the magnitude of the residues of substances in or on food at different stages of production, including use rate, for example, pounds of pesticide applied per acre of crop; milligrams per kilogram body weight dose of a drug to a food animal; parts per billion (ppb) or parts per million (ppm) in a processed food; the environmental fate of the substance, that is, rate and nature of conversion of the parent substance to degradate(s) via metabolism, photodegradation, aerobic or anaerobic conversion, and so forth; and point of introduction into the production process. Many of these factors, in addition to others, for example, physical and chemical characteristics of the substance and the nature of the food matrix, serve to determine the sources and routes of exposure. In the next sections of this chapter, the six categories of residues are followed through the key phases of their "life cycles," noting, for instance, where they might be introduced into the channels of food production; if, and in which direction, their residue levels may change as they traverse these channels; which food and other sources are likely to contain each type; what the routes of exposure would be as contributed by each source; if, when, and how they are measured in foodstuffs; and, finally, when measured, what level of residues are being found. Analysis of information on each of these phases can then contribute to the characterization of the distribution and magnitude of exposure and risk across the food sources and for segments of the population.

The generic scenario for the channel of production from farm to table of a food commodity might be described as consisting of three principal phases: (1) production or preharvest; (2) postharvest/processing; and (3) consumption. The site of production may be a farm, a feedlot, or a fishing or other harvest site. The second phase would include postharvest steps, including processing, with movement from processor to distributor, or the reciprocal, and then on through the distribution chain to the wholesaler and retailer and finally to the consumer. The final phase is preparation—trimming, washing, cooking—for consumption in a commercial, institutional, or residential setting. Substances from all six categories may be present, intentionally or unintentionally, at all three phases of production. Although substances approved as direct or indirect food additives will not likely be introduced during the growing of a crop or preparation of food animals for market, some indirect additives may be present in drinking water, soil, or air as a consequence of environmental contamination from their other, nonfood uses.

The level of residue might change as a food commodity moves through its life cycle. Residues of health concern, and their resulting potential risk, may degrade or be produced following exposure to the ambient natural or bacterial environment. Residues often are concentrated differentially in tissues of the body of a food animal. If the liver concentrates the chemical of interest, but muscle does not, the relative risk from eating the same amount of each tissue would be greater for liver than for filet mignon. Storage, washing, peeling, and cooking generally yield reductions in residues. Eating the portion of the commodity containing the highest residues would yield a higher exposure per gram of product than eating a blend of the whole food. Sequential sampling and analysis throughout a commodity's life cycle is key to understanding the changes that may occur in the nature and magnitude of the residue(s) of concern. Of greatest value for the characterization of potential risk to consumers is the analysis done "at the dinner plate" or point of consumption. In general, it appears that most residue levels of concern tend to decrease as the food moves from production to consumption.

Table 4.1 depicts potential sources of exposure to consumers of substances found within each of the six residue categories. It should be noted that, in addition to several traditional food sources, water is included. Under the current food safety system, particularly within the pesticide regulatory structure, water used for drinking and cooking is considered to be a food. Also, two nonfood routes/pathways of exposure are noted: air/inhalation and soil/direct-dermal. This is to remind the reader that people are exposed to certain of these substances in settings other than eating. Exposures could be the consequence of a food production–related use, for example, use of pesticides, or because these

TABLE 4.1. Potential Pathways for Consumer Exposure to Chemicals

	Residue Type					
Source of Exposure	Conventional Pesticide	Biopesticide	Direct/ Indirect/ Color Additive	Environmental Contaminant	Animal Drug	Naturally Occurring Toxin
Meat/milk	X		X (I)[a]	X	X	
Poultry	X		X (I)	X	X	
Fish/seafood	X	X	X(I)	X	X	X
Produce/grains	X	X	X(I)	X		X
Processed foods	X	X	X (D&I)	X	X	X
Water-ingestion	X		X(I)	X	X	
Air-inhalation	X		? (I)	X		
Soil/direct-dermal	X		X	X	X	

[a](I) refers to indirect food additives. Their presence as a source of exposure is likely to be the consequence of a nonfood additive use such as in an industrial or consumer product. (D) refers to direct food additives.

products have other uses in industrial or consumer products, for example, indirect/food contact additives, or because they are present in the environment naturally or as the consequence of prior use or handling, for example, environmental contaminants, naturally occurring toxins.

The Current U.S. Regulatory Scheme

Who Has Authority Over What?

Three federal agencies have defined regulatory responsibilities for the six categories of residue types. A patchwork of formal regulations and nonenforceable advisories or guidance is available for most of them. In theory, one could examine each one of these regulations and advisories, and develop a rough estimate of the upper bound level of exposure that could accrue to a particular chemical or class under worst-case circumstances. This, of course, presumes an understanding of the food consumption patterns of the population being evaluated and that no use, growing, or handling practices result in an exceeding of the allowable amount. One of the major deficiencies in this approach include the absence of sufficient data on misuse, food consumption, or actual residues found in foods, as in reality there may be no or nondetectable residues. Another is the fact that most of the regulations, in particular tolerances, were determined on a case-by-case basis without consideration of exposures, and therefore attendant risks, from other food uses or nonfood uses for that substance (aggregate exposure) or to substances with similar or toxicity-enhancing or mitigating mechanisms of action (cumulative effects).

FDA has regulatory authority for setting residue limits for and/or allowing the marketing of some genetically modified foods; direct, indirect, and color additives; and veterinary drugs used in food-producing animals and animal feeds (21 C.F.R. 170–199 2000). EPA has similar regulatory authority over all pesticides, of both conventional and biotechnological origin, for use in food and most other settings, including a few chemicals used on, but not in, animals (U.S. Congress 1996a). It also sets national drinking water standards under the Safe Drinking Water Act (U.S. Congress 1996b). States and tribes must enforce these standards; they apply to all drinking water treatment systems having at least 15 connections or serving 25 or more customers. FDA applies the same standards to bottled water. EPA, FDA, and USDA all have health advisories for drinking and bottled water and/or other guidance, for example, action levels or advisories for certain contaminants such as dioxins, PCBs, heavy metals such as mercury, cancelled organochlorine pesticides such as DDT, and natural toxins such as aflatoxin.

Given this regulatory structure, how many substances in the six categories are subject to formal regulations? The answer is roughly 7,000, if one does not include all of the direct and indirect food additives, substantially equivalent genetically modified foods, or no-/low-risk pesticides that are completely exempt from regulation and therefore never appear on the regulatory agencies' "radar screens." Currently, nearly 500 conventional and about 10 biotechnology-derived food use pesticides exist for which EPA has granted one or more tolerances or exemptions for a tolerance (U.S. EPA 2001d, e). FDA has completed more than 50 consultations on genetically modified foods, concluding that it had no further concerns about the introduction of these foods into the marketplace (U.S. FDA 2002). FDA's Center for Food Safety and Applied Nutrition's (CF-SAN) website notes that their database contains more than 2,000 direct and more than 3,000 indirect food additives (U.S. FDA 2001b, e). EPA has formal drinking water standards for more than 80 chemical substances, some of which are pesticides, while others are volatile organic chemicals (VOCs) and inorganic chemicals including heavy metals and disinfection byproducts (U.S. EPA 2000, 2001b). FDA has granted approval for about 100 veterinary drugs for use in or on animals that are a source of human food or animal feeds. No natural toxins such as the mycotoxins or seafood/fish toxins have formal residue limits, although guidance does exist for several of them (U.S. FDA 2001g, h, i). USDA has developed guidance levels for a number of environmental contaminants such as heavy metals, DDT, and other cancelled organochlorine pesticides and PCBs.

Federal Monitoring Programs

A brief review of the key federal monitoring programs of the three agencies, including both those that sample for enforcement/compliance and those designed to characterize residue levels as close to consumption as possible, will assist in understanding how well actual exposures and risk can be estimated and whether or not risk allocation can be implemented on a national scale.

FDA's monitoring programs encompass most foods, including seafood and some egg products. FDA is responsible for monitoring for compliance to pesticide tolerances as well as for those categories over which it also has approval authority, although, in actuality, ongoing monitoring programs exist only for conventional pesticides, environmental contaminants, animal drugs, and naturally occurring toxins (U.S. FDA 1995; 1997a, b; 1999a, b, c; 2000a, c, e; 2001a). Although compliance programs exist for direct, indirect, and color additives and dietary supplements, relatively little, if any, monitoring is conducted on a systematic, continuing, or even occasional basis (e.g., U.S. FDA 2000f). Between 100 and 200 environmental contaminants are monitored by all three agencies in food and drinking water (U.S. Congress 1996b; U.S. FDA 1993; 1995; 1997b; 2000a; 2001a; U.S. EPA 1999; 2000; 2001a, b, c; USDA 2000a, b) About 10 naturally occurring toxins are monitored by FDA and USDA in the commodities for which they have oversight (U.S. FDA 1992a, b, c; 1995; 1999a, b; USDA 2000a, b).

Regular, cyclical monitoring is conducted by FDA to determine tolerance compliance for about 200 of the nearly 500 food use pesticides, using multiresidue analytical methods that also can pick up nearly another 200 that do not have approved chemical/food use combinations (U.S. FDA 2000a, b).

Embedded in FDA's key compliance program components are several subprograms, such as those that sample bottled water, the National Drug Residue Milk Monitoring Program, the Toxic Elements in Foods Program, the Domestic and Imported Program, and the Pesticide Residue Monitoring Program. As noted earlier, the enforcement/compliance programs focus on determination of adherence to the approved residue limit. Therefore, the analytical methods used are designed to target the tolerance value, but not necessarily to determine the actual residue present. Nonetheless, in many cases, many of the methods, mostly multiresidue in nature, do have limits of detection that are 50 to 100 times lower than the tolerance. The monitoring programs include sampling of both domestic and imported foods. The number of imported samples generally exceeds that of domestic samples. As an example, the 1999 pesticide residue monitoring program included about 3,500 domestic and 6,000 imported samples. As noted earlier, this sampling program identifies nearly 400 pesticides in foods, about half of which have tolerances in place for those specific chemical/food combinations.

The Toxic Elements Program is a continuing, annual survey. Small in scale, it targets only a few food–contaminant combinations at a time, rotating these combinations over a cycle of years. Recent years have included targeted sampling for lead and cadmium in seafood, as well as natural toxins in a variety of products, for example, patulin in apple juice products. All three agencies also have been conducting extensive sampling of food for dioxins for the past several years, as a part of the comprehensive federal reassessment to understand more precisely the magnitude and distribution of exposure and risk to this class of substances from food sources.

In addition to its compliance programs, FDA conducts the Total Diet Study (TDS) (U.S. FDA 1997b, 2001f). The TDS is designed to determine residues in consumer-ready foods. About 260 foods, which serve as surrogates for more than 3,500 different foods that make up the items named in the USDA consumption surveys, are purchased and prepared for consumption as would be done in the home. The analytical methods are modified to measure residues 5 to 10 times lower than needed for compliance monitoring. Examples of the groups of analytes include:

Pesticides: organochlorines, organophosphates, carbamates, chlorophenoxys, pyrethroids, organosulfurs, EBDCs and ETU, substituted ureas, benomyl
Industrial chemicals: PCBs, VOCs
Elements: As, Cd, Ca, Cu, Fe, Pb, Mg, Mn, Hg, Ni, P, K, Se, Na, Zn
Radionuclides: Am, Ba, Ca, Co, I, La, K, Ra, Ru, Sr, Th
Other: Moisture, folic acid

The USDA maintains the monitoring for compliance program for all pesticides and veterinary drugs that may be found in meat, poultry, and some egg products (USDA 1998; 2000a, b, c; 2001a). USDA's Food Safety and Inspection Service (FSIS) samples meat, poultry, and egg products for about 150 pesticides in its enforcement/compliance program, as does USDA's Agricultural Marketing Service (AMS) in the Pesticide Data Program, which is not directed toward enforcement and compliance. USDA FSIS monitors animal drugs for compliance in meat, poultry, and some egg products. Both organizations conduct analyses for environmental contaminants such as heavy metals, organochlorine pesticides, PCBs, and dioxins.

As noted earlier, EPA sets national drinking water standards, in the form of maximum contaminant levels (MCLs), that the states and tribes must implement for all drinking water treatment systems serving 25 or more people. Currently, MCLs exist for 6 microorganisms, 7 disinfectants/byproducts, 16 inorganic chemicals, 3 radionuclides, and 53 organic substances (26 pesticides, 18 VOCs, and 9 others) (U.S. EPA 2001b). In addition, there are monitoring requirements for more than 35 unregulated substances, and nonenforceable Health Advisories (HAs) for nearly 200 inorganic and organic chemicals (U.S. EPA 1999, 2000). There is some overlap between the chemicals for which MCLs and HAs exist and for which monitoring requirements and HAs exist. States and tribes must collect monitoring data for individual systems but need report only the violations to EPA.

Results of Sampling and Analysis

For the purpose of this preliminary exposure analysis, residue data or their surrogates reported by the three agencies in the years 1998–2000 were used. These Pesticide Residue Monitoring Program results illustrate the types of commodities that are sampled; the numbers of samples, both domestic and imported, that are analyzed on an annual basis; and a profile of typical results (Table 4.2 [U.S. FDA 2000b]). As can be seen, although substantial percentages of most of the samples—milk, dairy, eggs being the exception—have detectable residues, only a very small percentage are violative; a total of 0.8% of domestic samples and 3.1% of imported samples either exceed tolerance or represent a "no-tolerance" situation for that chemical–commodity combination.

The Total Diet Study results show a different side of the story (Table 4.2 [U.S. FDA 2001f]). In the basic study with 1,040 samples, 104 different residues were found, representing 55 different individual pesticides or their degradates. The incidence of the top 20 pesticides ranged from 2% to 22%. In the special study with baby foods, 108 residues, representing 15 different pesticides, were noted in 78 samples. A similar range of occurrence, 1% to 26%, was noted.

TABLE 4.2. 1999 FDA Pesticide Residue Monitoring Program Results

Commodity	Domestically Produced Foods				Imported Foods			
	Number of Samples	Percentage of Samples with Detections	Percentage of Samples without Detections	Percentage of Samples with Violations	Number of Samples	Percentage of Samples with Detections	Percentage of Samples without Detections	Percentage of Samples with Violations
Grains and grain Products	468	38.5	61.3	0.2	276	23.9	75.4	0.7
Milk, dairy, eggs	116	2.6	97.4	0	22	4.5	95.5	0
Fish/shellfish	218	28.9	71.1	0	298	5.0	95.0	0
Fruits	1,063	60.6	38.8	0.6	2,290	10.7	57.5	1.8
Vegetables	1,414	29.1	69.7	1.2	2,768	31.3	64.8	3.9
Other	147	23.1	75.5	1.4	358	10.6	78.8	10.6
Total	3,426	39.0	60.2	0.8	6,012	31.9	65.0	3.1

FDA Total Diet Study Results

	Number of Samples	Number of Residues Found	Number of Pesticides Found	Percentage of Samples with Frequently Found Pesticides[a]	Number of VOCs Found	Number of Other Organic Chemicals Found
Total Diet Study	1,040	104	55	2–22%	18	10
Baby food	78	108	15	1–26%	N/A	N/A

Sources: U.S. FDA (2000b, 2001f).

[a]For each of the top 20 most frequently found pesticides, the percentage of samples that contained that pesticide.

N/A = not applicable.

As mentioned earlier, USDA's Food Safety and Inspection Service (FSIS) samples for at least 300 chemicals in its enforcement and compliance program—the National Residue Program (USDA 1998, 2000a). This program is implemented through an annual, continuing survey designed to evaluate compliance with EPA- and FDA-approved residue limits. It encompasses about 100 veterinary drugs and 150 pesticides that have tolerances in meat, poultry, and egg products and animal feeds. In addition, they analyze for certain environmental contaminants such as dioxins, heavy metals, and mycotoxins as well as processing contaminants such as nitrosamines, packaging migrants, and polyaromatic hydrocarbons (PAHs). Each year the Agency, in consultation with EPA, FDA, the Centers for Disease Control, and other USDA agencies, identifies priority public health compounds of concern. Information on these compounds' hazard profiles is considered along with previously generated violation data to develop the program for the next year. As does FDA in its monitoring programs, USDA rotates chemical–product combinations in cycles and increases or decreases the numbers of samples, as determined in the prioritization process.

Typical results from an annual survey in the National Residue Program are exhibited in Table 4.3 (USDA 1998b). Sample size is generally greater than that in the FDA Pesticide Monitoring Program, and the violation rate is substantially lower. In general, there is a higher rate of violations determined in the imported compared with domestic samples. This is consistent with the FDA findings, albeit for a different set of commodities.

USDA's Agricultural Marketing Service (AMS) manages the Pesticide Data Program, which is not directed toward enforcement/compliance (USDA 2000c, 2001a, b). Started in 1991, it is a collaboration between USDA AMS and the Office of Pesticide Programs at EPA. Created in response to the observations and recommendations anticipated to be included in the 1993 National Academy of Sciences report Pesticides in the Diets of Infants and Children, the initial emphasis was on sampling of the top 20 or 22 commodities consumed by infants and children younger than 7 years of age. These commodities were matched with those conventional pesticides thought to be "high hazard/risk." The organophosphorus and carbamate cholinesterase-inhibiting insecticides, Group B—Probable and Group C—Possible Human Carcinogens, and others shown to produce developmental or reproductive effects of concern in animal test species were among the first to be analyzed. To date, 34 commodities have been sampled, some in more than one survey or in more than one form, for example, fresh, frozen, and canned juice, and more than 100 pesticides have been identified in the samples. Most samples consist of composites, that is, 5 pounds of potatoes or apples, rather than single servings. Because concerns have been raised about the possibility of unacceptable risks occurring following a single, acute exposure to certain acutely toxic substances in some commodities, several special studies have been conducted in which split samples of single fresh

TABLE 4.3. 1998 FSIS National Residue Program Results

	Domestically Produced Food			Imported Food			
Residue	Number of Samples	Number of Samples with Violations	% of Samples with Violations	Number of Samples	Number of Samples with Detections	Number of Samples with Violations	% of Violations
Antibiotics	7,829	37	0.40	2,093	1	1	0.05
Sulfonamides	5,652	16	0.30	2,963	26	26	0.90
Arsenicals	2,542	1	0.04	182	0	0	0
Chlorinated hydrocarbons				1,290	72	72	5.60
Chlorinated organophosphates	5,613	4	0.07	1,290	5	5	0.40
Halofuginone	881	0	0	38	0	0	0
Ivermectin	3,672	8	0.20	1,488	0	0	0
Carbadox	699	0	0	212	0	0	0
β-Agonist: clenbuterol	218	0	0	N.D.[a]			
Phenylbutazone	N.D.	1		17	0	0	0

Source: USDA (1998).

[a]N.D. = not determined.

items such as apples, pears, or potatoes have been analyzed. Commodities are purchased at distribution points as close to the consumer's dinner plate as possible, washed, and peeled but not cooked before analysis. Analytical methods are designed for determination of low Limits of Detection/Limits of Quantification, rather than for tolerance compliance. As would be expected under these conditions, at least one pesticide residue has been detected in a significant percentage of samples. Occasionally, a sample will contain more than one residue, and very rarely a maximum of three or four. Because of the refined analytical methods, the violation rate is substantially higher—10-fold—than for domestic foods in the FDA Pesticide Residue Program. In this case, nearly all of the violations represent "no-tolerance" situations rather than those in which tolerances are exceeded. Results for 1998 and 1999 are shown in Table 4.4 (USDA 2000c, 2001a).

Drinking water is another food that may contain certain of the residue types that have been analyzed in this preliminary assessment. The national drinking water standards (MCLs) that EPA sets apply to bottled water that FDA monitors and to all drinking water treatment systems serving 25 or more people. As noted earlier, states and tribes must collect monitoring data for individual systems but need report only the violations to EPA. As a result, there is no simple way to access all of the existing occurrence data. In addition, in most cases, chemical residue levels need to be reported only for annualized values for a system; thus, if short-term peaks of exposure occur, they can be obscured by the reporting rules. A true profile of community or consumer exposure is virtually

TABLE 4.4. USDA Pesticide Data Program Results for 1998 and 1999

Year of Summary	Number of Commodities	Number of Samples	% of Samples with Detections	Number of Pesticides Targeted for Analysis[b]	Number of Pesticides Detected	Number of Detections of Pesticide Residues	# of Samples with Violations
1998 (F&V)[a]	11	7,017	61	57	87	8,494	270
1998 (Milk)	1	595	15	44	4	90	6
1998 (Corn syrup)	1	298	0	83	0	0	0
1998 (Soybean)	1	590	51	35	11	370	2
Total for 1998	14	8,500	55.1		92	8,954	3.85%
1999 (F&V)	12	8,637	67	106	87	12,431	260
1999 (Oats)	1	332	9	33	6	29	0
1999 (Corn syrup)	1	156	0	82	0	0	0
Total for 1999	14	9,125	64		90	12,460	4%

Sources: USDA (2000c, 2001a).

[a]F&V refers to fruits and vegetables.

[b]Number of pesticides targeted by USDA for analysis in the given year. Since analytical techniques detect a broad range of pesticides, they can, and do, find more pesticides than those targeted for analysis (see next column).

impossible to construct. Of interest, but only of marginal value in assessing actual exposures to drinking water contaminants, are the statistics on compliance with the MCLs in the year 2000. Health-based violations for several chemical classes and systems size are shown in Table 4.5 (U.S. EPA 2001c).

Conclusions

In conclusion, what does a preliminary analysis of the results of all this sampling tell us about the nature, magnitude, and distribution of exposure and risk in the food supply? It tells us that, generally, actual residues in food items other than water are most often found to be at levels several to 100 or more times lower than the legal limit, that is, the tolerance. Compliance monitoring tells us that violations are found in only a fraction of a percentage of domestic foods and up to about 3% to 4% in imported foods. Violations include a mix of cases in which tolerances are exceeded and "no-tolerance" cases (mostly, the latter) for the pesticide–commodity combinations. What all this sampling does not tell us is what the level of compliance is with regard to direct, indirect, and color additives, as little or no monitoring is done on most of these 5,000-plus substances. However, in general, based on our current understanding of their toxicological profiles, relatively little or no concern exists with regard to the hazard potential of these categories of residues, especially at the levels expected in foodstuffs. In ad-

TABLE 4.5. Safe Drinking Water Act Compliance Data: Health-Based Violations of Maximum Contaminant Levels (MCL)

Contaminant		25–500	501–3,300	3,301–10,000	10,001–100,000	>100,000	Totals
				System Size			
Organics							
Total	*Number of systems*						
Trihalomethanes	*with violations*	2	3		10		15
	Number of violations	2	6		20		28
	Pop. affected	146	2,890		206,809		209,845
Other Volatile	*Number of systems*						
Organic	*with violations*	28	8	3		1	44
Compounds	*Number of violations*	47	8	4	5	2	66
	Pop. affected	3,632	16,647	23,579	94,325	535,335	673,518
Synthetic	*Number of systems*						
Organic	*with violations*	5	4		1	1	11
Chemicals	*Number of violations*	8	5		1	2	16
	Pop. affected	790	4,579		14,390	180,000	199,759
Inorganics	*Number of systems*						
Nitrates	*with violations*	377	67	7	5	1	457
	Number of violations	624	157	13	9	1	804
	Pop. affected	44,431	87,287	30,444	142,829	158,000	462,991
Other	*Number of systems*						
Inorganic	*with violations*	43	8	7	2		60
Contaminants	*Number of violations*	67	15	8	2		92
	Pop. affected	8,615	10,549	35,924	42,058		97,146
Radionuclides	*Number of systems*						
	with violations	89	72	18	16		195
	Number of violations	166	130	25	25		346
	Pop. affected	18,685	100,322	98,611	356,727		574,345
Lead and copper	*Number of systems*						
	with violations	1,078	320	51	84	15	1,548
	Number of violations	1,381	390	76	100	15	1,962
	Pop. affected	158,200	388,147	285,072	2,666,466	4,577,567	8,075,452

Source: U.S. EPA (2001c).

dition, because the compliance programs are not statistically designed to determine the national profile for all commodities at a single point in time, and even though the Total Diet Study makes an attempt at doing this, but is limited by the numbers of samples that can be tested each year, we really do not have a very robust picture of the true characteristics of exposure, and thus risk, that food chemicals may pose to the population at large. Nonetheless, existing information indicates that dietary exposures to single chemicals are generally of low concern. Occasionally, "hot spots" occur that may yield higher risks, but they are an infrequent and often transitory occurrence, except for the persistent, bioaccumulative toxic (PBT) environmental contaminants, for example, dioxins, PCBs, organochlorine pesticides such as DDT, and the naturally occurring substances, for example, mycotoxins, seafood toxins, and so forth, that pose the greatest challenge. What we are less certain about is the potential for cumulative effects that may occur with coexposure to mixtures of substances. The Food Quality Protection Act of 1996 (U.S. Congress 1996a) has reminded regulators that, when setting food additive tolerances, consideration of both aggregate exposure and cumulative effects must be incorporated into the risk assessment and decision making processes. These requirements have been components of the Federal Food Drug and Cosmetic Act for many years, but have only recently been implemented, and only for pesticide tolerance-setting purposes. If the principles of aggregate exposure and cumulative effects were applied across the board for food additives, we may reach different conclusions about the potential for risk of these substances than we do at the present time.

Finally, as noted earlier, an accurate national profile of exposure remains elusive.

References

Unless stated otherwise, all online citations were accurate as of April 11, 2002.

21 CFR 170-199. 2000. Code of Federal Regulations. Food and Drugs. April 1. http://www.access.gpo.gov/nara/cfr/waisidx_00/21cfrv3_00.html.

40 CFR 180. 2000. Code of Federal Regulations. Subchapter E-Pesticide Programs. Tolerance and Exemptions from Tolerances for Pesticide Chemicals in Food. April. http://www.access.gpo.gov/nara/cfr/waisidx_00/40cfr_00.html.

U.S. Congress. 1996a. Public Law 140-170. The Federal Food Drug and Comestic Act as Amended in the Food Quality Protection Act of 1996. August 3. Washington, DC: U.S. Congress. http://frwebgate.access.gpo.gov/cgi-bin/multidb.cgi/useftp.cgi?Ip address=wais.access.gpo.gov&filename+publ170.104&directory+/diskc/wais/data/ 104_cong_public_laws.

————. 1996b. Public Law 140-182. The Safe Drinking Water Amendments of 1996. August 6. Washington, DC: U.S. Congress. http://frwebgate.access.gpo.gov/ cgibin/multidb.cgi/useftp.cgi?Ipaddress=wais.access.gpo.gov&filename+publ182.1 04&directory+/diskc/wais/data/104_cong_public_laws.

USDA (U.S. Department of Agriculture). 1998. 1998 National Residue Program. Domestic Residue Data Book. The "Red Book." Washington, DC: USDA. http://www. fsis.usda.gov/ophs/red98/index.htm.

————. 2000a. 2000 FSIS National Residue Data Program. The "Blue Book." Washington, DC: USDA. http://www.fsis.usda.gov/OPHS/blue2000/index.htm.

————. 2000b. 2000 FSIS National Residue Program Summary Tables. Washington, DC: USDA. http://www.fsis.usda.gov/OPHS/nrp2000/index.htm.

————. 2000c. Pesticide Data Program. Annual Summary Calendar Year 1998. Washington, DC: USDA. http://www.ams.usda.gov/science/pdp/download.htm.

————. 2001a. Pesticide Data Program. Annual Summary Calendar Year 1999. January. Washington, DC: USDA. http://www.ams.usda.gov/science/pdp/download.htm.

————. 2001b. Pesticide Data Program. Program Overview. Commodities Tested. Required compounds. Washington, DC: USDA. http://www.ams.usda.gov/science/pdp/overview.htm#pest.

U.S. EPA (U.S. Environmental Protection Agency). 1999. Office of Water. Revisions to the Unregulated Contaminants Monitoring Regulation for Public Water Systems; Final Rule. Federal Register: 64 (180): 50555–620, September 17.

————. 2000. Office of Water. Drinking Water Standards and Health Advisories. Summer. EPA 822-B-00-001. Washington, DC: U.S.EPA. http://www.epa.gov/OST.

————. 2001a. Office of Water. Document Related to Fish Tissue Quality. Revised February 19, 2001. Washington, DC: U.S.EPA. http://www.epa.gov/ost/pc/tissue.html.

————. 2001b. Office of Water. Current Drinking Water Standards. Updated May 31, 2001. Washington, DC: U.S.EPA. http://www.epa.gov/safewater/mcl/html.

————. 2001c. Office of Water. Factoids: Drinking Water and Surface Water Statistics for 2000. June. EPA 816-K-01-004. Washington, DC: U.S. EPA. http://www.epa.gov/safewater/data/getdata.html.

————. 2001d. Office of Pesticide Programs' website. Washington, DC: U.S. EPA. http://www.epa.gov/pesticides.

————. 2001e. Office of Pesticide Programs. Tolerance Index Files. Updated July 10. Washington, DC: U.S.EPA. http://www.epa.gov/opprd001/tolerance/tisinfo.

U.S. FDA (U.S. Food and Drug Administration). 1992a. Foodborne Pathogenic Microorganisms and Natural Toxins Handbook: Aflatoxins. Updated May 21, 2001.Washington, DC: U.S. FDA. http://www.cfsan.fda.gov/~mow/chap41.html.

————. 1992b. Foodborne Pathogenic Microorganisms and Natural Toxins Handbook: Various Shellfish-Associated Toxins. Updated May 21, 2001. Washington, DC: U.S. FDA. http://www.cfsan.fda.gov/~mow/chap37.html.

————. 1992c. Pesticides, Metals, Chemical Contaminants & Natural Toxins. Updated July 10, 2001. Washington, DC: U.S. FDA. http://www.cfsan.fda.gov/~lrd/pestadd.html.

————. 1993. Guidance Documents for Trace Elements in Seafood. Washington, DC: U.S. FDA http://www.cfsan.fda.gov/~frf/guid-sf.html.

————. 1995. The Food and Drug Administration's Seafood Regulatory Program. Washington, DC: U.S. FDA. http://www.cfsan.fda.gov/~lrd/sea.ovr.html.

————. 1997a. Food Compliance Program. National Drug Residue Milk Monitoring Program. December 18. Washington, DC: U.S. FDA. http://www.cfsan.fda.gov/~comm/cp03039.html.

————. 1997b. Food Compliance Program. Total Diet Study. December 18. Washington, DC: U.S. FDA. http://www.cfsan.fda.gov/~comm/cp04839.html.

————. 1998. Action Levels for Poisonous or Deleterious Substances in Human Food and Animal Feed. Washington, DC: U.S. FDA. http://www.cfsan.fda.gov/~lrd/fdaact.html.

————.1999a. Food Compliance Program. Mycotoxins in Domestic Foods. March 11. Washington, DC: U.S. FDA. http://www.cfsan.fda.gov/~comm/cp07001.html.

————. 1999b. Food Compliance Program. Mycotoxins in Imported Foods. January 20. Washington, DC: U.S. FDA. http://www.cfsan.fda.gov/~comm/cp07002.html.

————. 2000a. Food Compliance Program. Pesticides and Industrial Chemicals in Domestic Foods. February 16. http://vm.cfsan.fda.gov/~comm/cp04004.html.

————. 2000b. Food and Drug Administration Pesticide Program. Residue Monitoring 1999. April. Updated May 17, 2000. Washington, DC: U.S. FDA. http://vm.cfsan.fda.gov/~dms/pes99rep.html.

————. 2000c. Background Paper in Support of Fumonisin Levels in Corn and Corn Products Intended for Human Consumption. June 6. Washington, DC: U.S. FDA. http://vm.cfsan.fda.gov/%7Edms/fumonbg1.html.

————. 2000d. Elemental Analysis Manual for Food and Related Products. January. Washington, DC: U.S. FDA. http://www.cfsan.fda.gov/~dms/eam-toc.html.

————. 2000e. Food Compliance Program. Domestic Food Safety Program. February 2. Washington, DC: U.S. FDA. http://www.cfsan.fda.gov/~comm/cp03803.html.

————. 2000f. Food Compliance Program. Food Composition, Standards, Labeling and Economics. Dietary Supplements—Import and Domestic. February 17. Washington, DC: U.S. FDA. http://www.cfsan.fda.gov/~comm/cp21008.html.

————. 2000g. Total Diet Study Statistics on Element Results. April, 25. Revision 1, 1991-1998. Washington, DC: U.S. FDA. http://www.cfsan.fda.gov/~comm/tds-toc.html.

————. 2000h. Action Levels for Poisonous or Deleterious Substances in Human Food and Animal Feed. August. Washington, DC: U.S. FDA. http://www.cfsan.fda.gov/~lrd/fdaact.html.

————. 2001a. Consumer Advisory: An Important Message for Pregnant Women and Women of Childbearing Age Who May Become Pregnant About the Risks of Mercury in Fish. March. Washington, DC: U.S. FDA. http://www.cfsan.fda.gov/~dms/admehg.html.

————. 2001b. EAFUS: A Food Additive Database (Everything Added to Food in the United States). Updated January 24. Washington, DC: U.S. FDA. http://www.cfsan.fda.gov/~dms/eafus.html.

————. 2001c. Food Compliance Program. Domestic Fish and Fishery Products. April 3. Washington, DC: U.S. FDA. http://www.cfsan.fda.gov/~comm/cp03842.html.

————. 2001d. Mercury Levels in Seafood Species. May. Washington, DC: U.S. FDA. http://www.cfsan.fda.gov/~frf/sea-mehg.html.

————. 2001e. The List of "Indirect" Additives Used in Food Contact Substances. Inventory of Effective Premarket Notifications for Food Contact Substances. Updated April 3. Washington, DC: U.S. FDA. http://www.cfsan.fda.gov/~dms/opa-indt.html.

————. 2001f. Total Diet Study. April. Washington, DC: U.S. FDA. http://www.cfsan.fda.gov/~comm/tds-toc.html.

————. 2001g. Background Paper on Patulin in Apple Juice, Apple Juice Concentrates and Apple Juice Products. September. Washington, DC: U.S. FDA http://www.cfsan.fda.gov/~dms/patubck2.htm.

————. 2001h. Compliance Policy Guidance for FDA Staff. Apple Juice, Apple Juice Concentrates, and Apple Juice Products-Adulteration with Patulin. October 22. Washington, DC: U.S. FDA. http://www.fda.gov/ora/compliance_ref/cpg/cpgfod/cpg510-150.htm.

————. 2001i. Guidance for Industry: Fumonisin Levels in Human Foods and Animal Feeds. November 9. Washington, DC: U.S. FDA. http://www.cfsan.fda.gov/~dms/fumongu2.html.

————. 2002. List of Completed Consultations on Bioengineered Foods. March. Washington, DC: U.S. FDA. http://www.cfsan.fda.gov/~lrd/biocon.html.

5

The Current State of Play: Federal and State Expenditures on Food Safety*

Lawrence J. Dyckman

Foodborne illness in the United States is an extensive and expensive problem. Federal and state expenditures for activities to help ensure the safety of the nation's food supply are also significant. The cost of federal efforts alone exceeds $1 billion annually. To obtain a better understanding of federal food safety efforts, the U.S. General Accounting Office (GAO) has conducted a series of studies to determine the amount of resources that were expended by federal and state agencies for food safety measures and how the agencies used these resources (see U.S. GAO 1992; 1994; 1996; 1997a, b; 1998a, b; 1999, 2001).

Although 12 federal agencies located within 6 federal departments conduct food safety activities, the U.S. Department of Agriculture Food Safety and Inspection Service (FSIS) and the Department of Health and Human Services Food and Drug Administration (FDA) have primary regulatory responsibility for ensuring the safety of the nation's food supply. This chapter focuses on resource use by FSIS and FDA. To examine expenditures for FSIS and FDA, GAO analyzed the agencies' annual appropriations and financial documentation, which included information on actual food safety expenditures, activities, and accomplishments (U.S. GAO 2001). For food safety activities, GAO obtained and reviewed the associated costs and staff year levels and supplemented this information with agency program documents and discussions between GAO researchers and agency officials. Appendix A at the end of this book describes the role of each of the 12 federal agencies with food safety responsibilities (U.S. GAO 1998). Table 5.1 shows the food safety funding and staffing levels of the agencies for selected years.

---

* Adapted from two U.S. General Accounting Office (GAO) reports: *Food Safety: Overview of Federal and State Expenditures* (February 2001) and *Food Safety: Opportunities to Redirect Federal Resources and Funds Can Enhance Effectiveness* (August 1998).

TABLE 5.1. Changes in Funding and Staffing Levels for Food Safety at 12 Federal Agencies (1998 dollars in millions)

Agency	Funding (by fiscal year)			Staffing		
	FY1989	FY1994	FY1998[a]	FY1989	FY1994	FY1998
Food and Drug Administration (FDA)[b]	$158	$239	$254	2,648	2,999	2,796
Food Safety and Inspection Service (FSIS)	457	606	676	10,399	10,109	9,702
Animal and Plant Health and Inspection Service (APHIS)	*	*	*	*	*	*
Grain Inspection, Packers and Stockyards Administration GIPSA)[c]	42	44	0	860	685	0
Agricultural Marketing Service (AMS)[d]	9	14	10	183	33	42
Agricultural Research Service (ARS)	25	38	55	168	134	167
National Marine Fisheries Service (NMFS)[c]	12	16	13	265	285	174
Environmental Protection Agency (EPA)[e]	90	95	127	624	786	970
Centers for Disease Control and Prevention (CDC)	3	4	15	25	34	50
Federal Trade Commission (FTC)	2	2	†	29	23	†
U.S. Customs Service	*	*	†	*	*	†
Bureau of Alcohol, Tobacco, and Firearms (ATF)	*	*	†	*	*	†
Total	$798	$1,058	$1,150	$15,201	$15,088	$13,901

[a]Appropriated funds for FY1998.

[b] The FDA's data include funding and staffing for various programs across FDA that are involved with food safety activities, including the Center for Food Safety and Applied Nutrition, the Center for Veterinary Medicine, the field components for these centers, and overall agencywide support.

[c]Agencies' funding and staffing levels are for both safety and quality inspection activities.

[d]AMS' funding and staffing totals for FY1989 reflect egg inspection activities, which were transferred to the FSIS in 1994. Totals for FY1994 and FY1998 include data for the Pesticide Data Program, which began in 1991.

[e]Numbers for EPA are from the following sources: FY1991 President's Budget, 1989 Actuals; FY1996 President's Budget, 1994 Actuals; and FY1999 President's Budget, 1998 Enacted, and includes the total Office of Pesticides Programs.

Source: GAO's analysis of federal agencies' data. * indicates that the agency did not specify its food safety resources. † indicates that GAO did not review these agencies' food safety budgets because of the small amount of funds for these activities in previous years.

After a brief overview of the federal food safety funding in the first section, the second section presents the food safety activities undertaken by FSIS to attain these goals during fiscal year (FY)1998 and FY1999, the costs and staff years associated with each activity, and outcomes associated with selected activities. The third section presents similar data for FDA food safety activities undertaken by its units during FY1998 and FY1999. The fourth section reports the results of GAO's survey of state and territorial food safety programs. The fifth section discusses special appropriations under the President's Food Safety Initiatives for FY1998 and FY1999. The chapter ends with an evaluation of food safety expenditures and an assessment of reallocations that could enhance their effectiveness (U.S. GAO 2001).

An Overview of Federal Food Safety Expenditures

Public health officials believe that the risk of foodborne illness has been increasing over the past 20 years. Trends in the incidence of foodborne illness in the United States are linked, at least in part, to changes in Americans' eating habits and U.S. food production practices and import patterns. The U.S. Centers for Disease Control (CDC) estimates that unsafe foods cause as many as 76 million illnesses, 325,000 hospitalizations, and 5,000 deaths annually. The USDA estimates the medical costs and productivity losses attributable to foodborne illnesses associated with seven major pathogens at between $7 billon and $37 billion annually. These cost estimates are not comprehensive. They do not include the costs associated with other pathogens or those associated foodborne illnesses not caused by pathogens, such as allergies, or illnesses associated with chemical contamination. They also do not include the burden of pain and suffering placed on the U.S. population by these illnesses. In 1998, the GAO examined the food safety expenditures of these 12 agencies (U.S. GAO 1998). This structure necessitates extensive coordination to minimize duplication of effort, prevent gaps in regulatory coverage, and avoid conflicting actions. Past GAO reviews have shown inconsistencies and differences between agencies' approaches and enforcement authorities that undercut overall efforts to ensure a safe food supply (U.S. GAO 1992, 1993, 1994, 1997a). In the past, GAO has recommended a single food safety agency to correct the problems created by this fragmented system (U.S. GAO 1999).

Nearly 80% of consumer food expenditures are for foods under FDA's jurisdiction. FSIS is responsible for much of the remaining 20%. In FY1997, 85% of known foodborne illnesses were associated with products regulated by FDA, and the remaining 15% with products regulated by the FSIS. FSIS expended about 70% of FY1999 federal food safety moneys, or $712 million, to oversee about 20% of federally regulated foods. FDA expended about 30%, or $283 million, to oversee about 80% of federally regulated foods (Figure 5.1). Most

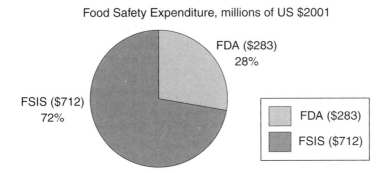

FIGURE 5.1. FSIS and FDA Food Safety Expenditures

Source: Prepared by GAO from FY1999 FSIS and FDA data and FY1997 U.S. Bureau of Labor Statistics Data.

of this expenditure was used to hire staff time. FSIS employed roughly 11,000 staff years, and FDA food safety activities employed about 2,500 staff years in FY1998 and FY1999. The distribution and use of federal food safety funds are in large part mandated by the statutes under which each agency operates.

Food Safety Inspections Service Expenditures

FSIS is responsible for ensuring that meat, poultry, and processed egg products moving in interstate and foreign commerce are safe, wholesome, and marked, labeled, and packaged correctly.[1] Each year, the FSIS oversees approximately 6,000 meat, poultry, egg product, and import establishments (Table 5.2). Under the governing inspection acts, FSIS is required to inspect continuously all meat and poultry slaughter plants and egg processing plants as well as to inspect meat and poultry processing plants daily. FSIS marks all inspected and approved meat, poultry, and egg products with a USDA inspection stamp. Without this marking, the products cannot be legally marketed. In effect, FSIS preapproves all meat, poultry, and processed egg products before they are marketed.

The statutes under which FSIS operates require carcass-by-carcass organoleptic, that is, sight, touch, and smell, inspections. These inspections involve more than 5,000 staff years of time, yet they cannot detect microbial pathogens, which are considered the most significant health risk associated with

[1] The Federal Meat Inspection Act regulates meat from cattle, swine, goats, sheep, and equines (horses); the Poultry Products Inspection Act defines poultry as domesticated fowl, which FSIS regulations define as chickens, turkeys, ducks, geese, and guineas. The Egg Products Inspection Act defines egg products as eggs removed from their shells for processing.

TABLE 5.2. Number of Establishments Inspected by the FSIS and Selected
Compliance Activities, Fiscal Year 1998 and 1999

Activity	FY 1998	FY 1999
Inspections		
Slaughter establishments	254	262
Processing establishments	4,297	4,343
Combination slaughter and processing establishments	985	968
State agreements[a]	256	254
Import establishments	135	129
Egg product establishments	78	75
Total establishments inspected	6,005	6,031
Compliance activities		
Compliance reviews	26,176	43,976
Warnings issued	1,520	2,778
Suspensions for Hazard Analysis and Critical Control		
Point Violations	77	118

[a]Funded through FSIS' headquarters Office of Field Operations at a cost of $40.6 million and
$44.4 million in fiscal years 1998 and 1999, respectively.

Source: GAO (2000).

foods. Since 1998, FSIS has required meat and poultry plants to implement
Hazard Analysis and Critical Control Point (HACCP) systems, which are considered to be the best available method of preventing microbial contamination.

FSIS also oversees domestic and foreign inspection of meat, poultry, and
processed eggs moving in interstate trade. FSIS reviews and assesses the effectiveness of intrastate meat, poultry, and egg product inspection programs
to ensure that their standards are at least equal to federal standards. FSIS also
reviews and assesses foreign inspection systems and facilities to ensure that
FSIS-regulated products imported to the United States have been inspected
under systems equivalent to those in the United States. FSIS reinspects imported meat, poultry, and egg products at ports of entry and at destinations
or other locations. In 1998, FSIS reviewed 7 of the 26 states with intrastate
inspection programs for meat or poultry and reviewed foreign inspection
programs in 22 of the 37 countries that were eligible to export products to
the United States. In addition to its inspection activities, FSIS conducts emergency responses, including retention, detention, or voluntary recall of adulterated foods and epidemiological investigations of foodborne hazards or
disease outbreaks. Finally, FSIS develops and implements cooperative strategies to prevent health hazards associated with animal production practices,
coordinating U.S. participation in international sanitary standard-setting activities, and providing safety information to food handlers and consumers.

Organizational Structure

FSIS accomplishes its mission through five program offices located in Washington, DC. The offices include the Office of the Administrator; Office of Public Health and Science; Office of Policy, Program Development and Evaluation; Office of Field Operations (headquarters and district offices); and Office of Management. In addition, FSIS operates a Technical Service Center in Omaha, Nebraska; three field laboratories located in Alameda, California, St. Louis, Missouri, and Athens, Georgia; and 17 district offices located throughout the United States.[2]

The food safety activities of FSIS can be separated into two major components—operations conducted in the field by district offices or in direct support of those district offices and operations conducted primarily in headquarters offices.[3] In aggregate, FSIS' field activities accounted for about 84% of the agency's expenditures (Table 5.3). Headquarters activities (the Offices of Management, Public Health & Science, Policy Program Development & Evaluation, and the Administrator) accounted for about 16% of aggregate expenditures.[4]

Office of Field Operations. The Office of Field Operations is responsible for managing a program of regulatory oversight and inspection for the meat, poultry, and egg product laws enforced by FSIS. As such, the office was responsible for about 84% of agency expenditures and more than 90% of staff years. The office is divided into two components—headquarters operations and field district operations.

The headquarters unit located in Washington, DC, sets policy and manages field operations. The headquarters unit accounted for about 10% of total FSIS expenditures. Included within this unit is the Technical Service Center, which serves as the agency's center for technical assistance and guidance for field operations personnel and industry. The center also reviews domestic and foreign inspection programs.[5]

---

[2]During FY1999, FSIS closed its Boston District Office, which changed the number of district offices from 18 to 17.

[3]FSIS' total expenditures included about $47 million in grants to states for inspection and other activities annually. These funds were likely reported as food safety expenditures by the state agriculture and health departments and thus may be double-counted in the federal and state total of $1.3 billion. In addition, in commenting on a draft of this report, the FSIS stated that some of its expenditures were for nonfood safety activities more related to food wholesomeness and quality issues, but provided no specific examples.

[4]The proportion of expenditures for each category of activity varied by less than 2% from FY1998 to FY1999.

[5]The Technical Service Center conducted review activities that accounted for about 12% of field operation's headquarters expenditures for FY1999. The center is responsible for

TABLE 5.3. FSIS' Expenditures and Staff Years for Food Safety Activities by Office, FY 1998 and 1999 (dollars in millions)

Office	Expenditures (percent of total)		Staff years (percent of total)	
	1998	*1998*	*1998*	*1998*
Field Operations				
Plant Inspections	463.3	486	9,441	9,330
	68%	68%	85%	85%
District Compliance,	35.4	34.1	521	517
Supervision and	5%	5%	5%	5%
Administration				
Headquarters	69.1	79.9	222	211
	10%	11%	2%	2%
Subtotal	567.8	600	10,184	10,058
	84%	84%	92%	92%
Headquarters Operations				
Management	62.7	61.8	406	382
	9%	9%	4%	3%
Public Health and Science	23.9	25.2	254	281
	4%	4%	2%	3%
Policy, Program Development,	18	18.9	149	162
and Evaluation	3%	3%	1%	1%
Administrator	5.3	6.1	64	68
	1%	1%	1%	1%
Subtotal	109.9	112	873	893
	16%	16%	8%	8%
Total	677.7	712	11,057	10,951
	100%	100%	100%	100%

Source: GAO (2001).

District Inspection and District Enforcement offices manage and direct both inspection and compliance activities. The field district offices accounted for about 73% of agency expenditures and about 90% of staff years (Table 5.3). Within the district offices, 93% of their expenditures were for in-plant inspections and 7% for the administration of those activities and compliance activities.

---

designing and implementing guidelines and procedures for review of foreign, state, and federal domestic inspection programs. The center also conducts special inquiries and reviews, such as reviews of state inspection programs, to ensure they are equivalent to the federal programs. In FY1999, the center reviewed the program documentation of 36 countries exporting to the United States to determine if they had implemented Hazard Analysis and Critical Control Point systems and *Salmonella* testing programs equivalent to U.S. requirements. In that same year, the center's review staff reviewed 96 state-inspected establishments in 11 states to determine their effectiveness and whether or not they were equivalent to the federal inspection programs.

District offices direct inspections of meat and poultry slaughter plants, processing plants, and plants that have combined slaughter and processing operations, as well as inspections of other establishments such as egg product plants and at import points. In FY1999, they inspected more than 99 billion pounds of meat and poultry and 3 billion pounds of egg products at about 6,000 domestic plants and 3.2 billion pounds of imported meat and poultry from 34 countries. FSIS estimates that carcass-by-carcass accounted for about $296 million of FY1999 inspection expenditures of $486 million. FSIS does not track expenditures specifically related to Hazard Analysis and Critical Control Point system inspections and thus could not provide that information.

The district offices also direct compliance reviews that are designed to (1) monitor businesses engaged in the production, distribution, and marketing of food products and (2) prevent the violation of laws and regulations. As a result of these reviews, in FY1999, the district offices detained approximately 20 million pounds of adulterated meat and poultry products and initiated 118 enforcement actions to stop inspection operations in federally inspected plants.

Office of Public Health and Science. The Office of Public Health and Science (OPHS) is responsible for conducting scientific analysis, providing scientific advice, collecting data, and making recommendations involving all public health and science concerns relating to products under FSIS jurisdiction. This includes mission activities such as epidemiology and risk assessment, surveillance, response to food safety emergencies, and laboratory analysis by the agency's three field laboratories. Three field laboratories located in Alameda, California; Athens, Georgia; and St. Louis, Missouri, accounted for half of OPHS expenditures, for $14 million of field activity expenditures, or 2%, of total expenditures, and almost 70% of the staff years. These laboratories coordinate and conduct analyses in microbiology, chemistry, and pathology for food safety in meat, poultry, and egg products. Among other reasons, they conduct these services to (1) support both domestic and import inspections done by FSIS, (2) support the agency's Hazard Analysis and Critical Control Point initiative, and (3) identify emerging pathogens in the food supply. In addition, the laboratories provide technical assistance to FSIS field staff.

Office of Policy, Program Development, and Evaluation. The Office of Policy, Program Development and Evaluation (OPPDE) is responsible for, among other functions, coordinating activities such as developing and recommending domestic and international policies for FSIS; reviewing product processes, standards, and labeling; and developing and evaluating inspection programs. The office accounted for about 3% of agency expenditures and 1% of staff years (Table 5.3). Within OPPDE, the Inspection Systems Development Division designs, develops, and tests new or modified inspection systems for food safety. This division works on developing specific changes to FSIS' inspection procedures, including work related to hazard analysis and critical control point procedures.

Office of the Administrator. The Office of the Administrator is responsible for overall management of the agency and activities such as public affairs, food safety education, and coordination of U.S. involvement in international standard setting for food safety and maintaining liaisons with trade organizations. As shown in Table 5.3, the office accounted for about 1% of agency expenditures and 1% of staff years.

A significant portion of the Office of the Administrator's funding, about 30% in FY1999, was expended on food safety education. These programs are designed to educate producers, distributors, food preparers, and consumers on the prevention of foodborne illnesses. This office also operates the agency's Meat and Poultry Hotline to answer consumer inquiries. In FY1999, this staff coordinated the agency's food safety education campaign, FightBAC!™, and handled about 36,000 consumer calls to the hotline.

Office of Management. In FY1998 and FY1999, the Office of Management accounted for about 9% (or $62–$63 million) of agency expenditures and used 4% of the total staff years to provide centralized administrative and support services to all other FSIS program offices, including human resource management, strategic planning, procurement, and financial management.

Food and Drug Administration

Food safety is one of FDA's many responsibilities, shared by multiple units within the agency. Under the Federal Food, Drug and Cosmetic Act (FFDCA), FDA is responsible for ensuring that (1) all foods moving in interstate and foreign commerce, except those under FSIS' jurisdiction, are safe, wholesome, and labeled properly; and (2) all animal drugs and feeds are safe, properly labeled, and produce no human health hazards when used in food-producing animals. FDA responsibilities include ensuring the safety of ingredients that make up foods, such as food additives that change a food's color or taste, and reviewing and approving new additives before they can be marketed. In administering the act, which generally follows the regulatory approach of allowing food products to enter the market without preapproval, FDA inspects and tests domestic and imported food products.[6] However, the FFDCA does not mandate or specify inspection frequencies for overseeing an estimated 57,000 domestic food establishments under FDA's jurisdiction (see Table 5.4). Products under FDA's

---

[6]Both the FDA and the FSIS have implemented hazard analysis and critical control point systems that are designed to identify and control foodborne hazards that are likely to occur. In December 1997, the FDA required seafood establishments to implement such systems, and in January 1998, the FSIS began requiring implementation at meat and poultry establishments.

TABLE 5.4. Number of FDA Food Safety Field Inspections, Examinations, and Samples Analyzed, Fiscal Years 1998 and 1999

Activity	1998	1999
Inspections		
Food Importers	940	765
Domestic food establishments[a]	11,922	14,680
Feed establishments[b]	4,182	3,128
Animal drug establishments	439	357
Total inspections[c]	17,483	18,930
Field examinations		
Imported foods	17,140	15,828
Domestic foods	2,172	1,992
Imported animal drugs/feeds	46	59
Total field examinations	19,358	17,879
Sample analyses		
Import food samples	16,802	15,439
Domestic food samples	10,894	9,335
Animal drug/feed samples[d]	1,580	1,784
Total samples analyzed	29,276	26,558

[a]Includes state contract inspections that are funded by the Center for Food Safety and Applied Nutrition at a cost of a little over $2 million each year.

[b]Includes state contract feed mill inspections that are funded by the Center for Veterinary Medicine at a cost of $833,000 and $614,000 in fiscal years 1998 and 1999, respectively.

[c]An individual importer, food, or feed establishment may be inspected more than once a year.

[d]FDA and the states also analyzed more than 200 bovine spongiform encephalopathy tissue residue samples each year.

Source: FDA.

jurisdiction do not require, and FDA does not place, any inspection mark on the products before they can be legally marketed. FDA is also responsible for maintaining surveillance of all animal drugs and feeds to ensure that they are safe and labeled properly and produce no human health hazards when used in food-producing animals and for overseeing more than 9,000 animal drug and feed establishments.[7]

FDA's food safety efforts are assigned to three centers: Center for Food Safety and Applied Nutrition (CFSAN) for the Foods Program; Center for Veterinary

[7]GAO's recently released report, *Food Safety: Controls Can Be Strengthened to Reduce the Risk of Disease Linked to Unsafe Animal Feed* (GAO/RCED-00-255, September 22, 2000), addresses concerns regarding the extent to which unsafe feed has been linked to human health problems in the United States and the actions FDA and the Department of Transportation are taking to ensure the safety of animal feed.

Medicine (CVM) for the Animal Drugs and Feeds Program; and National Center for Toxicological Research (NCTR) for research into the toxicity of products. In addition, the Office of Regulatory Affairs (ORA) is responsible for conducting field activities designated by the centers. ORA's compliance, inspection, and laboratory field staff manage, supervise, and conduct enforcement, compliance, inspection, sample collection, and analysis activities, as well as criminal investigation, education, and outreach activities.

As with FSIS, FDA's food safety activities can be separated into two major elements: (1) inspection and enforcement operations conducted in the field by district offices or at headquarters in direct support of those district offices and (2) operations conducted primarily in headquarters offices. As shown in Table 5.5, about 56% of FDA's food safety expenditures and more than 60% of its staff years were for food safety activities conducted in the field, and the remaining 44% of expenditures and nearly 40% of the staff years were for the headquarters-based activities of the centers. FDA expended $253 million in FY1998 and $283 million in FY1999 on food safety activities.

FDA food safety facilities are distributed nationwide. FDA headquarters and CVM are located in Rockville, Maryland, CFSAN is located in Washington, DC, and NCTR is located in Jefferson, Arkansas. The two centers, CVM and CFSAN, have a research facility in Beltsville, Maryland. CFSAN also has a fishery research center in Dauphin Island, Alabama, and a food technology research center in Chicago, Illinois. Field facilities, staffed primarily by Office of Regulatory Affairs personnel conducting inspections and laboratory activities, are distributed across 5 regional offices, 19 district offices, and 13 laboratories, and are supported by more than 120 resident posts.

FDA Field Operations

FDA Field Food Safety Activities for Foods and Animal Drugs and Feeds. Total field operations activity expenditures accounted for about 56% of total FDA food safety expenditures each year and 62% to 64% of FDA's staff years. CFSAN is responsible for directing field activities related to food products, and CVM is responsible for field activities related to feeds and drugs for food animals. These field activities, conducted by FDA's Office of Regulatory Affairs, include the inspection of food and animal feed and drug establishments under the agency's jurisdiction, field examination of food and feed products, and the collection and analysis of product samples to ensure that the products comply with applicable regulations.

CFSAN activities for foods accounted for about 85% of FDA's food safety field expenditures (Table 5.5). Using these funds, FDA conducted more than 14,600 domestic food establishment inspections, including those conducted by states under contract with FDA, at a cost of about $2 million; and about 765

TABLE 5.5. FDA's Expenditures and Staff Years for Food Safety Activities by Center, Fiscal Years 1998 and 1999 (dollars in millions)

Center	Expenditures (percentage of total)		Staff years (percentage of total)	
	1998	1998	1998	1998
Field operations				
Center for Food Safety and	127.2	145.2	1,426	1,535
Nutrition	50%	51%	57%	59%
Center for Veterinary Medicine	13.7	13.5	138	137
	5%	5%	6%	5%
Subtotal	140.9	158.7	1,564	1,672
	56%	56%	62%	64%
Headquarters operations				
Center for Food Safety and Applied	85.7	95.6	733	721
Nutrition	34%	34%	29%	28%
Center for Veterinary Medicine	25.9	27.7	203	206
	10%	10%	8%	8%
National Center for Toxicological	0.8	1.5	5	10
Research	<1%	1%	<1%	<1%
Subtotal	112.4	124.8	941	937
	44%	44%	38%	36%
Total[a]	253.3	283.5	2,505	2,609
	100%	100%	100%	100%

[a]Totals may not add because of rounding.

Source: FDA.

inspections of food importers. About $27 million, or 19%, of CFSAN food expenditures went to domestic and imported seafood hazard analysis and critical control point inspection activities. In FY1999, CFSAN spent more than $40 million for laboratory analysis of about 25,000 domestic and foreign product samples associated with field inspection activities.

Animal drugs and feeds field activity, that is, the ORA-conducted field activities in support of the Center for Veterinary Medicine expenditures, accounted for about 5% of FDA's total food safety field expenditures each year. With these funds, FDA conducted nearly 3,500 domestic animal drug and feed establishment inspections, including those conducted by states under contract with FDA. Also included in these expenditures is about $2 million for laboratory analysis of about 1,800 feed samples associated with field inspection activities.

FDA Headquarters Operations

CFSAN Headquarters Food Safety Activities. The center is responsible for FDA's Foods Program. CFSAN headquarters operations accounted for about 34% of total FDA food safety expenditures. CFSAN's FY1998 and FY1999 headquarters activities were divided into four major categories: premarket, postmarket, crosscutting, and FDA agencywide support expenditures.[8] CFSAN expenditures for management and administrative support of food safety activities are included in the expenditure amount for each activity.

Premarket activities to evaluate the safety of products such as food and color additives, infant formula, and medical foods before they are available to consumers accounted for about 11% (or about $10 million) of CFSAN's headquarters expenditures in FY1999. About $9 million, or nearly 90%, of premarket expenditures were for food and color additive premarket approvals activities. During the period studied, CFSAN implemented procedures to expedite the review of food additives intended to decrease the incidence of foodborne illness through their antimicrobial actions against pathogens that may be present in food. Other activities addressed food contact substances and irradiation labeling.

Postmarket activities to evaluate the safety of products, such as monitoring and response activities that are in the marketplace, accounted for about 18% of CFSAN's headquarters expenditures in FY1999. CFSAN's planning and policy implementation for microbial contaminants, which accounted for 39% of postmarket expenditures, included surveillance to assess antimicrobial resistance, microbiological research, and risk assessment to develop science-based solutions to detect and control microbial contamination. Another $3.5 million, or 21%, of postmarket expenditures were for cooperative programs with states addressing the safety of retail dairy and shellfish products.

Crosscutting activities that address both premarket and postmarket food safety issues, such as regulatory policy development and education and outreach activities, accounted for about 63% (or about $61 million) of CFSAN's headquarters expenditures in FY1999. CFSAN's food safety research and risk assessment, which accounted for $32.3 million, or 53% of crosscutting expenditures, included activities such as the completion of draft risk assessments for *Listeria, Vibrio parahaemolytics,* and methylmercury and food safety research in support of the National Food Safety Initiative.

FDA agencywide support accounted for about 8% of CFSAN's headquarters expenditures in FY1999. These expenditures represent CFSAN's allocation for its share of central direction and administrative services to ensure that FDA's efforts are effectively managed and that resources are put to the most efficient

[8]Differing from the CFSAN, the CVM did not identify crosscutting activities as a category.

use. Functions include agencywide policy, regulatory and legislative development, scientific coordination, planning and evaluation, consumer communication and public information, and management expertise and coordination in financial management, personnel, contracts and grants administration, and procurement.[9]

CVM Headquarters Food Safety Activities. The center is responsible for ensuring that only safe and effective animal drugs, feeds, and feed additives are marketed and that foods from animals that are administered drugs and food additives are safe for human consumption. The center maintains surveillance over all animal drugs and feeds to minimize threats to human health. CVM headquarters operations accounted for about 10% of total agency food safety expenditures, as shown in Table 5.5. The CVM headquarters activities are divided into three major categories: premarket, postmarket, and FDA agencywide support expenditures. CVM expenditures for management and administrative support for food safety activities are included in the total cost for each activity.

Within CVM, premarket activities accounted for about 46% of expenditures each year, and postmarket activities also accounted for about 46% of expenditures each year. CVM's epidemiological systems and surveillance activities, which accounted for about 34% of postmarket expenditures, included collaborative efforts with other federal agencies to monitor nationwide changes in susceptibilities to 17 antimicrobial drugs through the National Antimicrobial Resistance Monitoring System and efforts to monitor and reduce drug residues in meats. Intramural research to detect microbial and chemical contaminants that may be present in animal feeds and animal food products consumed by humans and research on antibiotic resistance accounted for 30% of postmarket expenditures. This included the development and validation of a test for detecting bovine protein in animal feeds, an important component of its bovine spongiform encephalopathy regulatory strategy.

NCTR Headquarters Food Safety Activities. The center's mission is to conduct peer-reviewed scientific research that provides the basis for FDA to make sound, science-based regulatory decisions and to protect the public health through pre- and postmarket surveillance. In FY1998, NCTR expended $842,000, including $75,000 from CVM, and 5 staff years on 8 food safety research projects. In FY1999, NCTR expended nearly $1.5 million and 10 staff years on 10 research projects, including $500,000 to expand food safety method

---

[9]NCTR also conducted food safety research funded through an interagency agreement with the National Institute of Environmental Health and Safety at a total cost of $8.4 million in FY1998 and FY1999.

development research. These expenditures accounted for no more than 1% of agency food safety expenditures.

National Food Safety Initiatives

National food safety initiatives announced by former President Clinton for FY1998–99 provided additional funds to strengthen identified weaknesses in the federal food safety system (U.S. GAO 1998). For FY1998, the administration's initiative received $43 million for specific food safety activities to improve the nation's food safety system. Prior to the initiative, these activities had competed with other agency priorities for funding. The $43 million in funding was aimed at, among other objectives, (1) improving a nationwide early-warning system for foodborne illnesses; (2) increasing seafood safety inspections; and (3) expanding research, training, and education in food safety. Under the initiative for FY1999, the administration has requested $101 million to build on the food safety efforts in the 1998 initiative and to enhance the safety of imported and domestic fruits and vegetables, among other goals. The CDC used initiatives funding to improve its monitoring of foodborne illnesses and will expand its surveillance locations throughout the country to eight. This program, now known as FoodNet, provides national data to better identify illnesses associated with foods; these data allow for more informed decisions about dealing with microbial contamination. Prior to FoodNet, CDC had very limited information on the extent of foodborne illnesses. Since this surveillance effort was undertaken, for example, CDC has learned that the incidence of one pathogen, *Campylobacter,* is far more frequent than previously known. Campylobacter is a pathogen that causes such food borne illnesses as chronic diarrhea, meningitis, and blood poisoning. It is the most common precipitating factor for Guillain-Barré syndrome, which is now one of the leading causes of paralysis from disease in the United States. Campylobacter can occur from contact with such foods as raw poultry and raw milk. Policy makers can now use this information to direct research and other activities to reduce illnesses caused by this pathogen.[10]

Although these food safety initiatives have addressed, and intend to address, some targeted problems, they do not deal effectively with the underlying fragmentation in the federal food safety system. As GAO has reported, past efforts to correct deficiencies in the federal inspection system for food safety have

---

[10]*Campylobacter* is a pathogen that causes such food borne illnesses as chronic diarrhea, meningitis, and blood poisoning. It is the most common precipitating factor for Guillain-Barré syndrome, which is now one of the leading causes of paralysis from disease in the United States. *Campylobacter* can occur from contact with such foods as raw poultry and raw milk.

fallen short, in part because they did not address the fundamental problems in the system (U.S. GAO 1997). Agencies operate under different regulatory approaches, have widely disparate budgets and staffs, and lack the flexibility needed to respond to changing consumption patterns and emerging food safety issues. These agencies' efforts are hampered by laws that were designed to address safety concerns in specific foods in a piecemeal fashion, typically in response to particular health threats or economic crises.

In addition, this fragmentation may have impeded the effective implementation of some of the activities funded through the food safety initiatives. For example, the initiatives for FY1998–99 included about $15.7 million to FSIS, FDA, and the Cooperative State Research, Education, and Extension Service, among other agencies, to develop jointly a national campaign to educate the public about the safe handling of fruits and vegetables. However, this effort excluded EPA, which spent about $230,000 in FY1998 and about $400,000 in FY1999 to develop and distribute its own brochure to educate the public about pesticides and foods. Although EPA attempted to coordinate its educational brochure with the other agencies, significant differences over the message still occurred. According to USDA and FDA officials and consumer groups, EPA's message implied that certain risks are associated with eating fruits and vegetables treated with pesticides. These groups said that EPA's message contradicted USDA's advice to eat more fruits and vegetables. At the same time, the other agencies developed a message that discussed the safe handling of fruits and vegetables and encouraged their consumption. After receiving comments from other agencies and the public on its draft brochure as published in the *Federal Register,* EPA revised its brochure to reflect the concerns of the other agencies.

Even when an activity under the initiatives has been designed to address a fragmentation problem, there is no assurance that it will be successful. For example, in January 1997, former President Clinton's Food Safety Initiative (Food Safety From Farm to Table: A National Food Safety Initiative) proposed improving seafood inspection activities by consolidating seafood inspections under one agency by October 1998. Under the proposal, NMFS' voluntary fee-for-service seafood inspection program would be moved to FDA. The transfer required granting FDA legislative authority to collect user fees. Congress has so far been unwilling to grant such authority.

Evaluation of Federal Food Safety Expenditures[11]

The scientific community recognizes that preventing contamination is the key to reducing the risk of foodborne illness. FSIS spent about $271 million annu-

---

[11]These evaluations are taken from GAO, *Opportunities to Redirect Federal Resources and Funds Can Enhance Effectiveness* (August 1998).

ally on inspectors who are present at each slaughter plant nationwide every day that it is in operation. These inspectors, under current FSIS rules and regulations, inspect each carcass—more than 8 billion birds and livestock annually—for visible defects, such as lesions and diseases. Under the traditional organoleptic inspection system, an inspector has about two seconds per bird, at the fastest line speeds, to determine whether the carcass meets federal standards for wholesomeness. Although these inspections fulfill the statutory requirements, they primarily identify defects in quality but do not detect microbial contamination.

As the threat of microbial contamination has increased, a Hazard Analysis and Critical Control Point (HACCP) system has come to be considered the best approach currently available for ensuring safe food because it focuses on preventing contamination rather than on detecting it once it has occurred. The HACCP system (1) identifies hazards and assesses the risks associated with each phase of food production,[12] (2) determines the critical points where the identified hazards can be controlled, and (3) establishes procedures to monitor these critical control points. Hazards include any biological, chemical, or physical property that may cause an unacceptable risk to consumers' health.

In January 1998, FSIS began to require meat and poultry plants to implement HACCP systems. The HACCP system requires FSIS' verification that a plant's overall system—not just the individual control points—is working. This verification relies on, among other things, microbial and other types of testing of product samples taken at various times throughout production. These tests contribute to verifying whether the plants meet food safety standards and alert the plants to deficiencies in the slaughtering process.

A User Fee May Be Appropriate to Cover Organoleptic Meat and Poultry Inspections

GAO previously reported that with the introduction of the HACCP system, the traditional system of organoleptic meat and poultry inspections of each meat and poultry carcass will become obsolete for improving the safety of meat and poultry because it does not prevent microbial contamination (U.S. GAO 1994). Moreover, experts have recognized that postmortem organoleptic inspections on every carcass must be changed because (1) they waste resources and cannot detect microbial pathogens, (2) the animal diseases for which they were originally designed have been eradicated in many countries, and (3) they result in unnecessary cross-contamination because the hands-on inspection techniques used virtually ensure that contamination spreads from one carcass to another.

---

[12]Hazards include any biological, chemical, or physical property that may cause an unacceptable risk to consumers' health.

However, this type of inspection may be useful to slaughter plants, as it primarily provides an assurance of quality, such as ensuring that feathers are removed and that tumors and blood clots are not present. Although these conditions do not generally threaten human health, they affect the quality of the product. Because the organoleptic inspections of slaughtered animals primarily help to ensure quality rather than food safety, these inspections are foremost in the slaughter plants' interest. Therefore, as GAO previously reported, it may be appropriate to charge user fees to cover the costs of these activities.

Resources from Daily Processing Plant Inspections Could Be Spent More Effectively

Federal food safety resources could also be used more effectively by adopting a risk-based approach rather than the approach currently used by FSIS, which requires daily inspections at all processing plants (U.S. GAO 1998). This inflexible, labor-intensive approach costs an estimated $109 million annually. In FY1999, daily meat and poultry processing inspections at about 4,300 establishments accounted for about $145 million of the agency's inspections expenditures. Under FSIS' current approach, an inspector must visit each meat and poultry processing plant every 8-hour operating shift to perform a number of tasks, such as monitoring the cleanliness of the workers' bathrooms and ensuring that the canning process operates under the right temperatures and pressures. An undetermined amount of funds could be made available by adopting a risk-based approach to determine the appropriate frequency for these inspections and to allow for more substantial inspections, if needed, when they do occur. Funds made available from this new approach could then be redirected to other food safety priorities. Developing a risk-based system to determine the frequency of daily inspections would result in fewer inspections but also in inspections that are more closely tied to risk.

Opportunities Exist to Redirect Budget Resources to More Effective Uses

If FSIS changes its current approach to carcass-by-carcass slaughter inspections, all or part of the $271 million annually spent on these inspections could be redirected to other federal food safety activities that better reduce the threat of food borne illness. A number of food safety concerns could be addressed, such as the following:

•   FSIS could help to install HACCP inspection systems at the smallest meat and poultry slaughter and processing plants. Because industry will bear most of the installation cost for these new systems and the smallest plants have a smaller volume over which to spread this cost, these plants will be disproportionately affected by the cost of the new inspection systems.

- FDA could increase the frequency of its inspections of other U.S. food-processing plants, such as nonmeat soup plants, cereal manufacturers, and canned fruit and vegetable processors. Currently, FDA inspects such plants under its jurisdiction only once in 10 years, on average. These inspections are not based on the health risks that these plants pose, but rather on available resources. FDA officials informed us that if they had increased resources, FDA could increase the frequency of inspections of high-, moderate-, and low-risk firms, in that order. In general, the inspections of lower-risk firms would be based on the availability of resources.

- FDA could improve its oversight of imported foods by assisting foreign countries in developing equivalent food safety systems or it could use the funds to improve its oversight of imported foods at ports of entry. In addition to these actions, the food safety agencies may have other priorities for the use of the funds that are made available from organoleptic slaughter inspections of meat and poultry plants or by basing the frequency of meat- and poultry-processing plant inspections on risk. For example, an Agricultural Research Service official stated that FDA could use additional funding to support an ongoing surveillance system of food animals. This system samples tissue from food animals that have been treated with antibiotics. The system monitors (1) the buildup of antibiotic tolerances in animals and (2) the mutation of pathogens resulting from antibiotic treatment. The health concern is antibiotic resistance to pathogens in humans as a result of consuming these food animals.

The Big Picture

More than 80% of the federal food safety budget goes to FSIS and FDA. Together FSIS and FDA spent nearly $1 billion annually to ensure the safety of the nation's food supply in FY1998 and FY1999. Expenditure patterns and activity vary widely across these agencies. FSIS's field inspection activities account for most of that agency's food safety expenditures (Figure 5.2). FDA's food safety expenditures are more closely divided between field inspection and headquarters activities (Figure 5.3). States report substantial expenditures, of nearly $300 million per year, of which 48% is spent on licensing and inspections (U.S. GAO 2001).

FSIS spends a large proportion of its funding on field inspections. This reflects the legislative mandate of the meat and poultry acts for continuous inspection of meat and poultry slaughter plants and of egg processing plants, and the agency's interpretation of federal law as requiring daily inspection of meat

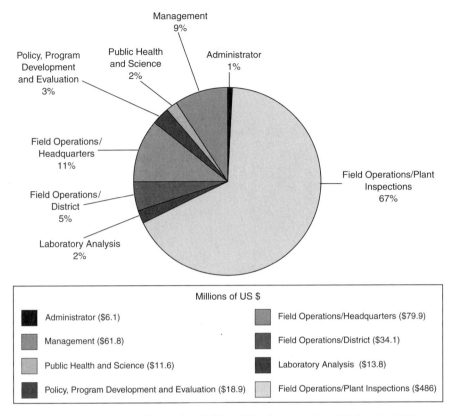

FIGURE 5.2. FSIS Expenditures for Field and Headquarters Food Safety Activities, FY1999

Source: Prepared by GAO from FSIS data (2001).

and poultry processing plants, for example, deboning and canning operations.[13] The two acts require that meat and poultry slaughter plants be under continuous FSIS inspection.[14] If a federal inspector is not present, the animals cannot be slaughtered. FSIS inspects animals both before and after slaughter. The acts also require FSIS inspectors to monitor processing plant operations,

[13]The Federal Meat Inspection Act requires a postmortem examination and inspection of the carcasses and parts of all livestock prepared at any slaughtering establishment. The Poultry Products Inspection Act requires a postmortem inspection of each bird processed.

[14]There has been an ongoing debate regarding the implementation of a system under which plant workers would assume more responsibility for the carcass inspections now conducted by federal inspectors. With guidance from recent court rulings, the FSIS is working to establish such a system while still meeting the requirements of the acts.

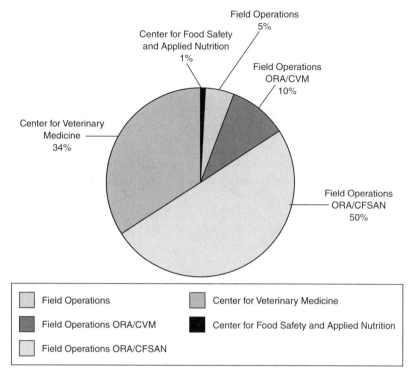

FIGURE 5.3. FDA Expenditures for Field and Headquarters Food Safety Activities, FY1999

Note: Percentages do not add up to 100 because of rounding. CFSAN, Center for Food Safety and Applied Nutrition; CVM, Center for Veterinary Medicine; ORA, Office of Regulatory Affairs. *Source:* Prepared by GAO from FDA's data.

such as deboning and canning, to ensure that plants are sanitary and adhere to approved procedures and label specifications. The acts do not explicitly set inspection frequencies for meat- and poultry-processing plants; however, FSIS has interpreted the acts as requiring the daily inspection of such plants and has established its regulations accordingly. That is, an FSIS inspector must visit each meat- and poultry-processing plant for an unspecified period of time—which may be as little as an hour—each operating day. As such, the majority of FSIS expenditures are directed to conducting inspection activities based on frequencies derived from the regulatory acts, rather than on the food safety risk of a specific plant or process.

Moving to a risk-based inspection system would allow for a more effective use of some of the resources currently expended on carcass-by-carcass and daily inspection activities. In 1998, GAO reported that FSIS' funds could be used more effectively if they were redirected using risk-based criteria (U.S. GAO 1998). Most of the almost $300 million—more than one fourth of the food safety budget—spent annually on FSIS' organoleptic, carcass-by-carcass slaughter inspections could be spent more effectively on other food safety activities that better address food safety risks. Once HACCP is fully implemented, the funds could become available through the Congress's (1) authorizing FSIS to impose user fees on meat and poultry plants for carcass-by-carcass slaughter inspections, (2) eliminating the legislatively mandated requirement for these federal inspections and allowing slaughter plants to hire their own inspectors, or (3) combining the above options—permitting the slaughter plants to either pay the user fees for federal inspections or hire their own inspectors. In addition, if daily inspections of the processing plants—at an annual cost of about $109 million—were replaced by inspections based on health risk, an undetermined amount of funds could be made available. All or part of the funds made available through the implementation of revisions to food safety inspections could be redirected to other food safety priorities.

FDA's relatively small proportion of expenditures on field inspection and supporting activities in comparison to FSIS' expenditures for those activities reflects the absence of specified inspection frequencies in the Federal Food, Drug and Cosmetics Act. The Act, which FDA has primary responsibility for administering, generally follows the regulatory approach of allowing almost all food products to enter the market without preapproval by federal agencies. Therefore, FDA is not required to inspect foods or food firms on a given schedule. As a result, FDA inspects the more than 57,000 food establishments under its jurisdiction about once every 5 years, on average, and according to FDA officials, inspected fewer than 1% of the 3.7 million imported food entries in FY1999.

In past reviews, GAO has identified a number of important food safety concerns that would require increased funding of FDA programs. An increase in the frequency of FDA inspections of U.S. food-processing plants following a risk-based monitoring program appears to have a potential for providing greater assurance of safe foods in the United States. Greater funding would also allow FDA to improve oversight of imported foods, both by assisting foreign countries in developing equivalent food safety systems and by improving inspection of imported foods at U.S. ports of entry. Increased funding could also allow FDA to expand its system for monitoring antibiotic use in food animals as a way of preventing antibiotic resistance.

Federal, state, and local governments share responsibility for ensuring the safety of the U.S. food supplies. Consumers also play a critical role, assisted by government food safety education programs. Although the U.S. food supply is generally of very high quality, the U.S. food safety system faces the challenge of adapting to changing market conditions, consumption patterns, and emerging pathogens. GAO reviews conducted over the past decade suggest that opportunities exist to redirect federal resources and funds in ways that can enhance the effectiveness of the federal food safety system.

References

U.S. GAO (General Accounting Office). 1992. *Food Safety and Quality: Uniform, Risk-Based Inspection System Needed to Ensure Safe Food Supply.* GAO/RCED-92-152, June 26.

————. 1993. *Food Safety: A Unified, Risk-Based System Needed to Enhance Food Safety.* GAO/T-RCED-94-71, November 4.

————. 1994. *Food Safety: Risk-Based Inspections and Microbial Monitoring Needed for Meat and Poultry.* GAO/RCED-94-110, May.

————. 1996. *Food Safety: New Initiatives Would Fundamentally Alter the Existing System.* GAO/RCED-96-81, March.

————. 1997a. *Food Safety: Fundamental Changes Needed to Improve Food Safety.* GAO/RCED-97-249R, September.

————. 1997b. *Food-Related Services: Opportunities Exist to Recover Costs by Charging Beneficiaries.* GAO/RCED-97-57, March.

————. 1998a. *Food Safety: Opportunities to Redirect Federal Resources and Funds Can Enhance Effectiveness.* GAO/RCED-98-224, August.

————. 1998b. *Food Safety: Federal Efforts to Ensure the Safety of Imported Foods Are Inconsistent and Unreliable.* GAO/RCED-98-103, April.

————. 1999. *Food Safety: U.S. Needs a Single Agency to Administer a Unified, Risk-Based, Inspection System.* GAO/T-RCED-99-256, August.

————. 2000. *Food Safety: Controls Can Be Strengthened to Reduce the Risk of Disease Linked to Unsafe Animal Feed.* GAO/RCED-00-255, September 22.

————. 2001. *Food Safety: Overview of Federal and State Expenditures.* GAO-01-177, February.

6

Industry Costs to Make Food Safe: Now and under a Risk-Based System

Laurian J. Unnevehr and Helen H. Jensen*

As food safety analysts, our goal is to identify food safety improvements that have the greatest net benefit to society. Other chapters in this volume examine emerging knowledge about the sources and incidence of foodborne risks. The purpose of this chapter is to examine the costs of reducing those risks. Our goal is to identify where food safety can be improved with least cost to society, as a step toward finding improvements with the lowest cost–benefit ratios. Such analysis is a fundamental part of regulatory decision making.

In the case of food safety, the dynamics of consumer and industry response to regulation and the mix of both private and public incentives to improve food safety make analysis of regulatory costs more complex. The reason is that the market failure in food safety is never a complete failure. Market incentives are offered to improve food safety and firms may adopt hazard control measures either to capture such incentives or in anticipation of more stringent regulation (Segerson 1999). Thus, it may be difficult to identify the additional or marginal costs of regulation. However, we presume that the goal is improved food safety, whether achieved through regulation or through market incentives, and that the key is to identify the most beneficial opportunities, and then to identify the type of mechanisms that will encourage consumers and industry to take advantage of those opportunities.

The literature about the costs of compliance with food safety regulation is conditioned by the kinds of regulation and how long the measures have been

* The authors acknowledge useful comments from David Hennessy and three anonymous reviewers.

in place. The regulations vary widely among hazards, food types, and stage of the production chain. We divide our review into two parts, reflecting fundamental differences between regulation of chemical and microbial hazards. The literature on the costs of pesticide regulation is the result of more than two decades of ex post experience with regulations initiated in the mid-1970s; it focuses mainly on how regulation alters crop production costs. The literature on microbial hazards is newer, and arises in response to more recent regulatory initiatives in the 1990s; it focuses on the livestock product subsector.[1]

The chapter begins with an overview of the types of costs at issue in regulatory cost–benefit analysis, the types of economic modeling tools that have been used to measure costs, and the lessons from environmental economics regarding regulatory alternatives. We provide an overview of whether and how those are applicable to food safety regulation. Next, we summarize the findings from studies of pesticide regulation and then we turn to studies of microbial regulation and draw lessons from each publication. We focus on what is known about the structure of costs and about the market incentives to improve food safety. We then explore how a systems approach can help to identify the most cost-effective means of improving food safety, particularly for microbial pathogens. Finally, we conclude by offering some questions for future data collection and research.

Cost–Benefit Analysis and Approaches to Measuring Social Costs

Once a science-based risk assessment has identified a public health risk, cost–benefit analysis can help to determine which regulatory option would most effectively address that risk. Other chapters in this volume discuss the measurement of benefits from food safety regulation. The most important benefits are those arising from improvements in human health, which include reduced medical costs and fewer productivity losses, as well as additional consumer utility from reduced risk of foodborne illness. Other potential benefits from safer food include reductions in market risks as a result of higher consumer confidence, reduced market volatility, access to foreign markets, and possible links between food safety and improved nutrition. Benefits estimation provides an initial criterion for ranking or prioritizing among interventions that address different public health hazards or interventions that result in different reductions in risk.

---

[1]A few studies have also been conducted on the cost impacts of regulations regarding growth hormones or antibiotic use in livestock production; we did not find any studies of mycotoxin or toxic waste regulatory costs (as they relate to food safety) in the published literature.

Complete assessment of the *net* benefits to society from any food safety improvement requires cost analysis. Cost estimates can show where market adjustments will reduce or increase costs, where and how regulation can alter existing market incentives, or how regulation will change investments in new technologies or inputs. Such adjustments may ultimately influence the risk reduction that can be achieved in practice, and thus cost analysis is an essential part of regulatory impact analysis.[2]

Cost–benefit analysis can aid in selection among alternative regulatory approaches, by showing which are most likely to achieve the greatest benefit with least cost to society. Alternatively, a public health goal may be selected and then cost analysis will be used to find the least cost alternative for achieving that goal.

What kinds of costs are considered? The Environmental Protection Agency (EPA) recently published guidelines for cost–benefit analysis of environmental regulation (U.S. EPA 2000). Table 6.1, adapted from EPA's exhibit 8-2, gives examples of the kinds of costs that result from regulation; we have added some examples specific to food safety. These include the costs incurred by firms that must change production processes in some way to meet new standards, labeled real-resource compliance costs. Costs can be either fixed costs that require an investment over several years or variable costs that are incurred with each unit produced. Costs can be very concrete and easy to measure, for example, the purchase of new equipment such as the steam pasteurizer used in beef packing plants, or less precisely defined, such as changes in labor organization to monitor temperatures. The simplest kind of cost analysis is simply an accounting for these costs within a static framework, for example, so many plants pay so much extra per unit of output.

These direct costs to firms lead to other changes in markets, such as social welfare losses from higher consumer prices for meat products, or transitional social costs, such as possible firm closings owing to the inability to meet standards competitively (Just et al. 1982). In measuring the latter two categories, both the distribution of real-resource costs and the adjustments to these costs are taken into account more fully. Adjustments may lead to lower costs over time as firms find more efficient ways to comply with standards, and understanding such adjustments is important for comparing regulatory alternatives. Market adjustments also distribute costs between consumers and producers, for example, through product price increases; among different kinds of producers, for example, firms of different sizes; or among different kinds of con-

---

[2]Sometimes confusion arises from the fact that a cost to one individual or firm may be a benefit to another. Thus, benefits of food safety regulation include the reduced costs of illness to consumers. In pesticide regulation, frequent reference is made to the "benefits" from chemical use in farm production. From a regulatory impact perspective, the values assigned to reduced chemical use in farm production would be the costs of canceling a chemical registration.

TABLE 6.1. Examples of Social Cost Categories

Social Cost Category	General Examples	Food Safety Examples
Real-resource compliance costs	Capital costs of new equipment	Steam pasteurizer
	Operation and maintenance of new equipment	Additional water needed for rinses
	Change in production processes or inputs	Higher price of new pesticides
	Maintenance changes in existing equipment	More frequent cleaning
	Changes in input quality, such as skilled labor	Training of employees in HACCP procedures
	Changes in costs attributable to product quality; can be positive or negative	Lower quality of product with reduced pesticide use
Social welfare losses	Higher consumer and producer prices leading to changes in consumer and producer surplus	Higher prices for crops with lost pesticide uses
		Higher prices for meat products
	Legal/administrative costs	Higher insurance costs against recalls
Transitional social costs	Firm closings	Regional shifts in crop production
	Unemployment	
	Resource shifts to other markets	Small meat processing plants shut down
	Transactions costs	Reduced stock value due to recalls
	Disrupted production	

Note that we have deleted Government Sector Regulatory Costs, as these are beyond the scope of our chapter.

Adapted from Exhibit 8-2, in U.S. EPA. 2000. Guidelines for Preparing Economic Analysis.

sumers, for example, consumers with degrees of health risks. Specifically, consumers may no longer incur costs of risk avoidance when these are shifted to industry as a result of regulation. Or, some firms may go out of business if they cannot compete owing to higher costs of compliance relative to the rest of the industry. These distributional considerations can be important in the regulatory decision-making process.

Table 6.2 shows the kinds of modeling tools used by economists to measure compliance costs and resulting market adjustments. Measuring direct compliance costs and their partial equilibrium impact on the market in question is usually the focus of regulatory analysis. Economists have extended this analysis in some cases to look more generally at impacts on several markets or at general equilibrium impacts in both factor and output markets. For example, Unnevehr et al. (1998) examined how Hazard Analysis and Critical Control Point (HACCP) costs would affect the three major meat product markets differently,

TABLE 6.2. Modeling Tools and Their Use in Food Safety Cost Analysis

Modeling Tools	Examples in Food Safety
Direct compliance costs	FSIS analysis for Pathogen Reduction Rule (USDA 1996) estimated costs of training, changes in production processes for meat and poultry plants
Partial equilibrium analysis	Roosen and Hennessy (2001) estimate the market effects of banning organophosphates for apples and compare welfare effects of different policies Lichtenberg et al. (1988) estimate market effects of banning ethyl parathion in three tree crops and show distribution of social welfare costs among producers, consumers, and export markets
Multi-market model	Unnevehr et al. (1998) analyze impact of Pathogen Reduction Rule on different meat product markets and find that substitution in demand reduces social welfare losses.
General equilibrium analysis	Golan et al. (2000) use a Social Accounting Matrix to see general equilibrium effects from changes in medical expenses and meat processing costs as a result of HACCP in meat/poultry; find that net benefits are higher among certain kinds of households.
Variable cost function	Antle (2000) estimates costs of improving quality and safety in meat plants based on past changes in input costs associated with higher product prices
Risk analysis model	Narrod et al. (1999) examine points of intervention to reduce *E. coli* O157:H7 in beef packing plants and find rising marginal costs of control.
Linear programming model	Onal et al. (2000) use a regional supply and demand optimization model to estimate the impact of *Salmonella* restrictions on hogs delivered to packing plants and find reallocation of regional supply. Jensen and Unnevehr (2000) evaluate the costs of alternative technologies in achieving food safety levels in pork processing and find rising marginal costs of safety and some technologies to dominate others.

Suggested by section 8.4 in U.S. EPA. 2000. Guidelines for Economic Analysis.

owing to differences in the incidence of costs and resulting substitutions in demand among beef, pork, and chicken. These substitutions reduced the total welfare cost of the regulation. Another example is the general equilibrium analysis of HACCP by Golan et al. (2000), who found that costs of implementation were almost fully passed through to households as a reduction in income, which was more than offset by a reduction in health care costs on the benefit side. The distribution of costs and benefits varied among household types, with the greatest net benefits going to households with children.

These kinds of modeling efforts are useful for illuminating the long-term effects of the regulation and its resulting costs. Such dynamics are important in determining incentives for innovation and compliance, and much of the economics literature has focused on the choice among regulatory approaches.

Choosing Regulatory Approaches that Result in Least Cost Compliance

Government interventions can take many forms. We distinguish between direct command and control (CAC) interventions and information-based interventions that provide incentives for private market solutions (Litan and Nordhaus 1983; Ippolito 1984). Direct interventions include CAC standards for performance, for example, pathogen counts or residue tolerances for products at some stage of the marketing channel. Such standards require the product's quality to be monitored, usually based on sampling and testing. In contrast, CAC processing standards achieve improved final product by directly specifying procedures to be followed in production. Examples include worker reentry restrictions for pesticide application or required sanitary operating procedures in meat plants. A third type of CAC approach is mandatory disclosure of information. Examples include requiring producers to provide information on any food safety processes they use, such as irradiation.

In contrast with CAC, incentive-based approaches are designed to induce either producers or consumers to identify and practice cost-effective methods that achieve improved food safety. Such interventions might include taxes on production inputs with food safety risks, for example, pesticides, which would encourage their use only where marginal value product is highest; or information to consumers to allow them to evaluate and avoid a hazard, for example, safe handling labels on meats; or facilitating private contracting through public certification of products that meet a minimum safety standard. For food safety, such approaches have limitations, as it may be desirable to protect vulnerable subpopulations that are unable to utilize or respond to information and incentives. For example, children are frequently more vulnerable to foodborne hazards of all kinds, and may be unable to utilize information or incentives about risk. Society may choose a CAC standard that protects this subpopulation.

The environmental economics literature demonstrates that there is a hierarchy among regulatory approaches in terms of the efficient use of society's resources (Cropper and Oates 1992). The most desirable is an incentive-based approach that allows producers and consumers to choose the level of pollution that balances social costs with social benefits. This is accomplished either by creating a market for the negative externality, for example, tradable pollution rights, or from the application of optimal pollution taxes. Incentive-based approaches are preferable to CAC, which increases social costs by constraining market choice. Among CAC approaches, process standards are less efficient than performance standards. Process standards specify how firms should achieve pollution reduction goals rather than specifying a performance level and allowing firms to choose the least expensive process for achieving it (Besanko 1987). Setting performance standards and allowing choice of production methods, and over time, innovation to meet standards, should allow greater efficiency in meeting a particular public health goal. Helfand (1991) demonstrated that setting a direct restriction on the level of pollution resulted in the highest level of economic returns and production efficiency among a set of five different performance and process standards.

Alternative regulatory approaches to achieve greatest risk reduction at lowest cost have been proposed in the food safety literature, as discussed later. But feasible incentive-based approaches differ among types of hazards. The presence of hazardous production inputs that are man-made, and are added as the result of producer decisions, can be influenced by incentive-based measures such as taxes. Naturally occurring hazards that can enter at any point in the food chain are expensive to test for and require different approaches, that is, they cannot be taxed. The high cost of information that creates the market failure for microbial hazards also makes a performance standard impractical. We discuss this issue further later in this chapter. Next we turn to a review of the literatures specific to these two general classes of hazards.

Costs of Pesticide Regulation

Pesticides are regulated by EPA, which registers chemicals for a particular use, that is, for a specific crop; regulates application procedures; and sets tolerances for residues. Food safety is one of many criteria used in these regulations; environmental and farm worker safety is also important. It is widely recognized that food safety risks are very important in determining whether a particular use is allowed. The 1996 Food Quality Protection Act (FQPA) set a consistent standard for risks from pesticide residues in food, eliminating the double standard created by the previous division of regulation between Federal Insecticide, Fungicide, and Rodenticide Act (FIFRA) for crop residues and the Delaney clause of the Federal Food, Drug, and Cosmetic Act (FFDCA) for processed foods (Osteen 2001). The FQPA standard requires reasonable certainty that no harm will result to infants and children from aggregate exposure to all residues, and also instructs that costs will not be considered in setting this standard. FQPA requires reassessment of pesticide tolerances for all currently registered

pesticides, and EPA gave priority to organophosphates because of their importance in children's dietary exposure. Organophosphates are widely used in field
crops and in fruits and vegetables important in children's diets, for example,
apples (Osteen 2001). Thus, food safety criteria continue to be important in
pesticide registration review, and will likely have significant economic impact.
Lessons from past analyses of pesticide regulation have continued relevance.

Three themes emerge from the pesticide literature: (1) there are small marginal costs to banning any particular use but these rise as more uses are banned
and fewer substitutes are available; (2) the practice of banning particular uses
makes regulation more costly and the same benefits could be achieved at lower
cost through different regulatory mechanisms that allocate pesticide uses
where they have highest value; and (3) the high costs of registration for new
pesticides has discouraged development of new alternatives. We examine each
theme in the following paragraphs.

The benefits from use of pesticides in crop production can be interpreted as
both significant and insignificant, depending on the standard being used.
Teague and Brorsen (1995) report that the ratio of the marginal value product
of pesticide use to pesticide price in three states is much greater than 1, indicating the strong profits attached to pesticide use. Gren (1994) found that a hypothetical 50% reduction in pesticide use in Sweden would result in a 6% reduction in farm incomes. Hanson et al. (1997) found that organic grain
production in the mid-Atlantic can achieve yields comparable with those from
conventional agriculture, but requires more family labor and management, the
value of which is difficult to quantify. Thus, although pesticides are found to
be profitable to use, the estimated costs of banning or restricting their use depend on the particular crop and the assumptions made.

Zilberman et al. (1991) and Osteen (1994) summarized the literature regarding the costs of banning pesticide uses and provided a number of insights
about why results of regulatory cost estimates can vary widely. First, the estimated costs of banning a pesticide use depend crucially on the availability of
substitute chemicals for that use. As entire classes of pesticides are restricted or
cancelled, fewer substitutes are available and the cost of the restrictions rises
(Roosen and Hennessy 2001). Second, a major effect of banning a pesticide is
to shift production to regions with less need for pesticide use. If this supply response is fairly elastic, there is less impact on market prices of the crop, but
there is also a clear regional redistribution of farm income (Lichtenberg et al.
1988). In particular, agriculture in the southern United States is more likely to
be impacted by pesticide restrictions than other regions, as the agroclimatic
conditions favor pests (Osteen 1994). Third, market price impacts of pesticide
bans depend on the elasticity of supply response, including the availability of
substitutes and the ease of shifting production to other regions. When the crop
is traded, the price effects in domestic markets are mitigated by changes in ex-

ports or imports, but the higher costs for domestic producers make them less competitive in world markets (Zilberman et al. 1991). Fourth, research and development to find substitutes or safer alternatives substantially reduce the cost of regulation in the long run (Osteen 1994).

Many economists have pointed out that the use of pesticide bans is an economically inefficient way of reducing risks from pesticides (Zilberman et al. 1991; Gren 1994; Zilberman and Millock 1997; Swinton and Batie 2001). Regulation that bans pesticide use often is more costly than other approaches that lead to similar reductions. Banning the use of a pesticide on a crop does not necessarily reduce use where its use causes the greatest harm. Equivalent or greater risk reductions could be achieved at lower cost by alternative policies that allocate pesticide risks toward their highest value uses. Such policies might include pesticide taxes, which might vary by crop or location of use, or tradable rights to use pesticides that producers could buy and sell. This would allocate pesticide use toward crops and regions where it has highest marginal value product while still achieving target average residues. Another alternative policy would be to set residue limits for food products, rather than for crops, in order to create incentives to address food safety risks directly (Swinton and Batie 2001). This would encourage a "systems"-based approach to reducing residues. Unfortunately, such alternatives are not authorized under FQPA.

A third theme in the pesticide literature is that the regulation has discouraged the development of new chemicals and sometimes the availability of existing chemicals. The high cost of supporting re-registrations for some pesticides discourages their support by manufacturers, especially for so-called minor uses, that is, crops with limited acreage (Osteen 1994). In a recent study, Ollinger and Fernandez-Cornejo (1995) estimated that development of a new pesticide takes 11 years and can cost manufacturers between $50 and $70 million. They also found that regulation encourages the development of less toxic pesticide materials and of biological pesticides as an alternative to chemical pesticides. But regulation discourages new chemical registrations, encourages firms to abandon registrations for minor crops, and favors large firms over smaller ones. The emphasis on reducing crop residues to meet a food safety standard also means that newer chemicals decay more rapidly, but may also be more toxic to farmworkers (Rola and Pingali 1993). Thus regulation creates incentives that influence the long-term pace and direction of new technology development.

The three themes in the pesticide literature provide important lessons. First, the redistribution effects among producing regions are likely to be more important than direct price effects in crop markets. Second, the choice of regulatory instruments has important implications for the costs of regulation. Third, the design of regulation influences long-term incentives for the development of new technologies. These lessons have some application in the emerging regulation of microbial hazards.

Costs of Regulating Microbial Hazards

Growing scientific awareness of the importance of foodborne pathogens led to new regulatory initiatives in the 1990s. Advances in public health, for example, improved information through faster and more sensitive tests for pathogens as well as better epidemiology permitted improved surveillance for foodborne illnesses, linked specific foods and companies with pathogen contamination, and identified known human illnesses as complications of acute foodborne infections. The new federal initiatives to address microbial hazards included HACCP regulations in seafood, meat and poultry, and fruit juices (U.S. FDA 1995, 2001; USDA/FSIS 1996); the development of Good Agricultural Practice (GAP) guidelines for produce (U.S. FDA 1998); and regulations regarding shell egg handling (U.S. FDA 2000). As these regulations and guidelines developed, a literature emerged to evaluate the impact on the food industry. This literature is relatively recent, and thus it is more difficult to establish "lessons" than in the case of pesticides.

In contrast to pesticides, which are man-made substances added during production, microbial hazards are naturally occurring organisms. Often, they can enter food products throughout the food supply and production chain, and once present, they can grow in numbers. Therefore control at one level does not ensure control at subsequent levels; and lack of control at one level has consequences for the subsequent stages in the food chain. This makes hazard control and the design of regulation more complex; it also complicates economic analysis of the costs of control.

One issue debated in the 1990s is the nature of HACCP as a regulatory standard. HACCP was initially developed in the 1960s by private industry as a management tool (Mazzocco 1996). As such, it provides efficiency in managing processes when the hazards and standards are clearly defined. That is, it can reduce the costs of testing, and of reworking or disposing of spoiled products, by preventing hazards and contamination. The focus on critical control points can lead to redesign of the production process to achieve control more efficiently. However, HACCP systems clearly entail costs, which are justified in private industry when there are market incentives for ensuring a particular standard of safety.

The costs of monitoring and testing are important for naturally occurring hazards, and are a motivation for an HACCP approach (National Research Council 1985). The high costs of obtaining information, that is, testing for microbial hazards ex post, make it more economical to emphasize prevention and monitoring of easily accessible indicators, in either private or public efforts to reduce such hazards (MacDonald and Crutchfield 1996; Unnevehr and Jensen 1996). In the 1990s, HACCP was mandated by federal regulation for firms in the seafood and meat/poultry industries, and in 2001 for the fruit juice industry. Specific HACCP plans are not mandated; under all three regulations individual firms are to develop plans that are relevant to their particular product mix and plant situation. These plans are then reviewed and approved by regulators. In the meat/poultry and fruit juice regulations, pathogen testing and reductions in pathogens are required. In the case of fruit juice, pathogen reduction is to be achieved through the use of a technology that meets a 5 log pathogen-reduction performance standard for reduction of generic *Escherichia coli*. The meat/poultry tests were successfully challenged in federal court in 2001, and can no longer be the basis for withdrawing inspections. However, they remain an important element in regulatory oversight of HACCP plans (Unnevehr 2003).

The flexibility in this type of regulation means that it is difficult to estimate its costs ex ante. For example, it is unclear what kind of changes in production processes might result from HACCP implementation. The flexibility in approach does not eliminate plant heterogeneity in terms of pathogen levels, which is one reason to also specify pathogen reductions as in the meat/poultry HACCP regulation (MacDonald and Crutchfield 1996). Thus, the nature of the HACCP regulation is unclear—is it a performance standard or a process standard? Unnevehr and Jensen (1996, 1999) and Antle (2000) describe the Pathogen Reduction Regulation in meat and poultry as a combination of performance and process standards. Helfand's (1991) analysis provides insights regarding use of mixed standards. In her terminology, this regulation combines the mandated use of a pollution control technology (HACCP) with a standard on pollution per unit of output (percentage of samples with pathogens). This combination will tend to maintain high levels of output but will reduce economic returns more than a direct restriction on the level of pollution. But this result depends on assumptions about the effect of the control technology on output and use of other inputs. For example, if the use of HACCP does not contribute to increased production, as its use changes only fixed costs and the change in marginal cost is zero, then its imposition is equivalent to a direct restriction on the level of contamination. Thus, whether HACCP allows for efficient firm response to regulation is unclear, and will depend on how well it helps firms to meet associated pathogen standards and whether it leads to significant changes in the variable costs of production.

Because ex ante costs are difficult to estimate and controversial in the food industry, there has been considerable interest in estimating HACCP costs as the regulations are implemented. For example, during the discussion period of the HACCP rule for meat and poultry, Texas A&M released an alternative cost estimate that showed much higher initial costs for industry than the FSIS estimate (see Crutchfield et al. 1997 for a review and comparison). A number of studies of HACCP have been undertaken (see collection in Unnevehr 2000) and it is now possible to make some ex post comparisons and generalizations, although more definitive answers will emerge only after longer experience. Studies of the costs of pathogen reduction show that both FSIS and FDA underestimated the costs of HACCP in their ex ante analyses. For example, Jensen and Unnevehr (2000) estimated that modifications of pork slaughter processes to reduce pathogens would cost $0.20 to $0.47 per carcass, substantially more than the FSIS estimate of $0.0056 for process modifications (Crutchfield et al. 1997). Antle (2000) analyzed past costs of quality improvement in the meat industry, and extrapolated that a 20% improvement in safety would have additional costs in the range of 1 to 9 cents per pound of product, which is several times larger than the FSIS estimates of less than one one hundredth of a cent per pound. Colatore and Caswell (2000) found that FDA underestimated the cost of HACCP in seafood plants, particularly the costs of plan design, training, corrective actions, and sanitation.

It is clear that the marginal costs of pathogen reduction are increasing and that complete control is quite costly. For example, Jensen et al. (1998) found that pathogen control marginal cost curves are steeply increasing for both beef and pork. Costs rise from 20 cents to $1.40 per beef carcass and from 3 cents to 25 cents per pork carcass as pathogen reduction increases from 1 log to 4 logs.[3] Figure 6.1 from Jensen et al. (1998), shows costs and pathogen reductions for pork carcasses with different combinations of water rinses and sanitizing sprays. Costs increase from 3 cents/carcass for a low-temperature (25°C) water rinse to more than 20 cents for the combination of hot (65°C) water rinse and sanitizing spray, which achieves the greatest pathogen reduction. This figure also shows that a cold water rinse plus sanitizing spray is more efficient than the 55°C rinse and spray, which lies inside the cost frontier.

Narrod et al. (1999) find rising costs of *E. coli* control in beef packing plants—costs rise from 5 cents to 45 cents per carcass as contamination is eliminated from 30% to 100% of production. Both of these studies emphasize that there is a frontier of efficient control technologies and technology combinations that provides least-cost pathogen reduction.

Under the 1996 meat and poultry HACCP regulation, plants showing higher than industry-average *Salmonella* levels must reduce these levels over time. The 2001 court ruling further weakens this provision. As plants are not required to implement high levels of pathogen control, actual costs incurred by meat and poultry firms likely are small relative to total costs and product prices. They may be around 1% to 2% of current processing costs (Jensen and Unnevehr 2000), and thus unlikely to lead to major increases in meat prices.

Although costs are small on average, they may still be enough to shift the distribution or scale of production at the margin. In both the seafood and

---

[3]One of the difficulties with evaluating interventions to control pathogens is that their effectiveness is generally measured under laboratory conditions where samples are intentionally inoculated with high levels of pathogens. In meat processing plants, levels of contamination are low, and many more samples would be needed to assess the effectiveness of a technology.

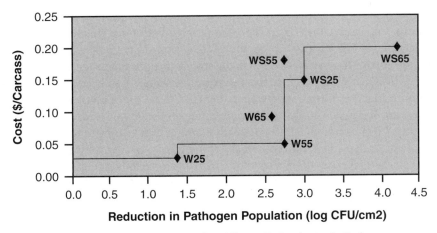

FIGURE 6.1. Total Enterics Reduction for Different Technologies in Pork
Source: Jensen and Unnevehr (2000).

meat/poultry industries, the impact of HACCP on small firms was an important consideration in the design of regulation. Both the meat/poultry and the fruit juice HACCP regulations were phased in with a longer adjustment period allowed for small plants. First-time implementation of HACCP requires large up-front investments in developing and implementing the HACCP plan; these costs are lower on a per-unit basis for larger food processors (Hooker et al. 2000; Nganje and Mazzocco 2000). Therefore, small firms' costs rise proportionally more than large firms with the implementation of HACCP, which may put them at a competitive disadvantage in the market. Furthermore, large firms frequently have more in-house resources at their disposal for design and implementation, for example, meat scientists on staff; diagnostic laboratories, and therefore have lower transactions costs in implementing an HACCP plan. Some small firms might be expected to go out of business as a result of higher relative costs.[4] Also, the need to have separate HACCP procedures for different products may also force small plants to drop some product lines (Hooker et al. 2000; Nganje and Mazzocco 2000). However, the ultimate impact on industry structure would be difficult to assign to food safety regulation alone, owing to the high rate of plant closings and other forces contributing to firm consolidation (MacDonald and Crutchfield 1996).

Another difficulty in assigning costs to regulation is that firms face a mix of market and regulatory incentives in adopting food safety measures. Certain markets increasingly demand evidence of hazard control from their suppliers

[4]Another source of higher costs might be greater sanitation and process control deficiencies in small plants. Ollinger (2000) found that such deficiencies were negatively associated with firm and plant size.

and this provides motivation beyond the minimum prescribed by regulation. Martin and Anderson (2000) report widespread adoption of HACCP and/or food safety control procedures among U.S. food processing firms. Almost 70% of large plants have an HACCP plan for at least one product; a majority of these firms also carry out food safety procedures associated with HACCP, such as monitoring temperatures of raw ingredients. Colatore and Caswell (2000) found most seafood plants implemented more extensive and costly HACCP plans than required by regulation, because they found other motivations to do so. The implication is that market incentives are driving firms to adopt food safety practices. This then raises the question of what additional food safety is provided by regulation and what additional costs can be assigned to this improvement.

Another issue in assessing costs is whether HACCP regulations in the processing industry will lead to greater demand for hazard reduction in farm level production. In many ways, HACCP reduces communication costs about the provision of safety. Fewer studies have been conducted at the farm level because there has been little regulatory activity, but the application of regulation to one part of the food chain can create incentives that are passed back to suppliers through the marketplace. An important theme from the European literature is that food processors and retailers are increasingly looking for assurances of food safety from their suppliers, creating incentives for improved safety throughout the food chain. In the United Kingdom, the passage of "due diligence" laws has forced food retailers to ask their suppliers for certification of hazard management (Henson and Northen 1998) and ISO 9000 methods for certification have been applied in the U.K. meat sector (Zaibet and Bredahl 1997).

In the United States, such contracts tend to be motivated entirely by market incentives and there is less reported evidence that regulation has played a role. In the meat subsector, fast food services specify food safety standards in their contracts with suppliers (Burgdorfer 2001). Suppliers of produce to major U.S. supermarket chains must certify food safety practices, and this is true for international as well as domestic producers (Calvin and Cook 2001). In the produce market, this certification has been facilitated by the use of FDA's GAP guidelines.

A few studies of hypothetical costs of adopting measures to reduce microbial hazards have been conducted at the farm level. Onal et al. (2000) examined the costs of restricting *Salmonella* contamination in hogs delivered to packing plants. Because there are differences in contamination levels by farm size and region, such restrictions would alter the regional distribution of production and increase costs for the system as a whole. Hayes et al. (2001) used Sweden's experience with banning antibiotic use in pork production to draw lessons for a possible ban in the United States. They found that such a ban would tend to reward producers who are already managing productivity and quality well. Wang et al. (2000) found similar results for control of toxoplasmosis in pork. Confinement production would have a slight cost advantage if control of this infection became mandatory. These findings reinforce the general theme that regulation can influence industry structure and may influence the regional distribution of production at the farm level.

An important structural issue that has not received much analysis is the outcome from new standards in markets with significant international trade. As trade in food products grows, the interaction of trade and regulation becomes more important (Roberts and Unnevehr 2003). Regulations should apply equally to both domestic and imported foods. For example, seafood exports to the United States, which account for more than half of the supply, should be processed under HACCP plans just as in domestic plants. However, enforcement of equivalent standards for foreign producers may be limited by the availability of resources for inspection and monitoring.

The presence of imports or exports will influence market response to regulation and the incentives for domestic food safety improvement. Worth (2000) calculated the reputation cost of a food safety outbreak from strawberries for domestic producers. When there are different supply sources, it is difficult for domestic producers to capture all of the benefits of safety improvement.

The microbial hazards literature raises several themes, but does not yet have well-documented results. These themes include the difficulties of assessing HACCP costs and impacts owing to the flexibility inherent in HACCP approaches; the likely rising marginal cost of food safety improvement; the presence of both private and regulatory incentives for improving food safety; and the likely structural implications of food safety regulation or market incentives for firm size, supply chain coordination, and international competitiveness.

In addition, several important questions have been raised in the literature, the answers to which will require multidisciplinary research in the future. These include what kind of regulatory approaches can best utilize incentives to increase food safety at least cost. In particular, can an enforceable standard be set for a naturally occurring hazard that is expensive to test for? If HACCP is flexible in implementation, then what improvement in food safety is actually achieved? Furthermore, given the difficulty of mapping pathogen reductions at one point in the food supply chain to illness outcomes in consumers, another question is how best to compare benefits and costs from HACCP regulations. All of these questions arise from the nature of microbial hazards and of process controls, and lead us to explore the question of whether a systems approach is the best way to find cost-effective improvements.

Looking at the Entire Food System

Greater attention to food safety highlights the integrated nature of the food production system. Assignment of costs and changes in the nature of costs depend on understanding this integration. As discussed in the preceding sections, the nature of the food safety risk depends on the product and type of contamination. Some hazards, such as pesticides applied at the farm, enter the food chain system in early stages. Processing and handling affect the hazards levels on the food product as it goes through the system until it reaches the final consumer. In contrast, microbial hazards are naturally occurring; contamination can enter the food production system at any stage, and unless it is eliminated at one stage in the production process, it can present problems at later stages of production. The controls of risks are linked across stages.

Probabilistic scenario analysis (PSA) and the closely related fault tree analysis (FTA) are tools used to account for multiple events and the probability of any event occurring in the food production system (Roberts et al. 1995). The PSA makes use of information on links in the food chain and events that may compromise the safety of the food: the type of hazard, the different ways it enters the food chain, for example, the specific link and linkages, and the full list of other, expected events. The "links in the food chain" are specialized, self-contained activities that are connected to events that determine the human health outcome. An "event tree" summarizes this information.

One example is the occurrence of *E. coli* O157:H7 in cattle at slaughter (Roberts et al. 1995). Cattle shipped to slaughter may carry threshold levels of the pathogen. The probability that *E. coli* O157:H7 contamination will occur in cattle at slaughter depends on whether, and how likely it is, that cattle carry the pathogen and whether the pathogen is detected at entry to the slaughterhouse. The slaughter operation is one "link" in the food chain or processing system. Later stages in the system include processing and fabrication, distribution and transport, wholesale/retailing, and finally the consumer level. In the food production system, each of these stages offers potential for contamination or recontamination. The PSA or FTA approach takes account of various linkages in the food system at a point in time, probabilities of occurrence, and all associated probabilities of failure, or, alternatively, effectiveness of control. Either the high-risk or most likely pathway becomes a promising candidate for control analysis.

In principle, information on the probabilities and paths in the production system can be used to assign expected costs to various control options, and identify the most cost-effective mitigation options. By identifying combinations of lowest cost interventions to achieve various levels of improved safety, the analyst can articulate optimal strategies. This approach combines risk outcomes and economic cost criteria to identify dominant solutions (McDowell et al. 1995). The outcome and cost dominance approach underlies the models used to evaluate beef processing (Jensen et al. 1998; Narrod et al. 1999) and pork processing (Jensen and Unnevehr 2000) that identify the cost-efficient combinations of interventions. In principle, however, such prescriptive economics is more likely to depend on a combination of methods from decision theory, risk analysis, and economics (McDowell et al.

1995).[5] Although the PSA/FTA approach describes system linkages in food production, it gives little guidance for identifying strategies to reduce hazards across the whole system because it fails to account for incentives that may lead to different behaviors and choices of technologies and controls among stages.

Food safety failures often stem from problems that are systemic in nature. The systemic failures occur in production systems characterized by interconnected stages in production and inputs, and this interconnectivity gives rise to the technological potential for failures. At the same time incentive problems provide the economic potential for failures (Narrod et al. 1999; Hennessy et al. 2001). The mixing of meat from a number of farm sources at the packer, processing, or intermediary levels illustrates both the interconnectivity in inputs and stages of production, and incentive problems. Ground meat may come from many different animal and farm sources. Problems that occur from the farm, or in handling of a single animal, can easily spread through the food product in the plant. Furthermore, when intermediaries comingle beef from several sources, failure in one large batch can quickly spread to consumers in a large geographic area (Hennessy et al. 2003). Testing of products at different stages is often difficult, and rapid tests are not available. Incentive problems occur because it is difficult for packers to reward farmers for care-taking, and farmers have no incentive to take additional care in production or transport to reduce the likelihood of problems at the packer level; nor do packers that sell product to intermediaries that comingle beef from several sources have market incentive to adopt technologies that reduce pathogens in the plant source.

Interconnectivity gives rise to complementarities in input use, that is, care in one area may increase the likelihood of taking care in other aspects of production. The presence of complementarities among activities means that benefits may arise from complementary activities that cannot be assigned to the marginal product of any individual activity (Goodhue and Rausser 1999). A change in the cost of one activity is likely to move a whole cluster of complementary activities in the food production system. This may explain Colatore and Caswell's (2000) finding that seafood plants implemented control measures beyond the minimum mandated by regulation.

A packer facing the problem of downstream risks might choose to provide incentives to input suppliers for documented production practices. With complementarity in inputs, a change in the price of one practice, for example, an incentive paid by the packer firm for feeding withdrawal, is likely to bring along other complementary practices, such as more careful tracking of transportation practices. An alternative to payment of incentives to input suppliers is to purchase control of the input supply, that is, shift ownership and control of

---

[5]Given the demand for data, application of probabilistic models is more realistically applied when confined to examining particular hazards and linkages, in contrast to the entire food production system.

production or transport to the packer firm. In this case, increasing vertical co-ordination can redistribute the risks and rents associated with reduced risk.

The complexity of most food production today suggests the importance of considering food safety problems from the systems perspective. A good example of such an approach is the action plan developed by FDA, FSIS, and Animal and Plant Health Inspection Service (APHIS) to eliminate *Salmonella enteritidis* (SE) illness caused by consumption of eggs (President's Council on Food Safety 1999). Underlying the action plan was a risk assessment model. The risk assessment model indicated that multiple interventions would achieve more reductions in SE illness than would a single point of intervention. The use of a risk assessment approach allowed combining information about the risk, sources of risk, and potential for controls throughout the egg production system and identified potential sites for intervention. The identified advantage of multiple interventions suggested following a broadly based policy approach across stages of production, instead of focusing on a single stage of production.

Figure 6.2, from the President's Council on Food Safety (1999), shows the stages of egg production and the agencies responsible at each stage. The action plan identifies a set of activities at each stage. Producers and packer/processors can choose between two strategies designed to give equivalent performance in terms of reduction in SE at the egg production and packer/processor stages. Strategy I focuses efforts at farm level testing and egg diversion; strategy II directs more resources to the packer/processor level and includes a lethal treatment, or "kill step" and HACCP plan at this stage. Both strategies include common features of regulatory presence on the farm, for example, control of chicks from SE flocks, and at the packer/processor, for example, mandated prerequisite programs of sanitary controls and washing. In addition to the interventions at production and packer processor stages, the action plan sets refrigeration standards for the distribution and retail stages to ensure that reductions in SE are preserved at later stages in the food supply chain. The flexibility offered to the industry in choosing between strategies for control at the producer and packing/processor levels allows for development of incentive structures consistent with the overall objectives of eliminating SE illnesses. The action plan identifies explicitly performance measures, that is, output standards, to be used, for example, reduced illnesses, SE isolates, and number of SE outbreaks and the responsible agency for each stage in the farm-to-table continuum.

The action plan for SE in eggs provides a good example of how a systemwide approach might be used. In this case, the systems approach facilitated the development and coordination of public and private strategies across the egg production system. The risk assessment model focuses on the desired public health outcome. The plan allows industry flexibility in developing and coordinating incentives across the production and processing/packing stages. Costs incurred under this systems approach are likely to be smaller than when interventions

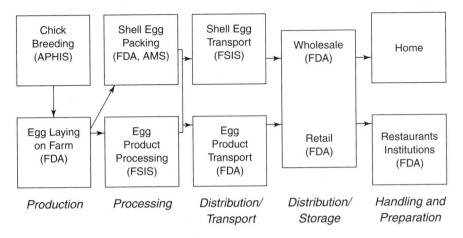

FIGURE 6.2. Egg Safety from Production to Consumption

Source: President's Council on Food Safety. Egg safety from production to consumption: an action plan to reduce *Salmonella enteritidis* illnesses due to eggs.

focus on only one point in the food chain. This is an example of how risk assessment can interface with economic incentives.

Conclusions Regarding Lessons and Future Directions for Research

We take away four lessons from this review of the literatures on pesticides and microbial hazards. The first lesson is that the distribution of costs is likely to be more important than market price effects, at least for the regulations imposed in the past. That is, food prices and availability for consumers are rarely the issue in food safety regulation impacts. This is partly because supply can be shifted to different regions, plants, or even countries. It is also partly a result of past balancing of costs and benefits in making regulatory decisions. The structural impacts that lead to painful economic adjustments, such as when production becomes infeasible in a particular region or when small firms in rural areas go out of business, are more important than market price impacts. A second lesson is that regulation has an impact on long-term incentives to invest in new technologies or inputs, and therefore is likely to bias the nature of productivity growth. Measuring these long-term costs and benefits to society is much more difficult, because the counterfactual cannot be observed; however, these impacts are important to consider in the design of new regulation. This leads to our third lesson—the most important reason to analyze costs is to choose among regulatory alternatives. Greater benefits can be achieved more quickly at lower cost to society with incentive-based measures. Allowing market adjustments to mitigate costs and improving on existing market incentives will be the most effective way to reach public health goals. Our fourth lesson is that a risk-based systems approach can be the best way to understand the costs, incentives, and risk outcomes resulting from alternative interventions. This approach is difficult owing to patchwork regulatory authority over different parts of the food chain and to the data required for risk assessment.

Given these lessons from the literature, what can we say about the need for research and data? Looking to the future, we can see increased attention to addressing microbial hazards, rising food safety standards, growing international trade of food products, emerging technologies that reduce information costs, and increased feasibility of public and private coordination. In that context, we have identified four areas for research and data collection. The first and most important is to adapt the conceptual framework for evaluating alternative regulatory instruments to the specifics of regulating risks from microbial hazards. We do not have any analysis of how alternative regulatory actions would alter microbial hazard reduction outcomes, incentives, innovation, or cost–benefit ratios. Some differences in implicit standards already exist that could provide data for analysis, such as the product specifications imposed on beef purchased for school lunches. Given the strong market incentives evident in microbial food safety, it will be important to identify the appropriate role for government intervention so as not to introduce inefficiencies through regulatory overkill. The second, and related, area for research is the impact of new information technologies, for example, rapid tests and genetic fingerprinting on the market failure in microbial food safety. We need to understand how such technologies can aid in setting performance standards and in helping the food industry to respond more efficiently to standards. A third area for economics research is to examine the interaction of higher domestic standards with international trade. In the future, the distributional effects of regulation are more likely to occur between domestic production and trade. We need to know whether standards are applied in equivalent ways to domestic production and imports and to understand better the U.S. comparative advantage in the production of safety attributes. Finally, a fourth area for future research is the interdisciplinary field of risk assessment applied to the entire food chain, which is still in its infancy. The SE risk assessment model for shell eggs and egg products illustrates the ability to assemble and analyze data across various stages of the food production system in order to achieve a science-based plan for food safety improvements. Because such research requires expensive data collection, efforts in this area should be directed toward the most important public health risks.

Our concluding comment is that economic analysis will be particularly useful for evaluating future policies to reduce microbial hazards, because it is directed toward understanding systemwide impacts and adjustments. We may not yet know what industry costs look like in a risk-based integrated system. But economists can help to identify the kind of system that will foster innovation and efficient use of society's resources in meeting public health goals.

References

Antle, J.M. 2000. No Such Thing as a Free Safe Lunch: The Cost of Food Safety Regulation in the Meat Industry. *American Journal Agricultural Economics* 82(May): 310–22.

Besanko, D. 1987. Performance Versus Design Standards in the Regulation of Pollution. *Journal of Public Economics* 34(October): 19–44.

Burgdorfer, B. 2001. Top US Beef Packers Can Meet McDonald's BSE Deadline. Reuters and FSNET, March 15.

Calvin, L., and R. Cook. 2001. *U.S. Fresh Fruit and Vegetable Marketing: Emerging Trade Practices, Trends, and Issues.* Economic Research Service, USDA, Agricultural Economic Report No 795 (Washington, D.C.).

Colatore, C., and J.A. Caswell. 2000. The Cost of HACCP Implementation in the Seafood Industry. In *The Economics of HACCP: Costs and Benefits,* edited by L.J. Unnevehr. St. Paul: Eagan Press, 45–68.

Cropper, M.L., and W.E. Oates. 1992. Environmental Economics: A Survey. *Journal of Economic Literature* 30 (June): 675–740.

Crutchfield, S.R., J.C. Buzby, T. Roberts, M. Ollinger, and C-T. Jordan Lin. 1997. *An Economic Assessment of Food Safety Regulations: The New Approach to Meat and Poultry Inspection.* Food and Consumer Economics Division, Economic Research Service, U.S. Department of Agriculture, Agricultural Economic Report No. 755, July 1997.

Golan, E.H., S.J. Vogel, P.D. Frenzen, and K.L. Ralston. 2000. *Tracing the Costs and Benefits of Improvements in Food Safety: The Case of the Hazard Analysis Critical Control Point Program in Meat and Poultry.* Economic Research Service, U.S. Dept of Agriculture. Agricultural Economics Report No. 791, October 2000.

Goodhue, R.E., and G.C. Rausser. 1999. Value Differentiation in Agriculture: Driving Forces and Complementarities. In *Vertical Relationships and Coordination in the Food System,* edited by G. Galizzi and L. Venturi. Heidelberg: Physica-Verlag, 93–112.

Gren, I-M. 1994. Cost Efficient Pesticide Reductions: A Study of Sweden. *Environmental and Resource Economics* 4(3, June): 277.

Hanson, J.C., E. Lichtenberg, and S.E. Peters. 1997. Organic Versus Conventional Grain Production in the Mid-Atlantic: An Economic and Farming System Overview. *American Journal of Alternative Agriculture* 12(1): 2–9.

Hayes, D.J., H.H. Jensen, L. Backstrom, and J. Fabiosa. 2001. Economic Impact of a Ban on the Use of Over the Counter Antibiotics in U.S. Swine Rations. *International Food and Agribusiness Management Review* 4: 81–97.

Helfand, G.E. 1991. Standards Versus Standards: The Effects of Different Pollution Restrictions. *American Economic Review* 81(June): 622–34.

Hennessy, D.A., J. Roosen, and H.H. Jensen. 2003. Systemic Failure in the Provision of Safe Food. *Food Policy* 28(February): 77–96.

Hennessy, D.A., J. Roosen, and J.A. Miranowski. 2001. Leadership and the Provision of Safe Food. *American Journal of Agricultural Economics* 83 (November): 862–75.

Henson, S., and J. Northen. 1998. Economic Determinants of Food Safety Controls in Supply of Retailer Own-Branded Products in United Kingdom. *Agribusiness* 14: 113–26.

Hooker, N.H., J. Siebert, and R.M. Nayga Jr. 2000. The Impact of HACCP on Costs and Product Exit: Evidence from Meat Processors in Texas. Abstract. *Journal of Agricultural and Resource Economics* 25(2): 727.

Ippolito, P.M. 1984. *Consumer Protection Economics: A Selective Survey of Empirical Approaches to Consumer Protection Economics,* edited by P. M. Ippolito and D. T. Scheffman. Washington, DC: Bureau of Economics, Federal Trade Commission, April.

Jensen, H.H., and L.J. Unnevehr. 2000. HACCP in Pork Processing: Costs and Benefits. In *The Economics of HACCP: Costs and Benefits,* edited by L.J. Unnevehr. St. Paul: Eagan Press, 29–44.

Jensen, H.H., L.J. Unnevehr, and M.I. Gomez. 1998. Costs of Improving Food Safety in the Meat Sector. *Journal of Agricultural and Applied Economics* 30(1, July): 83–94.

Just, R.E., D.L. Hueth, and A. Schmitz. 1982. *Applied Welfare Economics and Public Policy.* Englewood Cliffs, NJ: Prentice-Hall.

Lichtenberg, E., D.D. Parker, and D. Zilberman. 1988. Marginal Analysis of Welfare Costs of Environmental Policies: The Case of Pesticide Regulation. *American Journal of Agricultural Economics* 70(November): 867–74.

Litan, R.E., and W.D. Nordhaus. 1983. *Reforming Federal Regulation.* New Haven: Yale University Press.

MacDonald, J.M., and S. Crutchfield. 1996. Modeling the Cost of Food Safety Regulation. *American Journal of Agricultural Economics* 78(December): 1285–90.

Martin, S.A., and D.W. Anderson. 2000. HACCP Adoption in the U.S. Food Industry. In *The Economics of HACCP: Costs and Benefits,* edited by L.J. Unnevehr. St. Paul: Eagan Press, 15–28.

Mazzocco, M. 1996. HACCP as a Business Management Tool. *American Journal of Agricultural Economics* 78(August): 770–74.

McDowell, R., S. Kaplan, A. Ahl, and T. Roberts. 1995. Managing Risks from Foodborne Microbial Hazards. In *Tracking Foodborne Pathogens from Farm to Table: Data Needs to Evaluate Control Options,* edited by T. Roberts, H. Jensen, and L.J. Unnevehr. USDA, Economic Research Service, Miscellaneous Publication Number 1532, December: 117–24.

Narrod, C.A., S.A. Malcolm, M. Ollinger, and T. Roberts. 1999. Pathogen Reduction Options in Slaughterhouses and Methods for Evaluating Their Economic Effectiveness. Paper presented at the AAEA meetings and available on the web. (http://agecon. lib.umn.edu/) (accessed May 4, 2001).

National Academy of Sciences (NAS). 1985. *Meat and Poultry Inspection: The Scientific Basis of the Nation's Program.* Washington, DC: National Academy Press.

Nganje, W.E., and M.A. Mazzocco. 2000. Economic Efficiency Analysis of HACCP in the U.S. Red Meat Industry. In *The Economics of HACCP: Costs and Benefits,* edited by L.J. Unnevehr. St. Paul: Eagan Press, 241–66.

Ollinger, M. 2000. Market Influences on Sanitation and Process Control Deficiencies in Selected U.S. Slaughter Industries. In *The Economics of HACCP: Costs and Benefits,* edited by L.J. Unnevehr. St. Paul: Eagan Press, 171–85.

————, and J. Fernandez-Cornejo. 1995. *Regulation, Innovation, and Market Structure in the U.S. Pesticide Industry.* AER 719, USDA/ERS, June.

Onal, H., L.J. Unnevehr, and A. Bekric. 2000. Regional Shifts in Pork Production: Implications for Regional Competition and Food Safety. *American Journal of Agricultural Economics* 82(4, November): 968–78.

Osteen, C. 2003. What Are the Implications of the Current Assessment of Risks of Organophosphate Pesticides? USDA Economic Research Service website, (http://www.ers.usda.gov/Briefing/AgChemicals/Questions/pmqa7.htm) (accessed April 2001). Updated April 7, 2003.

————. 1994. Pesticide Regulation Issues: Living with the Delaney Clause. *Journal of Agriculture and Applied Economics* 26(1, July): 60–74, 90–96.

President's Council on Food Safety. Egg Safety from Production to Consumption: An Action Plan to Reduce *Salmonella enteritidis* Illnesses Due to Eggs. (http://www.foodsafety.gov/%7Efsg/ceggs.html%20) (accessed April 2001).

Roberts, D., and L. Unnevehr. 2003. Resolving Trade Disputes Arising from Trends in Food Safety Regulation. In *International Trade and Food Safety: Economic Theory and Case Studies.* Agricultural Economics Report 828, USDA Economic Research Service, October: 28–47.

Roberts, T., A. Ahl, and R. McDowell. 1995. Risk Assessment for Foodborne Microbial Hazards. In *Tracking Foodborne Pathogens from Farm to Table: Data Needs to Evaluate Control Options,* edited by T. Roberts, H. Jensen, and L.J. Unnevehr. USDA, Economic Research Service, Miscellaneous Publication Number 1532, December: 95–115.

Rola, A.C., and P. L. Pingali. 1993. *Pesticides, Rice Productivity, and Farmers' Health: an Economic Assessment.* Washington, DC: IRRI and World Resources Institute,

Roosen, J., and D.A. Hennessy. 2001. Capturing Experts' Uncertainty in Welfare Analysis: An Application to Organophosphate Use Regulation in U.S. Apple Production. *American Journal of Agricultural Economics* 83(1, February): 166–82.

Segerson, K. 1999. Mandatory Versus Voluntary Approaches to Food Safety. *Agribusiness* 15(1): 53–70.

Swinton, S.M., and S.A. Batie. 2001. FQPA: Pouring Out (In?) The Risk Cup. *Choices* (First Quarter): 14–17.

Teague, M.L., and B.W. Brorsen. 1995. Pesticide Productivity: What Are the Trends? *Journal of Agricultural Economics* 27(1, July): 276–82.

USDA (U.S. Department of Agriculture), Food Safety and Inspection Service. 1996. Pathogen Reduction Hazard Analysis and Critical Control Point (HACCP) Systems: Final Rule, Docket No. 93-016F. *Federal Register* 61(144, July 25): 38805–989.

U.S. EPA (Environmental Protection Agency). 2000. Guidelines for Preparing Economic Analysis. EPA 240-R-00-003. September 2000. (http://www.epa.gov/economics/) (accessed May 4, 2001).

U.S. FDA (Food and Drug Administration). 1995. Procedures for the Safe and Sanitary Processing and Importing of Fish and Fishery Products: Final Rule. *Federal Register* 60 (242): 65096–202.

————. 1998. Guide to Minimize Microbial Food Safety Hazards for Fresh Fruits and Vegetables. (http://www.foodsafety.gov/~dms/prodguid.html) (accessed May 2001).

————. 2000. Food Labeling, Safe Handling Statements, Labeling of Shell Eggs; Refrigeration of Shell Eggs Held for Retail Distribution; Final Rule. *Federal Register* 65 (234): 76091–114 (http://vm.cfsan.fda.gov/~lrd/fr001205.html) (accessed May 2001).

————. 2001. Hazard Analysis and Critical Control Point (HACCP); Procedures for the Safe and Sanitary Processing and Improving of Juice; Final Rule. *Federal Register* 66 (13): 6137–202. (http://www.fda.gov/OHRMS/DOCKETS/98fr/011901d.pdf) (accessed November 2003).

Unnevehr, L.J. (ed). 2000. *The Economics of HACCP: Costs and Benefits.* St. Paul: Eagan Press.

————. 2003. Food Safety: Setting and Enforcing Standards. *Choices* (First Quarter): 9–14. www.choicesmagazine.org (accessed July 15, 2004).

Unnevehr, L.J., and H.H. Jensen. 1996. HACCP as a Regulatory Innovation to Improve Food Safety in the Meat Industry. *American Journal of Agricultural Economics* 78(August): 764–69.

————.1999. The Economic Implications of Using HACCP as a Food Safety Regulatory Standard. *Food Policy* 24: 625–35.

Unnevehr, L.J., M.I. Gomez, and P. Garcia. 1998. The Incidence of Producer Welfare Losses from Food Safety Regulation in the Meat Industry. *Review of Agricultural Economics* 20(1, Spring): 186–201.

Wang, C., V. Diderrich, J. Kliebenstein, S. Patton, J. Zimmerman, A. Hallam, E. Bush, C. Faulkner, and R. McCord. 2000. *Toxoplasma gondii* Levels in Swine Operations: Differences Due to Technology Choice and Impact on Costs of Production. Paper presented at the International Association for Agricultural Economics meetings, Berlin, Germany, August.

Worth, T.W. 2000. The Cost of an Outbreak in the Fresh Strawberry Market. In *The Economics of HACCP: Costs and Benefits,* edited by L.J. Unnevehr. St. Paul: Eagan Press, 187–98.

Zaibet, L., and M. Bredahl. 1997. Gains from ISO Certification in the UK Meat Sector. *Agribusiness* 13: 375–84.

Zilberman, D., and K. Millock. 1997. Pesticide Use and Regulation: Making Economic Sense Out of an Externality and Regulation Nightmare. *Journal of Agricultural Economics* 22(2, December): 321–32.

Zilberman, D., A. Schmitz, G. Casterline, E. Lichtenberg, and J.B. Siebert. 1991. The Economics of Pesticide Use and Regulation. Science 25(August): 518–22.

7

The Value to Consumers of Reducing Foodborne Risks

Elise Golan, Jean Buzby, Stephen Crutchfield,
Paul Frenzen, Fred Kuchler,
Katherine Ralston, and Tanya Roberts

Policy makers have the difficult task of allocating government funds among different food safety programs. The risks targeted by these programs range from adverse health outcomes such as gastrointestinal illness, kidney failure, arthritis, and premature death to adverse economic outcomes such as reduced income for those who fall ill and loss of markets for food manufacturers. The primary populations benefiting from food safety programs range from children and the elderly to those engaged in food manufacturing.

The wide variety of potential outcomes and affected populations makes it difficult to rank risks and prioritize government spending on food safety. Should agencies prioritize on the basis of numbers of individuals who become ill or on the severity of illnesses? Should they put more effort into hazards in widely consumed foods? Do children's illnesses deserve more attention than those of the elderly? What is the trade-off between health and economic risks?

To provide a way to compare and rank the value of competing food safety programs, economists and public health analysts have designed a number of approaches for translating diverse outcomes to a common unit of measurement. The cost-of-illness and willingness-to-pay approaches translate diverse outcomes to dollar amounts, while the quality-adjusted life year approach translates diverse outcomes to healthy-time equivalencies. The approach that policy analysts use to compare the benefits of food safety programs can have an influence on the ranking of these programs. Programs that rank highest in terms of medical costs and human capital costs may be low ranking in terms of lost utility.

In this chapter, we examine the approaches that federal agencies have used to compare diverse outcomes and discuss the importance of adopting a common methodology to provide an accurate risk ranking. We also discuss the importance of incorporating risks other than health risks in the analysis. We argue that a risk ranking that is restricted to health outcomes may exclude one of the most important risks associated with foodborne illness: erosion of trust in the food supply system.

We begin the chapter with a description of failure in the market for food safety and the unreliability of market price as a measure of the value of food safety. In the second section of the chapter, we examine the methodologies developed by economists to translate diverse outcomes to a common unit of measurement. Next we present the empirical estimates of the value of reductions in foodborne health risks used by federal agencies to evaluate the benefits of food safety programs. In the third section of the chapter, we discuss non-health foodborne risks, such as market risk. We close by commenting on the usefulness of measures of the economic value of foodborne risk reductions.

Failure in the Market for Food Safety Obscures Economic Value

In an efficient market, price reflects the economic value of a good or service. As a result, for many products, determining economic value is simply a matter of determining market price. Unfortunately, although a market for food safety is slowly emerging, a market price for food safety does not exist yet. When similar foods differ in price and product safety, part of the price difference may be attributable to the difference in product safety. The price difference attributable to differences in product safety would be a market price for food safety. If consumers value food safety, then safer foods should demand a higher price, all else being equal. Foods with safety attributes such as pasteurized eggs, beef grown without antibiotics, and irradiated foods are beginning to appear on grocery store shelves. Nevertheless, aside from foods that are organically grown and produced, an attribute that is often perceived as a safety feature, product differentiation with respect to product safety is surprisingly uncommon. A number of observations explain the spotty food safety market and suggest that food manufacturers may have an incentive to supply less food safety than is optimal. That is, food producers may supply less food safety than consumers would demand if consumers knew the actual safety of the product and had to pay the cost of ensuring that level of safety.

First, for the most part, food safety is a credence attribute. Credence attributes are those that consumers cannot evaluate even in use (Darby and Karni 1973). Consumers usually cannot discern before purchase, or even after consumption, whether a food was produced with the best or worst safety procedures, or whether a food poses a health risk. For example, consumers are unable to distinguish between raw ground beef contaminated with *Escherichia coli* O157:H7 and uncontaminated ground beef. Consumers may be unable to identify the contaminated meat by either appearance, smell, or price, in which case they cannot gauge the true value of the food.

The fact that food safety attributes are difficult for consumers to detect means that firms producing high-risk food could charge low-risk prices, and because of their safety/cost cutting measures, have greater profits than low-risk producers. As a result, producers may have an incentive to provide food of lower quality and higher risk. Of course, if a firm is linked to an outbreak of foodborne illness, the loss in reputation and sales could outweigh the benefits of any food safety cost cutting. Highly publicized foodborne illness outbreaks have the potential to cut into profits, even in the long term, and could result in bankruptcy or distress sale.

Although the threat of negative publicity may curtail incentives to cut safety corners, difficulty identifying the contaminated food responsible for an illness lessens both this threat and the threat of litigation. Complex diets, long incubation periods, incomplete laboratory analyses, and the fact that the food evidence is usually destroyed (eaten) all reduce the chances of successful litigation (Buzby et al. 2001).

The fact that consumers, and prosecutors, have a difficult time ascertaining a food's safety attributes means that there is potential for market failure in the form of asymmetric or missing information. If consumers cannot tell how much safer one product is than another, market prices will not necessarily reflect their actual willingness to pay for food safety. However, the fact that an attribute is a credence attribute does not automatically mean that the market fails. Producers have developed a number of ways to provide consumers with credible information about credence goods. Firms could offer warranties or third-party certification (for a review of this literature see Golan et al. 2000). In addition, consumer skepticism and competition help reveal many credence attributes. If a label does not highlight a particular attribute, skeptical consumers may infer that either the product does not possess the desirable attribute or the attribute is of low quality. Grossman (1981) shows that this result occurs even where there is only one seller.

Competition among firms reinforces consumers' abilities to deduce relatively complete information about the hidden quality dimensions of products (Ippolito and Mathios 1990). For example, consumers will probably suspect that an unlabeled soymilk product contains genetically engineered (GE) ingredients if it is on a shelf next to a product labeled "non-GE." The product without the GE label not only leads consumers to assume that unlabeled products do not have the attribute, but it also makes consumers aware of the existence of the quality attribute. This competitive disclosure, which Ippolito and Mathios named the "unfolding" theory, results in explicit claims for all positive aspects of products and allows consumers to make appropriate inferences about foods without claims.

Unfortunately, the power of consumer skepticism and the unfolding theory are eroded when a whole class of products shares a negative characteristic: no producer gains through disclosure. In these cases, asymmetric information may lead to market failure. This could be the case for many food safety attributes. Private food producers may have difficulties advertising their products' superior food safety qualities. Claims such as "Our *Salmonella* count is 50% less than that of the leading brand," or "12% fewer recalls than last year," or "7% fewer rat hairs than allowed by FDA," although eye-catching, may not have the desired effect on sales. The ability to differentiate by safety attributes, particularly sanitary attributes, may be limited by the nature of the product (Kuchler [2001] examines this point). Firms may feel that any overt mention of safety risks could work to the disadvantage of a specific food product and to the industry as a whole.

The observation that producers may view safety disclosures as a negative attribute is illustrated by the history behind safe-handling labels on retail meat and poultry packages (Ralston and Lin 2001). In 1972, the American Public Health Association, individual consumers, and six other public health and consumer interest groups sued the U.S. Department of Agriculture (USDA), alleging that labels on meat and poultry products were false and misleading because (1) they failed to warn consumers against the dangers of foodborne illness, and (2) the official inspection seal certifying that the meat or poultry product was "USDA Inspected" could lead consumers to believe that a product was completely safe, regardless of how it was handled. USDA successfully fought the suit, arguing that consumer education was sufficient without a warning label on the product.

In 1993, following the lethal outbreak of *E. coli* O157:H7 in Jack-in-the-Box restaurants, another consumer group sued USDA to prevent the use of the official inspection seal on meat and poultry products unless it was accompanied by a label warning the consumer that the product may contain bacteria capable of causing infection, disease, or death and giving safe-handling instructions. This time, in a court-approved settlement, USDA agreed to begin developing a safe-handling label and issued an interim rule. However, on September 23, 1993, a collection of grocers' and food service distributors' associations filed a complaint alleging that USDA should have solicited comments before issuing the interim rule. USDA subsequently republished the rule as a proposal, and the final rule was published March 28, 1994 (FSIS 1994).

The actions of the grocers and food-service distributors suggests that food safety disclosure, even general statements for a whole class of products, were viewed as disadvantageous to the industry. Some industry members suggested that positive rather than negative information should be stressed on labels. They argued that the mention of bacteria should be dropped and that the label should read something like "Food products must be handled and prepared properly to prevent potential illness" (FSIS 1994, *14538*). Others argued that FSIS should refrain from offering advice on potential product liability (FSIS 1993, *52861*).

Approaches for Valuing the Benefits
of Reducing Morbidity and Premature Death

Market failure, including failure triggered by asymmetric information, may require government intervention. If so, policy makers need to know how much intervention in the market is warranted. They need to know how much consumers and society value food safety and what the value of government intervention is.

To target government spending to those programs of the most value to consumers, policy makers need a way to rank diverse risks affecting diverse populations. Economists and health policy analysts have developed three primary methodologies for translating diverse outcomes to a common unit of measurement for comparison purposes. The cost-of-illness and willingness-to-pay approaches convert diverse outcomes to dollar amounts and the quality-adjusted life years approach converts diverse outcomes to healthy-time equivalencies.

Cost-of-Illness

Cost-of-illness (COI) estimates are composed of two types of costs: direct and indirect. Direct costs are expenditures for medical goods and services such as medications, physician visits, and hospitalization. Indirect or human capital costs are the present value of labor earnings that are forgone as a result of an adverse health outcome. COI estimates provide policy analysts with an accounting of the economic flows resulting from illness and premature death and hence from government programs that improve public health. However, COI estimates do not provide a good measure of the full impact of disease on individuals or society and therefore do not provide a good measure of the value of reductions in illness and premature death. For example, COI does not measure the value of avoiding the pain and suffering associated with illness or the social benefit of lost nonmarket labor such as child care or community service. Economists and health policy analysts have critiqued COI estimates on a number of points, the most fundamental of which is that it equates the value of a life with forgone wages. Thus, COI estimates assign higher values of life to higher paid members of society and no value to members who are not part of the labor force (for a detailed critique of the COI approach see Kuchler and Golan 1999). A ranking based on such a premise diverges from most measures of disease severity or of social welfare.

Willingness-to-Pay

An entirely different approach to assigning value to risk reduction, an approach that provides a more accurate measure of the value of safety programs, is to estimate what risk reduction is worth to individuals whose health might benefit. With the willingness-to-pay (WTP) approach, analysts estimate consumers' willingness to pay for means to reduce health risk or to improve health.[1]

The WTP approach for estimating the benefits of public health programs rests on the observation that individuals can and do make trade-offs between health and other consumption goods and services. Individuals routinely and voluntarily accept many small risks in exchange for finite benefits. For example, driving a little faster than surrounding traffic may raise the risk of injury but usually results in reaching a destination sooner. Alternatively, a person might enjoy attending a popular movie at a crowded theater, recognizing that the activity raises the risk of contracting a contagious disease. People frequently make these trade-offs when purchasing goods. For example, car purchases frequently involve a price/safety trade-off.

An individual might suffer actual harm as a result of the decision to speed or to sit in a crowded theater or to buy a less safe car and might later regret the decision. However, WTP does not measure realized damages or capture the ex post valuation of an individual's changed health status. The WTP approach measures the resources individuals are willing and able to give up for a reduction in the probability of encountering a hazard that will compromise their health. The WTP approach is therefore concerned with measuring ex ante valuations, that is, valuations at the moment choices are made.

Some risks rank quite low when ex ante preferences are considered. For example, skiing carries a risk of injury and death, but very few skiers would welcome a government program that banned skiing on the basis of risk. Other risks rank quite high when preferences are considered. Magat et al. (1996) found that a significant proportion of the population values reductions in cancer risk much more highly than reductions in the risk of automobile fatality. Similarly, preferences provide a clear justification for assigning high priority to programs that reduce children's risks. In investigating risk preferences toward household chemicals, insecticides, and cleaning products, Viscusi et al. (1987) found a WTP to reduce risks to children 2.3 times higher than WTP to reduce risks to adults.

If funding is prioritized simply on the basis of outcome, without any regard to consumer preferences, then the deaths due to skiing would be ranked equal to the deaths due to childhood leukemia. The dollar values consumers attach to risk reduction help us to discriminate among risks to identify safety programs

---

[1]The use of WTP to determine consumer welfare is a basic benefits measure in neoclassical welfare economics. Where a demand curve can be estimated, total "willingness to pay" can be approximated by consumer surplus derived from a Hicksian demand curve (treating quantity demanded as a function of prices and a utility level, where income adjusts to maintain the utility level). When applied to changes in mortality risk, WTP measures the change in income, coupled with the change in the risk of mortality, that leaves the consumer's utility unchanged.

that are most valuable to consumers and to avoid funding risk reduction that
would actually make consumers worse off. The real strength of the WTP approach is that, unlike any other approach, it helps target funding toward those
programs providing the type of risk reduction most highly valued by society.
There are profound differences in the way that individuals value reductions in
different risks. WTP gives us a means of ranking diverse risks, not just by the
size of the risk, but by how uncomfortable individuals are about the risk.

Another strength of the WTP approach, one that it shares with the COI approach, is that because it uses money as the common unit of measurement, it
provides a full ranking of policy options *and* a context for determining social desirability. Not only does money translate health outcomes into a common unit
of account so that analysts can rank dissimilar programs with different health
outcomes—for example, the costs and benefits of a kidney machine can be compared with those of a nutrition program—but money also provides a measure
of costs of programs and therefore the net benefits of different policy options. If
the net benefits of a program were negative, the program would not be worthwhile, regardless of whether it was ranked higher than every other program.

In addition, because money is already in common use in ranking choices
and in conveying value, analysis based on a money scale allow us to compare
values and make trade-offs among all goods, whether produced in the public
or private sector. With a monetized account, analysts can compare not only the
relative value of various public health programs, but they can also compare the
value of these programs with alternative ways individuals might spend their
money, such as consumer goods. Moreover, these comparisons can be easily accomplished. If dollar benefits exceed dollar costs, the program is worth the
price. Such comparisons are not easily made with nonmoney measures. Analysts who, for philosophical reasons, do not choose dollars as the unit of measurement restrict the usefulness of their analyses for ranking policy options and
for determining the social desirability of policy.

A serious criticism of WTP as a measure of the value individuals place on
reduction in health risk is that it also reflects an individual's *ability* to pay. So,
for example, a consumer's WTP for car safety features is also a reflection of his
income or wealth as well as his preferences for safety and competing demands
on his resources. Use of WTP as a measure of the social welfare impact of government programs is based on the tacit assumption that the existing distribution of resources in the society is acceptable. For this and other reasons, some
analysts or policy makers may be uncomfortable with assigning dollar values
when the benefits are human health and safety.

Quality-Adjusted Life Years

To avoid using money as a unit of account, many turn to cost-effectiveness
analysis. With cost effectiveness analysis, adverse health outcomes are left in

physical terms, such as the number of cancer cases, or the number of premature deaths. Use of a physical outcome measure allows comparison of cost-effectiveness across programs with identical health outcomes, but does not allow comparison of the cost-effectiveness of programs that produce very different physical outcomes, such as cancer prevention and nutrition promotion. Similarly, cost-effectiveness analysis is not useful in comparing programs that affect very different parts of the population; for example, we have already seen that reduction of childhood cancer is viewed as different from reduction in cancer in the elderly.

Analysts have tried several ways of modifying cost-effectiveness to account for the variety of health outcomes programs yield. One of the most popular methods is to construct a health index, called quality-adjusted life years (QALY), that accounts for changes in both length and quality of life. To calculate QALYs, analysts use individual assessments of health outcomes arrayed on a 0–1 scale, with 0 indicating death and 1 indicating robust good health. With a QALY scale, adverse health outcomes that compromise both lifespan and functional ability are converted to a common unit of account. Because QALYs provide a common unit of account, they provide a means for ranking and prioritizing funding allocation across diverse types of programs, such as nutrition and dialysis programs. All things equal, those programs with the highest QALY per dollar calculation should be funded before those with lower QALY per dollar calculations.

Although the QALY approach imposes a certain logic to funding allocation, it is incomplete. With the QALY approach analysts could decide whether a nutrition or dialysis program should be funded first, but they would be unable to determine whether either program was worth the cost. QALYs do not provide a measure of net benefits. A QALY-per-dollar calculation does not provide information as to whether program benefits outweigh costs. In addition, because QALYs are used only by public health analysts, they do not provide a straightforward means for making comparisons with nonhealth goods and services. For example, analysts would be unable to say whether the QALYs generated by a nutrition program were more valuable than a college education.

Federal Agencies Use Different Value Estimates

To rank and prioritize government allocation of scarce resources among food safety programs and between food safety programs and other uses of government funds, federal agencies have employed a number of valuation methodologies. USDA, Food and Drug Administration (FDA), and Environmental Protection Agency (EPA) have all developed estimates of the value of food safety programs and all continue to revise and update their approaches.

All of the major estimates of the value of reductions in foodborne illness focus on measuring the value of reduction in adverse health outcomes. For these estimates, analysts begin by determining how many cases of disease should be attributed to food generally or to a specific food such as meat, poultry, or seafood. This is a data-intensive endeavor that involves determining contamination levels, the average dose of contaminant per food serving, and the probability of falling ill given the average dose per serving. (The chapters in Roberts et al. [1995] examine the difficulties in establishing the link between food and illness.)

The next step in the estimation procedure involves determining the outcomes associated with each foodborne disease and the probability of each outcome. The outcomes of foodborne illness range from mild gastrointestinal upset to death. Some foodborne illnesses result in long-term illnesses, or chronic sequellae, such as paralysis, arthritis, and mental retardation. For example, about 1.5% of *E. coli* O157:H7 disease patients develop hemolytic uremic syndrome (HUS), which usually involves red blood cell destruction, kidney failure, and neurological complications, such as seizures and strokes. Figure 7.1 is an example of an outcome tree for salmonellosis prepared by economists at Economic Research Service (ERS). Several other outcome trees are posted on the ERS website (http://www.ers.usda.gov/briefing/FoodborneDisease/).

Once researchers have determined the outcomes associated with a foodborne disease, the next step in the estimation procedure is to calculate the value of reductions for each type of adverse health outcome. The methodology for assigning an economic value to each outcome has generated a large theoretical and empirical literature. Researchers have used cost-of-illness, willingness-to-pay, and quality-adjusted life year techniques.

ERS Estimates

ERS economists conducted some of the earliest studies calculating the benefits of reductions in bacterial foodborne illness (Roberts 1980, 1985) and have updated and expanded their analysis repeatedly. In 1989, ERS published cost estimates for 16 foodborne bacterial diseases (Roberts 1989). For these estimates, Roberts extrapolated from earlier cost estimates for salmonellosis and listeriosis (Cohen et al. 1984; Roberts and Pinner 1990).

In 1996, ERS produced more detailed estimates of the costs of six bacterial foodborne pathogens, *Campylobacter jejuni, Clostridium perfringens, Escherichia coli* O157:H7, *Listeria monocytogenes, Salmonella,* and *Staphylococcus aureus* (Buzby and Roberts 1996; Buzby et al. 1996, 1998) and included estimates for a foodborne parasite, *Toxoplasma gondii* (Roberts and Frenkel 1990). These early estimates were the basis for the official regulatory impact analysis of the Hazard Analysis and Critical Control (HACCP) program for federally

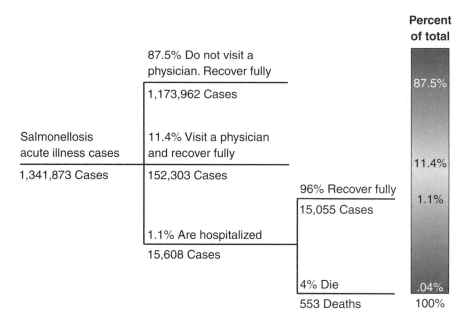

FIGURE 7.1. Distribution of Estimated Annual U.S. Foodborne Salmonellosis Cases and Disease Outcomes. Percentages are rounded.

Source: Prepared by Economic Research Service, USDA.

inspected meat and poultry slaughter and processing plants (Federal Register 1996), and are quoted in almost every discussion of the costs of foodborne illness (for a discussion of the HACCP analysis see Crutchfield et al. 1997a).

In 2000, ERS updated its estimates of medical costs and productivity losses for diseases caused by *Campylobacter* (all serotypes), *Salmonella* (nontyphoidal serotypes only), *E. coli* O157:H7, and *Listeria monocytogenes,* and added estimates for *E. coli* non-O157:H7 STEC (Table 7.1). These new estimates were based on updated CDC estimates of the number of cases, hospitalizations, and deaths for these foodborne pathogens (Mead et al. 1999) and account for age in the valuation of premature deaths.

ERS's methodology for calculating the costs of foodborne pathogens, and hence the potential benefits of food safety programs, involves first developing an outcome tree for each pathogen, showing the number of cases involving a physician visit, hospitalization, premature death, and chronic complications, although only selected chronic complications are included. For each outcome, medical costs are estimated for physician and hospital services, supplies, medications, and special procedures unique to treating the particular foodborne illness. Such costs reflect the number of days/treatments of a medical service, the average cost per service/treatment, and the number of patients receiving such service/treatment.

TABLE 7.1. Estimated Annual Costs (US$) Due to Selected Foodborne Pathogens, 2000

	Estimated Annual Foodborne Illnesses[a]			*Costs*[b] *Billion dollars (2000)*
Pathogen	*Number Cases*	*Number Hospitalizations*	*Number Deaths*	
Campylobacter spp.	1,963,141	10,539	99	1.2
E. coli O157:H7	62,458	1,843	52	0.7
E. coli, non-O157 STEC	31,229	921	26	0.3
Listeria monocytogenes	2,493	2,298	499	2.3
Salmonella	1,341,873	15,608	553	2.4
Total	3,401,194	31,209	1,229	6.9

[a] Data from the Centers for Disease Control and Prevention, Food-Related Illness and Death in the United States.

[b] Costs include medical expenses, the value of forgone or lost wages for nonfatal foodborne illnesses, and an estimate of the value of statistical life for each premature death that varies with age at death.

Source: Economic Research Service, USDA. http://www.ers.usda.gov/Emphases/SafeFood/features.htm.

For nonfatal illnesses, including those with chronic sequellae, ERS cost estimates include an estimate of the value of productivity losses for individuals who become ill and missed work. The value of lost productivity is set at the value of forgone wages. For fatal cases, ERS has used a number of methodologies to estimate the costs of premature death. For the 1996 cost estimates, ERS provided results from two different valuation methodologies: human capital and WTP. The human capital estimates of the cost of premature death were based on the individualized human capital approach developed by Landefeld and Seskin (1982). Landefeld and Seskin sought to approximate WTP by calculating an *individual's* human capital costs, that is, the value of forgone earnings. Unlike *social* human capital cost estimates, their estimates incorporate earnings net of taxes, nonlabor income, an individual rather than social discount rate, and a risk aversion factor. Landefeld and Seskin's estimates more closely approximate individual WTP measures than traditional human capital estimates, although such measures still do not incorporate preventive expenditures or the utility value of health.

For their estimates of "individualized" human capital costs attributable to foodborne pathogens, ERS researchers adjusted the Landefeld and Seskin measures of lifetime after-tax income by averaging across gender and interpolating between age groups to provide estimates on a wider range of ages (Buzby et al. 1996). Using the Landefeld and Seskin methodology, ERS estimates of the cost of a premature death ranged from roughly $15,000 to $1,979,000 (1995 dollars), depending on age.

ERS researchers based their second set of estimates for the 1996 cost calculations on WTP results from labor-market studies on wage differentials for jobs with health risks. These compensating wage studies calculate the amount of money workers would be willing to forgo in order to reduce job-related mortality risk. These numbers have been used to calculate the value of a statistical life. Two widely cited surveys of compensating-wage studies place the most reliable empirical results in the $1.6 to $8.5 million range (1986 dollars) (Fisher et al. 1989) and the $3 million to $7 million range (1990 dollars) (Viscusi 1993). ERS researchers chose a midpoint estimate of $5 million (1995 dollars) for their WTP estimates of the cost of a premature death. For the 1996 calculations, they used this value for every premature death, regardless of age at death or cause of death.

For the 2000 estimates, ERS researchers first adjusted the original 1990 mid-range compensating wage estimate for inflation to obtain a value of $6.5 million in August 2000 dollars. Then, researchers used information about the age distribution of deaths to adjust this value to account for age at death from each pathogen (Table 7.1, column 5). With this approach, the value of life was treated as an annuity paid over the average U.S. life span at an interest rate of 3%. Following the age-adjustment, the assumed cost of each death ranged from $8.9 million for individuals who died before their first birthday to $1.7 million for individuals who died at age 85 or older.

Because the five microbial pathogens have different health outcomes for different age groups, adjusting for the age at death raised the cost of some foodborne illnesses and lowered the cost of others. For example, the annual cost of foodborne illnesses caused by *Salmonella* decreased to $2.2 billion because more than two thirds of the deaths from salmonellosis occur among people older than 65 years of age. Adjusting foodborne illness costs for *E. coli* O157:H7 by age at time of death increased the estimates by $200 million because most deaths occurred in children younger than 5 years of age.

FDA Estimates

FDA has estimated the value of reductions in health risks due to consumption of contaminated seafood, juice, and milk products (e.g., see U.S. FDA 1993). The first step in the FDA estimation procedure is to estimate the incidence of disease and identify the most likely adverse health outcomes and duration of outcomes for each pathogen. For each health outcome, FDA researchers then calculate general costs of illness and disutility costs of illness. The general costs of illness include medical costs; lost productivity; transportation; household costs; costs of pursuing and defending liability suits, both pursuit of and avoidance of; and recalls, although in practice researchers may calculate only a subset of these costs. Disutility costs include the costs of pain and suffering borne directly by individuals as well as defensive expenditures borne by firms, individuals, and governments. FDA researchers argue that including both general costs and costs measured by WTP does not result in double accounting because

WTP measures capture only the individual's losses and not those borne by others such as insurance companies and employers.

To calculate the value of pain and suffering, FDA researchers use health status indices following the methodology suggested by the Research Triangle Institute (1988). These indices categorize adverse health outcomes by severity and duration of symptoms. Symptoms are ranked according to "functional states" describing the amount of mobility, physical activity, social activity, and the symptom/problem complex. Researchers then establish the relative disagreeableness of each health state and assign each one a disutility weight, ranging from 0 (as bad as death) to 1 (perfect health). In the last step of the procedure, FDA researchers convert the disutility value into a dollar measure. For these dollar estimates, FDA researchers use a compensating wage midpoint estimate, assigning a value of $5 million to premature death and a proportion of this amount to all other outcomes, depending on the outcome's disutility weight.

The total disutility cost of a nonfatal outcome depends on both its severity and duration. The total disutility of an illness is calculated by multiplying the value of the time spent sick by the disutility weight. Assuming that the average illness strikes a 40-year-old person with a remaining lifespan of 36 years, FDA researchers estimate the value of a "discounted life year" at $222,222 and the value of a "discounted day" at $609. Thus, the disutility of an illness with an average duration of 9 days, and a disutility weight of 0.52 would be $2,850. Each case is also weighted by the probability of death so that a case with very little possibility of death has a lower disutility cost than one with a high risk of death.

FDA's annual cost estimates for each type of illness associated with seafood are shown in Table 7.2. For these estimates, the probabilities associated with each health state were derived from the medical literature or from the results of a study performed for FDA by Research Triangle Institute (RTI 1993). It is assumed that consumers are equally likely to be exposed to all of the possible doses that are capable of causing illness. Medical costs include only the costs of hospitalization and emergency room care (U.S. FDA 1993).

EPA Estimates

EPA researchers are charged with monitoring and regulating levels of foodborne pollutants including pesticides. Foodborne pollutants are associated with a range of adverse human health effects, including effects on the nervous system, cancer, and reproductive and developmental problems. For many of these pollutants, such as mercury, dioxins, and polychlorinated biphenyls (PCBs), the populations most at risk are children and developing fetuses.

EPA researchers typically begin their benefit analysis with the National Research Council's four-step process for human health risk assessment (U.S. EPA 1999a). In the first step of this process, researchers identify the potential health effects that may occur from exposure to the hazard. In the second step, they calculate the dose levels necessary to trigger adverse outcomes for humans. In the

TABLE 7.2. Estimated Annual Costs (US$) of Illness Associated with Seafood, Per Case, 1993

Hazards	Disutility per Average Case[a]	Average Direct Medical Expenditures	Total Cost
Anisakis simplex	794	1,344	2,138
Campylobacter jejuni	1,934	0	1,934
Ciguatera poisoning	12,875	0	12,875
Clostridium botulinum	896,817	45,809	942,626
Clostridium perfringens	118,433	508	118,941
Diphyllobothrium latum	1,572	0	1,572
Giardia lamblia	3,166	3,048	6,214
Hepatitis A virus	3,329	0	3,329
Neurotoxic shellfish poison	269	0	269
Norwalk virus	572	0	572
Other *vibrios*	1,416	2,576	4,172
Paralytic shellfish poisoning	89,689	2,667	92,356
Salmonella non -*typhi*	564	1,270	1,834
Scombrotoxin poisoning	412	0	412
Shigella	61,981	8,890	70,871
Vibrio vulnificus	1,245,093	15,558	1,260,651

Source: FDA, Preliminary Regulatory Impact Analysis of the Proposed Regulations to Establish Procedures for the Safe Processing and Importing of Fish and Fishery Products, December 1993 http://www.cfsan.fda.gov/~djz/cfudpria.txt (accessed June 4, 2001).

[a] Disutility represents the cost associated with the pain and suffering from the illness, estimated using compensating wage measures.

third step, they conduct the exposure assessment. In the fourth step, researchers combine the hazard, dose–response, and exposure assessments to determine the overall health risk. Difficulties in estimating exposure, disease incidence, and outcomes arise because of the ability of these pollutants to travel long distances; to transfer rather easily among air, water, and land; and to linger for generations in people and the environment. In addition, the Food Quality Protection Act of 1996 stipulates that researchers consider exposure from all sources (food, water, air, etc.), evaluate cumulative risks, and consider special sensitivity of children.

For cost–benefit analysis, EPA researchers then determine the monetary value of averting health risks. EPA estimates of the cost of premature death are based on a mid-range estimate taken from 21 compensating wage studies and 5 contingent valuation studies conducted in the late 1970s and 1980s. The methodology for establishing the mid-range estimate is described in the *Guidelines for Preparing Economic Analyses* (EPA 2000a, *90*):

> To allow for probabilistic modeling of mortality risk reduction benefits, the analysts reviewed a number of common distributions to determine

which best fit the distribution of mean values from the studies. A Weibull distribution was selected with a central tendency (or mean) of $5.8 million (1997$). [Updating for inflation this number rose to $6.1 in 1999.]

Some EPA analyses include adjustments for age, although the *Guidelines for Preparing Economic Analyses* do not encourage such value adjustments, stating, "Age adjustments may be desirable from a theoretical standpoint, but the relationship between the value of risk reductions and expected remaining life span is complex" (U.S. EPA 2000a, *93*). For the analysis of the Clean Air Act (U.S. EPA 1999b), analysts varied the value of a statistical life by age group by assuming that the willingness to pay to save a life was the value of a single year of life times the expected number of years of life remaining for an individual and that the typical respondent in a mortality risk study had a life expectancy of an additional 25 years (methodology developed in Moore and Viscusi [1988]). For this analysis, EPA researchers also assumed that an individual discounts future additional life years using a 5% discount rate. These calculations yielded a value of $293,000 per life-year lost or saved (1990$).

To place a monetary value on reductions in morbidity and chronic sequellae, EPA researchers prefer the WTP approach, although they have used a variety of methodologies. In some cases, they calculate the present value of expected lifetime earnings lost due to the adverse health outcomes. For example, the benefit analysis for proposed effluent limitations for iron and steel includes an estimate of the effects of IQ loss caused by consumption of lead in fish, and other affected food sources) on lifetime earnings (U.S. EPA 2000b). In other cases, EPA researchers estimate morbidity costs by augmenting human capital estimates with estimates of the opportunity cost of time spent in hospital.

EPA cost estimates may also include direct medical expenses. In fact, EPA has issued a *Cost-of-Illness Handbook* containing information on the per capita incremental direct medical costs associated with the various illnesses linked to environmental pollutants (U.S. EPA 2001). The *Handbook* includes cost data for numerous cancers, developmental diseases and disabilities, respiratory diseases, acute diseases, and additional illnesses. Work on the *Handbook* began in 1991 and is ongoing. Despite the work reflected in the *Handbook,* EPA cost analyses do not necessarily include direct medical expenses. For example, the benefit analysis for proposed effluent limitations for iron and steel does not include costs of lead screening, medical treatment, or special education (U.S. EPA 2000b).

Customizing the Value of Health Risks for Food Safety Policy

An assumption underlying all of the outcome-based estimates is that the value of risk reduction is independent from the cause of an adverse outcome. This assumption implies that consumers place the same value on a specific adverse outcome regardless of whether the outcome is due to a congenital condition, contracted through consumption of undercooked hamburger, or a result of reckless skiing. An advantage of this assumption is that analysts who are charged with providing outcome-based estimates are able to use value estimates from health studies unrelated to food safety. Food safety analysts can borrow from the large number of environmental and health economics studies using a wide range of valuation techniques, such as contingent valuation, health production functions, hedonic pricing, and experimental markets, to calculate values for health outcomes (for a review and critique of this literature see Tolley et al. [1994]).

A disadvantage of the outcome-based approach is that it provides only a rough estimate of value, glossing over potentially large value differences stemming from risk-specific characteristics. Both empirical and theoretical studies support the conclusion that risk values are not "one size fits all." For example, one of the most striking observations that emerges from the compensating wage literature is the sensitivity of value-of-life estimates to the characteristics of the study population and to the level and type of risk. As a result, the general applicability of these estimates is questionable. As Viscusi states (1993, *1930*), "The value of life is not a universal constant, but reflects the wage-risk trade-off pertinent to the preferences of the workers in a particular sample." At best, compensating wage studies indicate a range for implicit value-of-life measures, but caution should be exercised in making general conclusions about the value of life.

A number of the characteristics of foodborne illness reduce the fit of most health benefit transfers. First, the characteristics of the population most vulnerable to foodborne risk are quite different from those of the population in many health-risk studies. Those most vulnerable to complications from foodborne illness are infants, the elderly, and immunocompromised individuals (Foegeding and Roberts 1994). This is a very different group than the sample of blue-collar men at the heart of the compensating wage studies. As a result, the values generated by compensating wage studies probably incorrectly estimate the value of reduction in foodborne risks. For example, empirical evidence suggests that consumers with children may allocate greater expenditures to reduce children's risks (Viscusi et al. 1987; Evans and Viscusi 1991). As a result, cost estimates for foodborne illnesses that primarily affect children will probably underestimate the value of risk reductions.

In addition to the impact of population characteristics on health-outcome values, the type and level of risk could also influence the estimates. For example, it can be argued that not all fatality risks represent the same utility loss, and that not just the likelihood but also the manner in which a person might die makes a difference. Magat et al. (1996) found that although the median respondent to their survey rated reduction in risks of terminal lymph cancer and death by automobile accident equally, 17% of respondents valued a reduction in terminal lymph cancer 33 times higher than a reduction in the risk of automobile accident fatality. Likewise, death from a foodborne illness such as a new variant of Creutzfeldt–Jakob disease, the human counterpart of "mad cow" disease, may generate much higher values than those generated by wage studies.

People may also be less willing to accept involuntary risk, such as most foodborne risks, than risk that is voluntarily assumed (Fischhoff et al. 1981). As a result, studies that measure response to voluntary risk, such as compensating wage studies, probably underestimate society's aversion to risk that is not contracted for, such as most foodborne risks. Other factors such as the possibility of defensive behavior, for example, longer hamburger cooking, and whether or not the risk produces consequences in the near or far distant future may also influence the value of the risk reduction.

The EPA white paper on valuing the benefits of fatal cancer risks (U.S. EPA 2000b) reviews many of the problems related to the blanket use of compensating wage estimates and suggests that measures of the cost of premature death borrowed from compensating wage and other studies be adjusted to account for the nature of the risks being valued and the socioeconomic characteristics of the affected populations. In their review of the white paper, the Environmental Economics Advisory Committee of the EPA Science Advisory Board concluded that estimates of the cost of premature death derived from compensating wage studies were not precise estimates of the value of reducing the risk of fatal cancers, but that the only risk characteristic for which adjustments can be made is the timing of the risk, that is, whether the risk produces consequences in the near or far future. The Advisory Board went on to state that despite the limitations of the compensating wage estimates, they "offer the best available basis for considering the value of fatal cancer risk reduction" (U.S. EPA 2000c, p. *2* of Letter to Administrator).

Despite EPA's Science Advisory Board's conclusions, many researchers are striving to move away from the direct use of compensating wage estimates and to better tailor these estimates to foodborne risks. To this end, researchers have conducted a number of contingent valuation and hypothetical market studies examining consumer preferences for food safety. Unfortunately, these studies have yet to provide a coherent set of guidelines with which to characterize foodborne risk values, although little systematic work has been done teasing out such guidelines. In many cases, the variety of attributes in contingent valuation (CV) and hypothetical market studies makes it difficult to compare results easily. For example, although CV surveys have been increasingly used to measure consumers' WTP for food safety risk reductions, it is extremely difficult, and often impossible, to meaningfully compare WTP estimates from these surveys as they tend to be tied to different foods, food safety risks, and levels of risk reductions. Even CV surveys that focus on the general area of pesticide residue risk reductions in produce have not successfully established a value range, primarily because they use different ranges of price premiums, different phrases describing the produce as residue-free, different elicitation methods, and different hypothetical scenarios.

Even CV pesticide surveys that estimated WTP for specific risk reductions are not easily compared because they focused on different goods (e.g., van Ravenswaay and Hoehn 1991; Weaver et al. 1992; Buzby et al. 1995, 1998). Buzby et al. (1995) found that consumers were willing to pay, on average, $0.19 more for a grapefruit that had lower risks from pesticide residues. In two versions of another CV survey, Buzby et al. (1998) elicited WTP for a reduction in exposure to pesticide residues on fresh produce. The first version of the survey found that the median WTP was $5.31 per household per week for fresh produce that meets government standards for pesticide residues, and $5.88 for fresh produce with no detectable pesticide residues. These estimates are large relative to other empirical estimates of the value of a mortality risk reduction and they are statistically insensitive to the size of the risk reduction, although the direction of the difference follows the prediction of theory.

Other CV surveys that focus on food safety issues have elicited consumers' WTP for reduced risk from a wide variety of risks in different foods, again complicating the comparison of WTP estimates. For example, surveys have estimated the value of risk reductions from toxins in shellfish (Lin and Milon 1995), nitrates in drinking water (Crutchfield et al. 1997b), and *Salmonella* in chicken and eggs (Henson 1996). Another survey elicited consumers' preferences for leaner pork produced with porcine somatropin (pST), a naturally occurring protein that some consumers feel poses a food safety risk (Halbrendt et al. 1995), and analyzed preferences for the different pork attributes with conjoint analysis.

Another method for estimating the value of food safety is the experimental markets approach. This approach eliminates the informational deficiency of nonmarket goods by placing the good in something akin to a market situation (Buzby et al. 1998). With this approach, real money changes hands for real goods under repeated real auction trials where market prices are revealed along the way. These experiments often take place in a laboratory setting with students as subjects. Application of experimental valuation to food safety is relatively new, compared to CV and cost-of-illness methods. The first published studies originated from research at the Iowa State University meat testing lab in the 1990s (Shin et al. 1992; Shogren et al. 1994a; Fox et al. 1995; Hayes et al. 1995), and since then this core group of researchers have been expanding the knowledge base on aspects such as study design and interpretation of results. Most of these studies have focused on WTP for meat products that are safer in terms of microbial food safety risks. However, the method has also been applied to bovine growth hormones in milk production (Fox 1995), reductions in pesticide risk (Roosen et al. 1997), and a number of food characteristics other than safety, including coloring, marbling, and size of pork cut (Melton et al. 1996a, b).

Buzby et al. (1998) presented results from an experimental auction market valuing food safety. This research used the Vickrey second price auction mechanism, much like that used on Ebay, in which the highest bidder obtains the product being auctioned for a price equal to the second highest bid. Over 10 repeated trial auctions, this experiment elicited WTP values for reductions in *Salmonella* risk in a pork sandwich from a sample of 50 undergraduate students. The average WTP bid, that is, the premium for the upgraded sandwich, was $0.54 for those students who received a $3 payment and were informed about the symptoms of salmonellosis and the odds of contracting salmonellosis from the original sandwich and the upgraded sandwich. This is very similar to the average WTP bids (approximately $0.55) for the same risk reduction by two other groups of students in Fox et al. (1995) but significantly less than that from two other groups in the same study whose WTP exceeded $1. For participants receiving no payment in Buzby et al. (1998), the average informed bid was $0.32.

An earlier study by Shogren (1993) found that participants paid roughly $0.70 to upgrade to a food product that had lower microbial food risks from a set of five pathogens, observed separately and combined. This estimate was robust in the experiment. In a similar experiment, Hayes et al. (1995) found that WTP values were relatively flat across a wide range of risks from the different pathogens although the marginal WTP decreases as the risk increases. After participants were informed about the food safety risks, mean informed WTP bids for an upgraded, safer sandwich ranged from $0.42 to $0.86 above the $3.00 cost of the original sandwich.

As with the CV studies, the experimental market studies are difficult to compare. The market studies often have different stages where different products are valued. For example, the experiments generally take place over 10 to 20 trials with new information sometimes provided in one of the middle trials such as the objective odds of the illness in the auctioned food product. This auction structure complicates the presentation of results, as each trial has its own mean and median values and averaging over all trials is seldom appropriate, particularly if new information is provided. The amount of money endowed to the subjects also varies and may influence bidding. Studies are often aimed to enhance understanding of different and very specific issues such as resolving differences in willingness to pay and willingness to accept (Shogren et al. 1994b) or calibrating contingent values with experimental auction markets (Fox et al. 1998).

As researchers analyze the results of more CV and hypothetical market studies, and refine outcome measures to reflect risk-specific characteristics, they will be able to choose among better tailored benefit estimates. For example, value estimates for a health outcome resulting from a fast-acting pathogen for which no defensive actions exist will be derived from similarly described outcomes. The fine-tuning of outcome measures is high on the agenda of many food safety analysts.

Scope and Cost of Nonhealth Foodborne Risks

Even when measured correctly, neither cost-of-illness nor willingness-to-pay estimates necessarily reflect society's preferences with respect to health or with respect to food safety policy. Both types of health estimates often move in the opposite direction from standard disease severity measures and from other rankings of social or risk alleviation programs (for a review of these issues see Kuchler and Golan [1999]). Society's value of food safety may include many benefits that are not accounted for by the standard measure of the value of health outcomes. In this section, we examine some of the nonhealth benefits attributable to safe food and a strong food safety system.

Value of Reductions in Market Risks

Food safety concerns may trigger market fluctuations that are only loosely related to the real value of health risks. Risks that have a very low ranking in comparison with other foodborne risks can trigger market reactions that rank high in terms of economic impact. For example, hypothetical health and environmental risks associated with the production and consumption of genetically modified foods have triggered measurable market response (Shoemaker et al. 2001). In addition, the global nature of food trade has the potential to amplify food safety scares. For example, in the mid 1990s, an outbreak of *E. coli* O157:H7, which was eventually traced to Japanese grown sprouts, caused U.S. exports of beef to Japan to drop temporarily by as much as 40%. (Buzby [2001] examines the impact of food safety perceptions on international trade.)

For cases like this, the value of reductions in foodborne risk has very little to do with reductions in health risks and almost everything to do with reductions in market risks. In volatile market situations, a human health risk ranking may not indicate the appropriate level of funding, or type of programs that should be funded to mitigate the foodborne risk. In these cases, the measure of the value of a food safety system should include its ability to reduce disruptions in domestic and international markets and in the economic losses these disruptions entail.

Value of Access to Foreign Markets

A strong food safety system may also reap benefits in terms of access to foreign markets. Many countries limit food imports to those countries with comparable or more stringent food safety systems. For example, the United States requires that countries wishing to sell meat and poultry products in the U.S. market have inspection systems equivalent to those of the U.S. For many food producers, access to foreign markets is vital to the success of their business. For these producers, the value of a strong food safety system goes beyond the value of reductions in foodborne health risks.

The benefits of access to foreign markets must be balanced against the costs of providing safer food—costs that may restrict access to food for low income consumers. Costly food safety requirements could result in high-priced food that low-income foreign (and domestic) consumers cannot afford. In these cases, high-cost safety standards may produce a "reverse Robin Hood effect" in which poorer consumers are forced to pay for safety or other quality attributes that they do not necessarily value (Mazis 1980, 8, makes this point with respect to food labeling requirements). In some cases, price increases may force poorer individuals to consume larger amounts of lower priced, riskier products.

Value of Consumer Confidence

A strong food safety system builds consumer confidence. Consumers' confidence in the food safety system makes them less susceptible to passing food scares and limits market volatility. For example, commentators have linked the collapse of the market for genetically engineered foods in the European Union to the lack of consumer confidence in the food safety system. As noted by Gaskell et al. (1999), although U.S. consumers tend to have confidence in USDA and FDA to regulate food safety, Europeans rank national bodies and industry far below international, environmental, and consumer and farm organizations in terms of trustworthiness.

Consumers' confidence in the food safety system and their general confidence in government regulatory oversight also serve to reinforce one another: a strong food safety system can lend credibility to other government programs and vice versa. For example, as noted in a 1999 Gallup Poll survey (Gallup 1999), "Another potentially important factor in Americans' confidence in the safety of the food on their grocery store shelves is their basic confidence in federal oversight."

A strong food safety system has spillover effects on general consumer well-being and general consumption choices. For example, in the preliminary Regulatory Impact Analysis for the seafood HACCP program, FDA researchers estimated large "consumer confidence" benefits. They argued that greater confidence in seafood safety would cause consumers to increase their consumption of lower fat/lower cholesterol seafood products and decrease consumption of higher fat meat and poultry. The overall decrease in fat consumed would cause a decrease in cases of coronary heart disease and cancer—which FDA researchers valued at between $3 and $14 billion (U.S. FDA 1993).

Food safety policy based on a human health risk ranking may not indicate the appropriate level of funding, or type of programs that should be funded when foodborne risks affect consumer confidence in the whole regulatory system.

Value of Safe Food—Is Food Special?

Is there something about food that conveys a value above and beyond any of its individual attributes? Is there a "foodness" quality that causes consumers to place a higher value on the integrity of the whole product so that changes in safety risks are valued differently than comparable risks for other products? A number of authors contend that food is special. Belonax (1997, *370*) describes the central role of food:

> There can be little doubt in anyone's mind that food occupies a crucial role in any society. Countries go to war over food. Economies revolve around food. Food is traded for political influence. Religions use food in their rituals. Food is used to celebrate life's passages. Food is shared to build friendships. Food bonds families.

Snowden (Snowden et al. 2002) goes so far as to describe food as a "significant non-durable art medium." Food ethnologists trace the importance of food in cultural identities. *Gastronomica,* from the University of California Press, is an entire magazine dedicated to the connection between food and culture.

Economic research into the value of specific food characteristics may provide information on the value of a "foodness" attribute. Hypothetical market studies such as those discussed previously are beginning to provide economists with information on consumers' preferences for a variety of food attributes. Market-based studies are also shedding light on consumers' attitudes toward food safety (and foodness). For example, Kuchler et al. (1996) illustrated the large difference between health benefits and costs of organic food by comparing the organic price premium for organic apple juice to the value of the reduced pesticide residue risk from replacing conventional apple juice with organic juice. They found that for adults, the price premium was between 138 and 461 times the value of cancer risk reduction, and for children, the price premium was between 27 and 90 times the value of cancer risk reduction.

Clearly, if consumers calculated risks as risk assessors do, the typical consumer would be unlikely to purchase organic apple juice for health reasons. The choice to consume organic foods may be a choice that goes beyond the specific attributes of the food, reflecting lifestyle choices as much as food choices. Likewise, the value of a strong food safety system may not be reflected in a simple tally of health or economic benefits.

The Economic Value of Foodborne Risk Is Only One Piece of the Puzzle

The reason that economists and policy analysts are interested in estimating consumer values, whether for reductions in food safety risks or reductions in environmental damages, is that markets have failed to calculate these values and to allocate resources accordingly. Economists use these value estimates to provide an indication of how society's resources should be allocated. In some cases, economists use these values in cost–benefit analyses. In other cases, econ-

omists use a ranking of these values to indicate a ranking of resource allocation. However, even when the value of risk reduction is correctly measured,
these values are not necessarily a meaningful guide to policy action. We discuss
two reasons why this may be true.

First, value estimates may not provide a correct project ranking unless they
are accompanied by cost estimates. The appropriate measure of the attractive-
ness of a project is net benefits, not just benefits. High-cost programs with large
benefits may not be as attractive or worthwhile as low-cost programs with
medium benefits. Efficient resource allocation depends on both benefits and
costs. Failure to balance benefits with costs is a sore point for many economists
(e.g., Morrall 1986). To underline the fallacy of considering only benefits and
not costs, economists have developed a methodology for translating monetary
costs into premature deaths. With health–health analysis, the count of fatalities *averted* by public sector programs is compared with the count of fatalities
induced by regulatory costs (Lutter and Morrall 1994). Regulatory costs induce
fatalities because they reduce the ability of the private sector to invest in health.
New regulatory compliance costs or taxes reduce disposable income. A consequence of reduced income is less ability to privately purchase goods and services, including those that reduce health risks and promote health. As a result,
additional adverse health outcomes may occur. With this methodology, wasted
money is translated into wasted lives.

Kuchler et al. (1999) used health–health analysis to calculate the mortality
effects of a potential oyster harvesting ban to protect consumers from the
pathogen *Vibrio vulnificus*. Given the income distribution of oyster harvesters
and processors, Kuchler et al. calculated that the income loss to the oyster industry would result in between 8 and 12 deaths. With 17 potential oyster-re-
lated deaths averted through the harvesting ban, the net benefit is between 5
and 9 lives. In this case, health is transferred *from* individuals in oyster communities *to* medically at-risk oyster consumers. If regulatory costs are ignored,
the value of these lives is overlooked.

The second reason value estimates may not provide a good guide to policy
makers is that case-by-case analyses may not provide the type of information
policy makers need. Case-by-case value estimates may provide important information for policy makers when they are confronted with externality and
public good problems. In these cases, value estimates help determine the
amount and type of regulation necessary to mitigate the problem. However, for
market failure springing from asymmetric information, the primary failure in
the market for food safety, policy makers may not necessarily have a use for
case-by-case value estimates.

For asymmetric information problems, policy makers have two primary
types of tools at their disposal. They could use direct regulation, such as establishing quality and safety standards, or they could use information policy, such
as labeling and education programs. If policy makers use direct regulation, value

estimates are useful in calculating cost thresholds. If policy makers choose to use information policy, their objective is to provide consumers with the relevant information and then let consumers calculate their own value trade-offs and allocate their own scarce resources as they see fit. Because most, if not all, of the costs and benefits of the consumption decision are borne by the consumer (no externality problems), fully informed consumers can determine the appropriate allocation of resources. In this case, the appropriate policy response is to facilitate the provision of information and the transparency of the food safety system. This type of policy response does not depend on a case-by-case calculation of the value of risk reduction the way that direct regulation does.

Researchers and policy analysts are becoming more aware of the importance of information and producer incentives in creating a strong food safety system. A number of government programs are targeted at increasing food safety information and the transparency of the safety system. For example, both FSIS and the FDA post a list of recalls for contaminated, adulterated, or misbranded products (http://www.fsis.usda.gov/OA/news/xrecalls.htm#Current, and http://www.fda.gov/opacom/7alerts.html). In another program, FSIS requires that the results of the HACCP *Salmonella* testing program for meat and poultry be published annually and made available to the public, although unfortunately results are not reported for individual firms as was originally proposed by FSIS. Other information programs that are under consideration include time/temperature indicators for each package of refrigerated food; harvest/lay/slaughter dates on each package of an animal protein product; pathogen performance information on each company and its products; identification of high-risk food products in a database that the immunocompromised individuals, pregnant women, and other high-risk people could consult; and a government certified label for low-risk foods so companies can compete on providing safety from pathogens. Advances in technology are supporting, and in many cases stimulating, information provision. For example, "DNA fingerprinting" technology makes it easier to link illness to specific firms. Such information may be key in health investigations of outbreaks and in food safety litigation (Buzby et al. 2001).

Improvements in food safety information provision will reduce the need for market intervention, and hence reduce the need for value estimates. Greater food safety information will provide producers with the incentives to provide the amount of food safety desired by consumers, thereby reducing the necessity for government intervention and regulation.

Conclusion

All of the major estimates (ERS, FDA, and EPA) of the value of reductions in foodborne illness measure the value of reduction in adverse health outcomes. For these estimates, analysts begin by determining how many cases of disease should be attributed to food. They then determine the outcomes associated with each foodborne disease and the probability of each outcome. The next step in the estimation procedure is to calculate the value of reductions for each type of adverse health outcome. ERS, FDA, and EPA all base their outcome values on value-of-life estimates borrowed from other studies, primarily compensating wage studies.

An advantage of the outcome-based approach to estimating risk values is that it provides analysts with a relatively expedient, formulaic method for calculating the benefits of food safety programs. With a risk or outcome mapping and a handful of outcome values, analysts can produce estimates for a wide variety of foodborne risks. However, there are two main disadvantages to this approach. First, the characteristics of both foodborne risk and of the population most vulnerable to foodborne risk are quite different from those in most empirical health-risk studies. As a result, estimates borrowed from the existing empirical studies are usually poor proxies for the value of reductions in foodborne risks. A main focus of current research into the value of foodborne risk reduction is on tailoring value estimates to reflect the characteristics of foodborne risks. Contingent valuation, real and hypothetical market, and preference calibration (Smith et al. 2001) studies are all shedding light on the value of foodborne risk reduction. The second disadvantage of the health-outcome approach is that society's value of food safety may include many benefits other than those resulting from reductions in adverse health outcomes. A strong food safety system promotes strong, stable food markets, access to foreign markets, and increased consumer confidence in government oversight. A strong food safety system helps ensure the integrity of the food system—something that may be valued more than a food's component attributes.

Better tailored health risk reduction values and value estimates that include more than health values will improve and most likely increase future estimates of the value of reduction in foodborne risks. Such estimates will provide impetus for higher food safety standards and increased regulation. They should also provide impetus for market-generated improvements in food safety. Increased awareness of the value of a strong food safety system should also increase efforts to improve the transparency of the food safety system and to correct general problems of asymmetric information in the market for food safety.

References

Belonax, J.J., Jr. 1997. *Food Marketing.* Needham Heights, MA: Simon & Schuster.

Buzby, J.C. 2001. Effects of Food-Safety Perceptions on Food Demand and Global Trade. In *Changes in Food Consumption and Global Trade,* edited by Anita Regmi. Washington, DC: U.S. Department of Agriculture, Economic Research Service, Agriculture and Trade Report, WRS-01-1, pp. 55–66.

————, and T. Roberts. 1996. ERS Updates U.S. Foodborne Disease Costs for Seven Pathogens. U.S. Department of Agriculture, Economic Research Service. *FoodReview* 19(3): 20–25.

————, R.C. Ready, and J.R. Skees. 1995. Contingent Valuation in Food Policy Analysis: A Case Study of a Pesticide-Residue Risk Reduction. *Journal of Agricultural and Applied Economics* 27(2): 613–25.

————, T. Roberts, C.-T. Jordan Lin, and J. MacDonald. 1996. *Bacterial Foodborne Disease, Medical Costs and Productivity Losses* U.S. Department of Agriculture, Economic Research Service, Agricultural Economic Report No. 741.

————, J.A. Fox, R.C. Ready, and S.R. Crutchfield. 1998. Measuring Consumer Benefits of Food Safety Risk Reductions. *Journal of Agricultural and Applied Economics* 30(1): 69–82.

————, P.D. Frenzen, and B. Rasco. 2001. *Product Liability and Microbial Foodborne Illness.* U.S. Department of Agriculture, Economic Research Service, Agricultural Economic Report No. 799.

Cohen, M.L., R.E. Fontaine, R.A. Pollard, S.D. Von Allmen, T.M. Vern, and E.J. Gangarosa. 1984. An Assessment of Patient-Related Economic Costs in an Outbreak of Salmonellosis. *New England Journal of Medicine* 229: 459–60.

Crutchfield, S., J. Buzby, T. Roberts, M. Ollinger, and C.-T.J. Lin. 1997a. *An Economic Assessment of Food Safety Regulations: The New Approach to Meat and Poultry Inspection.* U.S. Department of Agriculture, Economic Research Service, Agricultural Economic Report No. 755.

Crutchfield, S., J. Cooper, and D. Hellerstein. 1997b. *Benefits of Safer Drinking Water: The Value of Nitrate Reduction.* Department of Agriculture, Economic Research Service, Agricultural Economic Report No. 752.

Darby, M.R., and E. Karni. 1973. Free Competition and the Optimal Amount of Fraud. *Journal of Law and Economics* 16(1): 67–88.

Evans, W., and W.K. Viscusi. 1991. Estimation of State-Dependent Utility Functions Using Survey Data. *Review of Economics and Statistics* 73: 94–104.

Federal Register. 1996. Pathogen Reduction; Hazard Analysis and Critical Control Point (HACCP) Systems, Final Rule, 61,144 (July 25): 38805–989.

Fischhoff, B., S. Lichtenstein, P. Slovic, and D. Keeney. 1981. *Acceptable Risk.* New York: Cambridge University Press.

Fisher, A., L.G. Chestnut, and D.M. Violette. 1989. The Value of Reducing Risks of Death: A Note on New Empirical Evidence. *Journal of Policy Analysis and Management* 8(1): 88–100.

Foegeding, P.M., and T. Roberts, co-chairs, Council for Agricultural Science and Technology Task Force. 1994. *Foodborne Pathogens: Risks and Consequences.* Ames, IA: Council for Agricultural Science and Technology, 87 pp.

Fox, J.A. 1995. Determinants of Consumer Acceptability of Bovine Somatotropin. *Review of Agricultural Economics* 17:51–62.

Fox, J.A., J.F. Shogren, D.J. Hayes, and J.B. Kliebenstein. 1995. Experimental Auctions to Measure Willingness to Pay for Food Safety. In *Valuing Food Safety and Nutrition,* edited by J.A. Caswell. Boulder: Westview Press, 115–28.

————. 1998. CVM-X: Calibrating Contingent Values with Experimental Auction Markets. *American Journal of Agricultural Economics* 80(3): 455–65.

Gallup Poll. 1999. What Biotech Food Issue? <http://www.gallup.com/poll/releases/pr991005.asp)> (accessed August 6, 2001).

Gaskell, G., M.W. Bauer, J. Durant, and N.C. Allum. 1999. Worlds Apart? The Reception of Genetically Modified Foods in Europe and the U.S. *Science* 285(5426): 384–87.

Golan, E., F. Kuchler, and L. Mitchell (with contributions from C. Green and A. Jessup). 2000. *Economics of Food Labeling,* U.S. Department of Agriculture, Economic Research Service, Agricultural Economic Report No. 793.

Grossman, S.J. 1981. The Informational Role of Warranties and Private Disclosure About Product Quality. *Journal of Law and Economics* 24(3): 461–83.

Halbrendt, C., J. Pesek, A. Parsons, and R. Lindner. 1995. Using Conjoint Analysis to Assess Consumer's Acceptance of pST-Supplemented Pork. In *Valuing Food Safety and Nutrition,* edited by J.A. Caswell. Boulder: Westview Press, 129–53.

Hayes, D.J., J.F. Shogren, S.Y. Shin, and J.B. Kliebenstein. 1995. Valuing Food Safety in Experimental Auction Markets. *American Journal of Agricultural Economics* 77(1): 40–53.

Henson, S. 1996. Consumer Willingness to Pay for Reductions in the Risk of Food Poisoning in the UK. *Journal of Agricultural Economics* 47(3): 403–20.

Ippolito, P.M., and A.D. Mathios. 1990. The Regulation of Science-Based Claims in Advertising. *Journal of Consumer Policy* 13: 413–45.

Kuchler, F. 2001. Efficiency and Standard Setting in the Market for Processed Meats. *Consumer Interests Annual,* Volume 47 <http//consumerinterests.org/public/articles/> (accessed July 5, 2004).

————, and E. Golan. 1999. *Assigning Values to Life: Comparing Methods for Valuing Health Risks.* ERS, USDA, Agricultural Economics Report No. 784.

————, K. Ralston, L.J. Unnevehr, and R. Chandran. 1996. *Pesticide Residues: Reducing Dietary Risk.* U.S. Department of Agriculture, Economic Research Service, Agricultural Economic Report No. 728.

————, J.L. Teague, R.A. Williams, and D.W. Anderson. 1999. Health Transfers: An Application of Health-Health Analysis to Assess Food Safety Regulations. *Risk: Health, Safety, & Environment* 10(4): 315–32.

Landefeld, J.S., and E.P. Seskin. 1982. The Economic Value of Life: Linking Theory to Practice. *American Journal of Public Health* 72(6): 555–66.

Lin, J., and W. Milon. 1995. Consumer Valuation of Health Risk on Food Demand and the Implications for Regulation. In *Valuing Food Safety and Nutrition,* edited by J.A. Caswell. Boulder: Westview Press, 83–114.

Lutter, R., and J.F. Morrall III. 1994. Health-Health Analysis: A New Way to Evaluate Health and Safety Regulation. *Journal of Risk and Uncertainty* 8(1): 43–66.

Magat, W.A., W.K. Viscusi, and J. Huber. 1996. A Reference Lottery Metric for Valuing Health. *Management Science* 42: 1118–30.

Mazis, M. 1980. An Overview of Product Labeling and Health Risks. In *Product Labeling and Health Risks* (Banbury Report 6), edited by L. Morris, M. Mazis, and I. Barofsky. Cold Spring Harbor, NY: Cold Spring Harbor Laboratory Press.

Mead, P.S., L. Slutsker, V. Dietz, L.F. McCaig, J.S. Bresee, C. Shapiro, P.M. Griffin, and R.V. Tauxe. 1999. Food-Related Illness and Death in the United States. *Emerging Infectious Diseases* 5(5): 607–25. <http://www.cdc.gov/ncidod/eid/vol5no5/mead.htm> (accessed October 8, 1999).

Melton, B.E., W.E. Huffman, and J.F. Shogren. 1996a. Economic Values of Pork Attributes: Hedonic Price Analysis of Experimental Auction Data. *Review of Agricultural Economics* 18(4): 613–27.

Melton, B.E., W.E. Huffman, J.F. Shogren, and J.A. Fox. 1996b. Consumer Preferences for Fresh Food Items with Multiple Quality Attributes: Evidence from an Experimental Auction of Pork Chops. *American Journal of Agricultural Economics* 78: 916–23.

MIA (Meat Inspection Act). 1907. 21 U.S.C. 601-695 (1907), Public Law 59-242, 34 Stat. 1260, amended by Wholesome Meat Act Public Law 90-201, 81 Stat. 584 (1967), Meat Inspection (1994).

Misra, S.K, C.L. Huang, and S.L. Ott. 1991. Consumer Willingness to Pay for Pesticide-Free Fresh Produce. *Western Journal of Agricultural Economics* 16 (2): 218–27.

Moore, M., and W.K. Viscusi. 1988. The Quantity Adjusted Value of Life. *Economic Inquiry* 26(3): 369–88.

Morrall, J.F. III. 1986. A Review of the Record. *Regulation* (November/December): 25–34.

Ott, S.L. 1990. Supermarket Shoppers' Pesticide Concerns and Willingness to Purchase Certified Pesticide Residue-Free Fresh Produce. *Agribusiness* 6(6): 593–602.

Ralston, K., and C.-T.J. Lin. 2001. Safe Handling Labels for Meat and Poultry: A Case Study in Information Policy. *Consumer Interests Annual,* Volume 47 <http//consumerinterests.org/public/articles> (accessed July 5, 2004).

Research Triangle Institute. 1988. *Estimating the Value of Consumer's Loss from Foods Violating the FD&C Act.* Prepared for Dr. Richard Williams, Food & Drug Administration, FDA Contract No. 233-86-2097, September.

———. 1993. *A Sampling Aid for Implementing Risk-Based Import Inspection: Final Report.* Prepared for the Food and Drug Administration, September.

Roberts, T. 1980. Is Meat Inspection Worth the Cost? *National Food Review* 11 (Spring): 25-26.

———. 1985. Microbial Pathogens in Raw Pork, Chicken, and Beef: Benefit Estimates for Control Using Irradiation. *American Journal of Agriculture Economics* 67(5): 957–65.

———. 1989. Human Illness Costs of Foodborne Bacteria. *American Journal of Agricultural Economics* 71(2): 468–74.

———, and J.K. Frenkel. 1990. Estimating Income Losses and Other Preventable Costs Caused by Congenital Toxoplasmosis in People in the United States. *Journal of the American Veterinary Association* 196: 249–56.

———, and R. Pinner. 1990. Economic Impact of Disease Caused by *Listeria monocytogenes.* In *Foodborne Listeriosis,* edited by A.J. Miller, J. L. Smith, and G.A. Somkuti. Amsterdam: Elsevier, 137–49.

———, H. Jensen, and L.J. Unnevehr (eds.). 1995. *Tracking Foodborne Pathogens from Farm to Table: Data Needs to Evaluate Control Options.* U.S. Department of Agriculture, Economic Research Service, Miscellaneous Publication No. 1532.

———, J. Buzby, J. Lin, P. Nunnery, P. Mead, and P. Tarr. 1998. Economic Aspects of *E. coli* O157:H7: Disease Outcome Trees, Risk, Uncertainty, and Social Costs of Disease Estimates. In London School of Hygiene & Tropical Medicine Seventh Annual Public Health Forum's *New and Resurgent Infections: Prediction, Detection and Management of Tomorrow's Epidemics,* edited by B. Greenwood and K. De Cock. Chichester: John Wiley, 155–72.

Roosen, J., D.A. Hennessy, J.A. Fox, and A. Schreiber 1997. Measuring Consumers' Willingness to Pay for a Partial Banning of Pesticides on Apples. Working Paper. Department of Economics, Iowa State University.

Shin, S.Y., J.B. Kliebenstein, D.J. Hayes, and J.F. Shogren. 1992. Consumer Willingness to Pay for Safer Food Products. *Journal of Food Safety* 13: 51–9.

Shogren, J.F. 1993. Experimental Markets and Environmental Policy. *Agricultural and Resource Economics Review* 22(2): 117–29.

———, J.A. Fox, D.J. Hayes, and J.B. Kliebenstein. 1994a. Bid Sensitivity and the Structure of the Vickrey Auction. *American Journal of Agricultural Economics* 76(5): 1089–100.

———, S.Y. Shin, D.J. Hayes, and J.B. Kliebenstein. 1994b. Resolving Differences in Willingness to Pay and Willingness to Accept. *American Economic Review* 84(1): 255–70.

Shoemaker, R., J. Harwood, K. Day-Rubenstein, T. Dunahay, P. Heisey, L. Hoffman, C. Klotz-Ingram, W. Lin, L. Mitchell, W. McBride, and J. Fernandez-Cornejo. 2001. *Economic Issues in Agricultural Biotechnology.* U.S. Department of Agriculture, Economic Research Service, Agricultural Economic Report, No. 764.

Smith, V.K., G. Van Houtven, and S.K. Pattanayak. 2001. Benefit Transfer via Preference Calibration: 'Prudential Algebra' for Policy. Unpublished draft.

Snowden, J., J.C. Buzby, and T. Roberts. Forthcoming. Epidemiology, Cost, and Risk of Foodborne Disease. In *Foodborne Diseases,* edited by D. Cliver and Riemann. San Diego: Academic Press, 31–51.

Tolley, G., D. Kenkel, and R. Fabian (eds.). 1994. *Valuing Health for Policy.* Chicago: University of Chicago Press.

U.S. EPA (Environmental Protection Agency). 1999a. *Assessing Health Risks from Pesticides.* <http://www.epa.gov/pesticides/citizens/riskassess.htm> (accessed June 5, 2001).

———. 1999b. Appendix H: Valuation of Human Health and Welfare Effects of Criteria Pollutants (from The Benefits and Costs of the Clean Air Act, 1990 to 2010, EPA Report to Congress). <http://www.epa.gov/air/sect812/1990-2010/ch_aph.pdf> (accessed June 5, 2001).

———. 2000a. *Guidelines for Preparing Economic Analyses.* http://www.epa.gov/economics/ (accessed August 3, 2001).

———. 2000b. Environmental Assessment of Proposed Effluent Limitations, Guidelines for the Iron and Steel Industry. <http://www.epa.gov/waterscience/ironsteel/pdf/Iron-Steel-EA.pdf> (accessed May 17, 2001).

———. 2000c. An SAB Report on EPA's White Paper Valuing the Benefits of Fatal Cancer Risk Reduction. <http://www.epa.gov/sab/eeacf013.pdf> (accessed June 6, 2001).

———. 2001. *The Cost of Illness Handbook.* http://www.epa.gov/oppt/coi/ (accessed June 2001).

USDA ERS (Economic Research Service). 2000. ERS Estimates Foodborne Disease Costs at $6.9 Billion per Year. <http://www.ers.usda.gov/Emphases/SafeFood/features.htm#start> (accessed June 4, 2001).

U.S. FDA (Food and Drug Administration). 1993. Preliminary Regulatory Impact Analysis of the Proposed Regulations to Establish Procedures for the Safe Processing and Importing of Fish and Fishery Products. <http://www.cfsan.fda.gov/~djz/cfudpria.txt> (accessed June 4, 2001).

USDA FSIS (Food Safety and Inspection Service). 1993. Mandatory Safe Handling Statements on Labeling of Raw Meat and Poultry Products. Final Rule. *Federal Register* 58(195, October 12): 52856–873.

———. 1994. Mandatory Safe Handling Statements on Labeling of Raw Meat and Poultry Products. Final Rule. *Federal Register* 59(March 28): 14528–540.

van Ravenswaay, E.O., and J.P. Hoehn. 1991. Consumer Willingness to Pay for Reducing Pesticide Residues in Food: Results of a Nationwide Survey. Department of Agricultural Economics, Michigan State University, East Lansing, MI.

Viscusi, W.K. 1993. The Value of Risks to Life and Health. *Journal of Economic Literature* 31 (4): 1912–46.

———, W.A. Magat, and J. Huber. 1987. An Investigation of the Rationality of Consumer Valuations of Multiple Health Risks. *Rand Journal of Economics* 18(Winter): 465–79.

Weaver, R.D., D.J. Evans, and A.E. Luloff. 1992. Pesticide Use in Tomato Production: Consumer Concerns and Willingness-to-Pay. *Agribusiness* 8(2):131–42.

PART III

Tools for Risk-Based Assessment of Food Safety Policy Priorities

8

New Developments in Chemical and Microbial Risk Assessment*

ROBERT BUCHANAN AND BART SUHRE

The foundation for risk-based management of food safety is risk assessment. Without a sound assessment of the risks of foodborne illnesses—from chemicals, pathogens, or other biological agents—neither government nor industry can develop better approaches to preventing these potentially adverse health effects. This chapter examines the state of the art of chemical and microbial risk assessment, describing how two major food safety regulatory agencies, the U.S. Environmental Protection Agency (EPA) and the Food and Drug Administration (FDA), assess these risks.

The basic framework that most regulatory risk assessment follows was presented by the National Academy of Sciences in its 1983 report, *Risk Assessment in the Federal Government* (NAS 1983). The Council recommended that, in regulatory settings, risk assessment, a scientific evaluation of the factual nature of health or environmental risks posed by exposure to toxic substances, be separated from risk management, the evaluation of the information provided by risk assessment for the purpose of guiding risk management decisions. This separation was intended to protect the objectivity of the scientific assessment. Subsequent experience has shown that a greater level of communication between risk assessors and risk managers is needed to ensure that information generated by the risk assessment is organized so as to inform management decisions. For example, it is useful for the end-points of the risk assessments to be readily translatable to outcomes that are relevant to public health policy

*Senior authorship is not assigned. This chapter was adapted by Sandra A. Hoffmann from a presentation on chemical risk assessment by Bart Suhre and a presentation on microbial risk assessment by Robert Buchanan, both given at the RFF conference "Setting Food Safety Priorities: Toward a Risk-Based System," May 2001, Washington, DC.

goals. But the basic risk assessment framework outlined by the Council still guides federal agencies' regulatory assessment of chemical hazards in food and in the environment and has become the basis for international guidance on microbial risk assessment, as discussed in the following sections.

The NAS risk assessment framework envisioned a process with four distinct steps: hazard identification, dose–response assessment, exposure assessment, and risk characterization (Figure 8.1). Hazard identification involves collection of data and other evidence on the causal link between a particular chemical and a particular health or toxicological effect. Dose–response assessment determines the relationship between the level of exposure and the likelihood of the health effect. More recently the term "hazard characterization" has been replacing dose–response assessment, reflecting the increased consideration of multiple biological end-points and the concomitant consideration of toxicological effect severity. Exposure assessment involves determination of the extent of human exposure to the chemical, from the perspective of conditions with or without regulatory controls. Risk characterization describes the nature and magnitude of the human health or toxicological risk, drawing on evidence gathered in the three previous steps of the risk assessment. This usually involves characterization of the uncertainty inherent in the information assembled on the extent of the health risk (NAS 1983).

Chemical risk assessment has played an integral role in federal regulation of new food additives and pesticide residues in foods. In contrast, application of microbial risk assessment in support of federal regulatory decision making is in its infancy. Lessons learned from chemical risk assessment are being applied in developing the new science of microbial risk assessment.

New Directions in Chemical Risk Assessment

EPA's Office of Pesticide Programs regulates pesticide residues in or on food under the authority of the Federal Insecticide, Fungicide, and Rodenticide Act (FIFRA); the Federal Food, Drug, and Cosmetic Act (FDCA); and the amendment to these acts, the Food Quality Protection Act (FQPA).

FIFRA authorizes EPA to register or license pesticides. Under the Act, pesticide registrants must submit residue chemistry, toxicological, and environmental data for agency review. The Act also requires that the registration of a pesticide not cause "unreasonable adverse effects on people or the environment." EPA thus has a clear statutory mandate to conduct risk assessment before licensing a pesticide.

FDCA authorizes EPA to establish tolerances for pesticide residues in food. A tolerance is the amount of a pesticide legally allowed on a raw agricultural commodity. The Act also authorizes FDA and the Department of Agriculture (USDA) to monitor raw agricultural commodities for pesticide residues. Data

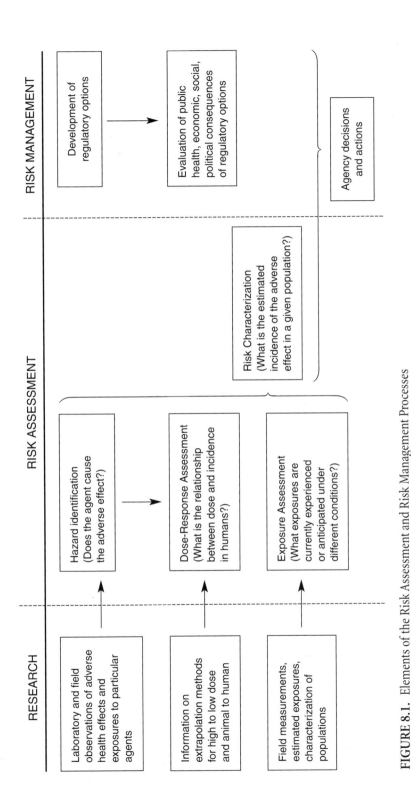

FIGURE 8.1. Elements of the Risk Assessment and Risk Management Processes

Source: NAS (1983).

collected through these surveillance efforts are used routinely by EPA to assess dietary risk from pesticides.

The 1996 Food Quality Protection Act (FQPA), which amended both FIFRA and FDCA, radically changed the way EPA's Office of Pesticide Programs (OPP) conducts risk assessments. Before FQPA was enacted, OPP's risk assessment paradigm was to conduct pesticide risk assessments on single-exposure pathways— dietary, agricultural worker, residential environment—independently, with the regulatory decision generally based on the dominant pathway and route of exposure. Among other considerations, FQPA required EPA to consider aggregate and cumulative risks to pesticides from multiple pathways and routes of exposure, endocrine effects, and the potential to enhance sensitivity of infants and children to pesticides. The Act mandated that these requirements be met before a pesticide tolerance was established on a raw agricultural commodity. In essence, EPA must consider the effects of exposure from pesticide applications in residential environments as well as in agricultural fields before setting a tolerance on a food. The Act also requires EPA to consider the cumulative health effects of multiple pesticides over multiple exposure pathways if they share a common toxicological mode of action. This introduces the very difficult task of evaluating the temporal and spatial parameters that must be considered to model co-occurrence of pesticide exposure from multiple chemicals, pathways, and routes of exposure and their impact on human health. Obviously, this risk assessment paradigm is quite different from the one that prevailed before passage of the Food Quality Protection Act. It is exemplified in changes to EPA's risk assessment research agenda (Table 8.1).

TABLE 8.1. New Directions for EPA Risk Assessment Research

Old Approach	New Approach
Single pollutant/single pathway	Aggregate and cumulative risks
Risk to the average individual	Risk to susceptible populations 　• High-end exposures　　• Genetic differences 　• Age-related differences　• Life style
Cancer versus non-cancer	Harmonized risk assessments
Descriptive, high-dose studies	Mechanistic, low-dose studies 　• Biologically based models
Focus on individual components of risk assessment	Focus on the linkages between elements 　• Predictive biomarkers　• Pharmacokinetic models
Research to inform risk assessment/ risk management decisions	Research to assess the public health impact of risk assessment/risk management decisions
Separate approaches to assessing health and ecologic risks	More holistic, integrated approach that incorporates health-ecologic dynamic

EPA's Tiered Approach to Exposure Assessment

EPA's Office of Pesticide Program defines risk as a function of a chemical's toxicity and exposure to the chemical. The agency takes a tiered approach to performing exposure and risk assessments, with the level of refinement dictated by regulatory need (Figure 8.2). For a dietary risk, for example, an initial screening assessment might start with assumptions that pesticide residues are present at tolerance levels on all crops for which the pesticide is registered and that the entire production of these crops were treated with the pesticide. Such an assessment can provide a screening level overview of whether a particular chemical poses a potential health risk. Typical refinements to a screening level assessment involve using residue monitoring data collected by USDA and FDA to estimate food residues and to consider the percentage of the crop that is usually treated, based on USDA data, to estimate exposure and risk. An additional refinement would be to use probabilistic rather than deterministic or point estimate techniques to estimate dietary residues on consumed food items and to use recently developed models to aggregate and cumulate exposure and risk to pesticides from multiple routes, including oral, dermal, and inhalation, and pathways—dietary, residential, drinking water—of exposure.

EPA's tolerance-setting process and related risk assessments are based primarily on toxicity and residue chemistry data provided by registrants in support of pesticide registrations. Toxicity data include dosing of laboratory animals by multiple routes (dermal, inhalation, oral) and durations—acute, subchronic, and chronic—and cover a full range of effects, including systemic toxicity, neu-

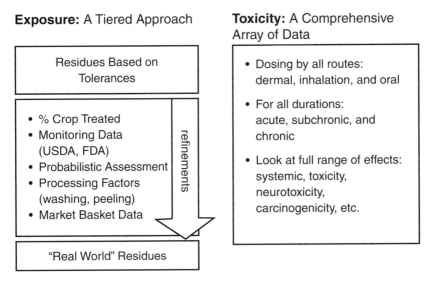

FIGURE 8.2. EPA Risk Assessment. Risk = f (exposure, toxicity)

rotoxicity, carcinogenicity, and so forth. If necessary, EPA can require pesticide registrants to submit very specific data to refine its risk assessments further.

This progressive series of refinements tailors the risk assessment to the needs of a particular regulatory decision, but it can also reduce the usefulness of risk assessments for setting regulatory priorities, as conducting a highly refined exposure assessment for one chemical and a simple screening-level assessment for another makes it difficult to compare the risk of two chemicals equitably. The level of refinement of the exposure assessment needs to be identical if meaningful systemwide comparisons are to be made.

Since the passage of the Food Quality Protection Act, EPA has developed a series of guidance documents focused on scientific issues related to probabilistic, aggregate, and cumulative risk assessments; common mechanisms of toxicity; and FQPA 10-fold safety factor to address concerns regarding exposure of infants and children to pesticides. These documents can be accessed on the EPA Web page, http://www.epa.gov/oppfead1/trac/science/.

The Emerging Science of Microbial Risk Assessment

Another arena for application of new developments in the life sciences is the emerging science of microbial risk assessment. Microbial risk assessment has become an important part of food safety regulation in recent years. This section describes how FDA approaches microbial risk assessment and assesses the usefulness of the information generated.

The challenge in conducting microbial risk assessment is twofold. Assessment must determine the frequency and extent to which consumers are exposed to pathogenic microorganisms, and it must convert those figures into a meaningful measure of public health impact.

Microbial risk assessment has been driven by the Sanitary and Phytosanitary Agreement and the accompanying Technical Barriers to Trade Agreement of the World Trade Organization. When food safety issues are the basis for a trade dispute, a country must be prepared to provide risk assessments to justify the scientific basis for its domestic food safety regulation. These agreements spurred development of microbial risk assessment.

In 1995 the World Health Organization (WHO) and the Food and Agriculture Organization (FAO) concluded that risk assessment techniques for microbial food safety issues were not likely to be available in the near term (WHO/FAO 1995). Their assessment proved wrong. Microbial risk assessment has progressed to the point where U.S. food safety regulatory agencies are using risk assessments for decision making. Five major regulatory risk assessments have been completed, or will be completed, in the United States alone in the next few years. These include assessments of *Salmonella enteritidis* in eggs and egg products (FSIS 1998), *Listeria monocytogenes* in ready-to-eat foods

(CFSAN/FSIS 2001), V*ibrio haemolyticus* in oysters (CFSAN 2001), *Escherichia coli* 0157 in ground beef (FSIS 2001), and fluoroquinolone resistance in *Campylobacter* (CVM 2001). Microbial risk assessment has also come into wider use in the international arena. FAO and WHO have conducted risk assessments of *Salmonella* in eggs and egg products, *Salmonella* spp. in broilers, *Listeria monocytogenes* in ready-to-eat foods, *Vibrio* spp. in molluscan shellfish, and *Campylobacter* in broilers (www.who.int/fsf/micro/index.htm).

Similarities and Differences Between Microbial and Chemical Risk Assessments

Microbial risk assessment methods have had the advantage of being able to draw on the many years of experience with chemical risk assessment. Like chemical risk assessment, microbial assessment involves identifying the hazard, assessing the exposure, characterizing the hazard, and characterizing the risk. This is essentially the framework that was developed at the behest of the National Academy of Sciences 30 years ago to assess chemical risks to public health (NAS 1983). Scientists and regulators working on food safety often refer to the microbial risk assessment framework as the *Codex Alimentarius* framework, but in reality, *Codex* adopted the earlier National Academy of Sciences framework developed for chemical risk assessment.

Some important differences exist between chemical and microbial risk assessments, however. Some of these differences are related to the regulatory context in which risk assessment is applied. First, unlike regulation of chemicals, food safety regulation focuses primarily on postmarket activities, not premarket approval. Second, because microbial risk assessment is very new, the evaluation of potential risk management decisions is only now being generally included in the assessments. Third, assumptions about chemical risk assessments have become so ingrained as to lead to concerns that chemical risk assessments are no longer transparent. Scientists and regulators developing microbial risk assessment at FDA, USDA, and elsewhere have made a conscious effort to try to make their risk assessments as transparent as possible.

Scientific differences also exist between chemical and microbial risk assessments. Chemical risk assessment must focus on identifying hazards, because effects often have long latency periods or have been incompletely established, particularly at low dose levels. In contrast, microbiological contamination usually creates an acute hazard, making identification much simpler. Microbial agents usually present a well-characterized syndrome, and a substantial body of relevant clinical and epidemiological information is often available. Well-defined clinical case studies that look at a variety of factors relevant to microbial risk assessment can also be drawn on. These differences mean that the hazard identification phase of microbial risk assessment is usually minimal compared with that in chemical risk assessments.

Exposure to pathogenic microorganisms also differs. The levels of pathogens can change dramatically in a short time because the organism can either grow or die. In just 6 hours at room temperature, for example, one *Vibrio* bacterium can produce billions of progeny. Conversely, a few seconds of cooking can destroy billions of *Vibrio* bacteria. The rapidity with which exposures can change and their sensitivity to environmental conditions confound exposure estimates.

Microbial risk assessors must also consider that they are dealing with a complex, three-part biological system. Risk is the result of the interaction among three highly variable biological systems: a pathogen, a host, and a food. In dealing with three major sources of variability, the situation can become very complicated very quickly.

Unlike chemical hazards, microbial hazards do not typically involve the build-up of a dose within the body; repeated exposure may actually reduce risk by increasing immunity. Disease caused by microorganisms is almost always associated with a single exposure. Even chronic syndromes associated with microbial infections, such as reactive arthritis or hemolytic uremic syndrome, are *sequelae* to acute episodes of illness caused by single exposures.

Microbial risk assessors assume that a single viable cell has a definable probability of producing an infection, a concept referred to as independence. As a result, they typically use nonthreshold models that can be extrapolated linearly or log linearly at low doses to estimate the probability of disease from infectious agents. These assumptions restrict dose–response models, with three models most often used: Beta-Poisson model, exponential model, and Weibull-Gamma model. The three models vary in terms of their complexity. The exponential model is a single-parameter model that is useful for looking at severe consequences of infections. It is fairly steep in shape. The Beta-Poisson model is a two-parameter model that is useful for studying infection. The three-parameter Weibull-Gamma model is the most flexible model, but it yields less certain results because it involves estimation of a greater number of parameters.

Types of Microbial Risk Assessment

Conducting risk assessment involves bringing increased sophistication to procedures food safety agencies have followed for years. FDA has addressed concerns of microbial risk assessment ever since the agency was founded. Over the years, however, it has shifted from relying solely on expert judgment to conducting safety assessments to using quantitative microbial risk assessment. Risk assessors have increased both the level of sophistication and the level of formality they bring to a problem. The hope is that they have increased the level of accuracy and transparency with which assessment of the risks of foodborne illness is addressed.

Four types of microbial risk assessments are currently in use. The first is risk ranking, a priority-setting activity in which investigators look at multiple foods for a single agent or multiple agents for a single food. An example of a recent risk-ranking exercise is the risk assessment of *Listeria monocytogenes,* described in the next section.

The second type of assessment is pathogen–pathway analysis, which involves looking at a single product–pathogen pair, following the movement of food through the production/consumption chain, seeing where the pathogenic organisms enter and exit, and where their populations rise and fall. This type of analysis is typically used to identify possible points for effective interventions or risk-control strategies.

The third type of assessment is risk–risk analysis, a risk-optimization process in which reducing one health risk increases the risk of another health outcome. In some of its applications, risk–risk analysis has focused on risks induced by increased costs associated with regulation (Lutter 1994). Of more immediate interest to food safety are analyses that focus on direct trade-offs across spin-off risks associated with efforts to target a hazard. For example, comparative risk analysis has recently been used to inform regulations governing control of *Cryptosporidium* and disinfection byproducts (U.S. EPA 1998). This type of analysis has not been conducted as part of a microbial food safety risk assessment, but could be used in assessments such as comparing the risk of chemical contaminants from the disinfection of raw foods versus the control of infectious diseases.

The fourth type of microbial risk assessments are often termed geographical risk assessments because they are generally employed to evaluate the risk of the introduction of a new infectious agent into a geographical region. This type of risk assessment has been used extensively in the past several years to assess the potential health consequences of introducing bovine spongiform encephalopathy (BSE) into a region.

Assessing the Risk of Listeriosis. The FDA undertook the *Listeria* risk assessment to compare the relative risk of serious illness and death associated with consumption of a variety of ready-to-eat foods (HHS/USDA 2001). The purpose of the assessment was to guide policy makers in evaluating the effectiveness of agency programs and regulatory measures aimed at reducing risk from *Listeria monocytogenes.*

Listeriosis is a relatively rare but severe life-threatening set of infections.[1] The disease affects four to eight people per million in the United States. Twenty percent of people hospitalized with the disease die (HHS/USDA 2001). Between

---

[1]A related disease, listerial gastroenteritis, is a mild, flulike illness. That disease is not modeled in the *Listeria* risk assessment, because little is known about it.

1988 and 1995 significant progress was made in reducing the risks associated with this organism. Since that time, however, no further reduction in incidence of the disease has been realized. *Listeria monocytogenes* is found in a wide range of ready-to-eat foods. Hundreds of foods are at least occasionally contaminated with this organism (U.S. FDA/USDA 2001).

The risk assessment looked at 20 groups of ready-to-eat foods. It then tried to determine consumers' exposure, develop a dose–response model based on annual disease statistics, and calculate the relative risk both per serving and per year for each of the 20 food groups. In effect, the assessment assumed that these 20 groups of food are responsible for foodborne listeriosis and then compared their relative importance.

In conducting the *Listeria* risk assessment, FDA/FSIS followed the *Codex* framework (WHO/FAO 1995). It started off by assessing exposure, determining the frequency of contamination for different foods and the number of *Listeria* found in the food when it was contaminated. FDA/FSIS relied primarily on retail data, allowing for the potential of growth between purchase and consumption. It then looked at the frequency of consumption and the amount of food consumed. Based on these figures, it estimated the number of *Listeria monocytogenes* ingested by the U.S. population for each of the food groups (Figure 8.3).

The next step was characterizing the hazard. FDA/FSIS started with data on dose–response relationships in mice to estimate the shape of the dose–response curve. Strains of *Listeria* differ in their virulence or ability to cause illness. FDA/FSIS took this variation into account and used a conversion factor to convert the mice data into data relevant for humans. These data were then anchored to actual disease statistics. This calibration ensured that the exposure and hazard characterization results were consistent with the actual number of cases per year.

FDA/FSIS came up with a series of dose–response curves for three subpopulations: the prenatal population, consisting of fetuses and babies up to 30 days old; the elderly, consisting of people 60 years old and older; and an intermediate age group consisting of people between 31 and 59 years of age. For each group it generated a dose–response curve with uncertainty limits. Figure 8.4 represents the dose–response curve for the neonatal group.

The last stage of the risk assessment was a risk characterization, which combined the exposure assessment and the dose–response models to estimate relative risk. This risk characterization was presented in three different formats. First, FDA/FSIS predicted the frequency of listeriosis per 100 million servings, an arbitrary number of servings (Figure 8.5). Second, it ranked the relative risk per serving for the 20 different food groups for three subpopulations (Table 8.2). Third, it estimated the relative annual risk ranking for the three subpopulations (Table 8.3). This ranking corrects for the total number of servings consumed in the United States per year. The per-serving risk ranking is the risk faced by an individual consumer; the annual risk ranking is the risk the nation faces.

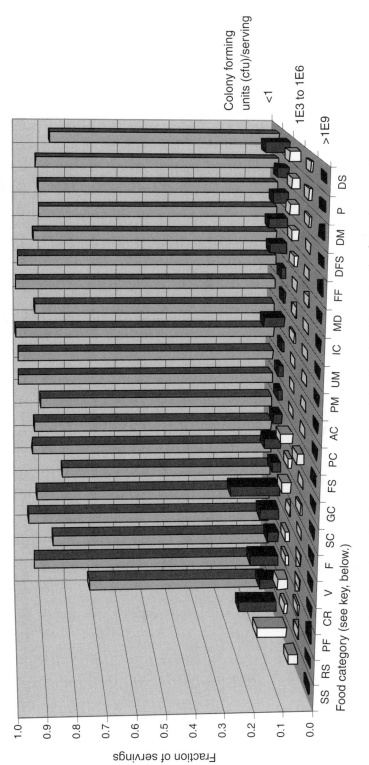

FIGURE 8.3. Predicted Number of Servings of Various Foods Consumed that Contain Different Levels of *Listeria monocytogenes*

Key: AC = aged cheese; CR = cooked ready-to-eat crustaceans; DFS = dry and semidry fermented sausages; DM = deli meat; DS = deli salads; F = fruits; FF = frankfurters; FS = fresh soft cheese; GC = goat, sheep, and feta cheese; IC = ice cream and frozen dairy products; MD = miscellaneous dairy products; P = paté and meat spreads; PC = heat-treated natural and processed cheese; PF = preserved fish; PM = fluid milk, pasteurized; RS = raw seafood; SC = soft, mold-ripened, and blue-veined cheese; SS = smoked seafood; UM = fluid milk, unpasteurized; V = vegetables.

Source: (WHO/FAO 1995).

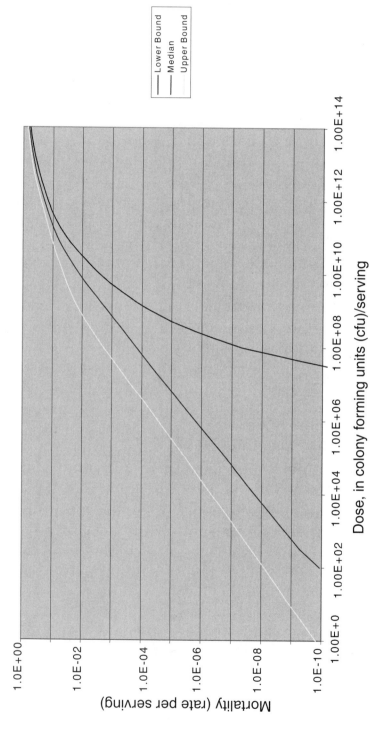

FIGURE 8.4. *Listeria monocytogenes* Dose–Response Relationship for Neonates with Estimated Uncertainty

Source: (WHO/FDA 1995).

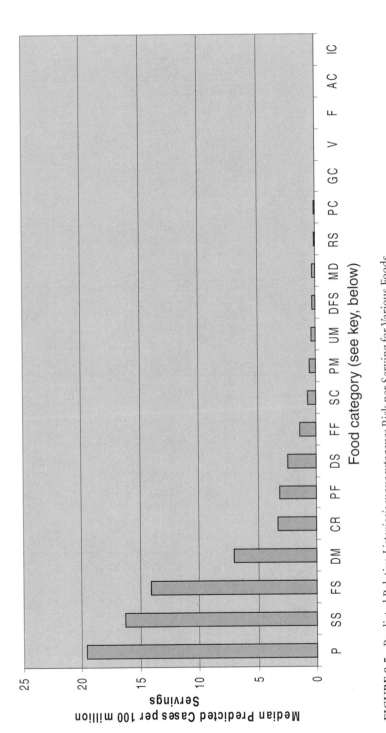

FIGURE 8.5. Predicted Relative *Listeriosis monocytogenes* Risk per Serving for Various Foods

Key: AC = aged cheese; CR = cooked ready-to-eat crustaceans; DFS = dry and semidry fermented sausages; DM = deli meat; DS = deli salads; F = fruits; FF = frankfurters; FS = fresh soft cheese; GC = goat, sheep, and feta cheese; IC = ice cream and frozen dairy products; MD = miscellaneous dairy products; P = paté and meat spreads; PC = heat-treated natural and processed cheese; PF = preserved fish; PM = fluid milk, pasteurized; RS = raw seafood; SC = soft, mold-ripened, and blue-veined cheese; SS = smoked seafood; UM = fluid milk, unpasteurized; V = vegetables.

Source: (WHO/FDA 1995).

TABLE 8.2. Listeriosis Relative Risk Ranking Per Serving by Food Category for Various Subpopulations

	Subpopulation		
Food Categories	Intermediate Age	Elderly	Perinatal
Seafood			
Smoked seafood	3	3	3
Raw seafood	14	14	14
Preserved fish	7	7	6
Cooked ready-to-eat crustaceans	6	5	5
Produce			
Vegetables	17	17	17
Fruits	18	18	18
Dairy			
Soft mold-ripened & blue-veined cheese	9	9	9
Goat, sheep, and feta cheese	16	16	16
Fresh soft cheese (e.g., queso fresco)	2	1	1
Heat-treated natural/process cheese	15	15	15
Aged cheese	19	19	19
Fluid milk, pasteurized	10	10	10
Fluid milk, unpasteurized	11	11	11
Ice cream and frozen dairy products	20	20	20
Miscellaneous dairy products	12	13	13
Meats			
Frankfurters			
All frankfurters	8	8	7
Only reheated frankfurters	[15]	[15]	[15]
Only non-reheated frankfurters	[1]	[2]	[2]
Dry/semidry fermented sausages	13	12	12
Deli meats	4	4	4
Pâté and meat spreads	1	2	2
Combination foods			
Deli salads	5	6	8

Source: (WHO/FDA 1995).

FDA/FSIS also endeavored to provide a detailed evaluation of the uncertainty associated with the *Listeria* risk assessment. The simulation employed in the risk assessment was based on 30,000 iterations of the model. However, because contracting listeriosis is a "rare event," the relative rankings among the food categories changed to some degree when the simulation was conducted again. The risk assessment used this approach to characterize uncertainty by running a simulation with its 30,000 iterations, determining the risk ranking for that simulation, and then repeating that process 4,000 times. These results

TABLE 8.3. Listeriosis Relative Risk Ranking Per Annum by Food Categories for
Various Subpopulations

	Subpopulation		
Food Categories	Intermediate Age	Elderly	Perinatal
Seafood			
Smoked seafood	6	6	7
Raw seafood	17	20	17
Preserved fish	13	13	13
Cooked ready-to-eat crustaceans	9	8	9
Produce			
Vegetables	11	9	11
Fruits	16	14	14
Dairy			
Soft mold-ripened and blue-veined cheese	14	15	15
Goat, sheep, and feta cheese	18	17	18
Fresh soft cheese (e.g., queso fresco)	7	11	6
Heat-treated natural cheese and processed cheese	10	10	10
Aged cheese	19	18	19
Fluid milk, pasteurized	3	2	2
Fluid milk, unpasteurized	15	16	16
Ice cream and frozen dairy products	20	19	20
Miscellaneous dairy products	5	4	5
Meats			
Frankfurters	4	5	4
Dry/semidry fermented sausages	12	12	12
Deli meats	1	1	1
Pâté and meat spreads	8	7	8
Combination foods			
Deli salads	2	3	3

Source: (WHO/FDA 1995).

allowed the uncertainty of the relative risk of each food category to be estimated. An example of the uncertainty analysis is provided in Figure 8.6.

The *Listeria* risk assessment provides an example of the kind of tool available for focusing regulatory effort. By identifying foods associated with increased risk, it helps decision makers know where to focus.

Conclusions

Chemical risk assessments have guided public health decisions in the United
States for at least 30 years. Yet with the development of better monitoring meth-

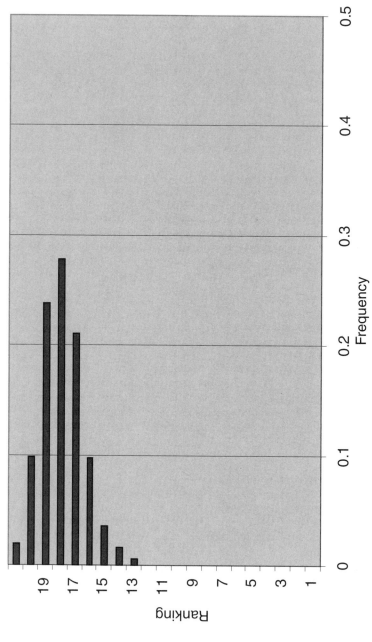

FIGURE 8.6. Uncertainty Analysis of the Predicted Relative Risk Ranking of Listeriosis Cases Caused by *L. monocytogenes* per Serving Associated with Vegetables

Source: (WHO/FDA 1995).

ods and rapid developments in the fields of toxicology, physiology, and genetics, chemical risk assessment remains a rapidly developing field. New statutory requirements that focus on the impact of cumulative exposure to environmental hazards along multiple exposure pathways and that require attention to subpopulation risks have radically changed the type of chemical risk assessment required for agency decision making. Despite more than a decade and a half of effort at EPA to use risk assessment and analysis to guide agency priority setting, challenges still remain in conducting risk assessments in a way that is useful for this process. Tensions remain between the goals of developing risk assessments that are tailored to inform individual regulatory decisions and use of those assessments to guide agency priority setting.

Microbial risk assessment is a new and rapidly emerging field. Significant progress has been made in the seven years since the first WHO/FAO consultation on microbial risk assessment. The need for microbial risk assessment, both to better guide domestic food safety policy and to satisfy demands of the Sanitary and Phytosanitary Agreement, has created great impetus for continued development in this field. Although microbial risk assessment starts from the same basic framework as chemical risk assessment, the nature of the hazard dictates that it differs in significant ways from the more established practices of chemical risk assessment.

Both chemical and microbial risk assessments are now expected to carry an increasingly heavy load in public health administration both domestically and in international forums. Although in the past assessments were relied on primarily to inform decisions about relatively narrowly focused interventions, they are increasingly being used to help inform program-wide priority setting. In the past chemical risk assessments focused on single chemicals and single pathways of exposure. Increasingly both chemical and microbial risk assessments are being asked to consider the "ecology" of exposure and possible interactions with other causal agents along a network of exposure routes.

Assessments that in the past were relied on solely to protect domestic public health are now being relied on to satisfy trading partners of the safety of U.S. products in international trade. This creates a heightened need for transparency in the way risks are assessed.

Increased knowledge about the presence of hazards, both chemical and biological, and advances in biological science present a constant challenge, as well as new opportunities. The individuals responsible for managing food safety risks lack much-needed information about exposure pathways, mechanisms that transport or transform hazardous agents, and about how these agents affect different parts of the U.S. population. All of these factors result in a science that is both changing rapidly and improving, yet characterized by high levels of uncertainty and incomplete information. Such an environment will only increase the need for risk assessment approaches that can systematically consider complex issue and estimate uncertainty.

References

CFSAN (Center for Food Safety and Applied Nutrition), U.S. Food and Drug Administration. 2001. Draft Risk Assessment on the Public Health Impact of *Vibrio parahaemolyticus* in Raw Molluscan Shellfish. January. http://vm.cfsan.fda.gov/~dms/vprisk.html.

CVM (Center for Veterinary Medicine), U.S. Food and Drug Administration. 2000 (updated Jan. 5, 2001). Risk Assessment on the Human Health Impact of Fluoroquinolone Resistant Campylobacter Associated with the Consumption of Chicken. (accessed October 18, 2003). http://www.fda.gov/cvm/antimicrobial/Risk_asses.htm

Federal Insecticide, Fungicide, and Rodenticide Act as amended by the Food Quality Protection Act of 1996. 7 U.S.Code, Secs. 136 *et seq.*

Federal Food, Drug, and Cosmetic Act. 21 U.S. Code Chap. 9.

Food and Agriculture Organization Expert Consultation/World Health Organization (FAO/WHO). 1995. *Application of Risk Analysis to Food Standards Issues.* Report of the Joint FAO/WHO Expert Consultation.

Lutter, R., and J.F. Morrall. 1994. Health–Health Analysis: A New Way to Evaluate Health and Safety Regulation. *Journal of Risk and Uncertainty* 8(1): 43–66.

NAS (National Academy of Sciences). Committee on Institutional Means for Assessment of Risks to Public Health. 1983. *Risk Assessment in the Federal Government: Managing the Process.* Washington, DC: National Academy Press.

SPS Agreement. 1999. Agreement on the Application of Sanitary and Phytosanitary Measures, April 15, 1994, Marrakesh Agreement Establishing the World Trade Organization, Annex 1A, World Trade Organization, The Legal Texts: The Results of the Uruguay Round of the Multilateral Trade Negotiations, 59–72.

TBT Agreement. 1999. Agreement on Technical Barriers to Trade, April 15, 1994, Marrakesh Agreement Establishing the World Trade Organization, Annex 1A, World Trade Organization, The Legal Texts: The Results of the Uruguay Round of the Multilateral Trade Negotiations, 59–72.

U.S. Department of Agriculture, Food Safety Inspection Service (FSIS). 1998. *Salmonella enteritidis* Risk Assessment: Shell Eggs and Egg Products. http://www.fsis.usda.gov/OPHS/risk/ (accessed April 29, 2004).

———. 2001. Draft Risk Assessment of the Public Health Impact of *Escherichia coli* O157: H7 in Ground Beef. www.fsis.usda.gov/OPPDE/rdad/FRPubs/00 023N/00-023NReport.pdf (accessed December 5, 2002).

U.S. Environmental Protection Agency. 1998. National Primary Drinking Water Regulations: Interim Enhanced Surface Water Treatment. *Federal Register.* 63(241): 69478–521.

U.S. Food and Drug Administration, Center for Food Safety and Applied Nutrition. (CFSAN). 2001. Draft Risk Assessment on the Public Health Impact of *Vibrio* parahaemolyticus in Raw Molluscan Shellfish. http://www.cfsan.fda.gov/~dms/vprisk.html (accessed December 5, 2002).

U.S. Food and Drug Administration, Center for Veterinary Medicine (CVM). 2000. Risk Assessment on the Human Health Impact of Flouroquinolone Resistant *Campylobacter* Associated with Consumption of Chicken. www.fda.gov/cvm/antimicrobial/Risk_asses.htm (accessed December 5, 2002).

U.S. HHS/USDA (Department of Health and Human Services, Food and Drug Administration, Center for Food Safety and Applied Nutrition and U.S. Department of Agriculture, Food Safety Inspection Service). 2001. Draft Assessment of the Relative Risk to Public Health from Foodborne *Listeria monocytogenes* Among Selected Categories of Ready-to-Eat Foods. www.foodsafety.gov/~dms/lmrisk1.html (accessed December 5, 2002).

9

Best Things First:
Rethinking Priority Setting
for Food Safety Policy

PETER NELSON AND ALAN J. KRUPNICK

Food safety professionals and policy makers widely agree that better analytical methods are needed to help allocate government resources to those investments that have the greatest impact on making our food system safer. We examine the issue of what kind of priority-setting system is needed for the government to improve its performance. Our discussion considers general issues and is not specific to food safety. Indeed, because of our experience in environmental regulation and the workings of EPA, it is the experience of setting priorities at EPA and other environmental agencies that drives this chapter. Thus this chapter first briefly discusses the traditional priority-setting, problem-based paradigm of comparative risk assessment and its use by EPA and various state governments, closing with a critique. It then describes a solution-based approach to priority setting and presents an outline of what such a process might look like. Finally, the discussion is brought back to food safety to examine the implications of the chapter for priority setting by the government in this area.

Although risk-based prioritizing emerged primarily in an environmental context, in many respects the process may be even better suited for prioritizing food safety interventions. As Hoffmann points out in the introductory chapter, the set of risks associated with the food safety issue is much narrower and more homogeneous than the range of risks falling under the jurisdiction of EPA. The issues confronting food safety agencies are for the most part limited to preventing illnesses among people currently eating food. Therefore many of the issues that have complicated environmental priority setting, such as comparing highly disparate risks and resolving how to treat future generations, do not arise in the food safety setting.

The Traditional Priority-Setting Paradigm

Scarcity of resources provides the justification for undertaking a priority-setting exercise. If resources were unlimited, it would be possible to achieve every environmental or food safety goal without making trade-offs. Given scarce resources, however, some form of priority setting is unavoidable. A basic assumption behind risk-ranking exercises is that it is better to set priorities explicitly and systematically, taking into account as much information as possible, rather than implicitly and in an ad hoc manner.

The traditional approach for setting environmental priorities begins with a comparative risk assessment, which provides policy makers with information on the relative magnitudes of different risks. The archetype is EPA's *Unfinished Business* (U.S. EPA 1987), which ranked 31 environmental threats in four categories and attempted to organize and prioritize risks through involvement of EPA staff, as well as to educate the public about the relative severity of different risks. In the intervening years, more than 50 studies have attempted to validate and extend this methodology (Morgenstern 1998). In addition, EPA engaged in round two of its pathbreaking effort, *Reducing Risk,* and these efforts spawned numerous comparative risk projects at the state level (see Konisky [2001] for a review of the results). Further, EPA continues to write in its strategic planning documents about prioritizing according to a risk paradigm.

The actual impact of all these exercises should be sobering for those seeking to move to a risk-based food safety system. With few exceptions the projects have failed to produce new strategies or rearrange budget priorities at either the federal or the state level. For instance, a 1997 review of several statewide comparative risk assessment (CRA) projects found that "no comparative risk project has resulted in a shifting of resources from lower to higher ranked issues" (Dea and Thomas 1997).[1]

Of course, statutory constraints and priorities can trump any nonregulatory initiative, such as comparative risk assessment, so in many cases it would be unrealistic to expect a dramatic shift in priorities. But other issues are involved as well. Often the design of the CRA effort did not include the follow-through necessary to turn high-priority problems into concrete regulatory actions and implementation (Feldman et al. 1996; Konisky, 2001). In the limited number of cases in which follow-up occurred, the risk strategies evolving from the CRA exercises were not realistic (Minard et al. 1993).

But perhaps the most fundamental reason for the lack of follow-through is the basic mismatch between the output of ranking exercises and the needs of policy makers. Comparative risk projects have focused on identifying and ranking environmental threats, rather than on evaluating risk *reduction* options. In

[1]One prominent exception is the Washington 2010 project, which led to several new regulatory and legislative initiatives (Minard 1996).

other words, the CRA approach embraced by state and federal governments has been oriented toward identifying *problems* rather than *solutions*. Goals are initially set based on overall risk levels, with little or no built-in linkage to important questions of budgets and regulatory implementation issues, such as cost and feasibility. After all, it is finding solutions that is the sine qua non of government.

The lack of focus on solutions should not be too surprising. As the phrase "worst things first" (Finkel and Golding 1994) indicates, the implicit assumption of many policy analysts is that the best way to establish priorities for risk protection is to address the largest, worst problems first. In the food safety arena, a good example is the recent pronouncement in a National Academy of Sciences report, *Ensuring Safe Food* (Institute of Medicine 1998), which said of an effective food safety system,

> First, it should be science-based, with a strong emphasis on risk analysis, thus allowing the greatest priority in terms of resources and activity to be placed on risks deemed to have the greatest potential impact.

Finding solutions is seen as the job of the regulatory offices of governments. It is they who are responsible for identifying and analyzing solutions to problems and performing risk assessments, cost–benefit analyses, cost-effectiveness analyses, and other analyses, usually at a depth and expense that go far beyond the typical CRA exercise.

But what if the largest problems are the most intractable? Or what if they are the most costly to address? What if in the aggregate, risk reductions achieved in many small problem areas turn out to be more cost-effective than those associated with the largest problems? There is no necessary connection between the overall severity of a problem and the ability to remedy it. For example, knowing that tornadoes kill a certain number of people each year does not tell us how many of these deaths could be avoided through government action, or how much it would cost to take such action. In fact, other threats may be present that pose less overall threat to society but are more amenable to governmental risk-reduction efforts. For example, it may cost $1,000 to address problem A, which poses 100 units of risk, but one might address 150 units of risk for the same $1,000 by solving lesser problems, B and C, each of which poses 75 units of risk but can be addressed for $500 each. Even assuming the only goal is risk reduction, as long as resources are limited, sound public policy must consider the costs of proposed measures.

An additional argument for ranking solutions rather than problems is that a number of policies have multiple benefits. A single-minded focus on problems may miss policy options that are highly effective because they deal with more than one risk simultaneously.

How would a solution-based orientation be different from a problem-oriented approach? At a general level, ranking policy options is a more integrated way to set priorities and provides clear guidance for implementation. In fact, it has been argued that the distinction between risk analysis and risk management is somewhat artificial because risk management issues often affect the shape of the risk analysis. As early as 1983, the National Research Council noted,

> Separation of the risk assessment function from an agency's regulatory activities is likely to inhibit the interaction between assessors and regulators that is necessary for the proper interpretation of risk estimates and the evaluation of risk management options. (NRC 1983)

Most importantly, CRA deals only with risk, and risk is only one of several factors that should enter into most government decisions. Cost, both to the government and to society generally, is an obvious other factor. A risk assessment gives only the benefit side of the equation and ignores feasibility and cost. Aside from risks and costs, public administrators need to consider such things as due process, administrative feasibility, legality, and political support. No one has yet developed a widely accepted analytical method for putting together all these factors.

Two important additional characteristics distinguish solution-based orientation. First, priorities are set based on *marginal risk reduction* rather than *total risk*. Because risk cannot be eliminated entirely, the focus should be on the benefits flowing from incremental risk reduction. Second, these improvements should be presented using a common metric that allows comparison with other possible improvements and their respective costs. Without such a comparison, we risk wasting our resources on misidentified priorities. In other words, we risk tackling the worst problems first rather than the problems with the best solutions, that is, addressing what we term the "best things first."

Yet a "best things first" approach may not be appropriate for all government priority-setting exercises. Agencies may wish to set priorities for research efforts and budgetary allocations, or to help define their regulatory agenda. A traditional comparative risk assessment is perhaps more applicable to setting research priorities. It makes sense to consider the risk posed by a problem in considering whether to invest research resources in that problem. In addition, much research effort traditionally goes into understanding the problem side, for example, why substance A causes effect B in rats. However, in contrast to most other contexts, lack of information generally increases the research priority of a topic. If we already have the information that is needed, the topic is a low priority for research.

A Solution-Based Process for Budgetary Priority Setting

Expanding or changing the comparative risk paradigm and the overall priority-setting process to make it work "better" and to give some standing to the best-things-first paradigm is not a new idea. Numerous attempts have been made to refine and redefine the stages of the priority-setting process, although most emphasize reconciling technical analyses with public participation (e.g., NRC 1996).

More to the point, some have called for a process that emphasizes finding policy solutions and estimating their costs at the priority-setting stage. For instance, in response to the Institute of Medicine (1998) report quoted earlier, the President's Council on Food Safety suggested that hazards be ranked based on their economic damage across hazard categories, then control measures evaluated, and finally net benefits for reducing the most significant risks in each hazard category evaluated.

Graham and Hammitt (1996) provide five suggestions for "refining the CRA framework," in the spirit of changing that framework to one that is solution based. These suggestions include the following:

- Rank both risk reduction options and baseline risk, the latter meaning total risks, as is typical in CRA.
- Rank according to the expected (mean) risk reduction.
- Use uncertainty as an information source.
- Rank according to competing and target risks. Competing risks are risks that may increase in the process of reducing other risks; today this phenomenon is referred to as risk–risk or health–health analysis.
- Rank according to both resource costs and savings.

These suggestions reveal a preference for the tool of cost-effectiveness analysis, in terms of resource costs per unit of risk reduction obtained by the policy option. Graham and Hammitt also make the important point that ranking by policy options resolves the vexing ambiguity of the categorization of risks. They use the example of the CRA debates over whether air pollution risks should be categorized separately under "criteria pollutants" and "hazardous air pollutants" or aggregated under "air pollutants." With the options approach, the scope of the policy options advanced determines the appropriate aggregation.

Finally, in terms of institution building, Graham and Hammitt believe that a new institution housed in Congress might be needed to correct the "national misprioritization of risks." Similarly, Justice Stephen Breyer, in *Breaking the Vicious Circle: Toward Effective Risk Regulation* (1993), considers institutional capabilities to prioritize risks, suggesting that an independent executive office similar to the Office of Management and Budget be set up to serve as a magnet for people with the relevant expertise and as a way of cutting across agencies in setting priorities.

More recently, EPA's Science Advisory Board tried to revamp the agency's priority-setting process (U.S. EPA 2000). It attempted to develop a process of integrated environmental decision making, which would add "a wider range of people to the decision-making process, . . . the use of the best science to assess cumulative, aggregate risks, to consider a broader range of options for managing or preventing risks, to make clear the role of societal values in deciding what to protect, to clarify the tradeoffs (including costs and benefits) associated with choosing some management scenarios and not others, and to evaluate progress toward desired environmental outcomes" (p. iii, Executive Summary).

An Example

For the sake of concreteness we present an illustrative example of what such a priority-setting process would look like. Imagine a food safety agency administrator seeking to establish budgetary priorities for her regulatory agenda and to respond to the requirements under the Government Performance and Results Act (GPRA) for strategic thinking and annual planning linked to budget priorities. We envision a two-pronged process in which the annual internal budgetary priority-setting process takes place using a best-things-first paradigm. Every four to five years or so, this process would be supplemented by a major priority-setting process with public participation, which would both feed into the budget process and meet GPRA requirements for strategic planning on this same schedule.

The annual budget process might be supplemented by experts but would otherwise be internal to the agency—that is, without public involvement—because of both historical precedent and because the process would otherwise become unwieldy. It would also focus on problem-based and solution-based categories that fit agency programs, because this is the way the agency is organized.

In addition to the annual budget priority process, we envision the administration engaging the general public every four or five years in a broader exercise to test its overall agenda against public perceptions, new research findings of which the agency may be unaware, and so forth. This process could be organized by pathogen, by root cause, or by any other means that is convenient and meaningful in obtaining public input. In so doing, we recognize that in a real sense, the agency's programmatic structure is a product of statutory activities and its own evolution and may not be the most appropriate means of organizing to manage risk and improve public welfare.

The priority-setting process we have in mind has five technical stages:

Identify current budgetary priorities in need of change and new problems to be considered, using a CRA approach with public participation.

Choose the solution-based tools, for example, cost–benefit analysis or cost-effectiveness analysis using quality-adjusted-life-years (QALYs).

Choose the policy options (solutions) to consider for each program element.
Evaluate each of the program elements using the tools chosen.
Develop final priorities based on technical analysis and other qualitative
   factors.

Step 1: Problem Identification

Although the solution-based model for priority setting is conceptually more
satisfying, the problem-based model is admittedly more practical; it is less expensive, faster, and more familiar. An initial sorting of the most serious problems may be an effective way to winnow the set of options for consideration.
Therefore, ranking by problems may substantially reduce the analytic burden
on policy makers—an important benefit, given scarce governmental resources.
At the same time, the narrowing down of the set carries a potentially large
cost, as it could lead to the failure to identify highly cost-effective risk reduction options.

An initial ranking of problems can help society avoid the potentially significant cost of missed opportunities for cost-effective risk reduction if the size of
the problem is positively correlated with the net benefits from its optimal solution. If this is the case, on average, society will be better off if the largest problems are tackled first. Whether this condition is reasonable depends on the degree of heterogeneity in risk sizes and policy costs.

When great heterogeneity across program elements exists in the sizes of
risks, the size of problems is more likely to be an acceptable proxy for a solution ranking. It is reasonable to expect that ameliorating a problem that affects
millions of people will produce greater overall benefits than remedying a problem affecting only a few. On the other hand, when the sizes of the problems are
relatively similar, the policy guidance from a single-minded focus on problems
will probably be limited.

Perhaps the most important benefit of beginning with at least a rudimen-
tary problem ranking is the potential for identifying previously ignored threats.
The search for solutions is predicated on the identification of problems. By first
surveying the problems to be ranked, it is possible that new problems or synergies among pollutants will be identified, paving the way for identification of
new risk-reduction options.

To be practical, the priority-setting process needs to be performed relatively
quickly and easily. For this reason, we suggest a streamlined version of the prob-
lem-ranking process. In particular, our illustrative process at this stage differs
from other CRA processes by working from existing rankings instead of developing de novo rankings. The agency first describes the implicit or explicit *current* regulatory priorities within a given program, as expressed in the budget
for that program or through other metrics, such as assigned staff or timing. The
next task is to identify any current priorities that need to be redefined or moved

up or down the priority list. The final task is to determine whether any new problems need to be ranked. Each change or addition to the current priority list would be justified, say by citing a statutory requirement.

The problems considered in *Unfinished Business* (U.S. EPA 1987) reflected how laws were written and environmental programs were organized. Although this approach had the advantage of linking areas over which EPA had jurisdiction, it did so at the cost of a somewhat narrow view of environmental problems, thereby missing the potential to identify important interactions and synergies among pollutants and their sources (Davies and Mazurek 1998).

In defining the problem set, it is important to think ahead. For example, in ranking food risks, the temptation might be to choose the problem set based on risk agents, that is, different pathogens, because the risk literature is largely organized this way. However, for the purposes of implementation, it might make more sense to define problems in terms of regulatory areas, such as hazards from poultry, beef, and so forth, or by food–pathogen combinations (see Taylor et al. 2003).

A complication is that solutions will not always fit neatly within problem categories. Some problems may require multiple solutions. An example from the environmental arena would be dealing with mobile and point sources of NO_x emissions. By the same token, some solutions have cross-cutting benefits. A rule implementing carcass sanitizing interventions at slaughterhouses would address multiple pathogen risks present from eating beef. Thus, decisions may need to be made up front about where to target the policy response. Alternatively, it may be necessary to recategorize problem areas on the basis of insights gained from the consideration of solutions.

One way through this thicket is to look at the underlying cause of the problem. A cause such as population growth is very difficult to address with policies, but if the cause is government or market failure, government policy may be relatively effective. For example, if government subsidies to polluting industries are indirectly exacerbating air pollution by encouraging increased output, removing the subsidies will eliminate an underlying cause of the problem. An advantage of beginning with an examination of underlying causes is that it can help identify factors that are the basis of multiple environmental problems. In these cases, potential policies may emerge that would be less apparent than if the focus were solely on the proximate causes, for example, emissions.

Step 2: Choosing the Analytical Tools

What sort of analytical approach should be used for weighing alternative policy options? Two leading candidates suggest themselves, cost-effectiveness analysis (CEA) and cost–benefit analysis (CBA). A major advantage of CBA is that it provides a common metric (dollars) for evaluating disparate benefits. The use of QALYs as the benefit measure in a CEA closes, but does not eliminate, the gap between CBA and CEA on this score. For a detailed discussion of issues around using monetization and willingness-to-pay (WTP) for valuing food safety improvements, see Hammitt's chapter in this book. For a similar discussion of using QALYs to analyze food safety interventions, see Weinstein's chapter. For discussion of the relevant strengths and weaknesses of CBA and CEA using QALYs for priority setting see Krupnick (2004). In this illustrative example, we assume that CBA is the tool of choice; however, the framework we outline could easily accommodate the use of CEA.

Beyond this, the analysis should address four supplemental elements:

- *Level of uncertainty:* The level of uncertainty regarding the results can be evaluated by expressing the results as numeric confidence intervals or through qualitative assessment of the level of precision of the analysis. The main idea is to describe the uncertainties for the decision makers appropriately and not bury them in the analysis.
- *Distribution of benefits and burdens:* Because equity is an important component for evaluating the desirability of different policies, policy makers need to know who benefits and who loses from the policies. If CBA is used to evaluate the options, the policies could be analyzed using alternative sets of equity weights. The analysis should also identify any vulnerable subpopulations who bear a large share of the burdens (or benefits) of a policy. Identifying vulnerable subgroups will enable the agency to design measures that counteract any disproportional impacts of either environmental threats or policies.
- *Nonquantified factors:* Factors not considered in the quantified analysis should be listed. Typically, irreversibility, catastrophic potential, and whether a risk is voluntary are not considered in CBA and CEA. Participants should know whether these are included in the technical analysis.
- *Legal constraints:* The analysis should present the relevant statutory requirements that might limit the options, analytical tools, deadlines, or standards. A requirement to implement best practicable technology in a particular program is the kind of constraint we have in mind; another example is a prohibition on using cost–benefit analysis. Such restrictions in a regulatory context would not necessarily apply in a budgetary priority-setting context.

Step 3: Identifying Policy Options

Clearly, a major challenge of a solution-based approach is narrowing the set of options to be considered. Any problem has many potential solutions, and a thorough and technically valid analysis of the effectiveness of even a single solution requires significant time and effort. An attempt to analyze every conceivable solution to each problem would cause the process to collapse under its own weight. The solutions must therefore be reduced to a manageable number.

In addition, we recognize that how fully the options will be analyzed determines, to an extent, how many options can be identified. More options can be realistically analyzed to the extent the analyses are less thorough. This circularity implies that options identification and analysis need to be decided together. For clarity, however, we keep the discussions separate.

In identifying options, we suggest first determining whether existing institutions, protocols, regulations, or laws limit the range of policy options that can be applied to a given program component. Where the agency administrator lacks discretion, perhaps the status quo is the only relevant option. This case is extreme and therefore probably rare, but in general, the more discretion the administrator has, the greater the range of policy options that need to be defined.

Another preliminary step is to define the baseline, or "do nothing" case. The cost and benefits of any policy cannot be modeled without first estimating what the world would look like without the policy. Insufficient attention to baseline issues can make a regulation seem more or less effective than it really is. For example, an examination of the benefits of Title IV of the 1990 Clean Air Act amendments, which limited sulfur dioxide and nitrogen oxide emissions from electric power plants, reveals that SO_2 emissions would likely have declined in the absence of regulation because low-sulfur coal became more available (Burtraw 1998). A second benefit of defining the baseline is helping to identify those threats that should not prompt government action.

Beyond those preliminary steps, we suggest several ways to limit the list of policy options, particularly when a relatively elaborate and tailored cost–benefit analysis is desired. We start by considering an approach taken by the European Union (RIVM 1999). The EU project had as its goal "to provide an economic assessment of priorities for European environmental policy planning." This emphasis on cost–benefit analysis comes directly from the Treaty of Amsterdam, which says that "potential benefits and costs" should be taken into account in the elaboration of environmental policy.

To analyze priorities, the EU defined a business-as-usual (baseline) scenario, along with a maximum feasible scenario (a technology-driven scenario) that was not to account for costs, and an "accelerated policy" (AP) scenario that goes beyond the baseline policies but falls short of the maximum feasible scenario. The AP scenario contains a less stringent set of targets than the maximum feasible targets. But within each scenario, the aim is to identify the least-cost means of reaching the targets. Thus, this approach varies stringency in defining policy options and, by using the least-cost means to meet the target, makes no explicit definition of the policy type being used, but implicitly assumes the policy permits maximum flexibility.

We agree with the implicit EU approach of defining policy options over these two dimensions—stringency and flexibility—and defining one of the options by limited flexibility and reasonably tight, if not maximum, stringency. We have in mind a best practicable technology (BPT) or best available technol-

ogy (BAT) standard, with its associated stringency. We chose this option because it is relatively easy to define and specify and is often used in regulatory
decision making. In addition, aggregate costs of meeting tighter and tighter
standards, in general, rise steeply after BPT/BAT, as costs are implicitly, if not
explicitly, being taken into account in defining BPT/BAT. The EU definition
of the maximum technology option could be an additional option if there is
some a priori reason to believe that its very high costs may be in the range of
the benefits.

We also agree with the EU that at least one more option is needed to allow
some idea of how net benefits respond to different policy options. In choosing
an additional option, we recommend modeling a flexible policy, for example,
a performance standard, with the same stringency as that implied by the policy with limited flexibility, the regulation of technology.[2]

Another approach to defining an additional scenario is suggested by the EPA
Science Advisory Board (U.S. EPA 2000). As part of its integrated risk project,
the board developed a protocol for identifying risk-reducing options from the
perspectives of stressors; geography, for example, risks in urban areas; and media. It defines options over seven categories that range from communication
and education to market incentives. Although no details are provided, the report notes that aggregation of stressors using "root cause" or "common
source/common pathway" analysis may make the task more manageable. Indeed, to the extent options can be found that address multiple stressors, a prima
facie case can be made for larger net benefits for such options than for options
operating on only a single stressor.

Step 4: Analyzing Options

No single "best" way of analyzing options exists, even within a cost–benefit or
cost–effectiveness paradigm. Some approaches are more qualitative than others, and where an accepted model exists to estimate costs and benefits, the
analysis can be both comprehensive and inexpensive. The simpler approaches
may be attractive when many policy options must be analyzed for each program element. More complex approaches may be attractive when rigorous and
credible results are needed.

The first approach is like a scorecard and is based on the interpretation of
cost–benefit analysis as a structured list of advantages and disadvantages of

---

[2]The percentage cost savings associated with the incentive approach relative to the technol-
ogy-defined approach may be assumed constant at alternative levels of stringency, leaving
one to estimate the benefits of alternative stringency levels. Even here, one can presume, as
is generally the case, that benefits are linearly related to stringency on a per-unit basis, recognizing that spatial or temporal effects at alternative stringency levels may be nonlinear.

particular courses of action. Elements of costs and benefits would be listed and given qualitative or perhaps quantitative scores, to describe the consequences of any particular policy option for any particular program element. Aggregation across scoring categories could be made—or not. If aggregation were desired, a set of weights would be used, recognizing its inevitable arbitrariness.

EPA's *Unfinished Business* (1987) used a variant of such an approach. Each program element was assigned a score along a seven-point severity scale. The scorecard incorporated the severity rating while adding the population at risk, the slope of the dose–response curve, and comments. Large programmatic areas were ranked using another type of scorecard, in which scores of high, medium, and low were assigned to the size of the susceptible population or the degree of concern according to catastrophic, serious, and adverse severity categories.

Another approach is the "sketch-planning model." Computer programs are already being used in the air pollution area that allow for relatively "quick and dirty" CBAs for nonregulatory purposes, as we mean for them to be used here. Such tools, although in no sense ideal, can be used when funds and time are highly constrained but analytical rigor and transparency are required. Because existing models do not address all applications, it might make sense to spend the resources necessary to create a network of sketch-planning models.

One such program is the rapid assessment model developed by the World Bank (Lvovsky et al. 2000). It addresses only air pollution damages to health and nonhealth end-points, but it needs very few data inputs—information on fuel use, population, and an air dispersion model are included in the package—to generate economic benefits from emissions reductions. The model itself has been used to estimate total damages in six cities around the world.

A model addressing both benefits and costs is the World Bank's Decision Support System for Integrated Pollution Control (DSS/IPC), described as "a rapid and rough assessment tool that can give only an indication of where problems are likely to occur, of relative significance of different pollution sources, and of the order of magnitude of costs and effects associated with alternative pollution control strategies." This model is available on the Web and is relatively user-friendly.

Another is the Tracking and Analysis Framework (TAF). This computer program was developed by several institutions, including Resources for the Future, for the National Oceanic and Atmospheric Administration and the Department of Energy to use in analyzing air pollution policy options. It incorporates detailed population tables, baselines, aggregated emissions inventories, simplified air quality source-receptor matrices, dose–response relationships, valuation functions from the standard epidemiological and valuation literatures, and a cost algorithm. It has been used recently to analyze, ex post, the costs and benefits of EPA's SO_2 trading program.

Step 5: Final Ranking

Although CEA or CBA will provide an initial ranking of the desirability of different policy interventions, this ranking should be regarded as one input, albeit an important one, into a larger budgetary decision-making process that we label risk management. Because these analyses are characterized by some uncertainty and not all costs and benefits of a policy can be quantified, it would be a mistake to accept uncritically the results of the technical ranking. Indeed, once the role of technical analysis is properly understood as providing information rather than creating rigid decision rules, many of the perceived problems of CEA and CBA recede. Technical analysis, in the proper perspective, is something that aids decision making rather than overriding it.

The mechanism by which the final ranking is made depends on the context. In many cases, the information from the technical analyses can simply be given to policy makers, who will make adjustments as they see fit. If the context calls for a greater degree of public participation, the rankings can be developed through a stakeholder process, such as consensus rankings or voting. A very promising although analytically intensive process is multiattribute utility analysis, in which the technical ranking is treated as an input along with other aspects, such as equity and voluntariness. Morgan et al. (1996) have shown how such a process would look in a risk ranking, and with minor adjustments it could be used for an integrated solutions ranking.

The Four-Year Public Priority Review

Because we envision a substantial public participation component in the four-year public priority review, this section discusses the roles the public might play during different stages of the process.

In recent years, the notion of a significant public participation component in CRAs, and by extension solution-based priority setting exercises, has become widely accepted. A recent National Research Council report (1996) described the process of risk characterization as an analytic-deliberative process, characterized by both rigorous, replicable methods, as well as by discussion, reflection, and persuasion to arrive at substantive decisions. Analysis frames public deliberation, but deliberation also frames analytic efforts, so the two processes are mutually supportive.

The importance of public participation in comparative risk projects, and by extension solutions-based projects, was expressed by EPA's Science Advisory Board in *Reducing Risk*.

> [B]ecause they experience those risks first-hand, the public should have a substantial voice in establishing risk-reduction priorities. Thus EPA should include broad public participation in its efforts to rank environ-

mental risks. Such participation will help educate the public about the technical aspects of environmental risks, and it will help educate the government about the subjective values that the public attaches to such risks. (U.S. EPA 1990)

Given the importance of problem definition to the agenda for the rest of the priority-setting exercise, a strong case can be made for public participation in this earliest stage of the process. On a substantive level, important problems that are of concern to the public may exist that have not been identified by experts, either because of lack of data, or because of insufficient attention by experts to important nonphysical attributes of risk. On a political level, it may be hard for any priority-setting exercise to maintain credibility if from the outset it completely ignores some issues that the public finds important.

The problem identification phase can receive public input through the convening of stakeholder panels and through public surveys. Early stakeholder involvement may be critical for ensuring the political viability of the process. Certainly, if part of the goal of a priority-setting exercise is to educate the public about the relative severity of risks, it makes sense to include for consideration the risks that it believes are important.

A second area where there is a potential role for the public is in helping to make policy judgments in the face of scientific uncertainties. Often controversies surrounding priority-setting exercises may not reflect differences in values as much as different evaluations of the underlying science. The spectacle of contesting interest groups waving about scientific studies purporting to show the superiority of their positions is all too familiar and has earned the title "adversarial analysis" (Busenberg 1999).

Risk assessments are a prerequisite for solutions-based priority setting. Although risk assessment is based on science, substantial uncertainties are often present that require the use of informed evidentiary judgments (Perhac 1998). The science underlying risk assessments may be sketchy in a number of areas, for example, level of exposure, toxicity, dose–response relationships, variations in susceptibility, and cumulative exposure. How to approach these uncertainties is not a question of pure science; it is a judgment call, and involving the public in these decisions is warranted.

The potential for the science itself to be a source of conflict in priority-setting exercises has received attention. A "collaborative analysis" model has emerged from the dispute resolution literature (Ozawa [1991] discussed in Busenberg [1998]). In this model, relevant stakeholders assemble a joint research group to conduct the technical analysis. Busenberg presents a case study of a 1996 risk assessment of the oil trade in Prince William Sound and argues that the use of a collaborative process "allowed the risk assessment participants to build a mutually acceptable foundation of knowledge that led directly and swiftly to major policy changes" (Busenberg 1998). Charnley (2000) surveys a number of case studies indicating that building a consensus on the appropriate science through early public engagement can significantly improve a project's credibility among stakeholders.

Finally, in the final ranking stage, the public could be included along with public officials in the sort of multiattribute utility-based exercise proposed by Morgan et al. (1996). They propose that a group of laypersons be selected by a quasi-random process. The panel should reflect the diversity of the United States. Two major requirements are that participants have at least a high school education and that they not be representatives of advocacy groups. The panels could then evaluate different candidate solutions, using the results of CBA or CEA studies as an input into the decision.

Implications for Setting Food Safety Priorities

The main idea of this chapter—that agencies should rank risk reduction opportunities, that is, solutions—comes out of our dissatisfaction with some attempts, particularly at EPA, to rank risks, rather than risk reductions. However, in the case of the food safety agencies, we have no evidence that they have a transparent, analytical process in place for ranking either risks or risk reductions. FSIS has very little discretion, but does attempt to rank risks. For instance, this group attempts to allocate resources in testing meat and poultry to minimize risks, while ignoring the larger issues of where in the farm-to-table chain risk reductions would be most cost effective (Taylor et al. 2003). FDA, under its CFSAN Program Priorities project, ranks risks using the best judgment of its staff, with factors such as past spending patterns, constituency demands, and fads playing a role (Taylor et al. 2003). Whether this lack of experience with analytically based prioritization is a drawback or an advantage in their adopting a prioritization strategy for risk reductions remains to be seen.

One of the major obstacles to moving toward a more risk-based food safety system is the presence of statutory mandates that govern how resources are deployed. For instance, FSIS must inspect every carcass passing through slaughter establishments and inspect every meat and poultry processing plant every day, without regard to the relative riskiness of the operations in these plants. In contrast, FDA is not required to inspect food establishments and lacks the resources to conduct even yearly inspections of all the plants under its jurisdiction. In other words, the types of solutions that may be pursued to improve safety are restricted by law and lack of resources.

But even with these constraints, both agencies have at least some discretion about where to devote their resources. For example, both FDA and USDA's Food Safety and Inspection Service (FSIS) have focused their efforts primarily on processing plants. However, for certain risks, it may be more effective to focus upstream, at the farm or fishing boat. Conversely, some risks may be present that are more effectively addressed downstream at the retail level or through consumer education. The kind of process outlined in the preceding discussion would greatly improve the analysis of such choices.

In addition, a solutions-based priority setting system could identify potential gains from changing the current regulatory structure. Ranking policy interventions by their effectiveness may highlight some approaches that are difficult to pursue given current law and regulation, such as developing a more risk-based approach to regulating food. In turn, this approach could provide guidance to legislative reforms where it is decided that they are necessary.

Implementing a solutions-based approach is not without major practical problems, let alone the political and legal issues. For instance, data gaps are large on attribution of risks by food–pathogen combinations; the risks associated with various stages of production; and the type, efficacy, and cost of risk reducing interventions. Particular problems include collection of surveillance data by outbreak, leaving the bulk of cases unreported, and the paucity of studies relating pathogen dose to health response.

The role of public participation—which we described in this chapter as a means for interjecting subjective risk preferences into the debate, and for other purposes—remains to be seen. Where the regulatory objects are reasonably homogeneous, public preferences, which tend to have a coarse scale, are unlikely to be very informative in further distinguishing risks. In this case, perhaps ranking risks or their solutions based on objective risk estimates might be acceptable. Where the agency is regulating "objects" heterogeneous in risks, such as carcinogens in pesticides and *Listeria* in food, public preferences could make a significant difference on rankings.

Finally, an initiative at USDA and a related one at RFF and the University of Maryland give some reasons for optimism regarding the penetration of analytical approaches to prioritization, whether they are risk rankings or solution rankings. The goal of both approaches is to provide a widely accepted and widely utilized tool that is transparent and objective, which will permit risk managers to compare risks using a variety of measures. The Economic Research Service of USDA has recently developed software called the Cost-of-Illness (COI) Calculator that enables users to examine the impact of different assumptions on cost estimates and risk rankings regarding the health effects of four foodborne pathogens. Outputs include numbers and types of cases, medical costs, productivity losses, and losses from premature death. Assumptions underlying these calculations can be changed by the user. This tool represents a step toward facilitating comprehensive, transparent, and replicable analysis of food safety policy benefits, although the costs or effectiveness of different policy interventions are not estimated in the program.

The RFF–University of Maryland effort, supported by The Robert Wood Johnson Foundation, is a more ambitious risk-ranking model called the Foodborne Illness Risk Ranking Model (FIFRM). This computer model permits the comparison and ranking of the relative public health impacts of specific food-borne hazards, including appropriate measures of the economic impact of illness. FIRRM compares the relative public health impacts of illness caused by 28 major foodborne pathogens. Using the model, users can produce rankings by pathogen, by food, and by pathogen–food combination, according to five measures of the impact on public health: number of cases of illness, number of hospitalizations, number of deaths, monetary valuation of health outcomes, and loss of quality-adjusted life years (QALYs). Rankings can be produced at the national level for the United States or, should data become available, for individual states, regions, or foreign countries. As for the COI Calculator, users can modify many assumptions and can also select the region and measures used for ranking and even choose methodologies for the attribution of pathogenic illness to food and the value of a multiplier to account for unreported illness. The model incorporates the data from the COI Calculator as well as information from many government and private sources. It also uses software for Monte Carlo simulation techniques to quantify the uncertainty of rankings and other results. In doing so, it integrates and furthers much of the research on the topic.

Acknowledgments

The authors are very grateful to J. Clarence Davies, Sandra Hoffmann, and Mike Taylor for excellent comments and suggestions. This chapter is based on research funded by the Richard Lounsbery Foundation.

References

Breyer, S. 1993. *Breaking the Vicious Circle: Toward Effective Risk Regulation.* Cambridge, MA: Harvard University Press.
Burtraw, D. 1998. *Appraisal of the SO$_2$ Cap-and-Trade Market. Workshop on Market-Based Approaches to Environmental Policy.* University of Illinois at Chicago.
Busenberg, G. 1999. Collaborative and Adversarial Analyis in Environmental Policy. Policy Sciences 32(1) 1–11.
Charnley, G. 2000. *Democratic Science: Enhancing the Role of Science in Stakeholder-Based Risk Management Decision-Making.* Washington, DC: HealthRisk Strategies, 36.
Davies, C., and J. Mazurek. 1998. *Pollution Control in the United States: Evaluating the System.* Washington, DC: Resources for the Future.
Dea, J., and S. Thomas. 1997. *Building a Foundation for Change: Opportunities and Challenges in State Comparative Risk Projects.* Montpelier, VT: Green Mountain Institute for Environmental Democracy.
Feldman, D., R. Perhac, and R.A. Hanahan. 1996. *Environmental Priority-Setting in U.S. States and Communities: A Comparative Analysis.* Knoxville, TN: Energy, Environment and Resource Center, University of Tennessee.

Finkel, A., and D. Golding (eds.). 1994. *Worst Things First? The Debate over Risk-Based National Environmental Priorities.* Washington, DC: Resources for the Future.

Graham, J., and J. Hammitt. 1996. *Refining the CRA Framework.* In *Comparing Environmental Risks: Tools for Setting Government Priorities,* edited by J. Clarence Davies. Washington, DC: Resources for the Future, 93–109.

Institute of Medicine. 1998. *Ensuring Safe Food: From Production to Consumption.* Washington, DC: National Research Council.

Konisky, D. 2001. Over a Decade of Comparative Risk Analysis: A Review of the Human Health Rankings. *Risk: Health, Safety, and Environment* 12(1/2): 41–58.

Krupnick, A., 2004. Valuing Health Outcomes: Policy Choices and Technical Issues, Washington, DC: Resources for the Future.

Lvovsky, K., G. Hughes, D. Madison, B. Ostro, and D. Pearce. 2000. *Environmental Costs of Fossil Fuels: A Rapid Assessment Method with Application to Six Cities.* Washington, DC: World Bank Environment Department, 104.

Minard, R. 1996. *CRA and the States: History, Politics, and Results.* In *Comparing Environmental Risks: Tools for Setting Government Priorities,* edited by J. Clarence Davies. Washington, DC: Resources for the Future, 23–61.

———, K. Jones, and C. Paterson. 1993. *State Comparative Risk Projects: A Force For Change.* Montpelier, VT: Northeast Center for Comparative Risk.

Morgan, G., B. Fischoff, L. Lave and P. Fischbeck. 1996. *A Proposal for Ranking Risk Within Federal Agencies.* In *Comparing Environmental Risks: Tools for Setting Government Priorities,* edited by J. Clarence Davies. Washington, DC: Resources for the Future, 111–147.

Morgenstern, R. 1998. *Comparing and Evaluating Different Environmental Risks.* Washington, DC: Resources for the Future, 31.

National Research Council. 1983. *Risk Assessment in the Federal Government: Managing the Process.* Washington, DC: National Academy Press.

———. 1996. *Understanding Risk.* Washington, DC: National Academy Press.

Ozawa, C. 1991. *Recasting Science: Consensual Procedures in Public Policy Making.* Boulder, CO: Westview Press.

Perhac, R. 1998. Comparative Risk Assessment: Where Does the Public Fit In? *Science Technology and Human Values* 23, 221-241.

Rijksinstituut voor Volksgezondheid & Milieu (National Institute for Public Health and the Environment). 1999. *European Environmental Priorities: An Environmental and Economic Assessment: Main Findings.* Netherlands: Netherlands Institute for Public Health and Environment, 131.

Taylor, M., M. Glavin, J.G. Morris, and C. Woteki. 2003. *Food Safety Updated: Developing Tools for a More Science- and Risk-Based Approach.* New York: Milbank Memorial Fund.

U.S. EPA (Environmental Protection Agency). 1987. *Unfinished Business: A Comparative Assessment of Environmental Problems.* Washington, DC: U.S. Environmental Protection Agency.

———. 1990. *Reducing Risk: Setting Priorities and Strategies for Environmental Protection.* Washington, DC: Science Advisory Board of U.S. Environmental Protection Agency.

———. 2000. *Toward Integrated Environmental Decision Making.* Washington, DC: Science Advisory Board of U.S. Environmental Protection Agency, 47.

10

Judgment-Based Risk Ranking for Food Safety

MICHAEL L. DeKAY, PAUL S. FISCHBECK,
H. KEITH FLORIG, M. GRANGER MORGAN,
KARA M. MORGAN, BARUCH FISCHHOFF,
AND KAREN E. JENNI

Escherichia coli outbreaks, pesticide residues, chemical additives, food irradiation, genetically modified crops, and "mad cow disease" are but a few of the food safety issues that make headlines. Many other risks, ranging from heart disease to acute life-threatening allergies, are associated with the consumption of foods that are considered safe by most people. Numerous additional health, safety, and environmental risks are related to food production and distribution.

Regardless of how broadly one defines the domain of food safety, limited resources restrict the number of risks that can be addressed and the extent to which risks can be mitigated. In the larger risk management context, numerous calls have been expressed for the systematic prioritization of risks or risk management strategies, so that limited resources may be allocated wisely (e.g., Finkel and Golding 1994; Davies 1996). In part, these calls are a reaction to the traditional approach, in which risks are evaluated separately, even sequentially. Events thrust a particular risk into the spotlight, resources are devoted to understanding or reducing that risk, and the process is repeated as events shift attention from risk to risk to risk. Although this sort of "muddling through" (Lindblom 1959; Bendor 1995; Long and Fischhoff 2000) has the potential to improve priorities gradually over time, it can also lead to alarming discrepancies in risk management policies (Tengs et al. 1995; van Houtven and Cropper 1996; Viscusi 1996).

Because food safety risks are borne by the public, and because the resources devoted to addressing these and other risks ultimately derive from the public, the public has an important role in establishing risk management priorities (M.G. Morgan et al. 1996; Stern and Fineberg 1996). Those interested in prioritizing food safety risks could learn a great deal from past prioritization efforts in other domains that rely on input from the public (e.g., U.S. EPA 1987, 1990, 1993, 2000; U.S. OSHA 1996; Institute of Medicine 1998). The primary goals of this chapter are to make food safety researchers and policy makers aware of several important issues that necessarily arise in such prioritization efforts, and to report on a specific risk-ranking method designed to address these issues.

Before applying any prioritization method in the domain of food safety, two key questions must be answered. First, what is the purpose of the prioritization exercise? Is it to help consumers make better choices in the marketplace; to help producers and distributors make more informed decisions regarding their practices; to help regulators know which foods, substances, practices, or facilities should receive the most scrutiny; or to more accurately place food-related risks in the larger context of health, safety, and environmental risks? All of these goals are worthy, and perhaps all should be pursued. But one should not hope that a single prioritization effort would address all of these issues simultaneously.

Second, what is the scope of the prioritization exercise? For example, does the exercise include risks from water as well as risks from food? A separate and perhaps more important component of the scope question concerns who or what is at risk. For example, does the exercise include only risks to consumers of food products, for example, the risks associated with the consumption of pesticide residues, or does it also include risks to the people directly involved in the production and distribution of food products, for example, risks associated with the application of pesticides? The importance of this distinction is evidenced by the fact that the "food and kindred products" industry has the highest rate of lost workdays resulting from injuries and illnesses (9.5 days per year per 100 workers) among the 38 industries analyzed by Matthews and Lave (2001). This rate is substantially higher than those for "high-risk" industries such as coal mining (7.7) or lumber and wood products (7.6), and more than triple the national average (3.1). Taking an even broader life-cycle approach would require consideration of risks in supporting industries as well, for example, risks associated with the production and transportation of pesticides. Finally, one must decide whether to include ecological end-points, for example, ecological effects of water pollution from agricultural fields and livestock facilities, or the effects of overgrazing or deforestation in addition to human health end-points. The narrower the scope of the exercise is, the easier it will be to set priorities. However, a narrower scope also increases the likelihood that the resulting priorities will not be in the public's best interest.

Once the purpose and scope of the exercise have been defined, numerous design decisions remain. Several of these are covered in greater detail later in this chapter, but two sets of decisions deserve special attention here. The first set concerns how various foods, substances, practices, or facilities are grouped or divided into categories for evaluation. For example, is "pesticide residues on food" considered a single risk category, so that it might be compared to "microbial risks from food," or is the category subdivided further? If the latter is the case, is the category subdivided according to food type, pesticide type, or both? How fine are the gradations? Are strawberries and apples in the same category, or in different categories? Are like pesticides lumped together, or is each pesticide considered separately? In our view, answers to such questions should reflect the goal of the ranking exercise (M.G. Morgan et al. 2000), but categorization decisions may be very difficult even if the goal is clear.

The second set of design decisions concerns the way in which the risk categories are described. What sort of information should be compiled, and how should it be presented? In particular, what risk attributes or end-points should be used? A common answer to the latter question is that expected mortality, expected morbidity, or some combination, such as the expected loss of quality-adjusted life years (see Chapter 11, this volume) is sufficient to capture the essence of riskiness. However, a great deal of research on risk perception suggests otherwise (Fischhoff et al. 1978b; Slovic et al. 1980, 1985, 1986; Slovic 1986). For whatever reason, people care about other features of risks, such as their controllability, their catastrophic potential, and whether the risks are natural or man-made. Any prioritization of risks or risk management options that ignores such concerns runs the risk of public opposition.

In the remainder of this chapter, we provide an overview of previous efforts to elicit individuals' risk-ranking efforts and describe the development and testing of a risk-ranking method designed to address a number of their shortcomings. Although the discussion does not focus on food safety, the proposed method is applicable to food-related risks. Specifically, the method may be used to rank food risks relative to each other or relative to nonfood risks; indeed, "food poisoning" is one of the risks considered in our studies.

Risk Ranking and Public Policy

Government agencies charged with regulating or otherwise managing health, safety, and environmental risks must somehow set priorities for addressing the many risks in their domain of responsibility. Although legislation and legislature-approved budgetary authority determine the broad outlines of an agency's mission, considerable latitude remains in the attention and resources that an agency devotes to particular problem areas. Over the past 10 or 15 years, risk management agencies have begun to experiment with more open prioritization processes in which input is sought from external experts, the lay public, and other stakeholders (Stern and Fineberg 1996).

The U.S. Environmental Protection Agency (EPA) has been especially active. In 1986, its staff ran the groundbreaking *Unfinished Business* project (U.S. EPA 1987), which compared the agency's actual allocation of regulatory attention with a ranked list of the risks that senior staff considered most important. This effort was followed by two agencywide risk-ranking projects conducted by EPA's Science Advisory Board (U.S. EPA 1990, 2000). In addition, EPA's Regional and State Planning Bureau has supported approximately 50 local and regional "comparative risk" projects (U.S. EPA 1993), the results of which have been summarized elsewhere (Minard and Jones with Paterson 1993; Davies 1996; Delhagen and Dea 1996; Feldman 1996; Feldman et al. 1996; Minard 1996; WCCR 1996; Feldman et al. 1997; Jones 1997; Jones and Klein 1999; Konisky 1999, 2001; GMI n.d.).

Elsewhere in the U.S. government, the Occupational Safety and Health Administration (OSHA) has undertaken a broad priority-setting exercise that involves considerable input from stakeholders in labor and industry as well as from the scientific community (U.S. OSHA 1996). The Federal Aviation Administration (FAA) has begun an effort to prioritize its safety initiatives (McKenna 1998), and a committee of the Institute of Medicine has recommended greater and more systematic public participation in the establishment of research priorities at the National Institutes of Health (Institute of Medicine 1998). Outside the United States, several countries have pursued rankings of their environmental priorities (e.g., Environment Canada 1993; New Zealand Ministry for the Environment 1996) and others have expressed interest in such ranking.

When done well, comparative risk efforts can simultaneously make risk management decision making more public and more systematic by providing an appropriate structure for integrating the public's values with relevant scientific information. As has been noted elsewhere (e.g., Davies 1996; Fischbeck et al. 2001), there is much to be gained from keeping the "big picture" in mind while focusing on the specifics of the various risks being evaluated. Of course, incorporating public opinion in a systematic manner is only one of several possible motivations that agencies might have for sponsoring risk-ranking exercises (Delhagen and Dea 1996; Feldman et al. 1996; Jones 1997). They also might hope to promote risk communication, foster dialog among stakeholders, or—more cynically—delay politically difficult choices. Nonetheless, these risk-ranking efforts represent a major shift in the way that risk management agencies integrate science and values to inform their policy decisions.

Despite the number and scope of such activities, risk ranking is still in an early stage of methodological development. In 1993, following a recommendation by the Carnegie Commission on Science, Technology, and Government (1993) for the wider use of risk ranking as an input to risk management decision making, the Office of Science and Technology Policy in the Executive Office of the President asked several research groups to propose methods for the federal government to rank risks within and across agencies. In response, members of our research group proposed a set of procedures that involve eliciting explicit preferences from lay groups (M.G. Morgan et al. 1996). In the sections that follow, we describe the conceptual and methodological challenges faced in developing the method and report results from four studies designed to assess its validity and usefulness.

Overview of the Carnegie Mellon Approach to Risk Ranking

Our proposed method for ranking risks has five interdependent steps (Figure 10.1). First, the risks to be ranked are grouped into a manageable number of categories (step A). Although risk management agencies typically are responsible for thousands of specific hazards, it is infeasible for laypersons, or even staff, to compare and rank such a large number. We refer to the resulting risk categories simply as "risks" to avoid cumbersome language.

Second, a set of attributes is selected as the basis for characterizing the risks (step B). These attributes include both quantitative measures such as expected mortality and more qualitative measures such as controllability. Because the way that risks are categorized depends in part on which attributes are used to describe them, these first two steps are likely to involve an iterative process.

Third, each risk is characterized in terms of each attribute. This information is combined with narrative descriptions to create risk summary sheets that provide concise, systematic information in a format that facilitates risk comparisons (step C). The technical literature and risk experts are used to ensure the accuracy and completeness of each risk summary sheet.

Fourth, participants in the exercise use the summary sheets to rank the risks (step D). Two different ranking procedures are used, and rankings are obtained both from individual participants and from groups of participants. In contrast to steps A–C, in which risk experts play a key role, the rankings in step D are performed by laypersons. The rationale for this division of labor is that the characterization of risk requires expert technical knowledge, whereas the ranking involves social value judgments that are more appropriately left to members of the public or their representatives (Hammond et al. 1992). Both good science and considered values are necessary for informed risk ranking; neither is sufficient individually.

Finally, when the ranking has been completed, a "thick description" of the results is prepared (step E) so that decision makers can interpret them appropriately, for example, with knowledge of which risks were contentious.

In developing this method, we have chosen to follow the Carnegie Commission, EPA, and others in ranking risks rather than risk management options. Although one would ultimately prefer to rank risk management options (Graham and Hammitt 1996), doing so would greatly complicate the ranking task, in part because the number of possible risk management options far exceeds the number of risks. Also, in cases where risks are more stable over time than management options, a ranked list of risks may have a longer shelf-life.

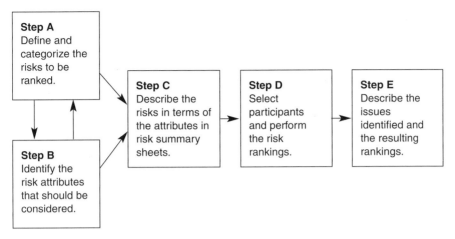

FIGURE 10.1. Steps in the Proposed Risk-Ranking Method
Source: Florig et al. (2001).

For example, sulfur air pollution has been a concern for many decades, during which time the technologies to control or remove it from the air have undergone frequent changes. Nonetheless, such a ranking is only one factor that decision makers need to consider when setting risk management priorities. Risks with middle and low ranks still deserve action if they can be effectively reduced at small cost. Conversely, if little can be done to reduce a highly ranked risk, managers should not spend resources on it that could provide more protection if invested elsewhere. However, the high rank could signal the need to invest in research that could eventually make cost-effective management possible.

In contrast to most of the state and local comparative risk exercises conducted to date, we have decided to focus on lay participants drawn from the general public rather than on "stakeholders" representing particular groups. (For an example of how the results of a ranking exercise might differ for laypersons, environmentalists, and members of the technical community, see Follin and Fischbeck 2001.) Our hope was to develop a method that would be broadly applicable to citizens willing to commit to learning about risk issues, despite their lack of prior involvement. Actual applications would depend on the setting. Sometimes, stakeholder rankings might provide a consensus that translates into political action. Other times, the goal might be to stimulate broader public discussion involving individuals who are not bound by their groups' public positions. We view our approach as being generally consistent with the National Research Council's analytic–deliberative process (Stern and Fineberg 1996; see also CSA 1997; Royal Commission on Environmental Pollution 1998) and with approaches that use stakeholders for the initial elicitation of concerns and evaluative criteria but use citizen groups for the final evaluation process (Renn et al. 1993; Renn 1999).

Development of the Centerville Middle School Test Bed

Although this project builds on theory and empirical results from behavioral social science, any proposed methodology for ranking risks requires empirical evaluation. To that end, we developed an experimental test bed concerning risks at the hypothetical Centerville Middle School (CMS). A school environment was selected because it involves a wide range of physical, chemical, biological, and social risks and because most adults have had extensive personal experience in the school setting, as former students and perhaps as parents.

In the information provided to participants, CMS is described as a public school that serves 430 seventh-, eighth-, and ninth-grade boys and girls and is located in a suburban residential community in the Midwestern United States. The two-story brick building was built in 1971 and is in a good state of repair. The first floor includes administrative offices, 14 classrooms, a cafeteria, an auditorium, a library, and utility space; the second floor includes 22 classrooms, several special-purpose rooms, a gymnasium, and a swimming pool. Cooking facilities and heating systems are provided with natural gas. The school grounds are fenced and include a parking lot, athletic fields, a track, basketball hoops, and some playground equipment. A two-lane suburban street, a four-lane divided expressway, railroad tracks, and a high-voltage power line are located nearby. The neighborhood has a low crime rate, and the school grounds are monitored by local police as part of their regular patrol route.

The sections that follow describe the design challenges addressed in applying our proposed method to the CMS test bed. Florig et al. (2001) provide additional detail on CMS, including links to a sketch and floor plan of the building and a map of the surrounding community. M.G. Morgan et al. (2000) and Florig et al. (2001) provide additional detail on the categorization of risks, the selection of attributes, the development of the risk summary sheets, and the procedures used to rank the risks.

Categorization of Risks

The problem of categorizing risks for ranking has received little formal attention in EPA's comparative risk exercises. They usually start with a list of environmental problems published in EPA's guidebook (U.S. EPA 1993), in which the basis for risk categorization is not described. In EPA's list, drinking water supplies and groundwater are singled out as resources that can be degraded, but air is not. Some point sources of pollution are categorized according to the entity responsible for creating the risk, but others are not. Municipal wastewater and solid waste are distinguished from industrial wastewater and solid waste, but a similar public–private distinction is not made for sources of air pollution. Accidental chemical releases are distinguished from routine releases, but this distinction is not made for other hazards. Several categories are defined by the physical or chemical agent directly responsible for harm, for example, radon, "other" radiation, particulate matter, sulfur dioxide, ozone, pesticides, lead, or carbon dioxide, but hundreds of other agents are not explicitly listed. Finally, Resource Conservation and Recovery Act hazardous waste sites are distinguished from Superfund sites, presumably because they are administered differently, even though other characteristics of the risks from the sites are very similar. A survey of participants in comparative risk projects revealed similar concerns, including claims that "problem areas were too broad, lacked common measurement criteria, and failed to distinguish past and present activities" (Feldman 1996, *12*).

Clearly, the results of risk-ranking efforts can be very sensitive to the way that risks are initially grouped. For example, small risks may escape attention if viewed separately, but not if aggregated; conversely, large risks may be divided into oblivion. Using mixed criteria for defining categories, for example, affected resources in some cases and human health end-points in others, can result in double counting. Such logical problems are perhaps less troubling if comparative risk exercises put "a higher premium on using the list as a risk-communication tool rather than on its intellectual consistency" (Minard 1996, *46*) or use the project as a vehicle to promote stakeholder interaction (Delhagen and Dea 1996; Feldman et al. 1996; Jones 1997), although confusing definitions still may erode support. Ultimately, it is difficult to imagine sound regulatory policy based on incoherent or inappropriate categories.

Some insights into the problem of categorization can be gleaned from the research literatures in psychology (Barsalou 1983; Medin and Smith 1984; Medin and Ortony 1989; Keil 1989; Komatsu 1992), natural science (Sokal 1974), and risk analysis (Cvetkovich and Earle 1985; Webler et al. 1995). Komatsu (1992) makes a key distinction between "similarity-based" and "explanation-based" approaches to categorization. *Similarity-based approaches* place a particular instance into a category based on the instance's similarity to an idealized category member (a "prototype"), to other specific category members ("exemplars"), or to both. *Explanation-based approaches* link category members together according to some underlying scenario, knowledge structure, or purpose. Barsalou (1983) provides the example of a category consisting of children, pets, photo albums, family heirlooms, and cash—the set of possessions one should grab when leaving the house in the event of a fire, time and safety permitting. Cvetkovich and Earle (1985, *7–8*) note that the explanation-based approach to categorization, or the "constructivist" approach, to use their term, "considers classification systems as aids to thinking and communicating and assumes that there is no single generally best classification system. The quality of a classification system depends on how well the functions of analysis and communication are performed. Thus, whether one system is better than another depends upon the specific aims of its user."

Given the wide variety of dimensions along which risks can be considered similar or dissimilar, similarity-based categorization of risks is inherently ambiguous. In an explanation-based approach, on the other hand, the goals of risk managers may be translated into categories relatively directly. We adopted the explanation-based approach while attempting to meet the additional goals that risk categories be logically consistent, compatible with administrative systems, equitable, and compatible with human cognition (Fischhoff 1995; M.G. Morgan et al. 2000). Table 10.1 provides additional detail on these desirable, but sometimes conflicting, goals.

Our specific approach conceptualizes the explanations underlying categorization strategies in terms of causally linked risk processes (M.G. Morgan 1981). These processes begin with human or natural activities, for example, the release of a pollutant or an accident-initiating event, that can give rise to environmental loadings. These loadings, in turn, lead to exposure and effects

TABLE 10.1. Desirable (but Sometimes Conflicting) Characteristics of an Ideal Risk-Categorization System for Ranking Risks

Categories for Risk Ranking Should Be

Logically consistent
    Exhaustive, so that no relevant risks are overlooked
    Mutually exclusive, so that risks are not counted twice
    Homogeneous, so that all risk categories can be evaluated on the same set
        of attributes
Administratively compatible
    Compatible with existing organizational structures and legislative mandates
    Relevant to management, so that risk priorities can be mapped into risk
        management actions
    Many, so that regulatory attention can be finely targeted
    Compatible with existing databases, to make best use of available information
        in the preparation of risk summary sheets
Equitable
    Fairly drawn, so that the interests of various stakeholders, including the general
        public, are balanced
Compatible with cognitive constraints and biases
    Chosen with an awareness of inevitable framing biases
    Simple, so that risk categories are easy to communicate
    Few, so that the ranking task is tractable
    Free of the "lamp-post" effect, in which more-understood risks are categorized
        more finely than less-understood risks

Source: Adapted from M.G. Morgan et al. (2000).

processes, which are then perceived and valued by people. Fischhoff et al. (1978a), Cvetkovich and Earle (1985), and Webler et al. (1995) have adopted similar strategies for risk categorization, although they did not consider the role of categorization in risk ranking per se. Figure 10.2 illustrates these causally linked processes and, using air pollution risks as an example, shows criteria that could guide categorization at each stage. Each element, in turn, could be expanded to include particular secondary categorization factors. For example, the kind of facility creating an environmental loading, for example, a power plant or steel mill, might be supplemented by the facility's organizational or legal status, for example, profit, nonprofit, cooperative, or municipal.

Categories are likely to be most useful when focused on the point in the chain of risk processes at which management intervention is most commonly or efficiently applied. For risk management organizations that concentrate on the early stages of the chain, risks should be sorted according to human activities, initiating events, and environmental loadings. However, this categorization may not directly address the risk end-points that concern many people. These might require secondary divisions, such as separating risks with chronic and acute effects, ones with significant catastrophic potential, or ones that have global versus local effects, for example, chlorofluorocarbons and greenhouse gases versus other trace pollutants. Because they involve very different regula-

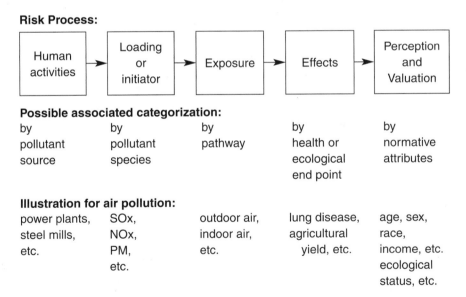

Risk Process:

| Human activities | → | Loading or initiator | → | Exposure | → | Effects | → | Perception and Valuation |

Possible associated categorization:

| by pollutant source | by pollutant species | by pathway | by health or ecological end point | by normative attributes |

Illustration for air pollution:

| power plants, steel mills, etc. | SOx, NOx, PM, etc. | outdoor air, indoor air, etc. | lung disease, agricultural yield, etc. | age, sex, race, income, etc. ecological status, etc. |

FIGURE 10.2. Examples of Alternative Categorization Schemes That Could Be Used at Different Points Along the Causal Chain of Risk Processes

Note: Examples given are for air pollution risks, but the basic categorization strategies can apply to any risk domain. *Source:* Adapted from M.G. Morgan et al. (2000).

tory authorities, indoor air pollutants and radionuclides might be considered separately from other air pollutants.

When categorizing risks for the CMS test bed, we considered several organizational principles for grouping the risks:

- Agent (e.g., radon, infectious disease, or school bus accident)
- Activity giving rise to the hazard (e.g., transportation, recreation, or education)
- Location (e.g., classroom, athletic field, or commuting route)
- Pathway (e.g., ingestion, inhalation, or physical trauma)
- End-point (e.g., injury, disease, or death)
- Group at risk (e.g., students, teachers, or maintenance workers)
- Entity responsible for creating the risk (e.g., students, school management, industry, or nature)
- Entity most responsible for managing the risk (e.g., students, parents, State Department of Education, or County Department of Health)

Primarily because of data limitations, we restricted the problem to risks to students and risks arising from action, but not from inaction, for example, not having antismoking programs or quality counseling services. Following the aforementioned logic, our categorization scheme began with the agents, for example, automobile accidents, that would initiate the processes leading to the undesirable consequences, for example, deaths and injuries. Many of the risks considered have multiple determinants. For example, the risks from hazardous materials transport on nearby highways or railroads may be caused by inadequate maintenance of the infrastructure or vehicle, a social or economic agent; drowsy or inattentive operators, a biological or psychological agent; or a specific chemical agent. For chemicals, we focused on the proximal agent, that is, hazardous chemicals, but aggregated across chemical types to keep the number of categories manageable and differentiated hazardous materials transport from on-site storage of swimming pool chemicals, which were included in the more general category "accidental injuries."

Additional distinctions separated risks that seemed substantially different. For example, we divided infectious diseases into "common" and "less common" categories, for example, colds versus pneumonia and meningitis, and separated commuting in school buses from independent commuting, for example, by car, by bike, or on foot, because of the different accident rates and responsible parties.

In the interest of simplification, we ignored interactions between different risks, for example, that school bus riders may be at greater risk of catching an infectious disease. Finally, our focus on risks at school obviously downplayed the more distal determinants of some risks, for example, the driving forces behind suicide or intentional injury. Table 10.2 shows the resulting list of 22 risk categories.

TABLE 10.2. Risk Categories for the Centerville Middle School Test Bed

Accidental injuries (excluding sports)
Airplane crashes
Allergens in indoor air
Asbestos
Bites and stings
Building collapse
Common infectious diseases
Commuting to school on foot, by bike, or by car
Drowning
Electric and magnetic fields from electric power
Electric shock
Fire and explosion
Food poisoning
Hazardous materials transport
Intentional injury
Self-inflicted injury or harm
Lead poisoning
Less common infectious diseases
Lightning
Radon gas
School bus accidents
Team sports

Selection of Risk Attributes

Although most, but not all, comparative risk projects have attempted to describe risks in terms of a common set of attributes to facilitate comparison, for example, cancer risks, noncancer risks, or risks to special populations (Jones 1997), the attributes selected have varied substantially across projects. Even when attributes are obvious, for example, deaths and injuries, the metrics for capturing them still require policy choices (Crouch and Wilson 1982; Fischhoff et al. 1984). For example, should expected mortality be reported as the number of deaths expected per year in a geographical area or an occupation, or as the chance in a million that an average person in that area or occupation will be killed?

The set of attributes that people care about has been the subject of extensive research (Fischhoff et al. 1978b; Slovic et al. 1980, 1985, 1986; Slovic 1986). As a first cut, this research suggests grouping attributes under two headings, or factors, on the basis of their intercorrelations. One of these factors reflects knowledge of the risk and captures attributes such as "known to science," "known to those exposed," "observability," "newness," and "immediacy of effects." The other factor, which has been called "dread," reflects attributes such as "controllability," "catastrophic potential," "severity," "risk to future generations," "equity," and "voluntariness." A third factor that reflects societal and personal exposure and is correlated with mortality and morbidity sometimes emerges in these studies.

Because the attributes associated with each factor are highly correlated, any of them could represent the factor. We selected two attributes from each factor to allow participants to attend to the one most relevant to their personal concerns and to gain a richer feeling for the factor as a whole. Our choice was guided by the strength of the normative argument for relying on the attribute, its comprehensibility to participants, and the quality of the data for assessing it (Fischhoff et al. 1978b; Jenni 1997). Specifically, we chose two attributes to represent the knowledge factor, "quality of scientific understanding" and "time between exposure and health effects," and two attributes to represent the dread factor, "greatest number of deaths in a single episode" and "ability of student or parent to control exposure". To these, we added three other attributes related to deaths. Two of these captured the expected risk of death to the average CMS student using different metrics—"number of deaths per year" and "chance in a million of death per year for the average student"—whereas the third addressed the equity issue by noting that not all students face the same level of risk—"chance in a million of death per year for the student at greatest risk." We also added three attributes for illnesses and injuries: "number of illnesses and injuries per year," "number of disability days per year," and "number of hospital days per year."

On the basis of several individual and group risk-ranking exercises, we made two major revisions to this list. First, because participants desired more information on the nature of injuries and illnesses, we dropped the three original attributes in favor of a two-by-two division distinguishing severity ("less serious" versus "more serious") and duration ("short-term" versus "long-term"). The four new attributes reported the number of cases of illnesses and injuries in each of these categories. Second, because some participants were confused by our presentation of uncertainty in the estimates for deaths, illnesses, and injuries, we created a third attribute to represent the knowledge factor. Labeled "combined uncertainty in death, illness, and injury," it was a weighted average of the uncertainties for these attributes. It was expressed quantitatively, as a number similar to a coefficient of variation, and qualitatively, as "low," "medium," or "high." These revisions yielded a final set of 12 attributes: 4 focused on mortality, 4 focused on morbidity, and 4 focused on other factors.

Development of Risk Summary Sheets

Although all comparative risk projects have provided information to participants regarding the risks to be ranked, these materials have seldom, if ever, been designed in a way that facilitates comparisons on all of the attributes under consideration. To make informed decisions, individuals must have adequate information, presented in a consistent, comprehensible format.

To this end, we prepared a summary sheet for each CMS risk, designed to be (a) concise, to allow subjects to learn about many risks in a short time; (b) nontechnical, to foster comprehension; and (c) consistent in terms of information and formatting, to facilitate comparisons. We arranged this information on pages small enough for participants to perform the ranking by sorting and resorting the risk summary sheets themselves. The first page of the 6.5-inch × 10-inch design is shown in Figure 10.3. At the top of the page is a simple identifying label, followed by a short qualitative description of the risk. The lower half of the page is a summary table with values for each of the 12 attributes, along with high and low estimates for death and illness or injury.

The second page (not shown) provides a general discussion of the risk, including what is known and not known about it, relative to the attributes. At the top of the third page (not shown) is a qualitative and quantitative discussion of the risk in the specific context of CMS, including comparisons with relevant risk norms, for example, the concentration of radon at which EPA recommends mitigation. At the bottom of that page is a description of what actions the school has taken to deal with the risk. This information attempts to (a) provide a realistic context; (b) make it clear that the exercise concerns residual risks; and (c) focus the ranking on how serious the risks are, regardless of the feasibility or cost of additional risk management.

In preparing these sheets, we drew on available literature, for example, U.S. Congress OTA (1995), supplemented by interviews with technical and school experts. Estimating mortality and morbidity often required both modeling and judgment. References, assumptions, and calculations were recorded in separate technical documents that served as internal references. Two technically trained risk analysts and two nonexperts reviewed each risk summary sheet. The nonexpert reviews included tape-recorded read-aloud protocols to allow us to identify miscommunications. We also asked nonexpert reviewers to offer suggestions for improving the presentations.

To facilitate consideration of all risk attributes, we also provided participants with an 11-inch × 17-inch chart with all 22 risks ranked separately, according to each attribute. For example, the list for "number of deaths per year" had the risk with the highest expected mortality rate, commuting to school on foot, by bike, or by car, at the top and the risk with the lowest expected mortality rate, lead poisoning, at the bottom. In addition to facilitating comparisons along each attribute, the chart emphasized the fact that risks that rank high on one attribute might rank low on another.

Procedures for Ranking Risks

Our ranking method includes both individual and group rankings. In all of these rankings, participants are instructed to rank the risks according to their levels of concern about those risks, without regard to the feasibility or cost of risk management options.

Food Poisoning

Summary:

About 80% of the students at Centerville Middle School eat lunches prepared in the school cafeteria. This carries some risk of food poisoning resulting from improper storage or preparation of food, such as cooking at temperatures that are too low to kill microorganisms or leaving prepared foods unchilled for long periods. Symptoms of food poisoning range from mild to serious and typically include diarrhea, nausea, vomiting, and abdominal cramps. In most cases, symptoms subside after a period of one or two days. In some cases, symptoms can be severe enough to cause death. Students who go home for lunch or who bring their lunch to school are also at risk from food poisoning, but those cases are not covered here.

Food poisoning risk for Centerville Middle School

Student deaths	Low estim.	Best estimate	High estim.
Number of deaths per year	.000007	.000015	.00003
Chance in a million of death per year for the average student	.015	.03	.05
Chance in a million of death per year for the student at highest risk	.02	.04	.06
Greatest number of deaths in a single episode		10–20	
Student Illness or injury			
More serious long-term cases per year	.00002	.0001	.0006
Less serious long-term cases per year	.0002	.001	.006
More serious short-term cases per year	.007	.025	0.1
Less serious short-term cases per year	0.1	1	10
Other Factors			
Time between exposure and health effects		hours to days	
Quality of scientific understanding		moderate	
Combined uncertainty in death, illness, injury		0.6 (low)	
Ability of student/parent to control exposure		high	

FIGURE 10.3. Example of the First Page of a Risk Summary Sheet

Notes: Additional information about the risk was included on the two inside pages. One risk summary sheet was prepared for each of the 22 risks at Centerville Middle School.

Participants first perform an *initial individual holistic* ranking procedure, in which they consider all of the materials described earlier and rank the risks by sorting the summary sheets. Next, participants perform an *initial individual multiattribute* ranking procedure, in which they make judgments about the relative importance of the various risk attributes (Keeney and Raiffa 1976; von Winterfeldt and Edwards 1986). In doing so, participants must indicate whether high or low levels of the last four attributes in Figure 10.3 are associated with greater concern, because these relationships may not be obvious (K.M. Morgan et al. 2001). For example, it may be unclear whether one should be more concerned about risks for which there is high scientific understanding or low scientific understanding. A simple spreadsheet is used to translate these judgments into multiattribute utility functions and implied rankings of the risks. In the standard version of the method, these multiattribute risk rankings are computed immediately and returned to the participants, who are then given the opportunity to reconcile differences between their holistic and multiattribute rankings to create *initial individual revised* rankings.

After completing these individual tasks, participants work in groups to produce a similar series of rankings: *group holistic* rankings, *group multiattribute* rankings, and *group revised* rankings. These groups provide opportunities for participants to hear and consider alternative opinions and thus evaluate and refine their own views.

After these group tasks, the individual participants characterize their groups' decision-making processes, and report their satisfaction with these processes and the resulting rankings. Finally, participants are allowed to dissent from their groups' rankings by producing a third series of rankings: *final individual holistic* rankings, *final individual multiattribute* rankings, and *final individual revised* rankings. These rankings are useful in tracking the effects of group discussion on individual judgments.

Thus, our standard method includes nine rankings of the risks: holistic, multiattribute, and revised rankings at the initial individual, group, and final individual stages. These multiple measures allow for several comparisons that provide insight into the quality of the risk-ranking process and results. In particular, assessing participants' opinions using different procedures provides an internal consistency check and may help allay concerns regarding the dependence of the results on the particular elicitation technique used to obtain the rankings.

Empirical Studies Using the Centerville Middle School Test Bed

In addition to the materials-development work described earlier, we have completed four studies designed to test and refine the materials and procedures that compose our method.

The first study involved 112 Carnegie Mellon undergraduates and assessed the contribution of the text and table portions of the risk summary sheets to individuals' rankings of 12 of the 22 risks (K.M. Morgan 1999). Participants received either text-only materials, consisting of a risk label plus a one-paragraph description; table-only materials, consisting of the attribute table from the risk summary sheet, with a generic risk label; text-plus-table materials, consisting of the risk label, the one-paragraph description, and the attribute table, but none of the additional narrative from the summary sheets; or full-summary-sheet materials. Participants also received information describing the CMS context, including the sketch, map, and floor plans. After reading all of the materials in the packet, participants ranked the risks according to their levels of concern.

The second study involved 24 laypersons from the Washington, DC and Pittsburgh, PA areas, and used the full set of 22 risks (K.M. Morgan et al. 1999). Both the holistic ranking procedure, in which participants ranked the risks directly, and several different multiattribute procedures, in which participants indicated the relative importance of the different attributes, used to construct implied rankings, were used. Specifically, each participant's attribute weights were used to construct concern scores for each risk using the following formula:

$$Concern_j = n \sum_{i=1}^{n} w_i \times v_i(x_{ij})$$

where j is a risk, i is an attribute, n is the number of attributes, w_i is the weight for attribute i, v_i is the value function for attribute i, and x_{ij} is risk j's level on attribute i. In a complete multiattribute assessment, the value functions are assessed separately for each attribute, and the attribute weights are assessed by using one of several techniques (e.g., "swing weights"; see Keeney and Raiffa 1976; von Winterfeldt and Edwards 1986). We elicited this information but also investigated several simpler, less time-consuming approximations. The concern scores were computed for each risk and then ranked for comparison with the holistic rankings.

All of the rankings collected in this study were from individual participants. Participants generated holistic rankings before providing the inputs necessary to construct the multiattribute rankings. The multiattribute rankings based on the complete assessment were shown to the participants, who then resolved the discrepancies between their holistic and multiattribute rankings to produce their final rankings of the 22 risks. Two informative analyses were performed on these judgments. The first used multiple regression to assess the extent to which participants used the results of the multiattribute exercise when generating their final rankings. The second assessed the extent to which a complete multiattribute utility assessment could be replaced by simpler estimation procedures without loss of fidelity. The level of consistency between the holistic and multiattribute rankings within individuals was used as a measure of convergent validity for this purpose; the higher the correlation between holistic and multiattribute rankings, the better.

The third study involved 218 risk management professionals enrolled in a short course entitled "Analyzing Risk: Science, Assessment, and Management" at the Harvard School of Public Health (K.M. Morgan et al. 2001). The study assessed (a) the consistency between holistic and multiattribute rankings at the individual and group levels, (b) participants' satisfaction with the ranking procedures and the results, (c) and the agreement among individuals and among groups. Participants were divided into 43 groups, each of which considered 9 or 11 of the 22 risks. Participants ranked the risks individually, then in groups, and again as individuals. The final individual rankings were included to assess changes of opinion and participants' dissent from their groups' rankings.

The fourth study involved 86 laypersons from the Pittsburgh, PA area, split among 11 groups, and used the full set of 22 risks (Fischbeck et al. 2000). We used several procedures in these sessions, looking for the one that captured the most information without unduly burdening the participants. In the standard procedure, participants completed their individual holistic rankings, provided information necessary to construct individual multiattribute rankings, and then reconciled the differences between these two rankings to generate individual revised rankings. They then repeated these procedures as groups and again as individuals to assess changes of opinion and participants' dissension from their groups' rankings.

Several key results from these four studies provide insight into the validity and usefulness of our proposed method for ranking risks. First, with the undergraduate participants in the first study, agreement among participants' holistic rankings, as assessed by the mean Spearman correlation (r_s) among rankings, was higher when the risk summary sheets included the attribute tables. Agreement was highest for the table-only condition (mean $r_s = 0.48$), second highest for the full-summary-sheet condition (mean $r_s = 0.44$), third highest for the text-plus-table condition (mean $r_s = 0.35$), and least for the text-only condition (mean $r_s = 0.15$). Participants in the other studies—all of whom received full summary sheets—typically had higher correlations among initial holistic rankings, ranging from 0.6 to 0.7, depending on the risk set. When average rankings were created for each of these four conditions, the table-only ranking was very similar to a ranking by expected mortality ($r_s = 0.94$). Average rankings for the full-summary-sheet and text-plus-table conditions were very highly correlated with each other ($r_s = 0.99$) but somewhat less correlated with expected mortality ($r_s = 0.78$ and 0.76, respectively). The average ranking from the text-only condition was essentially unrelated to expected mortality ($r_s = -0.11$) or to the rankings from the other conditions ($r_s = -0.10$ to 0.22). Thus, participants who are provided with both the text and the table information appear to incorporate both sources of information into their rankings of the risks and are more likely to agree regarding the appropriate ranking.

Second, the high levels of agreement between holistic and multiattribute rankings indicate that the multiattribute ranking procedure can be greatly simplified without loss of fidelity. Using the correlation with individuals' holistic rankings as a measure of convergent validity, simple multiattribute models that rely on estimation procedures for single-attribute utility functions and attribute weights perform as well as, or better than, more difficult and time-consuming elicitation procedures. Specifically, in one procedure that appears to work quite well, the weight for each attribute is based on the reciprocal of the attribute rank (Barron and Barrett 1996) and the value function for each attribute is based on the ranking of the risks' levels on that attribute. This result should encourage the use of multiattribute techniques in real-world comparative risk projects, because the procedure reduces the time and effort required from both participants and facilitators.

Third, we have used this simple procedure in our more recent risk-ranking exercises and have observed mean correlations of about 0.6 between individuals' initial holistic and multiattribute rankings. These correlations typically increase as the result of group discussion, but this result may depend on the set of risks under consideration. Agreement between the holistic and multiattribute procedures is similarly high when group rankings are considered. These results suggest that participants and groups have internally consistent views of the relative riskiness of hazards or that they construct internally consistent views as they work with the risk summary sheets.

Fourth, multiple regression results indicate that when given the chance, both individuals and groups revise their initial holistic rankings on the basis of their constructed multiattribute rankings. These revisions occur even among individuals and groups who have already been exposed to the attribute information when generating their holistic rankings. Thus, the multiattribute procedures may help participants to focus on the attributes in a way that is missing from the holistic procedure.

Fifth, individuals are quite satisfied with their groups' decision-making processes and would strongly support using these procedures and the resulting rankings in risk management decision making. Although participants often disagree with some aspects of their groups' rankings, their final individual holistic rankings usually are closer to their groups' holistic rankings than to their own initial individual holistic rankings. Thus, participants support their groups' rankings implicitly as well as explicitly.

Sixth, the level of agreement among individuals, as assessed by the mean Spearman correlation among individuals' holistic rankings, increases from about 0.6 to more than 0.8 as a result of the group discussion. Across groups considering the same set of risks, agreement is also quite high, with a mean correlation of about 0.8, regardless of whether the groups are composed of risk management professionals or laypersons. Such high levels of agreement indicate that the rankings that result from this process are quite replicable.

Seventh, regression analyses indicate that (a) individuals and groups pay substantial attention to expected mortality and expected illnesses and injuries and (b) they also incorporate other more qualitative risk attributes into their rankings. However, different individuals and groups do not always agree on which of these attributes should be included, or even which way they should be weighted. More work is needed to determine whether these attributes are viewed similarly in risk-perception and risk-ranking tasks.

Opportunities in Food Safety

Our experience eliciting risk rankings from the general public has shown that with a well-defined process a valuable input to policy makers can be captured. The value of these elicitations is evident at multiple levels of government and policy making. In this section, we demonstrate how such a risk-ranking procedure could be used at a county health department. Extrapolations to larger or smaller geographical regions follow naturally.

Before setting budgetary priorities for food safety programs, enlightened county officials might want to understand the concerns of the public. A well-constructed risk-ranking exercise can provide insights that would help not only with the allocation of funds but also with appreciating the variety of concerns held by the public and communicating information about the risks back to the community.

Following the steps of the risk-ranking process outlined in the previous section, the relevant risks first need to be categorized. A decision must be made as to what types of risks to consider. Even if the risks are limited to those faced by food consumers, not food providers, the list can be long, including biological contamination, for example, *Campylobacter, Listeria, Salmonella,* and *Cyclospora;* chemical contamination, for example, pesticides, toxic elements, naturally occurring toxins such as mycotoxins, and antibiotic residues in animal products; and allergens, for example, milk and milk products, eggs and egg products, and peanuts. Depending on the goals of the ranking exercise, it is conceivable that some of these broad categories could be "off the table" for political/bureaucratic reasons, although important insights might be gleaned with their inclusion. Further categorization by the health safety programs already in existence could be a logical next step, especially if funding decisions were pending. Risks could be divided into groups based on their position in the food production–consumption chain, for example, production, processing, preparation, storage, and disposal. Risks could then be further divided based on their location or source, for example, preparation in restaurants, public facilities such as schools and retirement homes, and family homes. Care must be taken so that risks are not counted twice. Bacteria that are introduced into food products early in the production–consumption chain may be controlled or eliminated at several later stages before they can affect a consumer. Should these risks be associated with the stage where they are introduced or with the stages where they could be controlled?

To develop complete descriptions (summary sheets) for the risks selected in the first step, risk attributes need to be defined. Measures of health outcomes such as morbidity and mortality statistics are important, but these must be presented so that other associated demographic variables are communicated, for example, age, income, health status, and geographical location of the people affected. Equity is often a very important dimension when the public ranks risks. Some illnesses have little effect on healthy adults, but are particularly dangerous for individuals who are immunocompromised, for example, individuals with AIDS, cirrhosis, or organ transplants, or those undergoing antimicrobial or cancer treatment; the very young; and the very old. Hybrid measures such as expected QALYs go only so far in accounting for the rich distribution of outcome measures that people actually use when they rank risks. Which is worse, a food risk that affects many elderly citizens or one that affects a few infants? The QALY values could theoretically be very similar, but how the public perceives the risks could be very different. A more complete description of who is being harmed by the risks will affect their rankings.

Ability to control the risk is another important dimension in ranking food safety risks. Risks that occur in the home because of improper food handling or preparation are likely to be viewed as less serious than those caused by illegal activities by food providers, all other risk dimensions being similar. Naturally occurring carcinogens such as acrylamide are much more likely to be accepted as part of everyday life than are synthetic substances such as Alar introduced into the food system for cosmetic or profit motives.

Measures that capture the amount of scientific understanding, the level of uncertainty, the catastrophic potential, trends over time, and the time between exposure and health outcomes could also all be significant factors in understanding how the public views food risks. One error made at a food processing plant that taints a large quantity of beef and in turn puts many people at risk would be perceived differently than a series of unrelated food storage errors made in many households. Likewise, risks for which we have little scientific understanding or wide uncertainty ranges, such as acrylamide, are likely to be viewed as riskier by the public than risks with similar but more certain outcome values. The addition of these measures in risk information material will affect how people view the risks. Is it important to understand how and to what extent this happens. Should policy and funding decisions be based on these concerns?

With the risks defined and described by these attributes, risk summary sheets need to be crafted. These should be aimed at the general public and written at a modest reading-comprehension level. These sheets have multiple purposes: as a consolidation of possibly divergent points of view with regard to local food safety issues, as a risk-communication mechanism targeted at the general public, and as the primary information source in risk-ranking exercises. The goal of the risk-ranking exercise must be to capture the concerns of an *educated* public. Fears based on rumors and anecdotal evidence can diminish the value of a ranking exercise. Information from trusted public sources needs to be well documented and placed in context. For example, recent stories in *Consumer Reports* on antibiotic-resistant *Campylobacter* and *Salmonella* are likely to be known by the public, and omission of the information may raise legitimate concerns of bias and selective reporting. To reduce such problems, summary sheets should include recent findings, discussions of common misconceptions, acknowledgment of what is not known, comparisons to other counties or regions, and accomplishments of various food safety programs to date. The sheets should be organized so that easy and direct comparisons between risks can be made. If hybrid measures are used to describe outcomes, for example, QALYs, they must be carefully and completely defined. Comprehension checks of the information content must be conducted before wide distribution of the sheets is allowed. Providing overly complex information to a public with limited knowledge will not benefit anyone involved in the process. On the other hand, basic but surprising facts can cause a major reevaluation of the relative risks. Does the public understand the relationship between the percentage of meals prepared at home (>70%) and the percentage of illness caused by home-cooked meals (>90%)? If these numbers were made salient for a county and several demographic groups, awareness and level of concern could change.

Depending on the goals of the ranking exercise, multiple detailed focus groups could be conducted from a cross section of the general population. As we have shown in our previous research, these surrogate groups often reach similar conclusions with high levels of satisfaction with the process and results. Several types of rankings can be collected, including individual and group, and holistic and formal multiattribute models, and possibly repeated at multiple time points in the process. This suite of rankings allows for a greater understanding of the public's concerns. How similar are the rankings before the group process? Can robust ranks be assessed directly from the general public? Are the same concerns held across multiple subgroups of the population? Understanding how minorities or the elderly view food safety risks is an important and necessary step in designing a comprehensive and effective risk-communication program. If high agreement is found between the rankings provided by multiattribute models and direct holistic procedures, then it may be possible to rank novel risks without having to conduct a new series of focus groups. For example, relative concerns about antibiotic-resistant bacteria found in chicken, the link between *Campylobacter* and Guillain-Barré syndrome, or *Salmonella* in unpasteurized frozen juice products could be determined directly from a documented multiattribute model.

At the federal scale, food safety policy choices become more complex and difficult to compare because of the multiple federal agencies competing for jurisdiction and funding. With food risks falling under the purview of the USDA, FDA, and EPA, a ranking exercise that ignored bureaucratic boundaries and focused instead on the actual risks could serve as a valuable input to senior administrators as they look beyond local decisions about specific programs and instead aim to understand the risks in a larger context.

Conclusions

Since EPA's initial effort some 15 years ago (U.S. EPA 1987), numerous comparative risk projects have been conducted at all levels of government. These projects represent a real step forward, not only because they strive to evaluate a variety of risks in a systematic way that allows regulators to see the forest as well as the trees but also because they recognize the interdependence of science and values in creating sensible policy. As we have noted, however, the methods used to conduct and document these risk-ranking efforts leave substantial room for improvement. The research reported in this chapter suggests several specific ways by which the state of the art can be advanced and applied to food safety risks.

First, much more attention needs to be paid to risk categorization, given the sensitivity of results to these early choices. Poor choices can increase the cognitive burden on participants and distort the results of the ranking exercise. It is often most useful to focus initial categorization efforts on those points in the chain of risk processes where risk management is most feasible. Thus, comparative risk projects may have greater influence on risk management decisions if the risk categories are based on activities, initiating events, and environmental loadings rather than on subsequent environmental and health effects.

Second, the information describing the risks should be provided in a concise, easy-to-understand format that facilitates direct comparisons of risks in terms of their important attributes. These attributes need to be determined at an early stage of a comparative risk project, so that suitable data can be gathered. Characterizing risks in a clear and consistent manner might have communication and management value, even if the materials are never used in formal risk-ranking exercises.

Third, comparative risk projects should strive to include multiattribute procedures. Doing so takes greater advantage of the effort spent on specifying the attributes of the risks, by increasing the chance that participants will attend to these details. The value of multiattribute procedures can be seen in the fact that our participants and groups revised their holistic rankings on the basis of constructed multiattribute rankings and expressed satisfaction with the process and the resulting rankings. It appears that these benefits can be obtained even with simplified multiattribute procedures that require less time and effort on the part of participants and facilitators.

Fourth, individuals' and groups' rankings and opinions should be assessed at several points during the exercise, because doing so provides insight into the quality of the risk-ranking process and results. These assessments measure participants' and groups' internal consistency, participants' implicit and explicit satisfaction, the sensitivity of rankings to procedural changes, and the stability of the decision processes and the resulting rankings across groups.

In our view, these improvements would greatly enhance the validity and usefulness of comparative risk projects in general and food safety risks in particular, and would increase the likelihood that meaningful and legitimate policy decisions would follow from the results of such efforts. Indeed, the rankings obtained in our studies of risks to middle-school students have several desirable features that would afford them credibility as inputs to risk-management decision making: rankings are highly correlated within and across individuals, levels of consistency and agreement increase as the exercise proceeds, and independent groups that consider similar sets of risks come to very similar conclusions about how those risks should be ranked.

Although our studies have focused on ranking health and safety risks in a rather limited domain, this promising approach may be expanded and adapted to address issues in a much wider range of settings, for example, all aspects of food production including pesticide use, and risks not only to consumers but also to farm laborers and the environment. Of course, these sorts of exercises do not have to be limited to government agencies. How would the managers of an individual food production facility, a firm, or an entire industry evaluate the risks associated with their operations? Although it certainly would be a huge challenge to compile and condense the data necessary to describe the relevant risks, we believe that a model of the type depicted in Figure 10.1 would be appropriate for such an undertaking.

Finally, it would seem desirable to move beyond "simply" ranking risks to ranking risk management options. However, ranking management options presents numerous difficulties, some of which were mentioned earlier in this chapter. The problem that the number of risk management options far exceeds the number of risks might be solvable through creative categorization of the options, particularly if some options can be used to address several different risks simultaneously. But that is far from given. A popular alternative is to compute cost-effectiveness estimates for a few management options for an individual risk, for example, comparing different interventions for treating or preventing illnesses caused by particular foodborne bacteria, but the cumulative application of this approach may never amount to the systematic, programmatic comparison of risk management activities that is the holy grail of researchers and policy makers alike. At this stage, simplification of the grand prioritization problem is absolutely necessary. Of the possible ways in which the problem might be simplified, ranking risks as opposed to risk management options seems a very reasonable choice, particularly if risk-ranking exercises are conducted in a way that maximizes their usefulness to risk management decision makers.

Acknowledgments

This work was supported by an EPA Science to Achieve Results (STAR) fellowship and by grants from the National Science Foundation (SRB-9512023 and SES-9975200), EPA (R8279200-1-0), the Electric Power Research Institute (W02955-12), the Alcoa Foundation, and the Chemical Manufacturers Association.

We thank Jun Long, Claire Palmgren, Patti Steranchak, and Henry Willis for advice and assistance.

References

Barron, F.H., and B.E. Barrett. 1996. Decision Quality Using Ranked Attribute Weights. *Management Science* 42: 1515–23.

Barsalou, L.W. 1983. Ad Hoc Categories. *Memory and Cognition* 11: 211–27.

Bendor, J. 1995. A Model of Muddling Through. *American Political Science Review* 89: 819–40.

Carnegie Commission on Science, Technology, and Government. 1993. *Risk and the Environment: Improving Regulatory Decision Making.* New York: Carnegie Corporation.

Crouch, E.A.C., and R. Wilson. 1982. *Risk/Benefit Analysis.* Cambridge, MA: Ballinger.

CSA (Canadian Standards Association). 1997. *Risk Management.* Report CSA-850. Ottawa, Ontario, Canada: CSA.

Cvetkovich, G., and T.C. Earle. 1985. Classifying Hazardous Events. *Journal of Environmental Psychology* 5: 5–35.

Davies, J.C. (ed.). 1996. *Comparing Environmental Risks: Tools for Setting Government Priorities.* Washington, DC: Resources for the Future.

DeKay, M.L., and H.H. Willis. 2000. Public Perceptions of Environmental Risks. Oral presentation at the Annual Meeting of the Society for Judgment and Decision Making, New Orleans, LA, November 18–20.

DeKay, M.L., H.K. Florig, P.S. Fischbeck, M.G. Morgan, K.M. Morgan, B. Fischhoff, and K.E. Jenni. 2001. The Use of Public Risk Ranking in Regulatory Development. In *Improving Regulation: Cases in Environment, Health, and Safety,* edited by P.S. Fischbeck and R.S. Farrow. Washington, DC: Resources for the Future, 208–30.

Delhagen, E., and J. Dea. 1996. *Comparative Risk at the Local Level: Lessons from the Road.* Boulder, CO: Western Center for Environmental Decision-Making.

Environment Canada. 1993. *Environmental Issue Ranking: A Proposed Priority Setting Methodology for Environment Canada.* Ottawa, Ontario, Canada: Conservation and Protection Service, Ecosystem Sciences and Evaluation, Economics and Conservation Branch.

Feldman, D.L. 1996. *Environmental Priority-Setting Through Comparative Risk Assessment*. Knoxville, TN: University of Tennessee, Energy, Environment, and Resources Center.

———, R. Perhac, and R.A. Hanahan. 1996. *Environmental Priority-Setting in the U.S. States and Communities: A Comparative Analysis*. Knoxville, TN: University of Tennessee, Energy, Environment, and Resources Center.

———, R.A. Hanahan, and R. Perhac. 1997. *Subnational Comparative Risk Projects: An Analysis of their Risk Management Phase*. Knoxville, TN: University of Tennessee, Energy, Environment, and Resources Center.

Finkel, A.M., and D. Golding (eds.). 1994. *Worst Things First? The Debate over Risk-Based National Environmental Priorities*. Washington, DC: Resources for the Future.

Fischbeck, P.S., M.L. DeKay, B. Fischhoff, M.G. Morgan, H.K Florig, C.R. Palmgren, and H.H. Willis. 2000. Evaluating a Risk-Ranking Methodology. Presented at the Annual Meeting of the Society for Risk Analysis, Arlington, VA, December 3–6.

———, R.S. Farrow, and M.G. Morgan. 2001. Introduction: The Challenge of Improving Regulation. In *Improving Regulation: Cases in Environment, Health, and Safety*, edited by P.S. Fischbeck and R.S. Farrow. Washington, DC: Resources for the Future, 1–16.

Fischhoff, B. 1995. Ranking Risks. *Risk: Health Safety and Environment* 6: 189–200.

———, C. Hohenemser, J.X. Kasperson, and R.W. Kates. 1978a. Can Hazard Management Be Improved? *Environment* 20: 16–20, 32–37.

———, P. Slovic, S. Lichtenstein, S. Read, and B. Combs. 1978b. How Safe Is Safe Enough? A Psychometric Study of Attitudes towards Technological Risks Benefits. *Policy Sciences* 9: 127–152.

———, S. Watson, and C. Hope. 1984. Defining Risk. *Policy Sciences* 17: 123–39.

Florig, H.K., M.G. Morgan, K.M. Morgan, K.E. Jenni, B. Fischhoff, P.S. Fischbeck, and M.L. DeKay. 2001. A Deliberative Method for Ranking Risks (I): Overview and Test-Bed Development. *Risk Analysis* 21: 913–21.

Follin, J.N., and P.S. Fischbeck. 2001. Trade-Offs among Environmental, Human Health, and Quality-of-Life Impacts. In *Improving Regulation: Cases in Environment, Health, and Safety*, edited by P.S. Fischbeck and R.S. Farrow. Washington, DC: Resources for the Future, 186–207.

GMI (Green Mountain Institute for Environmental Democracy). n.d. Comparative Risk Documents. http://www.gmied.org/PUBS/papers/crdocs/crdocs.html (accessed December 10, 2000).

Graham, J.D., and J.K. Hammitt. 1996. Refining the CRA Framework. In *Comparing Environmental Risks: Tools for Setting Government Priorities*, edited by J.C. Davies. Washington, DC: Resources for the Future, 93–109.

Hammond, K.R., L.O. Harvey, and R. Hastie. 1992. Making Better Use of Scientific Information: Separating Truth from Justice. *Psychological Science* 3: 80–87.

Institute of Medicine. 1998. *Scientific Opportunities and Public Needs: Improving Priority Setting and Public Input at the National Institutes of Health*. Washington, DC: National Academy Press, Committee on the NIH Research Priority-Setting Process.

Jenni, K.E. 1997. *Attributes for Risk Evaluation*. Doctoral Dissertation, Department of Engineering and Public Policy. Pittsburgh, PA: Carnegie Mellon University.

Jones, K. 1997. *A Retrospective on Ten Years of Comparative Risk*. Montpelier, VT: Green Mountain Institute for Environmental Democracy.

————, and H. Klein. 1999. Lessons from 12 Years of Comparative Risk Projects. *Annual Review of Public Health* 20: 159–72.

Keeney, R.L., and H. Raiffa. 1976. *Decisions with Multiple Objectives.* New York: Cambridge University Press.

Keil, F.C. 1989. *Concepts, Kinds and Cognitive Development.* Cambridge, MA: MIT Press.

Komatsu, L.K. 1992. Recent Views of Conceptual Structure. *Psychological Bulletin* 112: 500–26.

Konisky, D.M. 1999. Comparative Risk Projects: A Methodology for Cross-Project Analysis of Human Health Risk Rankings. RFF Discussion Paper 99-46. Washington, DC: Resources for the Future.

————. 2001. Over a Decade of Comparative Risk Analysis: A Review of the Human Health Rankings. *Risk: Health, Safety & Environment* 12: 41–58.

Lindblom, C. 1959. The Science of Muddling Through. *Public Administration Review* 19: 79–88.

Long, J., and B. Fischhoff. 2000. Setting Risk Priorities: A Formal Model. *Risk Analysis* 20: 339–51.

Matthews, D., and L.B. Lave. 2001. Evaluating Occupational Safety Costs and Policy in an Input-Output Framework. In *Improving Regulation: Cases in Environment, Health, and Safety,* edited by P.S. Fischbeck and R.S. Farrow. Washington, DC: Resources for the Future, 357–79.

McKenna, J.T. 1998. Industry, FAA Struggle to Steer Agenda. *Aviation Week and Space Technology* April 27: 60–61.

Medin, D., and A. Ortony. 1989. Psychological Essentialism. In *Similarity and Analogical Reasoning,* edited by S. Vosniadou and A. Ortony. New York: Cambridge University Press, 179–95.

Medin, D., and E.E. Smith. 1984. Concept and Concept Formation. *Annual Review of Psychology* 35: 113–38.

Minard, R.A., Jr. 1996. CRA and the States: History, Politics, and Results. In *Comparing Environmental Risks: Tools for Setting Government Priorities,* edited by J.C. Davies. Washington, DC: Resources for the Future, 23–61.

————, and K. Jones, with C. Paterson. 1993. *State Comparative Risk Projects: A Force for Change.* South Royalton, VT: Northeast Center for Comparative Risk.

Morgan, K.M. 1999. *The Development and Evaluation of a Method for Risk Ranking.* Doctoral Dissertation, Department of Engineering and Public Policy. Pittsburgh, PA: Carnegie Mellon University.

————, P.S. Fischbeck, and M.L. DeKay. 1999, November. Assessing a Multi-attribute Model for Ranking Risks. Paper presented at the Annual Meeting of the Institute for Operations Research and the Management Sciences, Philadelphia, PA, November 7–10.

————, M.L. DeKay, P.S. Fischbeck, M.G. Morgan, B. Fischhoff, and H.K. Florig. 2001. A Deliberative Method for Ranking Risks (II): Evaluation of Validity and Agreement among Risk Managers. *Risk Analysis* 21: 923–37.

Morgan, M.G. 1981. Choosing and Managing Technology-Induced Risk. *IEEE Spectrum* 18(12): 53–60.

————, B. Fischhoff, L. Lave, and P. Fischbeck. 1996. A Proposal for Ranking Risk within Federal Agencies. In *Comparing Environmental Risks: Tools for Setting Govern-*

ment Priorities, edited by J.C. Davies. Washington, DC: Resources for the Future, 111–48.

———, H.K. Florig, M.L. DeKay, and P.S. Fischbeck. 2000. Categorizing Risks for Risk Ranking. *Risk Analysis* 20: 49–58.

New Zealand Ministry for the Environment. 1996. *Towards Strategic Environmental Priority Setting: Comparative Risk Scoping Study.* Wellington, New Zealand: Ministry for the Environment.

Renn, O. 1999. A Model for an Analytic-Deliberative Process in Risk Management. *Environmental Science and Technology* 33: 3049–55.

———, T. Webler, R. Horst, P. Dienel, and B. Johnson. 1993. Public Participation in Decision Making: A Three-Step Procedure. *Policy Sciences* 26: 189–214.

Royal Commission on Environmental Pollution. 1998. *Setting Environmental Standards.* London, U.K.: Her Majesty's Stationery Office.

Slovic, P. 1986. Perception of Risk. *Science* 236: 280–85.

———, B. Fischhoff, and S. Lichtenstein. 1980. Facts and Fears: Understanding Perceived Risk. In *Societal Risks Assessment: How Safe is Safe Enough?* edited by R.C. Schwing and W.A. Albers. New York: Plenum Press, 181–216.

———. 1985. Characterizing Perceived Risk. In *Perilous Progress: Managing the Hazards of Technology,* edited by R.W. Kates, C. Hohenemser, and J.X. Kasperson. Boulder, CO: Westview Press, 91–125.

———. 1986. The Psychometric Study of Risk Perception. In *Risk Evaluation and Management,* edited by V.T. Covello, J. Menkes, and J. Mumpower. New York: Plenum Press, 3–24.

Sokal, R. 1974. Classification: Purposes, Principles, Progress, Prospects. *Science* 185: 1111–23.

Stern, P.C., and H.V. Fineberg (eds.). 1996. *Understanding Risk: Informing Decisions in a Democratic Society.* Washington, DC: National Academy Press, National Research Council, Committee on Risk Characterization, Commission on Behavioral and Social Sciences and Education.

Tengs, T.O., M.E. Adams, J.S. Pliskin, D.G. Safran, J.E. Seigel, M.C. Weinstein, and J. Graham. 1995. Five-Hundred Life-Saving Interventions and their Cost Effectiveness. *Risk Analysis* 15: 369–89.

U.S. Congress, OTA (Office of Technology Assessment). 1995. *Risks to Students in School.* OTA-ENV-633. Washington DC: U.S. Government Printing Office.

U.S. EPA (Environmental Protection Agency). 1987. *Unfinished Business: A Comparative Assessment of Environmental Problems.* Washington, DC: U.S. EPA, Office of Policy Analysis.

———. 1990. *Reducing Risk: Setting Priorities and Strategies for Environmental Protection.* Washington, DC: U.S. EPA, Science Advisory Board.

———. 1993. *Guidebook to Comparing Risks and Setting Environmental Priorities.* Washington, DC: U.S. EPA, Office of Policy, Planning, and Evaluation.

———. 2000. *Toward Integrated Environmental Decision-Making.* Washington, DC: U.S. EPA, Science Advisory Board, Integrated Risk Project Steering Committee.

U.S. OSHA (Occupational Safety and Health Administration). 1996. The OSHA Priority Planning Process. http://www.osha.gov/oshinfo/priorities/index.html (accessed December 10, 2000).

van Houtven, G., and M.L. Cropper. 1996. When Is a Life Too Costly to Save? The Evidence from US Environmental Regulations. *Journal of Environmental Economics and Management* 30: 348–68.

Viscusi, W.K. 1996. The Dangers of Unbounded Commitments to Regulate Risk. In *Risks, Costs, and Lives Saved: Getting Better Results from Regulation,* edited by R.W. Hahn. New York: Oxford University Press, 135–66.

von Winterfeldt, D., and W. Edwards. 1986. *Decision Analysis and Behavioral Research.* New York: Cambridge University Press.

WCCR (Western Center for Comparative Risk). 1996. *A Review of Ecological Assessments from Five Comparative Risk Projects.* Boulder, CO: WCCR.

Webler, T., H. Rakel, O. Renn, and B. Johnson. 1995. Eliciting and Classifying Concerns: A Methodological Critique. *Risk Analysis* 15: 421–36.

11

Quality-Adjusted Life Years: Application to Food Safety Priority Setting

MILTON C. WEINSTEIN

Decisions that set priorities for food safety regulation must be made in the face of considerable uncertainty regarding the probabilities of health risks, the effectiveness of interventions to reduce those risks, and the health consequences for people who face these risks. More generally, public health priorities involve not only the choice of which food safety risks to focus on, but also the relative value of applying resources toward food safety as compared with other public health measures, such as environmental regulation, transportation safety, and medical care. The premise of this book is that systematic, scientific approaches to assessing and quantifying those risks, and of responses to them, are appropriate in guiding those resource allocations.

This chapter concerns the potential role for a quantitative, risk-based measure that has been widely advocated and increasingly used to inform priority setting in other domains of public health policy: quality-adjusted life years (QALYs). The underlying philosophy of QALYs, like that in decision science generally (Raiffa 1968), is that it is better to be explicit and quantitative about one's knowledge and values, even in the face of tremendous uncertainty, than to rely on unaided intuition. This chapter concerns the potential applicability of QALYs to guide priorities for food safety regulation.

Quality-adjusted life expectancy is equal to the expected number of years of life expectancy gained, but with each year of potential life adjusted by a weight that reflects preferences for the quality of life during that year (Torrance 1986; Patrick and Erickson 1993; Gold et al. 1996). The construct of disability-adjusted life years (DALYs) is a variant of the QALY construct that has been used to inform health care priority setting in the developing world (Murray and Acharya 1997).

In setting priorities for research or policy attention, it is often useful to assess the "burden of illness" potentially attributable to a condition or health risk. For such purposes, as in setting priorities for food safety regulation, the measure of potential QALYs lost might be used. For example, a burden of disease analysis based on QALYs was used as the basis of an analysis performed by the Institute of Medicine for the National Institute of Allergy and Infectious Diseases, to recommend priorities for new vaccine development (Stratton et al. 1999).

Estimating the expected number of QALYs lost due to a health risk, or gained from an intervention, can be challenging, as the process requires explicit estimates of the probabilities of different consequences for mortality and morbidity, as well as assessment of the values or weights attached to different possible health outcome states. It requires estimates of the survival and health status of a population of interest, both with and without the exposure or intervention under evaluation. Health states—such as time spent with acute illness, chronic physical impairments, pain and discomfort, or cognitive and emotional impairment—are assigned weights, on a 0–1 scale, that reflect the preferences of the affected population. These weights reflect the value of time spent in these less than ideal health states relative to time spent in perfect health. Quality-adjusted life expectancy is calculated by weighting the number of QALYs under different scenarios by their probabilities of occurrence. The calculation of quality-adjusted life expectancy should reflect both the health benefits and harms of the program being considered.

Cost-effectiveness analysis (CEA) extends this analytical process a step further by considering not only the health consequences of actions but also their costs. The purpose of CEA in health care is to structure information about the consequences and costs of health interventions in a form that can guide decision making about resource allocation for health (Russell et al. 1996). CEA entails the use of scientific data and theory, as well as mathematical modeling, to develop quantitative estimates of the health impact of an intervention or program—measured in QALYs—and relates this measure of health benefit to the cost of the program. The result is a cost-effectiveness ratio, typically expressed in units of dollars per QALY gained (Gold et al. 1996; Drummond et al. 1997). If the policy objective is to allocate resources to achieve the most health benefit, then programs with low ratios of cost per QALY would receive higher priority than interventions with higher cost-effectiveness ratios. When two or more intervention options are being evaluated, such as different tolerance levels for food contaminants, or different cancer screening strategies, incremental cost-effectiveness ratios must be used to calculate the additional cost per additional QALY gain between the increasingly costly and effective options. The reciprocal of the cost-effectiveness ratio can also be used as an index of value for money, or "bang for the buck": Which programs can be expected to save the most QALYs for a given allocation of resources such as $1,000,000?

CEA using QALYs is now widely used in evaluating medical and public health technologies and programs. Examples of CEA may be found regularly in the pages of the leading medical journals, such as the *Journal of the American Medical Association,* the *New England Journal of Medicine,* and the *Annals of Internal Medicine.* Guidelines for clinical practices, developed under the auspices of medical specialty organizations, appeal to CEAs as the basis for the recommendations on clinical practices. Public health agencies such as the U.S. Centers for Disease Control and Prevention (CDC) use CEA to inform decisions ranging from screening practices to vaccination priorities to food supplementation (U.S. CDC 1999). CEAs are also required by agencies in many countries, from Australia to Canada to the United Kingdom, that regulate the reimbursement of pharmaceuticals under public insurance programs. Analysis using QALYs is the preferred methodology for submissions to the National Institute of Clinical Excellence (NICE), the agency responsible for those determinations in the United Kingdom.

In response to the demand for, and increasing supply of, CEAs in the United States, guidelines for the conduct of CEA were formulated by a USPHS-sponsored panel, in which numerous federal agencies concerned with health resource allocation participated as observers (Gold et al. 1996; Weinstein et al. 1996). These guidelines call for QALYs to be the standard, or reference, measure of health improvement in CEAs intended to inform health care resource allocations from a societal perspective.

A number of measurement systems have been developed to assign QALY values to important health conditions. These systems, such as the Health and Activity Limitation Index (HALex) (Gold et al. 1996) and the Health Utilities Index (HUI) (Torrance et al. 1996), serve as a resource for future burden-of-illness analyses and CEAs.

The advantage of QALY-based CEA that has earned the method favor among decision scientists and, to some extent, policy makers in public health and medicine is that, unlike its analytical cousin cost–benefit analysis (CBA), CEA does not require that health impacts be valued in monetary terms. In CEA, one does not have to place a dollar value on life and health to estimate a QALY gain and a cost-effectiveness ratio. The dollar value of a QALY does come into play in making absolute determinations of whether the cost per QALY is too high to justify the adoption of a program, but it is not required in order to draw conclusions as to whether one program should receive higher priority for resources than another. This has made CEA more popular as a tool for economic evaluation in health care than CBA, which involves measuring all costs and benefits in economic terms.

The principal question addressed in this chapter is the following: Can QALY assessment and CEA be used to inform regulatory priorities in food safety? Following a brief review of the methodology for estimating gains in quality-adjusted life expectancy is a review of some applications of QALY-based CEA that have been influential in policy formation in health care. We give special attention to the Institute of Medicine study of priorities for new vaccine development, which used QALYs as the central method. Then we turn to some of the challenges in using quality-adjusted life years, including the need to estimate health consequences and health-related preferences separately and explicitly. We also give a brief discussion of some of the theoretical limitations of QALYs as a summary measure of health consequences. We then turn to the central question: What are the advantages and disadvantages of QALY-based CEA as a methodology for guiding food safety priorities, particularly as compared with CBA based on willingness-to-pay? The chapter concludes with some remarks on research needs for making the QALY methodology useful for food safety decision making.

Methodology for Estimating QALY Gains

The greatest strength of QALY analysis also presents the major challenge to its use: It requires explicit, quantitative, and separate estimates of the *probabilities* of various possible consequences of alternative actions, and of the *values* attached to those consequences.

The probabilities required include disease incidence and progression, as well as those of death from the disease and from other causes. Sources of these probabilities may include experimental studies such as clinical trials and animal bioassays, nonexperimental data such as follow-up studies and case-control studies, clinical databases, public health statistics, and expert judgment.

Models may be used to combine data from various sources and to achieve calibration among different probability estimates. For example, estimates of the incidence of a foodborne infection could be obtained either by constructing a model that combines data on the dose–response function between exposure and incidence with data on the population distribution of exposure, or directly from public health data on incidence of the infection among persons exposed. Models may also be needed to extrapolate from a proximal event such as incidence of disease to the lifetime consequences of that event in terms of survival probabilities and quality of life.

In a QALY calculation, the expected durations of time in various health states are weighted by utilities that reflect the preferences of the affected population. A utility weight of 1.0 corresponds to perfect health (1 year = 1 QALY), and utility weights less than 1.0 correspond to less perfect health states. One year spent in a health state with utility weight u would be equivalent to u QALYs, or a loss of $1 - u$ QALYs compared to perfect health.

To reflect true preferences regarding the relative values of different health states, the weights should be based on responses to questions of the following types (Torrance 1986; Patrick and Erickson 1993; Gold et al. 1996):

How many years of life, *Y*, in perfect health would you consider to be equivalent to *N* years of life in health state *S*? This is the "time trade-off" method, and the implied utility weight for health state *S* would be *Y/N*.

What probability of death, *P*, would you be willing to accept in order to improve your health for the rest of your life from health state *S* to perfect health? This is the "standard gamble" method, and the implied utility weight for health state *S* would be 1–*P*.

If a societal perspective is used for policy making, then the relevant preferences may be those of the general population. In other words, the utility estimates for a population would be based on the responses to these types of questions in a sample of that population. Fortunately, a number of such surveys have been performed, so that it is now possible to obtain utility weights specific to a number of common disease states (Fryback et al. 1993; Gold et al. 1996).

The preferred method of assigning utilities to health states is to use utility weights that have been obtained from one of several general health-state classification systems (Gold et al. 1996). These systems define health in terms of a small number (four to eight) of domains, such as ambulation, cognition, emotion, and pain. Commonly used systems of health-state weights are the Health Utilities Index (HUI) (seven or eight domains) (Torrance et al. 1996); the EQ-5D (five domains) (Dolan et al. 1996); the Quality of Well-Being Scale (QWB) (four domains) (Kaplan and Anderson 1988); and the SF-6D (six domains) (Brazier et al. 2002). The utility weights associated with these systems were obtained from community surveys. To apply one of these systems of weights to an assessment of QALY gain or loss from an intervention or exposure requires a mapping from the disease states of interest to the general health-state classification system from which the weights are drawn. Such mappings can be done either by administering the classification questionnaire to a sample of patients in the disease states of interest or by the use of clinical judgment. This approach, using expert judgment, was used in the Institute of Medicine study of vaccine priorities; we describe the approach in the next section.

Other utility-weighted health-state classification systems have been developed for specific diseases or conditions. Notable among these is the Functional Classification Index for trauma (MacKenzie et al. 1996). The Functional Classification Index has been used to assign utility weights to a broad range of specific injuries caused by motor vehicle accidents, classified by body region.

Disability-adjusted life years provide a closely related method for assigning weights to health states. With DALYs, health states are classified into disability categories, and weights have been assigned to each disability level by a panel of clinical experts (Murray and Acharya 1997). The principal difference between QALYs and DALYs, apart from the fact that DALYs run in the reverse direction—from 0 for unimpaired health to 1 for dead—is that DALYs multiply the disability weight by another weight that reflects age of the affected person. Years of life at very young and older ages are weighted less than years of life in the years of highest productivity.

In calculating QALY or DALY gains or losses, future years are discounted to present value, using an appropriate economic discount rate. Current recommendations are to use a discount rate of between 2% and 7% per annum, with one consensus position being 3% (Gold et al. 1996). To this extent, QALYs handle the future similarly to willingness-to-pay and other economic measures of health outcome.

Uses of QALYs and DALYs in Health Care

Analyses of health impacts and benefits using QALYs and DALYs are increasing. QALYs and DALYs have been used to measure health status in the U.S. population (Gold et al. 1998) and in developing countries (Murray 1994). They have been used in CEAs to inform the development of clinical practice guidelines for cholesterol management (Goldman et al. 1992), and a variety of preventive health services (U.S. CDC 1999). As the result of a CEA is a ratio of cost per QALY, and compendia of similarly derived ratios for wide ranges of health interventions have been compiled (Tengs et al. 1995; Graham et al. 1998).

An increasing number of studies have applied one or more of the available sets of health-state preference weights to assign utilities to time spent with health conditions such as paralysis, asthma, renal failure, and arthritis. The Beaver Dam Health Outcomes Study surveyed citizens of Beaver Dam, Wisconsin, using both a time trade-off questionnaire and the Quality of Well-Being Scale (Fryback et al. 1993). As part of that survey, individuals also responded whether they were currently affected by one or more health conditions from a list that included arthritis, hypertension, stroke, asthma, ulcer, colitis, allergies, and many others. The implied utility weights were stratified by age. For example, the mean QWB utilities for time spent with arthritis ranged from 0.64 to 0.72, depending on age.

In an effort to link the National Health Interview Survey (NHIS) to health-state preferences, the Health and Activity Limitation Index (HALex) was developed to assign QALY weights to the health conditions included within the NHIS (Gold et al. 1996). The HALex was constructed by linking the responses to the NHIS questions on limitation of activity (six levels, from no limitation to limited in Activities of Daily Living) and on self-rated health (Excellent, Very Good, Good, Fair, Poor) to self-reported health conditions. The preference weights for each of the 30 combinations of limitation of activity and self-rated health were based on an adaptation of the Health Utilities Index. By this process, QALY weights were obtained using the HALex for a wide range of conditions defined by the International Classification of Diseases. The conditions include many that are relevant to food safety: partial or full paralysis; mental retardation; migraine headaches; digestive problems ranging from constipation and diarrhea to ulcer and gastrointestinal cancer; respiratory problems such as asthma; endocrine problems such as diabetes and kidney stones; cardiovascular problems such as stroke, ischemic heart disease, and hypertension; and many others. The HALex study reports means, medians, and interquartile ranges of utility weights for all of these conditions (Gold et al. 1996).

More research will be needed to make it possible to associate a loss of QALYs with an incident case of foodborne illness. One requirement for QALY analyses will be epidemiological estimates of the mortality (lost life years) and morbidity (time spent in symptomatic health states) associated with these diseases. The task of assigning utility weights to symptoms and disability also requires more work. Although the HALex study represents a useful source of data on utility weights for some relevant conditions, unfortunately the HALex is no longer being used by the National Center for Health Statistics as a measure of health status based on the National Health Interview Survey. In addition, although preference weights for other scales such as the Health Utilities Index, EQ-5D, and SF-6D are available, no source of data is generally available that would enable a "mapping" from the set of conditions associated with foodborne diseases into these scales. Surveys of individuals experiencing symptoms and disability associated with foodborne diseases, using instruments such as the HUI, EQ-5D, and SF-6D, would make it possible to evaluate the loss of QALYs associated with durations of time spent with each of these conditions.

The Institute of Medicine Study of Vaccine Priorities

An example that bears some important similarities to the task of setting priorities for food safety regulation was the Institute of Medicine's (IOM's) study of priorities for new vaccine development (Stratton et al. 1999). This study was the second in a series of studies commissioned by the National Institutes of Health, with the purpose of providing guidance to the NIH on priorities for research and development of new vaccines. The first study, published in 1985, concentrated on vaccines against infectious diseases (Institute of Medicine 1985), but the second study, published in 1999, expanded the scope to include many chronic diseases whose etiology has been linked to infectious agents, including various cancers and forms of arthritis (Stratton et al. 1999).

The IOM analysis was structured as a burden of illness analyses, in which the expected annual health burden was estimated for a number of potentially vaccine-preventable diseases. Public health data, including published and unpublished estimates from the Centers for Disease Control and Prevention, were used as the basis for estimating disease incidence and mortality. The epidemiological and medical literatures were used to extend these estimates to assign probabilities to specific health consequences, such as acute episodes of illness, chronic disabilities, and impairments of health-related quality of life such as pain or emotional distress. Thus, for each potential vaccine, a combination of data and expert judgment was used to assign probabilities to the duration of time spent or avoided in various disease-related health states.

The valuation of these health states was accomplished using QALYs. Specifically, the second revision of the Health Utilities Index (HUI-2) was used to assign preference weights to each of the health states associated with the diseases of interest. The mapping from disease-specific health states to the generic health-state classification in the HUI was accomplished by expert judgment. The domains of the HUI-2 include sensation (vision, hearing, and speech), mobility, emotion, cognition, self-care, pain, and fertility. For example, the numbers of persons experiencing retinopathy associated with cytomegalovirus (CMV) were distributed by the experts into the cells in the HUI matrix that corresponded to its possible effects on sensation and on other domains of health such as emotion and ambulation. The QALY weight assigned to time spent in those health states were obtained from the published scoring of the HUI-2, which had been based on a community preference survey using the standard gamble method. Finally, the HUI-2 weights across all health states associated with CMV were weighted by their durations and probabilities of occurrence, and summed up to yield the expected QALY loss associated with CMV.

Challenges in Using QALYs

One question addressed in this book is whether QALYs or willingness-to-pay (WTP) offers a more appropriate methodology for measuring food safety risks and setting food safety priorities. Clearly, there are advantages and limitations to both, and both present challenges.

QALY assessments require explicit estimates of both the probabilities of health outcomes and valuations of health states. Whereas WTP requires estimates of only the probability of the proximal health event of concern, such as the incidence of a disease or morbid event, QALY estimation requires a complete specification of the downstream consequences of that outcome, including transitions between health states over time. Prior to preference assessment in QALYs, one needs an estimate, albeit sometimes only a rough estimate, of the probability distribution of a population into numerous health-state scenarios, or health profiles, which can then be valued by assigning utility weights to periods of time spent in various health states. Complex simulation models are often used to estimate these lifetime probabilities for clinical decision analyses (e.g., see Samsa et al. 1999; Prosser et al. 2000; Freedberg et al. 2001), but simplified decision tree models are often sufficient, as exemplified in the IOM vaccine study.

Once the probabilities of experiencing health states over time have been estimated, the next task is to assign utility weights to the health states. This can be a complex undertaking if the number of distinct health states is large. If a mapping from problem-specific health states to a system of generic preference weights is used, and such a mapping has not been done previously, then the options for the analyst are either a dedicated cross-sectional survey of persons experiencing those health states or reliance on expert judgment either to perform the mapping or to assign utilities to health states directly. Such a task was performed successfully in the IOM vaccine study, using experts in the diseases of interest.

Theoretical Limitations of QALYs

A number of theoretical limitations of QALYs deserve attention, although they should not deter us from using them if the alternative is unaided intuition or an alternative method that has its own limitations.

The calculation of aggregate or expected QALYs in a population is based on the assumption that citizens are risk neutral with respect to survival time (Bleichrodt et al.1997). Risk neutrality means that life expectancy—the average number of years of survival—is the only summary statistic needed to rank order risks that vary in terms of the resulting probabilities of living to various lengths of life. An alternative hypothesis is that individuals are risk averse with respect to length of survival, which means that they would prefer a smaller length of life for certain to a probability distribution with a higher average life expectancy. While evidence exists that individuals are not risk neutral for individual health decisions under risk (McNeil et al. 1978), a compelling case can be made that for societal decisions, the total or average health impact should be the basis for policy (Gold et al. 1996). It is also possible that what may appear to be risk aversion in responses to utility surveys may actually be attributable to cognitive distortions of the probabilities of consequences, so that the degree of true risk aversion may be much less than it appears to be (Bleichrodt et al. 2001).

Another criticism of QALYs as a basis for health priorities is that they tend to ignore the psychological consequences of health decisions. By focusing on the health state, any utility or disutility associated with the context of the risk or risk reduction may be excluded. For example, it has been shown that individuals are willing to pay large amounts of money for the peace of mind associated with donating one's own blood for transfusions during surgery, rather than to take the very small risk of acquiring a serious infection from donated blood (Lee et al. 1998). The value of the QALY gain cannot possibly account for the expressed value to individuals of avoiding this risk, which suggests a large psychological component. In the food safety context, the value of avoiding dreaded and unknown risks of foodborne pathogens would not be captured in a QALY calculation of the potential specific diseases that might occur. Whether the appropriate policy response is to give credence to these psychological concerns, or to try to overcome them through information and counseling, is debatable.

Still another limitation of basing priorities on aggregate expected QALYs is that it ignores distributional and equity issues. The distribution of risks and benefits of a food product or of interventions to reduce its risks is not uniform. The persons harmed by the intervention may be poor farm workers or consumers forced either to pay higher prices or forgo nutritional benefits, while the beneficiaries may be those fortunate enough to be concerned about small risks rather than basic nutrition. Surely these considerations enter the political process, but there is a risk that they may be given inadequate attention if only the aggregate magnitudes of risks and benefits are considered. This equity limitation applies, of course, as much or more to willingness to pay as a basis for priorities. With QALYs, each QALY counts the same, regardless of wealth, gender, or age, whereas WTP tends to be correlated with these attributes. Nonetheless, priorities based on QALYs are still subject to the criticism that the measure of health risk ignores important distributional concerns.

Advantages of QALYs for Food Safety Decision Making

The most important strength of the QALY approach is that it incorporates scientific evidence on the health consequences of diseases and health conditions and thereby makes explicit the reasons for valuing risk reductions. Consistent with the spirit of decision analysis, the task of estimating the probabilities of the consequences of action (risk assessment) is separated from the task of valuing those consequences (risk valuation).

Scientific evidence drives the risk assessment task. In the risk assessment, the accumulated evidence on the epidemiology, natural history, and treatment of the relevant health conditions is brought to bear on the problem of modeling and forecasting the relevant consequences. The result of the risk assessment step is a set of probability distributions of time spent in various health states, with or without the risk of concern.

Citizens' value judgments dominate the risk valuation task, where utility weights based on community surveys are applied to the health states of importance to the problem. The resulting measure of expected QALYs lost or gained reflects values that are assigned by citizens to the ultimate health consequences of foodborne risks, and the evidence and expert judgment that inform the probabilities that specific health consequences will occur.

QALYs versus WTP, DALYs, and Burden of Illness Studies

CEAs that use QALYs as a measure of health outcome can be used to rank order interventions that expend resources to protect human health. Thus, CEA would seem to lend itself to the task of guiding priorities for food safety. QALYs have a marked advantage over measures sometimes used in CEAs, such as number of lives saved or years of life saved, because they reflect citizen trade-offs between many dimensions of health. However, because CEA stops short of assigning monetary value to health outcomes, it is silent on the question of how much it is worth spending to gain a QALY. CBA, based on WTP, does provide a monetary measure of health benefit, but it does so with some pitfalls.

One problem with WTP is that willingness to pay for health improvement tends to increase with increasing wealth. This tends to produce greater values of life saving and health improvement at older ages and in more affluent segments of the population (Krupnick et al. 2002). In food safety, this might lead, for example, to higher priority for prevention of foodborne risks to the elderly and the more affluent, compared to QALY-based priorities.

In contrast to the decomposed approach inherent in the QALY method, WTP procedures require laypersons to synthesize both their beliefs and their attitudes regarding the consequences of risk. Laypersons generally do not understand the probabilities and consequences of a condition such as "kidney failure" or "diabetes," whereas they may be better able to assign values to specific health states such as pain, confinement to bed, or visual impairment. An assessment of willingness to pay for a reduction in the probability of one of these holistically described conditions, for example, may introduce noise into the assessment process, owing to the imperfect knowledge of the respondent.

On the other hand, QALYs, assigned to health states rather than to actions, generally do not reflect psychological values, which may include regret, dread, and risk aversion. WTP can incorporate these psychological values, which may be both an advantage and a disadvantage. It is an advantage to the extent that these factors are considered normatively relevant to policy making, but it is a disadvantage to the extent that these factors are considered irrational or artifacts of cognitive distortions.

As mentioned earlier, disability-adjusted life years (DALYs) are a variant of QALYs, which may also be used to rank risks and to guide priorities for resource allocation. One feature of DALYs that may be objectionable to some potential decision makers is that they weight different ages differently, generally assigning lower weight to the earliest and latest years of a life span. The rationale for this procedure comes from the use of DALYs in developing countries, where the external benefits of increased economic productivity tend to be much more important than in industrialized economies with full or near full employment. Nevertheless, the effect of using DALYs with their age weighting in food safety priorities would be to give relatively higher priority to foodborne risks affecting persons in their most productive years, relative to their formative and retirement years of life, and relative to prevention of infant and child deaths.

QALYs, DALYs, or WTP can be used in burden-of-illness analyses, which estimate the aggregate impact of conditions in an affected population, rather than in economic evaluations, such as CEAs and CBAs, whose purpose is to assess the value of interventions that reduce risks. Burden-of-illness studies, by their nature, ignore the potential of policy changes or health interventions to actually achieve health improvements. Thus, for example, a disease with a major public health impact but for which there is no known way to reduce its incidence would rank higher in a burden-of-illness study than a condition with a lesser burden but for which public health measures are available. For this reason, burden-of-illness studies are more appropriate in the context of decisions regarding research and development of new technologies than in priority setting for programmatic resources.

Research Needs Toward Using QALYs and CEA in a Food Safety Priority Setting

The following steps may be considered part of a research agenda that can make QALY assessment a practical tool for priority setting in food safety.

One step would be to develop a database of incidence-based QALY impacts of diseases and conditions typically associated with foodborne risks. Much of this information already exists in databases such as the Beaver Dam Health Outcomes Study and the Health and Activity Limitations Index. However, many conditions relevant to foodborne risks may not be captured by these sources. A study akin to the Institute of Medicine's vaccine priorities project could be a worthwhile undertaking. Such a project would entail collecting evidence from public health data, epidemiological and clinical studies, and expert judgment, to assess the health consequences of the conditions of interest. Patient surveys and expert judgment would then be used to map the resulting health states into a preference-weightable form, such as the classifications of the Health Utilities Index.

A second research area motivated by food safety concerns would be to conduct preference surveys to compare values based on holistic perceptions of the consequences of risk and on explicit specifications of health consequences of risk in terms of mortality and morbidity. The comparison would be between holistic utility assessments for diseases such as "renal failure" and those based on explicit valuation of specific health states associated with those diseases. The former task could be repeated, first, by giving the respondent no information about the probabilities of specific health consequences and, second, by providing such information. Through such a study design, it might be possible to infer to what extent differences between holistic and state-specific utilities are attributable to incomplete knowledge of the health consequence of disease, as opposed to values not captured by the health-state-specific utilities. The design could be applied to both QALY and WTP assessments.

Conclusion

Priority setting based on estimation of the expected burden on quality-adjusted life expectancy can be a useful policy tool in food safety. This approach makes use of both scientific evidence and expert judgment on the health consequences of the conditions of concern, and citizen preferences regarding the relative value of those consequences. Further research is needed, both on health-state preferences and on the mapping from risks to health consequences, in order to assemble the information that would permit the assignment of QALY losses to foodborne risks. This information can be incorporated into analyses of burden of disease measured in terms of QALY losses, and into CEAs of the cost per QALY gained by various regulatory interventions. Because of their inherent limitations, neither the QALY approach nor any other analytical approach should completely replace the judgments of policy makers, which are sensitive to political, behavioral, and ethical considerations.

References

Bleichrodt, H., P. Wakker, and M. Johannesson. 1997. Characterizing QALYs by Risk Neutrality. *Journal of Risk and Uncertainty* 15: 107–1.

Bleichrodt, H., J.L. Pinto, and P.P. Wakker. 2001. Making Descriptive Use of Prospect Theory to Improve the Prescriptive Use of Expected Utility. *Management Science* 47: 1498–1514.

Brazier, J., J. Roberts, and M. Deverill. 2002. The Estimation of a Preference-Based Measure of Health from the SF-36. *Journal of Health Economics* 21: 271–92.

Dolan, P., C. Gudex, P. Kind, and A. Williams. 1996. The Time Trade-off Method: Results from a General Population Study. *Health Economics* 5: 141–54.

Drummond, M., B. O'Brien, G.L. Stoddart, and G.W. Torrance. 1997. *Methods for the Economic Evaluation of Health Care Programmes,* 2nd edit. Oxford, UK: Oxford University Press.

Freedberg, K.A., E. Losina, M.C. Weinstein, A.D. Paltiel, C.J. Cohen, G.R. Seage, D.E. Craven, H. Zhang, A.D. Kimmel, and S.J. Goldie. 2001. The Cost-Effectiveness of Combination Antiretroviral Therapy in HIV. *New England Journal of Medicine* 344: 824–31.

Fryback, D.G., E.J. Dasbach, R. Klein, B.E. Klein, N. Dorn, K. Peterson, and P.A. Martin. 1993. The Beaver Dam Health Outcomes Study: Initial Catalog of Health-State Quality Factors. *Medical Decision Making* 13: 89–102.

Gold, M.R., J.E. Siegel, L.B. Russell, and M.C. Weinstein (eds.). 1996. *Cost-Effectiveness in Health and Medicine.* New York: Oxford University Press.

Goldman, L.D.J. Gordon, B.M. Rifkind, S.B. Hulley, A.S. Detsky, D.W. Goodman, B. Kinosian, and M.C. Weinstein. 1992. Cost and Health Implications of Cholesterol Lowering. *Circulation* 85: 1960–68.

Graham, J.D., P.S. Corso, J.M. Morris, M. Segui-Gomez, and M.C. Weinstein. 1998. Evaluating the Cost-Effectiveness of Clinical and Public Health Measures. *Annual Review of Public Health* 19: 125–52.

Institute of Medicine, National Academy of Sciences. 1985. *New Vaccine Development: Establishing Priorities.* Washington, DC: National Academy Press.

Kaplan, R.M., and J.P. Anderson. 1988. A General Health Policy Model: Update and Applications. *Health Services Research* 23: 203–35.

Krupnick, A., A. Alberini, M. Cropper, N. Simon, B. O'Brien, R. Goeree, and M. Heintzelman. 2002. Age, Health, and the Willingness to Pay for Mortality Risk Reductions: A Contingent Valuation Survey of Ontario Residents. *Journal of Risk and Uncertainty* 24: 161–86.

Lee, S.J., B. Liljas, P.J. Neumann, M.C. Weinstein, and M. Johannesson. 1998. The Impact of Risk Information on Patients' Willingness to Pay for Autologous Blood Donation. *Medical Care* 36: 1162–73.

MacKenzie, E.J., A.M. Damiano, T.S. Miller, and S. Luchter. 1996. The Development of the Functional Capacity Index. *Journal of Trauma* 41: 799–807.

McNeil, B.J., R. Weichselbaum, and S.G. Pauker. 1978. Fallacy of the Five-Year Survival in Lung Cancer. *New England Journal of Medicine* 299: 1397–1401.

Murray, C.J.L. 1994. Quantifying the Burden of Disease: The Technical Basis for Disability-Adjusted Life Years. *Bulletin of the World Health Organization* 72:429–445.

———, and A.K. Acharya. 1997. Understanding DALYs. *Journal of Health Economics* 16: 703–30.

Patrick, D.L., and P. Erickson. 1993. *Health Status and Health Policy.* New York: Oxford University Press.

Prosser, L.A., A.A. Stinnett, P.A. Goldman, L.W. Williams, M.G.M. Hunink, L. Goldman, and M.C. Weinstein. 2000. Cost-Effectiveness of Cholesterol-Lowering Therapies According to Selected Patient Characteristics. *Annals of Internal Medicine* 132: 769–79.

Raiffa, H. 1968. *Decision Analysis: Introductory Lectures on Choices Under Uncertainty.* Reading, MA: Addison-Wesley.

Russell, L.B., M.R. Gold, J.E. Siegel, N. Daniels, and M.C. Weinstein. 1996. The Role of Cost-Effectiveness Analysis in Health and Medicine. *Journal of the American Medical Association* 276: 1172–77.

Samsa, G.P., R.A. Reutter, G. Parmigiani, M. Ancukiewicz, P. Abrahamse, Lipscomb, J., and D.B. Matchar. 1999. Performing Cost-Effectiveness Analysis by Integrating Randomized Trial Data with a Comprehensive Decision Model: Application to Treatment of Acute Ischemic Stroke. *Journal of Clinical Epidemiology* 52: 259–71.

Stratton, K.R., J.S. Durch, and R.S. Lawrence (eds.). 1999. *Vaccines for the 21st Century: A Tool for Decisionmaking.* Washington, DC: National Academy of Sciences.

Tengs, T.O., M.E. Adams, J.S. Pliskin, D.G. Safran, J.E. Siegel, M.C. Weinstein, and J.D. Graham. 1995. Five Hundred Life-Saving Interventions and Their Cost-Effectiveness. *Risk Analysis* 15: 369–90.

Torrance, G.W. 1986. Measurement of Health State Utilities for Economic Appraisal. *Journal of Health Economics* 5: 1–30.

———, D.H. Feeny, W.J. Furlong, R.D. Barr, Y. Zhang, and Q. Wang. 1996. Multiattribute Utility Function for a Comprehensive Health Status Classification System: Health Utilities Index Mark 2. *Medical Care* 34: 702–22.

U.S. CDC (Centers for Disease Control and Prevention). 1999. An Ounce of Prevention. *American Journal of Preventive Medicine* 16: 248–63.

Weinstein, M.C., J.E. Siegel, M.R. Gold, M.S. Kamlet, and L.B. Russell. 1996. Recommendations of the Panel on Cost-Effectiveness in Health and Medicine. *Journal of the American Medical Association* 276: 1253–58.

12

Willingness-to-Pay Measures of Food Safety Regulatory Benefits

James K. Hammitt

The value of improvements in food safety can be measured by consumers' "willingness to pay" (WTP), defined as the amount of money that consumers would voluntarily exchange for specified reductions in risk of foodborne illness. WTP for food safety depends on characteristics of the consumer, including total mortality risk, wealth or income, health, and other factors. This chapter reviews the economic theory of WTP for reductions in risk of fatality and chronic and acute morbidity, and considers issues that arise in the use of revealed-preference and contingent valuation methods for estimating WTP to reduce foodborne health risks.

The basic economic approach to quantifying the value of food safety is to determine the quantity of other goods and services that individuals would willingly give up to obtain greater food safety. This idea of value comes from the observation that individuals and families, like society as a whole, must operate under financial and time constraints. The trade-offs individuals make between alternative possible uses of their limited resources indicate the relative value they attach to these uses. It is usually convenient to measure these other goods and services in monetary units because this provides a common unit of measure. One way to think about this idea of value is to ask how much money would a budget-constrained individual be willing to shift from other uses to pay for a little more safety? This is referred to as the individual's "willingness to pay" (WTP) for greater safety. Another way to conceptualize it is to ask how much larger an income would a budget-constrained individual be willing to accept at the cost of having a little less safety? This is referred to as the individual's "willingness to accept" (WTA) compensation for less safety. Usually, WTP and WTA are used to measure the value of *small,* or marginal, changes in safety, as most policies that affect food safety produce only small changes in risk to individuals.

The definition of value as a rate of substitution between food safety and other goods has several immediate consequences. The value of food safety may differ among individuals, depending on their preferences for safety relative to other goods; their wealth and income, which affect their ability to pay; and the set of alternatives available to them, which influence their ability to manage food-related and other health risks they face.

When evaluating public policies, it is society's willingness to pay for improved food safety that is of concern. Social WTP is usually viewed as the sum of the willingness to pay of all individuals in society. The policy benefits measured by social WTP for improved food safety include three components. First, individuals are less likely to experience the "pain and suffering" and other disutility associated with illness or fatality in each time period. This component is typically the largest factor in individual WTP, at least for severe illness and fatality. Second, medical and other resources that would have been used caring for victims of foodborne illness can be diverted to other uses. Third, productivity losses that occur when people are sick or die are reduced. Typically, the individual bears only part of the costs associated with the second and third components, because some of the medical costs are paid by health insurers, either private or public, and some of the lost productivity is compensated through sick pay or public assistance.

In estimating the value of food safety to society, it is important to recognize that individual WTP may not include parts of the medical costs or productivity losses when these are paid by others. If so, the shares of these components paid by sources other than the individual should be added to individual WTP in order to estimate social WTP. Treatment costs and lost productivity are the focus of the "cost of illness" approach (Rice 1967), which counts the social value of these components regardless of who bears these costs. The cost of illness approach provides an incomplete measure of the value of reducing illness because it omits the individual utility loss. It is this individual disutility that is the focus of this chapter.

The value of improvements in food safety is likely to be sensitive to the set of foods affected. Improvements in the safety of one food may be relatively small, as it may be easy to avoid risks associated with this food by substituting others. In contrast, improvements in safety of a broad class of foods, for example, seafood, may be of much greater value, as the alternative method of avoiding these risks is to avoid consumption of the whole class of foods. This implies that the value of a program to improve the safety of a broad class of foods may be substantially greater than the sum of the values of programs to improve safety of selected food types.

The next section describes the economic theory describing individual WTP for changes in health and health risks. The third section describes the two major approaches for obtaining empirical estimates of individual WTP to reduce risks of foodborne illness and fatality: revealed-preference and stated-preference or contingent valuation (CV) methods. Conclusions are presented in the last section.

Theory of WTP for Food Safety

This section describes the economic theory of WTP for changes in risk of adverse health effects. The risks of fatality, chronic morbidity, and acute morbidity are described in each subsection.

Risk of Mortality

The WTP approach to valuing changes in mortality risk was proposed by Schelling (1968) in an article suggestively titled "The Life You Save May Be Your Own." Schelling observed that for improvements in food safety and other policies that reduce mortality risk, one cannot know whose life will be "saved." The question is not how to value postponement of a specific death but how to value small changes in mortality risk across a population.

The individual's rate of trade-off between wealth and risk in a specified time period, for example, the current year, can be represented graphically as the slope of the individual's indifference curve between his wealth (w) and the probability ($1 - p$) that he will survive a specified time period, for example, the next year, at the individual's current wealth and survival probability (Figure 12.1). The slope represents the amount he would be willing to pay (his change in wealth, Δw) for a small change in his probability of survival ($\Delta 1 - p$), given his current wealth (w_0) and probability of survival ($1 - p_0$). For small changes in the probability of survival, WTP is approximately the change in probability times the individual's marginal rate of substitution between wealth and the probability of survival, that is, $\Delta w \approx \frac{dw}{dp} \Delta p$. The marginal rate of substitution $\frac{dw}{dp}$ (holding utility constant) is called the "value of a statistical life" (VSL). VSL is something of a misnomer because it is really the individual's willingness to pay for a small change in his probability of survival for a specified time period, such as the next year in this example. If an individual's VSL is $5 million, he would pay up to $\Delta w = \$50$ to reduce his risk of dying this year by $\Delta p = 1$ in 100,000. Because VSL is not constant over the range of the probability of survival, this value applies only to small changes in risk. It does not imply the individual would pay $5 million to avert certain death this year, or that he would accept certain death in exchange for $5 million. It does imply that 100,000 similar people would together pay $5 million to eliminate a risk that would be expected to randomly kill one among them this year.

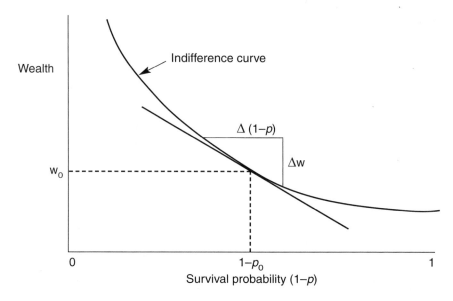

FIGURE 12.1. Preference Trade-Off Between Wealth and Survival Probability

VSL is not a universal constant but varies by individual and circumstance. The dependence of VSL on total mortality risk, wealth, health, competing mortality risk, background financial wealth, age, and life expectancy are described in the following paragraphs.

The standard economic model (Drèze 1962; Jones-Lee 1974; Weinstein et al. 1980) considers mortality risk within a single period and assumes that the individual's welfare can be represented as the expected state-dependent utility of wealth

$$U(p, w) = (1 - p)\, u_s(w) + p\, u_d(w - L) \tag{1}$$

where p is the individual's chance of dying during the current period and $u_s(w)$ and $u_d(w)$ represent his utility as a function of wealth conditional on surviving and dying, respectively. The state-dependent expected utility model is widely used in modeling individual preferences over risky alternatives. In this case, it makes the assumption that the utility that the individual derives from wealth when he dies does not depend on the utility he derives from wealth while living. The function u_d incorporates the individual's preferences for bequests, and the utility of consumption during the part of the time period he survives. The wealth loss L represents any financial consequences of dying such as medical bills or life-insurance benefits. In this one-period model, wealth and income are treated as equivalent, but the difference between them can be important in multiperiod models.

The individual's VSL is derived by differentiating equation (1) holding utility constant to obtain:

$$VSL = \frac{dw}{dp} = \frac{u_s(w_0) - u_d(w_0 - L)}{(1 - p_0)u'_s(w_0) + p_0 u'_d(w_0 - L)} = \frac{\Delta u(w_0)}{Eu'(w_0)} \qquad (2)$$

where the prime indicates the first derivative, w_0 is current wealth, and p_0, which is between 0 and 1, is total current mortality risk. The numerator in equation (2) is the difference between utility if the individual survives or dies in the current period. The denominator is the expected marginal utility of wealth, that is, the utility associated with additional wealth conditional on surviving (u_s') and on not surviving (u_d') the period, weighted by the probabilities of these events. Assuming that life is preferred to death [$u_s(w) > u_d(w - L)$ for all w] and that greater wealth is preferred to less [$u_s'(w) > 0$ and $u_d'(w - L) \geq 0$ for all w], both numerator and denominator are positive and so VSL is positive.

Baseline Risk. It is natural to assume that the increased utility from additional wealth is larger if the individual survives and has the opportunity to spend it than if he dies, that is, $u_s'(w) > u_d'(w - L)$. If so, an increase in the baseline risk of death, p_0, decreases the value of the denominator in equation (2), representing the expected utility-cost of spending. The difference in utility between survival and death, represented by the numerator, is unaffected by baseline risk, so the individual would be willing to spend more to reduce his mortality risk. For small changes in risk, the effect of baseline risk, christened the "dead-anyway" effect by Pratt and Zeckhauser (1996), cannot be large.[1] Assuming that $u_d'(w) \geq 0$, that is, the individual never prefers to leave a smaller bequest, the proportional effect of a change in baseline risk on VSL cannot be greater than the proportional change in the survival probability $(1 - p_0)$ (Hammitt 2000a).

Wealth or Income. As with most goods, WTP for a reduction in mortality risk depends on ability to pay and is likely to increase with wealth or income. The assumption that additional wealth is more valuable in life than as a bequest [$u_s'(w) > u_d'(w - L)$] implies that the numerator of equation (2) increases with wealth. Most individuals are averse to financial risk. If so, the denominator declines with wealth—the second derivatives of $u_s(w)$ and $u_d(w)$ are negative—and VSL increases. If the individual is indifferent to financial risk, the denom-

---

[1] If the individual gets more utility from additional wealth if he survives than dies, he sacrifices little utility by spending profligately on reducing his risk of dying when the probability is large, as he is likely to be dead anyway.

inator is constant and again VSL increases with wealth. Only in the unlikely event that the individual prefers to bear greater financial risk, for the same expected return, can the denominator increase with wealth, making the effect on VSL indeterminate. Empirical evidence about the relationship between income and VSL is limited. The most numerous and credible estimates of VSL come from studies of compensating wage differentials (Viscusi 1993). These studies estimate wages as a function of workplace-fatality risk, human-capital variables, and other factors. Because income or the wage rate is the dependent variable, it cannot be used as an explanatory variable, and so these studies typically do not provide information about income elasticity, the percentage change in VSL in response to a 1% change in income.

The income elasticity can be estimated by meta-analysis of compensating-wage-differential studies in which the study populations differ in income, risk, and other factors, but these studies lack power. Liu et al. (1997) estimated the relationship between VSL, income, and workplace-fatality risk for a sample of 17 compensating-wage-differential studies in the United States and other industrialized countries. Their point estimate for the income elasticity is 0.54, with a standard error of 0.85. Mrozek and Taylor (1999) expanded on this approach by including multiple VSL estimates from each of 23 wage studies and controlling for the average wage, risk, and other factors. They report four specifications yielding estimated elasticities of VSL with respect to the wage rate between 0.50 and 0.88 with standard errors of 0.26 and above (a fifth model yields a negative but insignificant estimate).

Because contingent valuation studies elicit WTP directly, they can be used to estimate the income elasticity of VSL. Typical estimates range from 0.2 to 0.5. For example, Jones-Lee et al. (1985) estimated values of 0.25 to 0.44, Mitchell and Carson (1986) estimated 0.35, and Corso et al. (2001) estimated 0.41.

Health. VSL may depend on the quality of health the individual expects to experience if he survives. Although one might anticipate that WTP to reduce mortality risk will be greater if the individual anticipates surviving in good health rather than poor, the reverse is also possible. If poor health limits the individual's opportunity to improve his well-being by spending money, the marginal utility of wealth may be smaller if he survives in poor health than if he survives in good health. If so, the denominator of equation (2) is smaller if survival will be in poor health than if it will be in good health. As the numerator is also smaller, VSL for survival in poor health may be larger or smaller than VSL for survival in good health, depending on whether the effect of health on the marginal value of wealth outweighs its effect on the total utility of survival.

There is some empirical evidence to suggest that the marginal utility of income may be lower in poor health than in good health. Sloan et al. (1998), using a survey-based approach, found that the marginal utility of income is lower for an individual having multiple sclerosis (MS) than for an otherwise similar healthy individual. The estimated value of the factor by which marginal utility is decreased is sensitive to whether the estimate is obtained from people with or without MS; estimates are 0.08 for people without MS and 0.67 for people with MS.

Competing Mortality Risk. At any point in time, individuals face a variety of competing mortality risks. WTP to reduce one risk, such as the threat from microbial contaminants in food, depends on the magnitude of the competing risks. Competing mortality risk reduces the chance that the individual will survive the period, and thus reduces the value of the numerator in equation (2). It also reduces the value of the denominator in equation (2), the dead-anyway effect. Eeckhoudt and Hammitt (2001) showed that, if larger bequests are preferred to smaller $[u_d'(w) > 0]$, the effect in the numerator dominates and so WTP to reduce a target risk decreases as competing mortality risk increases. In contrast, if the individual is indifferent to the size of his bequest $[u_d'(w) = 0]$, competing mortality risk has no effect on WTP.

Financial Risk. Over both the short and the long run, an individual's wealth is uncertain. Hence current wealth, w_0, in equation (2) is more accurately viewed as a random variable rather than a fixed quantity. Moreover, different individuals face different degrees of uncertainty about their wealth, either because of investment choices or because of differences in education and other factors that affect earning prospects. The effects of a pure increase in financial risk, holding the expected value of wealth constant, depend on the difference between the individual's degree of risk aversion conditional on survival and conditional on death, and on whether or not he is prudent in each state, that is, whether the third derivatives of the state-dependent utility functions u_s and u_d are positive (Kimball 1990). Under the reasonable conditions that the individual is weakly risk averse and prudent in both states, and no more risk averse regarding his bequest than regarding his wealth conditional on survival, increasing financial risk reduces VSL (Eeckhoudt and Hammitt 2001).

Age and Life Expectancy. The effect of age on VSL has been examined in theoretical models and, to a limited extent, by empirical studies. Theoretical models (e.g., Shepard and Zeckhauser 1984; Rosen 1988; Ng 1992) represent the individual's lifetime utility as the expected present value of his utility in each time period. Utility within a period depends on consumption, which is limited by current income, savings and inheritance, and ability to borrow against future earnings. The individual seeks to maximize lifetime utility by allocating his wealth to consumption, savings, and reductions in current-period mortality risk.

Two factors influence the life-cycle pattern of VSL. First, the number of future life years at risk declines as one ages, so the benefit of a decrease in current-period mortality risk (the numerator in equation [2]) declines. Second, the opportunity cost of spending on risk reduction (the denominator in equation [2]) also declines with age as savings accumulate and the investment horizon approaches. The net effect may cause VSL to fall or rise with age.

In models that assume an individual can borrow against future earnings, VSL declines with age. For example, Shepard and Zeckhauser (1984) calculated that VSL for a typical American worker falls by a factor of three from age 25 to age 75. If individuals can save but not borrow, VSL rises in early years as the individual's savings and earnings increase before it ultimately declines. In this case, Shepard and Zeckhauser found that VSL peaks near age 40 and is less than half as large at ages 20 and 65.

Ng (1992) argued that the rate at which individuals discount their future utility is likely to be smaller than the rate of return to financial assets, whereas Shepard and Zeckhauser (1984) assumed these rates are equal. If the utility-discount rate is less than the rate of return, individuals should save more when they are young and consume more when old. Under these conditions, VSL may not peak until age 60 or so (Ng 1992). Even if individuals discount future utility at the rate of return, if they are prudent (Kimball 1990), younger people might be anticipated to save more, and spend less on reducing mortality risk, because of the greater range of future financial contingencies they face.

Although many CV studies include age as one of several explanatory variables in a regression model describing WTP for risk reduction, these studies typically have not focused on estimating the effect of age on VSL. The results of these studies are somewhat contradictory, with several finding VSL increases with age (e.g., Gerking et al. 1988; Johannesson et al. 1997; Lee et al. 1997) and others finding VSL decreases with age (e.g., Buzby et al. 1995; Hammitt and Graham 1999). Jones-Lee et al. (1985) included both linear and quadratic age terms in their regression models and concluded that VSL peaks at about the mean age in their sample, which is not reported.

Two recent empirical studies are specifically directed toward estimating the effect of age on VSL. Krupnick et al. (2002) and Alberini et al. (2002) conducted CV studies of WTP for a hypothetical intervention that would reduce the respondent's risk of dying in the next 10 years by either 1 or 5 in 1,000. The samples were restricted to individuals 40 years of age and older. For a sample of Canadian respondents, Krupnick et al. (2002) estimated that VSL is roughly constant for ages 40 to 69, and is about 30% smaller for individuals 70 years of age and older. For an American sample, Alberini et al. (2002) found no statistically significant effect of age, although their point estimate suggests that VSL is about 20% smaller for respondents older than 70 years of age than for younger respondents.

The amount of money an individual would pay to reduce his chance of dying in a specified time period by a small amount, called his VSL, depends on his individual characteristics. In addition to his preferences for survival probability relative to other goods and services he could purchase, VSL depends on wealth, initial survival probability, age, health, and other factors. In theory, larger wealth and smaller survival probability increase VSL but the effects of the other factors may be positive or negative.

Risk of Chronic Morbidity

The standard model of WTP for reductions in mortality risk can be reinterpreted as a model of WTP for reductions in risk of chronic illness. Under this interpretation, $u_s(w)$ represents utility for wealth if the individual remains healthy, and $u_d(w)$ represents utility for wealth if the individual develops a chronic disease.

The assumption that the person prefers to be healthy than to develop a chronic disease, $u_s(w) > u_d(w - L)$, is not problematic. It also seems reasonable to assume that the marginal utility of wealth is greater when one is healthy than when one is chronically ill, $u_s'(w) \geq u_d'(w)$, with strict inequality resulting if opportunities for gaining enjoyment through purchase of goods and services are diminished by chronic disease. As noted earlier, limited empirical evidence exists to suggest that the marginal utility of income is smaller in a state of chronic poor health than in good health (Sloan et al. 1998). However, if the individual is liable for substantial medical expenses or suffers substantial uncompensated loss of income, the resulting wealth loss L could be great enough so that the marginal utility of wealth when one is healthy is less than the marginal utility of wealth less the financial costs of chronic illness when one is ill, $u_s'(w) < u_d'(w - L)$; this requires risk aversion in the event of chronic disease, that is, $u_d''(w) < 0$).

If the standard model of VSL is reinterpreted as a model of WTP to reduce risk of chronic disease and if $u_s'(w) > u_d'(w - L)$, then all of the results described in the section on risk of mortality carry over. In particular, WTP to reduce the risk of chronic disease increases with the total probability of disease and with wealth or income, and it decreases with competing risks of chronic disease and financial risk. If the marginal utility of income is unaffected by chronic disease, then WTP to reduce the risk is unaffected by the total risk. In contrast, if the wealth loss from morbidity is large enough so that $u_a'(w) < u_d'(w - L)$, then an increase in baseline risk reduces WTP, the opposite of the dead-anyway effect, and the effect of wealth on WTP is ambiguous, even if the individual is risk averse in both healthy and unhealthy states.

Risk of Acute Morbidity

The economic theory of WTP to reduce the risk of acute morbidity has received relatively little attention. Moreover, the single-period model that has been used to study mortality risk is less useful for studying acute morbidity.

A defining characteristic of acute morbidity is that one recovers from it, returning to the state of health experienced before the acute morbidity. This suggests that the effects of adverse health on the marginal utility of income are less important, because of the possibility of substituting consumption between periods of morbidity and full health. It also suggests that the duration of morbidity is important.

Empirical results suggest that WTP to reduce the risk of acute morbidity increases with the duration and severity of the morbidity. In a meta-analysis of five health-related CV studies, Johnson et al. (1997) provided empirical evidence of a nonlinear relationship between WTP and both duration and severity of acute illness. Severity was measured using an index of health-related quality of life (HRQL), the Quality of Well-Being scale (QWB; Kaplan and Anderson 1988). Such indices are used to weight duration of morbidity to calculate the quality-adjusted life years (QALYs) associated with an illness. They are in principle von Neumann–Morgenstern utility functions for health (Pliskin et al. 1980). By examining the relationship between empirical WTP and QWB value for 53 short-term health conditions, Johnson et al. (1997) found a weak relationship for mild conditions but a strong negative relationship for more serious conditions. These findings support the common-sense notion that WTP to reduce the risk of illness is larger for more severe illnesses. Similar results were obtained by two studies that used CV to estimate WTP to prevent acute illness in Taiwan. Liu et al. (2000) estimated mothers' WTP to protect themselves and their children from suffering a cold. WTP increased with the severity of symptoms, where symptoms were represented using either dummy variables or the QWB. Alberini et al. (1996), in a study of the value of reducing illness associated with air pollution, also found that WTP to avoid acute morbidity increases with the number of symptoms.

CV studies of WTP to avoid acute morbidity suggest that WTP increases with duration of the illness to be avoided, but at a rate that is less than proportionate to duration. Johnson et al. (1997) estimated an elasticity of WTP with respect to duration of about 0.5. Tolley et al. (1994) used CV to estimate WTP to prevent each of seven symptoms and various combinations of symptoms, for 1 day or for 30 days. Comparing estimates of WTP to avoid 1 day or 30 days of individual symptoms implies an elasticity of WTP with respect to duration of about 0.5 to 0.7. Liu et al. (2000) and Alberini et al. (1996) estimate somewhat smaller elasticities of WTP with respect to duration of about 0.2.

Nonhealth Attributes

Consumers' WTP for food safety may reflect preferences over attributes in addition to health risks, including nonhealth consequences and methods of food production. In contrast, QALY measures, described later, depend on the health consequences alone. For example, organically grown foods are valued by some consumers for a number of reasons in addition to perceived health benefits. These include perceived reductions in risks to ecosystems and biodiversity, support for small family farms rather than large agricultural corporations, and a belief that organic production methods are inherently more desirable (Hammitt 1990; Williams and Hammitt 2000). Similarly, some consumers appear to have strong preferences with regard to other food-production technologies, such as the use of genetically modified crops and irradiation. These preferences may reflect perceived risks to health and ecosystems, but to some extent they seem to reflect judgments that these technologies are inherently less desirable than more traditional technologies, regardless of their consequences. Donaldson et al. (1996) found that 75% of a sample of consumers reported a positive WTP for a hypothetical technology to reduce the risk of illness from eating poultry, but only 50% reported a positive WTP for irradiation to reduce the same risk. One third of those who would not purchase irradiated poultry report they would be willing to pay a positive amount to prevent irradiation.

Comparison with QALY

Economic theory suggests that WTP for food safety may depend on a variety of characteristics of the individual and the risk. The effects of individual-specific characteristics on WTP are quite different than the effects of these characteristics on an alternative method for valuing risks of foodborne illness, QALYs. Some of these differences are summarized in Table 12.1. When foodborne risks are measured using QALYs, the value of a mortality risk reduction is independent of total mortality risk, wealth, or income[2]; in contrast, these factors increase WTP. Health impairment decreases the QALY measure, but its effect on WTP is ambiguous. Competing mortality risk is the only factor considered here that has the same effect on both WTP and QALYs: it reduces the value of a mortality risk reduction. Financial risk decreases WTP and has little or no effect on QALYs, and life expectancy increases the QALY value but its effect on WTP is ambiguous. Finally, concerns about the technology by which a change in risk of foodborne illness is produced—"organic" production methods, genetically modified cultivars, irradiation—may affect WTP for the risk reduction, but do not affect QALYs, which depend only on health outcomes.

---

[2]Wealth or income may affect the QALYs lost to illness when wealth ameliorates the effect of health impairment or when the effect of health impairment on income-earning potential is incorporated in the Health-Related Quality of Life measure, as recommended by Gold et al. (1996).

TABLE 12.1. Effects of Individuals' Characteristics on the Value of Reducing a Current Mortality Risk

	WTP	*QALYs*
Baseline risk	Increase	No effect
Wealth	Increase	No effect[a]
Impaired health	Ambiguous	Decrease
Competing risk	Decrease	Decrease
Financial risk	Decrease	No effect
Life expectancy	Ambiguous	Increase
Technology	May affect	No effect

[a]Wealth may affect QALYs if it affects ability to cope with health impairment or if health impairment reduces income-earning capability.

Methods for Estimating WTP for Food Safety

Two broad classes of methods are used for estimating WTP for food safety: revealed-preference and stated-preference methods. Both methods have been used to estimate WTP for food safety. Each method has its strengths and weaknesses. These are described in the following subsections.

Revealed Preference

Revealed-preference methods measure WTP from actual behavior. These methods are based on the assumption that people make choices that are in their best interests. By observing the choices people make in situations in which they are implicitly trading health risk against either money or other goods that can be valued in monetary terms, for example, time, one can infer what their preferences must be for them to have preferred the choice they made to the available alternatives.

Revealed preference has traditionally been judged by economists to provide more valid estimates of WTP than other methods, because it is based on behavior in consequential situations, in which individuals have incentives to identify and understand the alternative choices. Revealed-preference methods require the existence of situations in which people are choosing among alternatives that differ in risk and other attributes, and in which the analyst is able to identify the alternatives that were not chosen and their attributes as perceived by consumers. Moreover, the individuals must be making informed choices. Choices based on misperceived alternatives do not reveal the individual's preferences among the accurately measured attributes of the alternatives. Because revealed-preference methods require situations in which choices can be observed, they are limited in their ability to estimate separately the values of co-occurring risks. For example, if a food contaminant creates risks of both morbidity and mortality, it may be possible to estimate consumers' WTP to avoid the specific bundle of these risks created by the contaminant, but not to estimate WTP to reduce each risk individually.

A number of revealed-preference studies of WTP for food safety have been conducted. Some rely on cross-sectional data in which different consumers choose different foods, while others rely on time-series data and examine how consumer choice responds to changing information about foodborne risks.

Cross-sectional studies have examined consumers' choices between different types of food. For example, one can compare consumer WTP for organically and conventionally grown produce. Hammitt (1986, 1993) obtained retail price data for organic and conventional versions of 27 types of fresh produce sold in supermarkets and other grocery stores in Los Angeles. He estimated that the organic versions were priced 6% to 84% higher than the conventional versions, which implies that consumers who purchased the organic versions were willing to pay this amount more for organically grown produce. Dividing the present value of lifetime WTP by the estimated reduction in lifetime cancer risk yields a value per statistical cancer case of about $5 million, which is similar to other estimates of VSL; it is assumed that most cancers are fatal.

A difficulty in interpreting cross-sectional estimates as measures of WTP for food safety is that the analyst must identify the attributes of the alternative foods that matter to consumers. Organically and conventionally grown produce differ on several attributes that are potentially relevant to consumers, including appearance and taste.[3]

Organically grown produce is widely perceived to present smaller risks of foodborne illness, because synthetic pesticides are not used in its production. Whether these consumer beliefs are accurate is uncertain, as the risks associated with consuming organically grown produce have not been analyzed and the risk-perception literature suggests individuals tend to overestimate the effects of man-made technologies relative to "natural" risks. There is some reason to suspect that the risk-lowering benefits of reduced exposure to synthetic pesticides may be offset by exposure to greater quantities of toxic plant constituents, "natural pesticides," owing to farmers' choice of cultivar or greater pest-induced stress on the plants, exposure to nonsynthetic pesticides such as sulfur, and exposure to greater microbial risks as a result of using manure as a fertilizer (Ahl 1997; Williams and Hammitt 2000).

Data from a risk-perception survey in the Boston area (Williams and Hammitt 2000) suggest that consumers differentiate among several types of risk. They perceive that the risks of cancer and other adverse health effects from pes-

---

[3]Schutz and Lorenz (1976) conducted blind taste tests among experimental crops grown under organic and conventional conditions. They found that subjects favored whichever version was labeled organic, but could not distinguish between versions without labeling.

ticide use are smaller for organically grown than for conventional produce, but that the risks from microbial contamination and toxic constituents of the plant are similar. Consumers who prefer organically grown produce also believe that it differs on attributes of the production process that are of concern to them, independent of any effects on their own health. For example, the production process is perceived as better in that it presents smaller risks to ecosystems and farmworkers and promotes small "family" farms in contrast to large "corporate" farms (Hammitt 1990; Williams and Hammitt 2000).

Other revealed-preference studies examine changes in consumption of specific foods in response to information about risks. For example, van Ravenswaay and Hoehn (1991) examined how WTP for Alar-free apples changed once health risks from use of the growth regulator were publicized. They estimated that WTP for Alar-free apples ranged from 10% to 30% of the apple price. Because the mortality risks associated with Alar are uncertain, the implied VSL ranges between about $1.5 million and $27 million. Other studies of the effect of risk information on food demand include those of Shulstad and Stoevener (1978), who examined the effect of information about mercury contamination on demand for pheasant hunting in Oregon; Swartz and Strand (1981), who examined the effect of information about kepone contamination in the James River on demand for James River and Chesapeake Bay oysters; Johnson (1988), who examined the effects of information about ethylene dibromide (EDB) use as a grain fumigant on demand for baked-goods mixes; and Smith et al. (1988) and Foster and Just (1989), who examined how demand for Hawaiian milk shifted with information about contamination by heptachlor, a pesticide that remained on pineapple husks used to feed dairy cattle.

These time-series studies appear to provide better evidence of consumer WTP for food safety than do the cross-sectional studies. Many of the differences between alternative foods are controlled by the time-series design and there is less danger of confounding estimates of WTP for risk reduction with WTP for other attributes, such as characteristics of the production process. A disadvantage of the time-series studies is that consumers may overreact to new information suggesting risks of foodborne illness, and so estimates of WTP soon after release of the news may be substantially higher than estimates obtained after the information has been assimilated. Alternatively, time-series studies may underestimate WTP if consumers find it relatively easy to avoid one type of food for a limited period until concerns about its safety have been resolved, but avoiding the food for a longer period would entail greater hardship.

Stated Preference

The other major class of methods for estimating WTP for food safety relies on consumers' statements about their preferences and behavior in surveys. Contingent valuation (CV) (Mitchell and Carson, 1989) is the most commonly used of these stated-preference approaches.

CV and other stated-preference methods are much more flexible than re-vealed-preference methods, as survey respondents can be presented with questions about what choices they would make in a wide variety of hypothet-ical circumstances. A concern about CV is that survey responses are not as credible an indicator of preferences as is behavior in more consequential set-tings, because the respondent has little incentive to analyze the choice or to report truthfully. Respondent incentives to accurately characterize and report their preferences may be sensitive to details of the CV study, including respon-dents' perception that the results will influence government behavior and the format of the WTP question, for example, open-ended, binary choice (Carson et al. 2000).

Economic experiments provide a third alternative that combines some de-sirable features of revealed- and stated-preference methods. In experiments by Hayes et al. (1995), for example, participants were required to consume food items that differed in risk of illness, and to pay money to obtain the safer food item. Behavior in such experiments may differ from routine behavior that is the subject of revealed-preference studies because of the novelty of participat-ing in an experiment, the fact that it is a one-time rather than recurring deci-sion, and other factors.

A central difficulty in using CV to estimate WTP for changes in food safety is to communicate the difference in risk between alternative choices to survey respondents. The standard theory of WTP for reductions in risk of fatality or other serious health effects (see the second section) implies that WTP should be nearly proportional to the absolute change in the probability of the adverse event. For example, WTP to reduce fatality risk in the current year by 2 in 100,000 should be almost exactly twice WTP to reduce fatality risk by 1 in 100,000. The incremental WTP to reduce risk by the second increment, that is, from 1 in 100,000 to 2 in 100,000, should be smaller than WTP for the first in-crement, from 0 to 1 in 100,000, for two reasons: VSL declines with increasing survival probability (the dead-anyway effect) and with the decline in wealth that results from purchasing the first survival increment. For relevant param-eter values, both effects are trivial: the dead-anyway effect reduces VSL by no more than the proportional increase in survival probability, and WTP for these small risk increments is a very small fraction of income, so the wealth effect cannot be large (Hammitt 2000b).

In almost every CV study of WTP for risk reductions of differing magni-tude, estimated WTP is inadequately sensitive to the difference in magnitude. Hammitt and Graham (1999) identified 14 CV studies published from 1980 through 1998 that either reported a test of sensitivity to magnitude or provided enough information to enable them to conduct such a test. They found that al-though estimated WTP was sensitive to the magnitude of risk reduction, that is, the estimated value of a larger reduction exceeded the estimated value of a smaller reduction, in 11 cases, WTP was inadequately sensitive, that is, less than proportionate to the magnitude of risk reduction, in all cases.

To test whether inadequate sensitivity to magnitude is a result of difficulties in communicating small risk changes to survey respondents (Baron 1997), Corso et al. (2001) asked respondents to value reductions in automobile fatality risk. Respondents were presented with one of three visual aids—a field of 25,000 dots, a logarithmic or hierarchical linear risk ladder—or no visual aid, and values for reducing annual risk by 5 in 100,000 or 10 in 100,000 were elicited from separate subsamples. Corso et al. found that estimated WTP was sensitive to the magnitude of risk reduction for respondents presented with any of the visual aids, but not for the control group. Moreover, the hypothesis that estimated WTP was proportionate to the risk reduction could not be rejected for the groups of respondents presented with either the dots or the logarithmic risk ladder. This study suggests that CV can yield estimates of WTP for small risk reductions that are consistent with economic theory, and hence that near-proportionality of estimated WTP to risk reduction may be used as a test for the validity of CV estimates (Hammitt 2000b).

Inadequate sensitivity of WTP to magnitude of risk reduction can be an important concern in estimating WTP for health effects of differing severity. Because the probability of mild cases of foodborne illness far exceeds the probability of severe cases, it is reasonable to anticipate that programs to improve food safety will yield much larger decreases in the probability of mild effects than of severe effects. If CV is used to estimate WTP for decreases in these risks, differences in the stated magnitudes of risk reduction may confound estimates of the sensitivity of WTP to severity of end-point.

Henson (1996) used CV to estimate WTP for safer eggs, which would reduce the probability of mild, moderate, and severe illness, and death, by 1 in 800, 1 in 3,000, 1 in 22,000, and 1 in 6 million, respectively. Mean estimates of the value per statistical case (WTP divided by reduction in probability) are £500, £6,500, £68,000, and £4.6 million, respectively. Whereas Henson interpreted these estimates as plausibly related to the severity of the health effect, Covey et al. (1998) suggest an alternative explanation that is supported by interviews with survey respondents and testing for the sensitivity of WTP to differences in magnitude of risk reduction. The alternative explanation is that respondents' reported WTP is determined primarily not by evaluating the benefits of the risk reduction, but rather by determining how much of an increase in expenditure for eggs the respondent could tolerate without significant disruption of his or her budget. This mechanism is consistent with the rough similarity of WTP estimates for the different risk reductions Henson (1996) obtained, which range between £0.63 and £3.10. Dividing roughly the same WTP by a small risk reduction in the case of fatality and by a larger risk reduction in the case of mild illness produces very different values per statistical fatality and per case of mild illness. Henson (1996) also noted that WTP for the same risk reductions was substantially (50% to 100%) greater when it was to be achieved by reducing risks associated with eating chicken rather than eggs. He suggests this difference might reflect anchoring WTP to the higher price of chicken.

Both revealed-preference and contingent valuation methods have been widely used to estimate the monetary value of reducing health risks, with several studies focusing on risks from consuming different types of foods. Although a number of important methodological concerns are present in both types of studies, the existing literature suggests that plausible estimates may be obtained using either method. Given the methodological difficulties, however, these estimates should be interpreted as suggesting the order of magnitude rather than the exact value of the risk reduction.

Conclusions

WTP measures provide a convenient method for summarizing individuals' preferences about the benefits of reducing foodborne risks of illness and death. By quantifying the benefits of food safety in monetary units, WTP measures provide a method to compare the benefits of food safety programs with the costs of these programs and with the benefits that could be obtained through alternative uses of resources. Because WTP compares the benefits of reducing foodborne risk with the benefits that individuals could obtain by spending their resources on other goods and services, it depends on the individuals' ability to pay—his wealth—and also on the other opportunities that are available to him. As a result, WTP may differ between individuals, and may be influenced by aspects of the risk other than the probability and health consequences.

Empirical estimates can be obtained using both revealed-preference and contingent valuation methods, although each approach has limitations. A number of estimates of WTP to reduce specific risks of foodborne illness as well as other health effects have been reported in the literature. Despite their limitations, these methods appear to provide useful estimates of the value of food safety.

References

Ahl, N. 1997. Director's Corner. USDA Office of Risk Assessment and Cost-Benefit Analysis. *ORACBA News* 2(6): 5–7.

Alberini, A., M. Cropper, T.-T. Fu, A. Krupnick, J.-T. Liu, D. Shaw, and W. Harrington, 1996. What Is the Value of Reduced Morbidity in Taiwan? In *The Economics of Pollution Control in the Asia Pacific,* edited by R. Mendelsohn and D. Shaw. Cheltenham, UK: Edward Elgar, 108–49.

————, M. Cropper, A. Krupnick, and N.B. Simon. 2002. Does the Value of a Statistical Life Vary with Age and Health Status? Evidence from the United States and Canada. Discussion Paper 02-19. Washington, DC: Resources for the Future.

Baron, J. 1997. Biases in Quantitative Measurement of Values for Public Decisions. *Psychological Bulletin* 122: 72–88.

Buzby, J., R. Ready, and J. Skees. 1995. Contingent Valuation in Food Policy Analysis: A Case Study of a Pesticide-Residue Risk Reduction. *Journal of Agricultural and Applied Economics* 27: 613–25.

Carson, R.T., T. Groves, and M.J. Machina. 2000. Incentive and Informational Properties of Preference Questions. University of California, San Diego, http://www.econ.ucsd.edu/~rcarson/ (accessed July 9, 2004).

Corso, P.S., J.K. Hammitt, and J.D. Graham. 2001. Valuing Mortality-Risk Reduction: Using Visual Aids to Improve the Validity of Contingent Valuation. *Journal of Risk and Uncertainty* 23: 165–84.

Covey, J., M.W. Jones-Lee, G. Loomes, and A. Robinson. 1998. Valuing the Prevention of Food-Borne Illness: Some Limitations of Consumers' 'Willingness to Pay.' *Risk Decision and Policy* 3: 245–59.

Donaldson, C., T. Mapp, M. Ryan, and K. Curtin. 1996. Estimating the Economic Benefits of Avoiding Food-Borne Risk: Is 'Willingness to Pay' Feasible? *Epidemiology and Infection* 116: 285–94.

Drèze, J., L'Utilitè Sociale d'une Vie Humaine. 1962. *Revue Française de Recherche Opèrationelle* 6: 93–118.

Eeckhoudt, L.R., and J.K. Hammitt. 2001. Background Risks and the Value of a Statistical Life. *Journal of Risk and Uncertainty* 23: 261–79.

Foster, W., and R.E. Just. 1989. Measuring Welfare Effects of Product Contamination with Consumer Uncertainty. *Journal of Environmental Economics and Management* 17: 266–83.

Gerking, S., M. De Haan, and W. Schulze. 1988. The Marginal Value of Job Safety: A Contingent Valuation Study. *Journal of Risk and Uncertainty* 1: 185–99.

Gold, M.R., J.E. Siegel, L.B. Russell, M.C. Weinstein (eds.). 1996. *Cost Effectiveness in Health and Medicine: Report of the Panel on Cost Effectiveness in Health and Medicine.* New York: Oxford University Press.

Hammitt, J.K. 1986. *Estimating Consumer Willingness to Pay to Reduce Food-Borne Risk.* R-3447-EPA, RAND Corporation, Santa Monica.

————. 1990. Risk Perceptions and Food Choice: An Exploratory Analysis of Organic-Versus Conventional-Produce Buyers. *Risk Analysis* 10: 367–74.

————. 1993. Consumer Willingness to Pay to Avoid Pesticide Residues. *Statistica Sinica* 3: 351–66.

————. 2000a. Valuing Mortality Risk: Theory and Practice. *Environmental Science and Technology* 34(8): 1396–1400.

————. 2000b. Evaluating Contingent Valuation of Environmental Health Risks: The Proportionality Test. *Association of Environmental and Resource Economists Newsletter* 20(1): 14–19.

————, and J.D. Graham. 1999. Willingness to Pay for Health Protection: Inadequate Sensitivity to Probability? *Journal of Risk and Uncertainty* 18: 33–62.

Hayes, D.J., J.F. Shogren, S.Y. Shin, and J.B. Kliebenstein. 1995. Valuing Food Safety in

Experimental Auction Markets. *American Journal of Agricultural Economics* 77: 40–53.

Henson, S. 1996. Consumer Willingness to Pay for Reductions in the Risk of Food Poisoning in the UK. *Journal of Agricultural Economics* 47: 403–420.

Johannesson, M., P-O. Johansson, and K-G. Lofgren. 1997. On the Value of Changes in Life Expectancy: Blips Versus Parametric Changes. *Journal of Risk and Uncertainty* 15: 221–39.

Johnson, F.R. 1988. Economic Costs of Misinforming About Risk: The EDB Scare and the Media. *Risk Analysis* 8: 261–69.

———, E.E. Fries, and H.S. Banzhaf. 1997. Valuing Morbidity: An Integration of the Willingness-to-Pay and Health-Status Index Literatures. *Journal of Health Economics* 16: 641–65.

Jones-Lee, M. 1974. The Value of Changes in the Probability of Death or Injury. *Journal of Political Economy* 82: 835–49.

———, M. Hammerton, and P.R. Philips. 1985. The Value of Safety: Results of a National Sample Survey. *The Economic Journal* 95: 49–72.

Kaplan, R.M., and J.P. Anderson. 1988. A General Health Policy Model: Update and Applications. *Health Services Research* 23: 203–35.

Kimball, M.S. 1990. Precautionary Saving in the Small and in the Large. *Econometrica* 58: 53–73.

Krupnick, A., A. Alberini, M. Cropper, N. Simon, B. O'Brien, R. Goeree, and M. Heintzelman. 2002. Age, Health and the Willingness to Pay for Mortality Risk Reductions: A Contingent Valuation Survey of Ontario Residents. *Journal of Risk and Uncertainty* 24: 161 –86.

Lee, S.J., P.J. Neumann, W.H. Churchill, M.E. Cannon, M.C. Weinstein, and M. Johannesson. 1997. Patients' Willingness to Pay for Autologous Blood Donation,. *Health Policy* 40: 1–12.

Liu, J.-T., J.K. Hammitt, and J.-L. Liu. 1997. Estimated Hedonic Wage Function and Value of Life in a Developing Country. *Economics Letters* 57: 353–58.

———, J.K. Hammitt, J.-D. Wang, and J.-L. Liu. 2000. Mother's Willingness to Pay for Her Own and Her Child's Health: A Contingent Valuation Study in Taiwan. *Health Economics* 9: 319–26.

Mitchell, R.C., and R.T. Carson. 1986. *Valuing Drinking Water Risk Reductions Using the Contingent Valuation Method: A Methodological Study of Risks from THM* and *Giardia.* Washington, DC: Resources for the Future.

———. 1989. *Using Surveys to Value Public Goods: The Contingent Valuation Method,* Washington, DC: Resources for the Future.

Mrozek, J.R., and L.O. Taylor. 1999. What Determines the Value of Life? A Meta Analysis. Unpublished manuscript, Department of Economics, Georgia State University, May 1.

Ng, Y.-K. 1992. The Older the More Valuable: Divergence Between Utility and Dollar Values of Life as One Ages. *Journal of Economics* 55: 1–16.

Pliskin, J.S., D.S. Shepard, and M.C. Weinstein. 1980. Utility functions for life years and health status. *Operations Research* 28: 206–24.

Pratt, J.W., and R.J. Zeckhauser. 1996. Willingness to Pay and the Distribution of Risk and Wealth. *Journal of Political Economy* 104: 747–63.

Rice, D. 1967. Estimating the Cost of Illness. *American Journal of Public Health* 57: 424–40.

Rosen, S. 1988. The Value of Changes in Life Expectancy. *Journal of Risk and Uncertainty* 1: 285–304.

Schelling, T.C. 1968. The Life You Save May Be Your Own. In *Problems in Public Expenditure Analysis,* edited by S.B. Chase. Washington, DC: Brookings Institution: 127–62.

Schutz, H.G., and O.A. Lorenz. 1976. Consumer Preferences for Vegetables Grown Under "Commercial" and "Organic" Conditions. *Journal of Food Science* 41: 70–73.

Shepard, D.S., and R.J. Zeckhauser. 1984. Survival versus Consumption. *Management Science* 30: 423–39.

Shulstad, R.N., and H.H. Stoevener. 1978. The Effects of Mercury Contamination in Pheasants on the Value of Pheasant Hunting in Oregon. *Land Economics* 54: 39–49.

Sloan, F.A., W.K. Viscusi, H.W. Chesson, C.J. Conover, and K. Whetten-Goldstein. 1998. Alternative Approaches to Valuing Intangible Health Losses: The Evidence for Multiple Sclerosis. *Journal of Health Economics* 17: 475–97.

Smith, M.E., E.O. van Ravenswaay, and J.P. Hoehn. 1988. Sales Loss Determination in Food Contamination Incidents: An Application to Milk Bans in Hawaii. *American Journal of Agricultural Economics* 70: 513–30.

Swartz, D.G., and I.E. Strand, Jr. 1981. Avoidance Costs Associated with Imperfect Information: The Case of Kepone. *Land Economics* 57: 139–50.

Tolley, G., D. Kenkel, and R. Fabian. 1994. *Valuing Health for Policy: An Economic Appraisal.* Chicago: University of Chicago Press.

van Ravenswaay, E.O., and J.P. Hoehn. 1991. The Impact of Health Risk Information on Food Demand: A Case Study of Alar and Apples. In *Economics of Food Safety,* edited by J.A. Caswell. New York: Elsevier Science, 155–74.

Viscusi, W.K. 1993. The Value of Risks to Life and Health. *Journal of Economic Literature* 31: 1912–46.

Weinstein, M.C., D.S. Shepard, and J.S. Pliskin. 1980. The Economic Value of Changing Mortality Probabilities: A Decision-Theoretic Approach. *Quarterly Journal of Economics* 94: 373–96.

Williams, P.R.D., and J.K. Hammitt. 2000. A Comparison of Organic and Conventional Fresh Produce Buyers in the Boston Area. *Risk Analysis* 20: 735–46.

PART IV
Assessing Opportunities

13

Opportunities for Risk Reduction: A Public Health Perspective

J. Glenn Morris, Jr.

The past decade has witnessed substantive advances in efforts to reduce the risk of foodborne disease. Driven in part by the *Escherichia coli* O157:H7 outbreaks that occurred in the western part of the United States in 1993 (U.S. CDC 1993; Bell 1994), there was strong public pressure to understand better the factors contributing to occurrence of foodborne illness and to develop regulatory strategies to minimize the risk of infection. These efforts led, in 1995, to implementation of the U.S. Food and Drug Administration's Final Rule on Procedures for the Safe and Sanitary Processing and Importing of Fish and Fishery Products ("Seafood HACCP")(CFSAN 1995), followed shortly by the Pathogen Reduction: Hazard Analysis and Critical Control Point (HACCP) Systems; Final Rule for meat and poultry, from the U.S. Department of Agriculture's (USDA's) Food Safety and Inspection Service (FSIS)(FSIS 1996). While serving as major milestones in moving toward a risk-based regulatory approach to food safety, these regulations also highlighted the existing deficiencies in data on frequency, routes of transmission, and economic impact of foodborne illness. This, in turn, led to creation of FoodNet, for collection of surveillance data on human foodborne disease; to an increasing commitment of funds by multiple agencies to food safety research; and to a renewed emphasis on accurately determining cost of illness, and the costs and benefits associated with regulatory interventions.

We are now the beneficiaries of these efforts: the chapters in this volume provide critical new data; evaluations of progress to date, including data on economic impact; and discussions of methodologies to assess risk. However, it is legitimate to ask whether major opportunities for improved risk reduction in food safety still remain, and where these opportunities might lie. This chapter explores these opportunities, with a particular focus on issues related to microbial food safety.

Underlying Concepts

It should be emphasized that microbes and chemicals are different—and often require different conceptual approaches in risk assessment and risk management. Outcomes are much easier to recognize in microbial foodborne illness, as there are almost always "bodies in the road" : effects of infection are usually immediately apparent, or become apparent within a matter of months, such as Guillain-Barré syndrome in *Campylobacter* infections, reactive arthritis in *Salmonella* infections, or congenital neurological and other deficits after *Toxoplasma* infections in pregnant women. In contrast, illnesses associated with chemical contaminants often have a long (multiyear) latency period, and it is much more difficult to link these back to specific exposures.

Microbial systems, dealing, as they are, with living organisms, are inherently highly complex. Foodborne illness can be caused by dozens or perhaps hundreds of possible pathogens, including pathogens that have yet to be identified (Tauxe, this volume). Each of these pathogens has a unique epidemiology, with its own reservoirs where the microorganism "lives," and modes of transmission. Change is an integral part of this system. Bacteria can reproduce rapidly: multiplication of a single bacterium can result, within a matter of hours, in millions, or billions, of bacteria. Because of this, the concepts of threshold, or tolerance, have less meaning in microbial as compared with chemical risk assessment/risk management. Bacteria also tend to be highly promiscuous, with strains and species having the ability to change their characteristics rapidly based on exchange of genetic material. This, in turn, can lead to the emergence of new strains that may have increased virulence or the capacity for epidemic spread.

As but one of many examples of the latter phenomenon, the epidemiology of *Vibrio parahaemolyticus* has undergone substantive changes in the last 5 to 10 years, with increasing numbers of cases being reported worldwide, including in the United States (WHO 1999; Chiou 2000; Chowdhury 2000; Daniels 2000). In the United States there has also been a shift in the mode of transmission. Prior to 1990, outbreaks generally occurred in the setting of cross-contamination of foods by raw seafood; since 1990, in contrast, 69% of outbreaks have been associated with consumption of raw oysters (Daniels 2000). Preliminary studies suggest that these changes are related to the emergence and global spread of a new, more virulent *V. parahaemolyticus* clone (O3:K:6, and the related groups O4:K68 and O1:KUT), associated with transfer or acquisition of genetic material by the clonal strain (Chang 2000; Chowdhury 2000).

Microbial risk can be introduced or modified at multiple points along the "food continuum." For some pathogens, the farm or the growing waters are the primary points of introduction. Examples include *Toxoplasma* in swine, with prevalence rates approaching 50% for some small producers (Gamble et al. 1999); and *Vibrio* species in shellfish, with virtually all summer-harvested oysters carrying these organisms (Wright 1996; Motes 1998). In feedlots, pathogens such as *E. coli* O157:H7 may be acquired or increase in number in feedlots, with feedlot practices, including feeding practices, having a potential impact on risk (Armstrong, 1996). Slaughter provides a number of opportunities for contamination of meat and poultry, based on transfer of microorganisms from gut contents or skin, and subsequent spread to other, uncontaminated carcasses through cross-contamination, as may occur with *Salmonella* and *Campylobacter* during rinse procedures. Processing may permit spread of contamination through an entire lot, as has been described with *E. coli* O157:H7 during the batch grinding and mixing that occurs in hamburger preparation (Armstrong 1996); it may also provide an opportunity for introduction of pathogens such as *Listeria* from the immediate plant environment. Microorganisms may also spread to other food items within kitchens and food service establishments. Variables in these instances include kitchen practices and sanitation, and the ability of a specific microorganism to grow in or on a particular food item under the conditions in which the food is kept.

Given the size and complexity of the system, its interlocking nature, and the constant change seen in dealing with microorganisms, it becomes very difficult to develop a clear picture of the risk inherent in food and how to minimize it. Although some excellent work has been done on development of risk assessment models, these models have tended to focus on single pathogen–food combinations, such as *Salmonella enteritidis* in eggs. Tauxe, in his chapter, has provided a conceptual framework for further exploring and integrating the risk of various food–pathogen combinations, incorporating data from outbreak reports and expert opinion. At this point, however, there has not been an effort to integrate food, pathogen surveillance, and economic data into a single model for prioritizing opportunities to reduce risk—a function of both technical limitations in modeling and the limited availability of data on many food–pathogen combinations.

Current Regulatory Approaches to Food Safety

As currently configured, food safety regulation and surveillance are scattered across multiple government departments and agencies (Merrill, this volume): as outlined in the recent National Research Council report, *Ensuring Safe Food from Production to Consumption* (NRC 1998), at least a dozen federal agencies administer more than 35 statutes and are overseen by 28 congressional committees. Furthermore, much of the system is ossified; retains significant command and control components; and utilizes approaches that, while they may have been "cutting edge" at the time of their original introduction close to 100 years ago, do not reflect our current understanding of foodborne risks. The most obvious example of this is the continued use of organoleptic, carcass-by-carcass inspection by FSIS. The U.S. General Accounting Office (GAO) has reported that, in fiscal year 1999, FSIS spent approximately $296 million, representing 42% of its total budget, and approximately 30% of the federal food safety budget, on carcass-by-carcass inspection (U.S. GAO 2001). As originally envisioned, organoleptic inspection was intended to eliminate dead, diseased, dying, and disabled animals from the food supply, in keeping with the widely prevalent concept at the beginning of the 20th century that illness occurred because of the presence of "filth" and dead animals. Although the in-plant presence of USDA inspectors may be beneficial, numerous studies have indicated that organoleptic inspection does not address the primary human health risks currently associated with meat and poultry (IOM 1990; NRC 1985, 1997).

The introduction of HACCP concepts into the regulatory framework has presaged the increasing acceptance of a risk-based regulatory structure. However, placement of HACCP systems has tended to reflect the site of traditional regulatory authority, or the site where regulatory authority can be best maintained, rather than, necessarily, the optimal site for intervention. FSIS has had its primary presence in slaughter and processing plants: when HACCP for meat and poultry was introduced, it focused on control of pathogens in these plants. This had clear advantages, as these plants served as a "choke point" through which all product moved; in this instance, available data also suggested that the plants were a primary source for introduction of pathogens (NRC 1985, 1987), making a regulatory focus at this point reasonable. When FDA implemented seafood HACCP, the focus was also on plant activities. In this instance, however, available data indicated that pathogenic microorganisms, such as *Vibrio* species, were acquired primarily in harvest waters (IOM 1991); critical control points in plants were clearly of secondary importance, as compared with the "production" control points, over which FDA had much less control.

HACCP is also, by its nature, a highly flexible and, in many ways, industry-oriented system: it encourages processing plants and producers to identify specific hazards associated with their processes, and to identify critical control points at which risk can be minimized or eliminated. In the USDA Pathogen Reduction/HACCP Final Rule plants were required to implement HACCP, but, in an effort to provide plants with flexibility in design of risk reduction strategies, specific details of the HACCP plan were left to the industry. To provide a basis for regulatory control, the rule also articulated microbial performance standards, in this case, performance standards for *Salmonella* and generic *E. coli* in the final product. This use of a performance standard has generated its own set of problems relating to how such standards should be set, and modified, as industry practices change (IOM 2003). Initial *Salmonella* performance standards in the USDA Pathogen Reduction/HACCP Final Rule were based on the national mean levels of contamination of product categories with *Salmonella*, as determined by surveys conducted in the early 1990s. The USDA intended that, as the incidence of contamination and the national mean declined, the *Salmonella* standards would be reduced accordingly, thereby inducing further reductions in *Salmonella* within the demonstrated capacity of the industry, as reflected in the new national mean. This has not occurred, owing both to the difficulties inherent in changing existing regulations and to uncertainties about how to correlate standards with desired public health outcomes—the latter being a critical, unanswered question that has underscored the need for sophisticated risk modeling capabilities.

How Do We Improve Risk Reduction?

Act on Identified Problem Areas

Although a great deal still needs to be done in assessing and ranking of food-associated microbiological risks, sufficient data are currently available to allow us to pinpoint particular problem areas. Since the implementation of FoodNet by USDA/FDA/CDC in 1995, there has been a substantive improvement in the quality and quantity of data on foodborne illness in the United States; this has been paralleled by increasing efforts to define the associated cost of illness. Work such as that presented by Golan and colleagues in this volume reflects these advances. In keeping with this work, substantial regulatory interventions have been targeted toward control of *Salmonella,* with a secondary focus on *E. coli* O157:H7 and *Campylobacter,* and, most recently, *Listeria.* In contrast, very little attention has been given to control of foodborne *Toxoplasma,* despite the fact that it is associated with the third highest estimated cost of illness, after *Campylobacter* and *Salmonella* (Table 13.1).

In this instance, we have the necessary data, but have not been able to focus resources on the problem. This, in part, reflects the current division of regulatory authority: *Salmonella* and *Campylobacter* are microorganisms susceptible to control during slaughter and processing, where FSIS has authority. Foodborne toxoplasmosis, in contrast, is best controlled by on-farm programs, targeted toward reducing infection rates in herds. Such programs have generally fallen under the auspices of USDA's Animal and Plant Health Inspection Ser-

TABLE 13.1. Estimated Annual Costs Due to Selected Foodborne Pathogens, 1996[a]

Pathogen	Estimated Annual Costs (billion dollars)
Campylobacter jejuni or *coli*	0.8–5.6
Clostridium perfringens	0.1
E. coli O157:H7	0.3–0.7
Listeria monocytogenes	0.1–0.3
Salmonella	0.9–3.5
Staphylococcus aureus	1.2
Toxoplasma gondii	3.2

[a]Derived from Buzby (1996).

vice (APHIS), an agency that has traditionally focused its efforts on animal health rather than food safety (www.aphis.usda.gov/oa/aphissp/spmissio. html), and that has had comparatively limited resources to commit to food safety. A national *Toxoplasma* control program could have a major public health impact, but will require that someone, or some agency or group, "take ownership" of the problem, with adequate resources and regulatory authority to implement necessary changes.

Invest in Science

Despite the improvements in data availability noted earlier, we have only scratched the surface in terms of the underlying data needed to develop a truly risk-based prevention program: if we want to reduce risk further, we have to know what we are doing and where we are going. This translates into a continuing, urgent need to invest in science. We lack a great deal of data on pathogens, their reservoirs, and transmission pathways (Tauxe, this volume). We need to be able to develop attributable risk data for specific foods: that is, what percentage of illness caused by a specific pathogen, such as *Salmonella,* can be linked with a specific food (such as chicken or raw broiler chickens)(Tauxe, this volume). A need exists to better define health outcomes, long-term effects of illness, and the costs associated with these outcomes. As interventions are undertaken, the need for ongoing disease surveillance is also present. If we do not know who is getting sick, we cannot monitor changes that may occur in response to specific interventions and, in turn, cannot evaluate the efficacy of the intervention.

Pathogens are currently identified in only a minority of suspected foodborne disease cases. In some instances this reflects the lack of an adequate laboratory infrastructure to identify pathogens, such as Shiga-like toxin producing *E. coli,* or viral agents such as norovirus. In other instances, even with the best currently available technology, no pathogens are identified. This highlights the following needs. There is a need for further technologic improvements to facilitate identification of currently recognized pathogens, including development and use of molecular techniques such as multiplex PCR and microarrays.

A need exists to look for other, as yet unidentified, pathogens. Again, this will almost certainly require use of molecular techniques to screen for possible microbial toxins (which may be in species not currently recognized as toxigenic), to look for new viruses, and to compare patterns of microbial flora in patients with and without diarrhea.

A need exists to better understand and identify non-infectious causes of diarrhea, so that these cases can be differentiated from infectious, foodborne illness.

Development of food-attributable risk data also involves substantive challenges. Currently, outbreak investigations provide the primary source of such data. When an outbreak is recognized an investigation may be initiated by the local health department; as part of such an investigation, efforts will be made to identify both the causative microorganism and the food responsible for the outbreak. When summed across multiple outbreaks, data of this type can be used to estimate the percentage of illness caused by a specific pathogen that is attributable to a specific food—a critical element in estimating risks associated with a food and in prioritizing interventions. However, exclusive reliance on outbreak data can introduce a significant bias into such calculations: outbreaks are frequently not representative of "routine" sporadic cases; may not be recognized unless a large number of people are involved in a single geographical location; and may not be investigated unless the health department in the jurisdiction in which the outbreak occurred has the resources and motivation to conduct an investigation. Food-attributable risk can be obtained as a part of case-control studies of sporadic cases; in its initial design, it was anticipated that FoodNet would serve as a source of such data. However, because of budgetary limitations and changing priorities, these data have generally not been forthcoming. Given the critical nature of these data to development of a science-based regulatory system, it is essential that there be ongoing studies to determine the contribution of specific foods to illness.

A need also exists to develop sophisticated analytical methods to describe risk within these complex natural systems. Traditional risk-assessment approaches, based on chemical hazards, do not always lend themselves to an understanding of microbial problems. Even practitioners of microbial risk assessment have not reached a consensus on the "best" approach or methodology. On one hand, some groups have focused on development of detailed, "sequential" analyses, tracking a single microorganism through a series of carefully defined steps from farm to human intestinal tract. Others have taken more global, ecological approaches (Smith 2001). Although there is a tendency among risk managers at times to deal with all problems by saying, "We'll do a risk assessment," there needs to be recognition that the model employed may have a profound impact on the outcome, resulting in the potential for "dueling risk assessments." As one example, the outcome of a recent risk assessment of quinolone-resistant *Campylobacter* sponsored by the FDA's Center for Veterinary Medicine (CVM) (CVM 2001) has been challenged by a risk assessment conducted by a private company (Cox Associates, www.cox-associates.com) sponsored by industry groups. Although a movement has emerged at an international level to standardize methodology, efforts to force all work into a single model structure carry their own set of problems. Instead, support, and funding, should be provided for model development and methodology assessment, with an emphasis on both utility and creativity.

Develop the Capacity for a Unified Approach

Foodborne pathogens do not recognize the boundaries built into our current regulatory system: Vibrios blithely contaminate shellfish in harvest waters, unaware that they are doing so outside of a formal FDA HACCP program. If risks are to be appropriately managed, it is necessary to reorganize our regulatory structure/approach so that it can deal in a unified way with risk reduction opportunities within the entire continuum from harvest to consumer. In particular, there is a need to be able to redirect resources to "high-risk" areas, such as foodborne toxoplasmosis, not just areas of risk that happen to fall under one agency's jurisdiction.

This need for a unified approach extends to industry: ideally, regulatory systems would allow companies to target their risk reduction efforts at the most critical points in the food continuum, not just focus food safety efforts in slaughter and processing, if more cost-effective interventions can be undertaken elsewhere. This concept is consistent with HACCP, and could be accomplished, while maintaining regulatory control, by shifting of performance standards toward the consumer end of the continuum. This would be most applicable to industries that are highly vertically integrated, such as poultry. More creative approaches will be needed to allow this type of unified approach for products for which no one single company has primary product control from farm to supermarket shelf. This has become particularly evident in the case of ground beef, in which clear difficulties have been encountered in "pushing back" performance standards at the grinding level to earlier parts of the food chain (IOM 2003).

Develop a Regulatory System that Is Flexible

To be effective in reducing risk, regulatory systems must be flexible. This is of particular importance given the complexity and changing nature of microbial risk. As previously noted, regulatory systems tend to become ossified, developing a life of their own that goes well beyond the intent of those who initially wrote the regulations. This lack of flexibility does not permit systems to respond to new pathogens and new challenges; it also drives resource allocation, severely hobbling the ability of government to respond to new problems. At a concrete level, this translates into a need for creativity in design of new regulatory systems, as well as the political will to change the old ones.

Carcass-by-carcass inspection of meat and poultry, and the organoleptic inspection system that evolved to perform this function, provides an obvious example of this problem. As a method for removing dead and diseased animals from the food supply in 1906, it was highly effective. However, it has only limited value in minimizing contamination of meat and poultry by pathogenic microorganisms. Ideally, food safety resources committed to organoleptic inspection could be seamlessly shifted to other, more relevant interventions. The inability of FSIS to do this is tied both to the underlying enabling legislation, underscoring the critical importance of such legislation, and to long-standing labor and political issues.

As another example, screening of harvest water for fecal coliforms was initially used as a means of reducing the risk of acquisition of typhoid fever from shellfish. Given the disappearance of chronic typhoid carriers from the U.S. population, it was highly unlikely that anyone would ever contract typhoid fever from U.S.-harvested shellfish in the year 2001. Fecal coliforms are not relevant in assessing risk of contamination with *Vibrio* species (Kaper et al. 1979; Motes et al. 1998), and *Vibrio* species have been implicated as the major current risk associated with eating raw shellfish (CFSAN 1995). However, monitoring of fecal coliforms does have potential value as a surrogate marker for reducing risk of infection with other enteric pathogens, such as hepatitis A and possibly norovirus. Substantial state resources are directed toward monitoring for fecal coliforms; ideally, a flexible regulatory structure would allow these resources to be apportioned in relation to risk.

The HACCP food safety regulations put in place beginning in the mid-1990s have the advantage of being risk based. However, the risk data on which they were based are changing. For example, meat and poultry HACCP includes the assumption that all *Salmonella* species/serotypes represent a comparable human health hazard. As recently reported by investigators in our group and FSIS (Sarwari et al. 2001), a comparison of *Salmonella* isolated from humans and animals suggests that certain serotypes are potentially of less importance as a human health risk. Table 13.2 shows data developed with a mathematical model designed to predict the "expected" rate of human infection with specific serotypes, based on rates of isolation of *Salmonella* and food consumption data; as can be seen for serotypes such as *Salmonella* Kentucky, a major colonizer of chickens, the actual rate with which they cause human illness is much lower than would be expected based on the frequency with which they are isolated from food animals. Unfortunately, HACCP regulations, as currently structured, do not allow easy incorporation of these and other changing risk data.

As a permutation on this issue, the cumbersome nature of the current regulatory process also complicates the ability of agencies to take rapid action to respond, either positively or negatively, to an immediate or perceived public health threat. As an example, data collected through the National Antimicrobial Resistance Monitoring System (NARMS) have shown a rapid increase in resistance to quinolone antibiotics since the mid-1990s, when they were first approved for use in agriculture. By 1999, the rate of resistance to quinolones in human *Campylobacter* isolates was approaching 18%, up from the 13% range in 1997 and 1998 (CDC 2000), and from a projected 1% to 2% level in the early 1990s (based on data from Minnesota [Smith et al. 1999]). When confronted with these problems, FDA/CVM was in the midst of a multiyear process to develop a framework document to provide a basis for decisions of this type. CVM has now proposed to withdraw approval for quinolones in poultry (www.fda.gov/cvm/antimicrobial/NOOHB.htm); however, pending hearings and further appeals, the drug continues to be used. In this instance, a regula-

TABLE 13.2. Actual Distribution of Major *Salmonella* Serotypes Isolated from Humans, as Compared with Human Serotype Distribution Predicted by the Mathematical Model Using Data on *Salmonella* Serotypes in Food Animals and Food Consumption[a]

Serotype	Actual Percentage of All Human Salmonella Infections Due to this Serotype	Based on Serotype Distribution in Animals, Predicted Percentage of All Human Salmonella Infections that Should Be Due to this Serotype (95% Confidence Interval)[b]
Typhimurium	29	12 (10, 14)
Heidelberg	9	15 (13, 16)
Hadar	5	13 (11, 14)
Newport	6	0.7 (0.2, 1.1)
Thompson	2	5 (4, 6)
Kentucky	0.1	14 (12, 16)
Derby	<0.1	5 (4, 6)
Other	49	36 (34, 38)

[a]Table taken from Sarwari et al. (2001). The mathematical model assumes that each product category (i.e., chicken, beef, pork) has equal risk, and that each serotype has equal likelihood of causing human illness. As described in Sarwari et al. (2001), the model is only minimally affected by subsequent manipulation of product category risk, leading to the hypothesis that serotypes differ in their likelihood of causing human illness. Human *Salmonella* isolates reported through the Centers for Disease Control and Prevention, *Salmonella* Surveillance System; chicken data from USDA *Salmonella* spp. in Broiler Study (1990–1992) and USDA Baseline Broiler Study (1994–1995); beef data from USDA Baseline Steer/Heifer Study (1992–1993) and USDA Baseline Cow/Bull Study (1993–1994); pork data from USDA Baseline Market Hog Study (1995–1996). The analysis excludes *S. enteritidis* isolates because of their strong association with eggs.

[b]Expected proportions based on model described in Sarwari et al. (2001). Confidence intervals are based on a percentile bootstrap method.

tory system that measures response in years was not optimally prepared to deal with a situation in which changes were occurring in a much shorter time frame.

Anticipate the Unexpected

No system can anticipate the completely expected. However, given the fact that we are dealing with natural systems, the unexpected will occur. Bovine spongiform encephalopathy (BSE) serves as a classic example: there was nothing in our experience to suggest that prion disease would jump the species barrier into cattle, and then into humans, in the form of a new variant of Creutzfeldt–Jakob disease (Prusiner 2001). Although such events may not be predicted, the food safety system should have sufficient resources to deal with them. This translates into two key concepts. The system must have immediately available resources to deal with a newly emergent pathogen or disease, including the ability to undertake key scientific studies, without having to wait for the next budget cycle, as nature is seldom considerate enough to work in budget cycles. The system must also be able to handle the situation without diverting critical resources from existing risk-based programs, thereby reducing current food safety capabilities.

Conclusion

To summarize: microbial systems underlying occurrence of foodborne disease are complex, constantly changing, and hard to model. Risk-based systems for control of microbial pathogens are being developed, and should provide a means of improving food safety. However, as outlined in this and earlier chapters in this volume, for such systems to have an optimal impact on the health of the public there are certain key needs and requirements:

- A willingness on the part of government to respond to identified risks, even if they do not fit current regulatory frameworks or agency flow charts.
- A willingness to underwrite investments in science, to obtain and analyze data needed to characterize risk factors for illness, establish regulatory standards, and prioritize interventions.
- A recognition of the need for a unified approach, seeking to minimize risk in the context of the entire continuum of food production, from farm to consumer.
- Flexibility: Regulatory systems must be able to respond to changing science and changing patterns of risk, that is, one needs to be able to shift resources from a problem that has been solved or has moved to a lower risk priority.
- An ability to accommodate the unexpected: not only may patterns of risk change, but new, totally unexpected risks may appear, which must be dealt with and, in turn, incorporated into the regulatory system.

It will be of interest to see how these challenges will be met in the coming decade.

References

Armstrong, G.L., J. Hollingsworth, and J.G. Morris, Jr. 1996. Emerging Foodborne Pathogens: *E. coli* O157:H7 as a Model of Entry of a New Pathogen into the Food Supply of the Developed World. *Epidemiologic Reviews* 18: 29–51.

Bell, B.P., M. Goldoft, P.M. Griffin, M.A. Davis, D.C. Gordon, P.I. Tarr, C.A. Bartleson, J.H. Lewis, T.J. Barrett, J.G. Wells, R. Baron, and J. Kobayashi. 1994. A Multistate Outbreak of *Escherichia coli* O157:H7-Associated Diarrhea and Hemolytic Uremic Syndrome from Hamburgers. *Journal of the American Medical Association* 272: 1349–53.

Buzby, J., and T. Roberts. 1996. ERS Updates U.S. Foodborne Disease Costs for Seven Pathogens. *FoodReview* 19: 20–25.

CFSAN (Center for Food Safety and Applied Nutrition). 1995. Procedures for the Safe and Sanitary Processing and Importing of Fish and Fishery Products; Final Rule. *Federal Register* 60: 65095–202.

CVM (Center for Veterinary Medicine). 2001. The Human Health Impact of Fluoroquinolone Resistant *Campylobacter* Attributed to the Consumption of Chicken. Document date: October 18, 2000; revised January 5, 2001. www.fda.gov/cvm/antimicrobial/Risk_asses.htm (accessed July 6, 2004).

Chang, B., S. Yoshida, H. Miyamoto, M. Ogawa, K. Horikawa, K. Ogata, M. Nishibuchi, and H. Taniguchi. 2000. A Unique and Common Restriction Fragment Pattern of the Nucleotide Sequences Homologous to the Genome of Vf33, a Filamentous Bacteriophage, in Pandemic Strains of *Vibrio parahaemolyticus* O3:K6, O4:K68, and O1:K Untypable. *FEMS Microbiology Letters* 192: 231–36.

Chiou, C.S., S.Y. Hsu, S.I. Chiu, T.K. Wang, and C.S. Chao. 2000. *Vibrio parahaemolyticus* serovar O3:K6 as a Cause of Unusually High Incidence of Food-Borne Disease Outbreaks in Taiwan from 1996 to 1999. *Journal of Clinical Microbiology* 38: 4621–625.

Chowdhury, N.R., S. Chakraborty, T. Ramamurthy, M. Nishibuchi, S. Yamasaki, Y. Takeda, and G.B. Nair. 2000. Molecular Evidence of Clonal *Vibrio parahaemolyticus* Pandemic Strains. *Emerging Infectious Diseases* 6: 631–36.

Daniels, N.A., L. MacKinnon, R. Bishop, S. Alkekruse, B. Ray, R.M. Hammond, S. Thompson, S. Wilson, N.H. Bean, P.M. Griffin, and L. Slutsker. 2000. *Vibrio parahaemolyticus* Infections in the United States, 1973–1998. *Journal of Infectious Diseases* 181: 1661–66.

Gamble, H.R., R.E. Brady, and J.P. Dubey. 1999. Prevalence of *Toxoplasma gondii* Infection in Domestic Pigs in the New England States. *Veterinary Parasitology* 82: 129–36.

IOM (Institute of Medicine). 1990. *Cattle Inspection.* Report of the Committee on Evaluation of USDA Streamlined Inspection System for Cattle. Washington, DC: National Academy Press.

———. 1991. *Seafood Safety.* Washington, DC: National Academy Press.

———. 2003. *Scientific Criteria to Ensure Safe Food.* Washington, DC: National Academy Press.

Kaper, J.B., H. Lockman, R.R. Colwell, and S.W. Joseph. 1979. Ecology, Serology, and Enterotoxin Production of *Vibrio cholerae* in Chesapeake Bay. *Applied and Environmental Microbiology* 37: 91–103 .

Motes, M.L., A. DePaola, D.W. Cook, J.E. Veazey, J.C. Junsucker, W.E. Garthwright, R.J. Blodgett, and S.J. Chirtel 1998. Influence of Water Temperature and Salinity on *Vibrio vulnificus* in Northern Gulf and Atlantic Coast Oysters. *Applied and Environmental Microbiology* 64: 1459–65.

NRC (National Research Council). 1985. *Meat and Poultry Inspection: The Scientific Basis of the Nation's Program.* Washington, DC: National Academy Press.

———. 1987. *Poultry Inspection. The Basis for a Risk Assessment Approach.* Washington, DC: National Academy Press.

———. 1998. *Ensuring Safe Food: From Production to Consumption.* Washington, DC: National Academy Press.

Prusiner, S.B. 2001. Shattuck Lecture – Neurodegenerative Diseases and Prions. *New England Journal of Medicine* 344: 1516–26.

Sarwari, A.R., L.S. Magder, P. Levine, A.M. McNamara, S. Knower, G.L. Armstrong, R. Etzel, J. Hollingsworth, and J.G. Morris, Jr. 2001. The Serotype Distribution of *Sal-*

monella from Food Animals After Slaughter Differs from that Seen Among Human Isolates. *Journal of Infectious Diseases* 183: 1295–99.

Smith, D.L., A.D. Harris, J.A. Johnson, E.K. Silbergeld, and J.G. Morris, Jr. 2002. Animal Antibiotic Use Has an Early but Important Impact on the Emergence of Antibiotic Resistance in Human Commensal Bacteria. *Proceedings of the National Academy of Sciences of the United States of America* 99 (9): 6434–9.

Smith, K.E., J.M. Besser, C.W. Hedberg, F.T. Leano, J.B. Bender, J.H. Wicklund, B.P. Johnson, K.A. Moore, and M.T. Osterholm. 1999. Quinolone-Resistant *Campylobacter jejuni* Infections in Minnesota, 1992–1998. Investigation Team. *New England Journal of Medicine* 340: 1525–32.

U.S. CDC (Centers for Disease Control). 1993. Update: Multistate Outbreak of *Escherichia coli* O157:H7 Infections from Hamburgers – Western United States, 1992–1993. *Morbidity and Mortality Weekly Reports* 42: 258–63.

———. 2000. National Antimicrobial Resistance Monitoring System (NARMS) for Enteric Bacteria Participants (Human Isolates). http://www.cdc.gov/narms/ (accessed July 6, 2004).

USDA FSIS (Food Safety and Inspection Service). 1996. Pathogen Reduction; Hazard Analysis and Critical Control Point (HACCP) Systems; Final rule. *Federal Register* 61: 38806–989.

U.S. GAO (General Accounting Office). *Food Safety: Overview of Federal and State Expenditures.* GAO-01-177, February 2001.

WHO (World Health Organization). 1999. *Vibrio parahaemolyticus*, Japan, 1996–1998. *Weekly Epidemiology Record* 74: 361–3.

Wright, A.C., R.T. Hill, J.A. Johnson, M.C. Roghmann, R.R. Colwell, and J.G. Morris, Jr. 1996. Distribution of *Vibrio vulnificus* in the Chesapeake Bay. *Applied Environmental Microbiology* 62: 717–24.

14

Opportunities for Risk Reduction: An Economist's Perspective

JULIE A. CASWELL

More systematic use of risk analysis is the key to setting food safety priorities more effectively. The preceding chapters discuss several elements of
effective risk analysis including assessment of different types of risks, design
and evaluation of policies and institutional arrangements to manage those
risks, and measurement of the benefits and costs of different risk management
strategies. Each element offers opportunities for contributing to more effective
risk reduction. However, the greatest opportunity will likely come from better
management of the system as a whole.

When we think about opportunities for more effective risk reduction, we are
on fairly well trodden paths in the sense that we can delineate the universe of
information needed to make good regulatory decisions. This universe includes
knowing the range and relative seriousness of foodborne risks, what incentives
private and public parties have to reduce this risk, which risks are of the highest priority, which regulatory mechanisms and organizations work best and
when, and how to communicate about risk issues. However, management of
the overall foodborne risk portfolio is a difficult job. If it were not, we would
likely have many fewer opportunities to improve the performance of the U.S.
food safety system.

Moving forward requires focusing more clearly and with more discipline
on conducting risk analysis and on using it as a framework to rationalize approaches to risk. This means that we need good risk assessment, but not only
risk assessment. It also requires a strong emphasis on strategies for risk management and communication. It further requires a recognition that risk
analysis, especially risk assessment, are tools for making decisions that better
reflect society's values. In other words, risk analysis should be the servant and
not the master.

A comprehensive approach to managing the foodborne risk portfolio is lacking in the United States. The question is, why is it lacking? Conceptually it is not too difficult a task. Although data to make ideal decisions are often missing, information to make better decisions is available. Organizational and political impediments to effective management of the overall risk portfolio exist, however. The opportunities for more effective risk reduction lie along the path of better risk assessment, management, and communication.

Opportunities in Risk Assessment

The chapters by Tauxe and Fenner-Crisp offer comprehensive overviews of what we currently know about microbial, chemical, and other types of foodborne risks. Their bottom line is that although we know a great deal and our knowledge is expanding, many gaps exist. Clearly a crucial gap in microbiological analysis is in measuring the incidence of foodborne illness and linking cases to specific pathogens and foods. In estimates of the incidence of foodborne disease per year by the Centers for Disease Control and Prevention (CDC), the pathogenic agents are not known in more than 80% of the approximately 76 million illnesses, in more than 80% of the 325,000 hospitalizations, and in about 65% of deaths (Mead et al. 1999).

In addressing gaps in the knowledge of foodborne risks and their sources, Tauxe argues for using an additive approach to building information. Knowledge about risks would be built up by pathogen, by food category or other routes of infection, and by the production phases in which they occur or multiply. The result would be an overall view of the importance of different pathogens and different paths of infection stated in terms of human health outcomes including illnesses, hospitalizations, and deaths. Tauxe emphasizes the rapid evolution of knowledge in this area as, for example, with *E. coli* O157:H7, which has only relatively recently been recognized as a foodborne pathogen and traced to its main sources. Adding a health outcome tree that differentiates various severities of illness would enrich Tauxe's framework.

On the chemical and other foodborne hazards side, Fenner-Crisp concludes that an accurate national profile of hazards remains elusive. She describes multiple residue monitoring efforts undertaken by government agencies for specific risk sources. It is clear, however, that nothing on the chemical side is comparable in scope to Tauxe's proposal for an integrated picture of microbial risks, although the Food Quality Protection Act moves toward looking at groups of risks for pesticides. In fact, the picture that emerges is of several disjoint sampling regimens for different types of chemical risks in different food and water sources. On the chemical side, an integrated picture would involve evaluating adverse health outcomes across risks, including interactions between risks, across foods, and across the supply chain. Tracking over time is especially important for these risks where health impacts are likely to be chronic and latent, given that current regulatory efforts have mitigated acute effects. A better overall picture of risks on the chemical side is also clearly important because of the suspicion that some long-term risks associated with chemical use are not being adequately assessed.

There are real opportunities to improve overall risk reduction performance through the use of risk assessment. The first opportunity is to build a bridge between the, to date, largely separate areas of microbial and chemical risk assessment. Managing the foodborne risk portfolio requires being able to compare relative risk rankings from all sources, not only ranking within risk types, for example, within foodborne pathogens. A relative ranking across the whole portfolio of foodborne risks could be developed at different levels of detail or quality. These levels range from a crude ranking, to a better but more expensive ranking, to a deluxe (very good) ranking. Given current knowledge and capabilities, the aim should probably be for a ranking that is somewhere between crude and better in detail and quality.

The problem is that the United States is in a no person's land regarding risk assessment for the purposes of risk ranking and overall program management. A very few, very high quality risk assessments of individual risks have been performed, usually for specific foods. Examples include the risk assessments for Salmonella enteritidis in shell eggs and egg products (U.S. FSIS 1998), Vibrio parahaemolyticus in shellfish (U.S. FDA 2001), and Listeria monocytogenes in ready-to-eat foods (U.S. FDA et al. 2001). Overall, these may be the most serious risks and the agencies may have succeeded in gathering information on the worst things first. But in the absence of a global risk ranking, how do we know?

The federal government does not have information above the crude, or very crude, level that allows comparisons to be made across the whole spectrum of risks for management purposes. More attention needs to be given to improving the quality of this overall ranking for policy makers to have better information to inform their decisions and risk managers in agencies to do a better job. The question in the current fragmented U.S. food safety system is, whose responsibility is it to produce this across the board risk ranking? Is it because it is no one's responsibility that we do not have one?

Opportunities in Risk Management and Communication

Risk management and risk communication are central functions of policy makers and the agencies they charge with responsibility for food safety assurance. Risk assessment and relative risk rankings tell us the impacts of different foodborne risks, usually in terms of counts of adverse health outcomes. Risk management and communication add diverse other considerations in order to evaluate which approaches to risk reduction are likely to be most effective. When deciding which risks to address and how, policy makers and risk managers need to:

- Understand private (e.g., company, consumer) and public incentives to reduce risk.
- Set priorities for risk reduction using input from risk assessment.
- Choose the most effective regulatory organization and mechanisms.
- Understand the costs and benefits of choices.

These areas are not in hierarchical order because the process is iterative. Similarly, risk analysis is an iterative process, with risk assessment, management, and communication informing each other.

The key point that policy makers and risk managers need to internalize regards the degree of market failure in the provision of food safety. The chapters by Unnevehr and Jensen on costs and by Golan et al. on benefits emphasize this point. The test for whether government should become involved is frequently stated in terms of whether there is a market failure. But as Unnevehr and Jensen note, "The market failure in food safety is never a complete failure." The fact that there is a private market for food safety, however imperfect it may be in particular cases, means that policy makers and risk managers always have to focus on the total effect of a regulatory option on private and public incentives to secure food safety.

For a company, private incentives to secure food safety include protecting its reputation and that of its brand names, building market share, meeting buyer requirements, and protecting itself from legal liability for unsafe products. For consumers, the obvious incentive to undertake protective measures, for example, hand washing and avoiding cross-contamination between foods, is to avoid illness. As a result of these private incentives in the area of food safety, there is more scope to work with the market than, for example, in the area of environmental quality improvement. In this sense, the food safety budget that the government is working with extends beyond the federal and state dollars spent on food safety.

The mix of private and public provision of food safety makes for a more complex set of incentives to reduce risk. Consequently, the number of private and public approaches that can be used to reduce risk is larger. In turn, this makes measuring the costs and benefits of a particular regulation a difficult job. For example, to what extent would companies in an industry have adopted the Hazard Analysis and Critical Control Points (HACCP) approach to ensuring food safety because of private incentives, if it had not been required by the government? Assessing the costs and benefits attributable to a HACCP regulation, and therefore its effectiveness, requires an answer to this question. It is estimated that the total annual public food safety regulatory budget in the United States is in the range of $1 to $1.5 billion (U.S. GAO 2001). Clearly this amount is dwarfed by private expenditures on securing food safety but we do not know by how much.

Unnevehr and Jensen take the full range of private and public incentives for reducing risk into consideration in their survey of research on the costs of food safety provision. They draw several lessons from this research. First, as noted, measuring the costs of a particular regulation is more difficult for foodborne risks because of the mix of private incentives. Second, the research shows that the marginal cost of risk reduction likely increases with successive improvements in food safety. Thus further reductions become more expensive to accomplish. Third, flexible regulatory approaches that allow choice in how to meet quality standards will likely be more cost effective than prescriptive process standards. However, the costs of flexible standards are more difficult to estimate. Fourth, because industries as a whole have a wide range of ways to adjust to new regulations, the impact of a regulation may be less in the absolute size of its costs than in the distribution of those costs across areas of the country or companies. Although the industry may adjust well overall, some segments may be advantaged or disadvantaged by the new regulation. Finally, regulation has a potentially strong effect on the direction and pace of technological and structural change in industries and on competitiveness.

A systems approach to cost analysis offers a key opportunity for improving the management of foodborne risk by going beyond a risk ranking based on counts of adverse health outcomes to bring in consideration of which risks might be more or less costly to address. As an example of such a cost-effectiveness analysis (CEA), suppose that pathogen A tops the list in a relative risk ranking, causing 20% of the counts of adverse health outcomes as a result of foodborne risks. Based on risk assessment, this pathogen might appear to be the top priority for action. However, further suppose that it costs $1 billion a year to eliminate illness related to pathogen A, whereas for $500 million one could eliminate illness related to chemical B, which causes 14% of adverse health outcomes related to food. Assuming the severity of illness in both cases is the same, control of chemical B is more cost effective than control of pathogen A. We would not know this without the perspective of cost analysis. CEA can inform risk management without a full-blown benefit–cost study that attempts to quantify both benefits and costs in monetary terms.

Beyond overall CEA, Unnevehr and Jensen argue that the most important reason to analyze costs is to choose among regulatory alternatives aimed at reducing a particular risk. They cite the *Salmonella enteritidis* risk assessment and management plan for shell eggs and egg products as an example in which the costs of control at different stages of the supply chain were successfully used to choose the most effective management strategy. In Tauxe's framework for assessing risks, this is a fairly simple case: one pathogen, one food product, and all stages of the supply chain. But even so, the type of analysis carried out for the *Salmonella enteritidis* management plan is rarely done. Instead, regulatory analyses frequently focus on the cost of a single intervention that has already been chosen for implementation. Little actual CEA or benefit–cost analysis comparing alternative control strategies is currently performed. As a result, analysis may suggest that a particular regulatory approach has benefits greater than its costs but it will give little perspective on whether alternative strategies would be more effective.

The *Salmonella enteritidis* case also illustrates that cost analysis is very important in designing regulatory approaches that facilitate and strengthen private incentives, that is, those that work with the market. Unnevehr and Jensen argue that economists have much to contribute here because it is their job to understand and quantify the systemwide impacts and adjustments that are likely to occur or have occurred from use of different regulatory alternatives.

CEA is in itself a very useful tool in risk management. However, in its simple form it continues to rely on counts of adverse health outcomes to measure the benefits of a particular risk reduction. As Golan et al. point out, "Policymakers need to know how much intervention in the market is warranted. They need to know how much consumers and society value food safety and what is the value of government intervention." Golan et al. make the bedrock point that we need benefits estimation because, with partial, or in some cases more complete, failure in the market for food safety, the market prices of food products do not reflect the value that individuals and society place on food safety.

Golan et al. draw several lessons from their review of research that estimates the benefits of reducing foodborne risks. The predominant emphasis in this work has been on measuring the value of avoiding adverse health outcomes, including, of course, death. This value can be measured in several ways, including in terms of quality-adjusted life years (QALYs); the monetary value of avoided costs of illness, for example, avoided medical costs and losses in productivity; or the market or stated willingness to pay of consumers for safer foods. Of these, they note that the willingness-to-pay method has not yet yielded comprehensive results. The federal food safety agencies have employed a variety of these methods to value benefits, including efforts to count other types of nonhealth benefits such as continued market access. Improving the quality of information on the adverse health outcomes of foodborne risks is important to improving the quality of benefit estimates because these estimates focus in large part or totally on adverse health outcomes as the benefit being valued.

The predominant emphasis on adverse health outcomes in benefit estimates means that estimates are roughly comparable across FDA, USDA, and EPA, although methodologies differ considerably. Golan et al. call attention to the fact that the extensive work on health outcomes and their costs has shown how important it is to look behind simple counts of health outcomes, for example, deaths and illnesses, in evaluating different risks. Although a death may be a death—although that is not certain because there are many ways to die—an illness is certainly not an illness. For example, an illness that causes a long-term disability is very different from one that causes two days of flulike symptoms. Priorities for risk reduction based on benefits could be significantly different from rankings based on counts of adverse health outcomes or even on QALYs. This is especially true when we take into account other types of benefits that may arise from safer food including reductions in market risks resulting from higher consumer confidence, lower market volatility, access to foreign markets, and possible links between food safety and improved nutrition.

Benefit estimation offers two key opportunities for improving management of foodborne risks, both of which mirror opportunities in the cost analysis area. The first opportunity is to use a systems approach to identify the full range of benefits that may come from risk reduction, including their sources and distribution. Although frequently difficult to do quantitatively, qualitative identification of the range of benefits can enhance the effectiveness of decision making. The second opportunity is in facilitating the design of regulatory approaches that work with the market by strengthening private incentives for food safety production.

Bringing together insights from cost and benefit analyses indicates real opportunities for better risk reduction strategies on the risk management and communication fronts. Again, there is a clear need to bridge knowledge from the microbial and chemical areas. As we found with risk assessment, these areas have been separate spheres, which impedes overall management of the entire foodborne risk portfolio. Someone needs to mind the entire store and manage the entire risk portfolio for food safety. This management includes using risk assessment/risk rankings, applying cost-effectiveness or benefit–cost criteria to a range of control options, and developing an action plan. In other words, it involves establishing a risk-analysis–based system.

This system should generate an overall portfolio analysis with relative benefit–cost or cost-effectiveness rankings across regulatory options. As in risk assessment, the options for this portfolio analysis are a crude, a better but more expensive, or a very good analysis. Again, the goal initially should be the crude to better type of analysis. Producing such an analysis and overall plan involves having a better understanding of the interaction between regulatory standards and private actions. For example, when will information (labeling) work and when will it not? Given that food safety is a partially private good—that is, a private market for it exists, although it may work imperfectly—more options for regulatory approaches are available and use of information is potentially very important.

The question remains: in the U.S. federal government, whose job is it to produce the across-the-board evaluation of regulatory options and risk reduction opportunities? Is the fact that it is no one's job the reason that we do not have this comprehensive approach?

Means and Ends: How Separate Can They Be?

Setting U.S. food safety priorities involves many complicated management questions. Both means and ends need to be considered in improving the food safety system. The means include statutes, the organization of the regulatory agencies, regulations, enforcement mechanisms, budgets, and systematic use of risk analysis. The ends include risk reduction, cost-effective risk reduction, and, ultimately, risk reduction with the most favorable benefit–cost ratio. How closely do means and ends need to be aligned to achieve better performance? Do current means impede our ability to reach our ends?

A much discussed example of the means/ends question is the evident disparity in funding of risk reduction activities between the Food Safety and Inspection Service (FSIS) in the United States Department of Agriculture and the Food and Drug Administration (FDA) in the Department of Health and Human Services. Data from a recent General Accounting Office (GAO) study (U.S. GAO 2001) yields the picture shown in Table 14.1. Here the means are the agencies and their programs/budgets and the end is risk reduction. The data suggest that FSIS uses 72% of the federal food safety "budget," defined here as the total of FSIS and FDA food safety expenditures in FY99, to regulate 22% of the food system, as measured by value of sales. Food products regulated by FSIS were associated with 15% of the 7,000 cases of foodborne illness reported by CDC in 1997 for which the food sources of the illness were known, out of a total of 12,000 cases. Meanwhile, FDA uses 28% of the "budget" to regulate 78% of the food system in terms of sales, and products it regulates account for 85% of the 7,000 illnesses with known food sources. Analysis of outbreaks by the Center for Science in the Public Interest (CSPI

TABLE 14.1. FSIS and FDA Shares of Budget, Food Sales Regulated, and Known Causes of Foodborne Illnesses

Agency	Share of FY1999 "Budget" (%)[a]	Share of Food Sales Regulated (%)	Share of Reported Illnesses with Known Causes (%)[b]
FSIS	72	22	15
FDA	28	78	85

[a]The budget here is the sum of food safety expenditures in FY1999 by the FSIS and the FDA as reported by the GAO.

[b]Based on CDC data for 12,000 cases reported in 1997, of which approximately 7,000 were linked to a particular food source. Percentages shown here are of the 7,000 cases with known causes (U.S. GAO 2001, 5).

Source: U.S. GAO (2001).

2000) suggests a similar pattern regarding foodborne sources of illness, with foods regulated by FDA causing nearly four times as many outbreaks as foods regulated by USDA.

Although everyone knows the story is more complicated than this table portrays, the temptation is strong to draw conclusions. But what conclusions can be drawn? Is FSIS overfunded and FDA underfunded? Is FSIS appropriately funded and FDA under funded? Could more risk reduction be achieved with the same "budget" if resources were reallocated? In reality, this table tells us either nothing or very little. For example, the fact that FSIS's share of illnesses with known causes is lower than its share of the food system regulated (15% versus 22%) may be the result of heavier funding for food safety activities in the meat and poultry sector. The outcome measure, illnesses, may be dependent of the input measure, funding. Further, the control case for comparison is not clear. Meat and poultry may be riskier than the products regulated by FDA. In this situation, say we might expect that with an equal intensity of funding, for example, share of budget equal to share of food system sales, meat and poultry would account for 40% of known causes of illness. The fact that the FSIS share of illnesses is less than its share of food sales may be an indicator of the success of the agency's food safety program. The table imparts even less information when we recall that the numbers for the share of known causes of illness are based on 7,000 reported cases when CDC estimates there are 76 million cases annually, of which more than 80% have unknown causes.

So what can be concluded? It may be safe to conclude that FDA, with its 1999 food safety budget of about $300 million, was underfunded. Several critiques of FSIS inspection programs, particularly of its carcass-by-carcass inspection system (e.g., U.S. GAO 1998), argue that FSIS spends too much on in-plant inspection of this type. But this does not indicate whether FSIS's budget is too large or simply needs to be reallocated to more effective activities. The federal government's overall risk reduction effort cannot be evaluated without better understanding of private and public incentives to reduce foodborne risks, risk rankings and priorities based on input from risk assessment, and the cost-effectiveness or benefits and costs of different control options.

What is needed to answer the resource allocation question is all the elements of risk analysis. These include analysis of foodborne risks:

- By pathogen or chemical/other source
- By food category (and other routes of exposure)
- By production phase(s)
- Over time
- By health and other risk outcomes
- By incentives for reduction and regulatory mechanisms
- By the cost-effectiveness and/or benefit–cost analysis of control options.

The challenge is organizing to conduct an effective risk analysis, particularly from a risk portfolio perspective. Additional questions then arise regarding desirable organization that are addressed briefly in the next section.

The Boundary Questions

Food has a variety of quality attributes, for example, safety, nutrition, taste, shelf life, produced at different stages in the supply chain; is traded internationally; and poses risks to safety that are dynamic and ever changing. All of these characteristics lead to boundary issues in organizing the regulatory activities of the federal government. First, how should regulatory boundaries be drawn as food with a mix of quality attributes flows from farm to table? For example, control of foodborne risks associated with hamburger may require changes in practices in farms/feedlots related to animal health, pathogen loads, and animal drug use; in slaughter and processing facilities; in distribution in the retail chain and in handling in food service operations; and in the handling and cooking of food in the home.

As another example, how should boundaries be drawn between regulation of safety and other quality attributes such as nutrition, the absence of economic adulteration, or truthful packaging and labeling? This boundary question is becoming more pressing as the lines between foods, functional foods, nutraceuticals, and drugs become blurred. Given that the supply chain is increasingly integrated and quality attributes may be closely related, how should boundaries be drawn in the regulatory organization regarding who should be in charge of oversight of what? Integrated inspection systems may be more cost effective but require more diverse expertise. Some regulatory decisions are inherently related across different product attributes. For example, label space is limited so the highest priorities for labeling need to be identified across risk and other quality issues.

A second major boundary question relates to international trade in food products. Increased trade means that more food products are being imported into the United States and that the United States is trying to increase its exports to other markets. Domestic regulatory decisions on food safety are now subject to some discipline under the World Trade Organization (WTO). The WTO's Agreement on Sanitary and Phytosanitary Standards sets standards for countries, including requiring that they do not discriminate against products from other countries (national treatment); base regulations on sound science, particularly on risk assessment; and operate systems that are transparent. Thus domestic regulatory programs have to be able to withstand international scrutiny, while providing protection to the domestic market. In addition, in the future the quality of regulatory programs is likely to have a larger influence on competitiveness and access to international markets.

A third boundary question regards new or unknown food safety risks. Who is keeping an eye on the monsters in the closet? The European Union's recent experience with "mad cow" disease suggests a tendency to avert one's eyes or pull the blanket up over one's head. With the fragmented regulatory system in the United States, there is a real potential that new risks will be ignored until it is too late, will not have a constituency, or will fall through the cracks in the mosaic of regulatory responsibility.

Organization of Federal Food Protection Activities

How serious is the problem of making the means of the U.S. regulatory system serve the end of effective risk reduction? Does the current system have fatal flaws, major inefficiencies, or minor inefficiencies? Reformers have suggested that significant reallocation of regulatory resources based on risk analysis may require statutory change, for example, elimination of requirements for carcass by carcass inspection; consolidation of regulatory responsibility in a single agency; or both.

Merrill and Francer essentially argue that simultaneous statutory and organizational reform is too large a task. Their argument is based on political considerations and the likely administrative manageability of a consolidated agency. If both were attempted, either they would not be accomplished or a great deal of dislocation would be present, which might actually impede risk reduction, at least in the short run. Merrill and Francer are agnostic about the usefulness of consolidation of responsibility into a single agency. They argue that, "Reform advocates have not yet been able to portray a new system that could model total foodborne risk and calibrate regulatory requirements accordingly." In contrast, a series of reports by the GAO argues that both statutory reform and consolidation of responsibility are necessary for improvement in the system's performance. A significant move toward management of the foodborne risk portfolio cannot be made when parts of the portfolio are controlled by different agencies in different executive departments.

My conclusion is that opportunities for improvements in the performance of the regulatory system lie with more systematic and disciplined use of risk analysis. This would begin with updating the statutes to recognize risk analysis principles, particularly the use of risk assessment, cost-effectiveness, and cost–benefit analysis to identify means of achieving desired levels of risk reduction as efficiently as possible. These principles should also be included in new legislation. An example where this was not the case is the Food Quality Protection Act passed in 1996, which makes one step forward and one to three steps backward. The step forward was setting a consistent standard for risks from pesticide residues in food. A first possible step backward was setting the standard as a reasonable certainty that no harm will result to infants and children from aggregate exposure to all residues. This is essentially a zero risk standard. A definite step back was the instruction that costs will not be considered in setting this standard. A further step back is limiting the regulatory options to banning pesticides that do not meet the standard. Agencies cannot pursue risk analysis based regulation unless Congress and the President support this approach.

Arguing for disciplined use of risk analysis is not, as concerned consumers fear, a carte blanche to go slow, delay taking action when information is incomplete, or put considerations of costs to industry above benefits to consumers from improved risk reduction. Instead it is a means of assuring that we devote our resources to the important risks, use those resources effectively, and have capacity available to address new risks quickly as they arise.

We clearly need a two-tiered approach to generating better information for effective regulation. The two tiers are (1) broad and shallow information on risks, health outcomes, incentives, benefits, and costs and (2) narrow and in-depth information on risks that appear to be high priority to address. The federal government is generating the second type of information through high-quality risk assessments such as those performed for Salmonella enteritidis, Vibrio parahaemolyticus, and Listeria monocytogenes. However, no one in the federal government is clearly responsible for generating the first type of information, and it is sorely lacking.

Based on this two-tiered system of information, policy makers and risk managers can make judgments on actions that need to be taken by the federal government to address foodborne risk effectively in the United States. Effectiveness can be framed as less risk for the same budget (cost-effectiveness) or in terms of designing a risk reduction portfolio with the lowest cost–benefit ratio. The need for organizational reform can be judged based on how much progress the current system makes toward establishing a risk-analysis–based system of regulation. Of course, the question is, what is the chicken and what is the egg? Can we achieve statutory reform and a stronger move toward a risk-analysis–based approach without consolidation of regulatory authority for food safety?

References

CSPI (Center for Science in the Public Interest), C. Smith DeWaal, L. Alderton, and M.F. Jacobson. 2000. Outbreak Alert! Closing the Gaps in Our Federal Food-Safety Net. August 2000. http://www.cspinet.org/reports/outbreak_alert/index.htm (accessed July 12, 2004).

FSIS (Food Safety and Inspection Service). 1998. Salmonella enteritidis Risk Assessment: Shell Eggs and Egg Products. Final Report Submitted June 12, 1998. Revised with editorial corrections August 10, 1998. http://www.fsis.usda.gov/ophs/risk/index.htm (accessed July 12, 2004).

Mead, P.S., L. Slutsker, V. Dietz, L.F. McCaig, J.S. Bresee, C. Shapiro, P.M. Griffin, and R.V. Tauxe. 1999. Food-Related Illness and Death in the United States. Emerging Infectious Diseases 5 (September–October). http://www.cdc.gov/ncidod/eid/vol5no5/mead.htm (accessed July 12, 2004).

U.S. FDA (Food and Drug Administration), Center for Food Safety and Applied Nutrition. 2001. Draft Risk Assessment on the Public Health Impact of Vibrio parahaemolyticus in Raw Molluscan Shellfish. January 2001. http://www.cfsan.fda.gov/~dms/vprisk.html (accessed July 12, 2004).

———, USDA/FSIS (Food Safety and Inspection Service), and CDC (Centers for Disease Control and Prevention). 2001. Draft Assessment of the Relative Risk to Public Health from Foodborne Listeria monocytogenes Among Selected Categories of Ready-to-Eat Foods. January 2001. http://www.foodsafety.gov/~dms/lmrisk.html (accessed July 12, 2004).

U.S. GAO (General Accounting Office). 1998. Food Safety: Opportunities to Redirect Federal Resources and Funds Can Enhance Effectiveness. GAO/RCED-98-224.

———. 2001. Food Safety: Overview of Federal and State Expenditures. GAO-01-177, February.

15

Toward an Integrated, Risk-Based Food Safety System: Constructing the Analytical Tools

Michael R. Taylor

The preceding chapters of this book document some important shifts that have occurred over the past 20 years in how food safety experts think about achieving food safety. These include the much-expanded focus on microbial hazards in the food supply, the increasing use of risk assessment and risk analysis in food safety decision making, and a new emphasis on prevention of foodborne hazards and illnesses. These shifts are grounded in an improved understanding of the health consequences of foodborne hazards and associated costs, the emergence of new technologies to enhance food safety, and a corresponding public demand for continuous improvement in the food safety performance of government, as well as the performance of private sector food producers, processors, and retailers.

Two seminal reports of the National Academy of Sciences (NAS) chart these developments and their implications for the federal government's food safety program. The 1998 report *Ensuring Safe Food From Production to Consumption* (IOM 1998) called for a more integrated effort among the federal food safety agencies and the pursuit of a more science- and risk-based approach to reducing foodborne illness. It recommended that a single responsible official be charged with directing the federal food safety effort and allocating its resources in ways most likely to reduce the risk of illness. The 2003 NAS report *Scientific Criteria to Ensure Safe Food* (FNB 2003) discussed the need to link food safety hazards and interventions throughout the food production and processing system with health outcomes. It recommended that the federal government establish performance standards at appropriate points in the system as measures of accountability and success in controlling foodborne hazards.

The shifts documented in this book, coupled with the recommendations in the two NAS reports, point toward a food safety system of the future that is much improved in four key areas: (1) prevention of foodborne illness, (2) accountability for the effectiveness of interventions, (3) integration of food safety efforts, and (4) risk-based allocation of resources. The 1998 NAS report recommended fundamental statutory and organizational modernization of the federal food safety system to achieve these improvements, as have, in various forms, the General Accounting Office (U.S. GAO 2001), the President's Food Safety Council (2001), and a number of commentators, including this author (Taylor 2002).

Significant political and practical barriers exist to fundamental statutory and organizational change in the nation's food safety system. With or without such change, however, government and private sector policy makers can benefit from new analytical and decision tools to design and manage a more science- and risk-based food safety system. This concluding chapter explains why such tools are needed, briefly describes the tools, and suggests some of the questions that should be considered in developing them. This chapter draws on the work of the Food Safety Research Consortium (FSRC), whose plans to develop priority-setting and resource allocation tools for a more science- and risk-based food safety system were described in a report issued in 2003 by The Milbank Memorial Fund and Resources for the Future (Taylor 2003).[1]

An Integrated, Systems Model of Foodborne Illness

The need for and the nature of the tools discussed in this chapter are grounded in an integrated "systems" understanding, or model, of foodborne illness. This model has a *causation* element and a *prevention* element and portrays the causation and prevention of foodborne illness as products of the interaction among multiple factors that occur across the entire spectrum from on-farm production to in-home consumption. This integrated understanding of foodborne illness is not new from a scientific perspective, but, as discussed in Chapter 2, it has not been an important factor in the evolution and design of the government's current food safety activities (Taylor 2003).

Causation

The causation element of the integrated, systems model of foodborne illness involves consideration of all the conditions, events, and behaviors that con-

---

[1] Additional information on the Food Safety Research Consortium and its agenda are available on its website at http://www.rff.org/fsrc/fsrc.htm (accessed November 23, 2003).

tribute to a person becoming ill from a foodborne hazard. In the end, whether a foodborne hazard—such as a microbial pathogen or chemical contaminant—makes a person ill depends on the inherent pathogenicity or toxicity of the hazardous agent, the level and duration of exposure, and the sensitivity of the consumer to the agent. The interaction of these factors is labeled here the *exposure event.*

For chemical hazards, such as lead, mercury, and dioxins, the interaction of these factors at the point of consumption is generally considered and described in a predictive way by the science of toxicology and familiar approaches to risk assessment and food safety evaluation, based largely on data from animal studies (Rodricks 1992). For microbiological hazards, the causation of illness at the point of consumption is generally described retrospectively through clinical or epidemiological observation, although predictive risk assessments have been conducted in several important cases, such as *Listeria monocytogenes* (U.S. FDA 2003), *Escherichia coli* O157:H7 (FSIS 2001), and *Salmonella enteriditis* in eggs (FSIS 1998).

In addition to the exposure event at the point of consumption, the causation component of an integrated foodborne illness model requires consideration of the factors that lead to the presence of the pathogen or chemical contaminant in food at a level capable of causing illness (labeled here the *transmission pathway*). For chemical contaminants, these factors include (1) the human activities and natural processes that produce the chemical and result in its presence in food; (2) any bioaccumulation that might occur through the food chain, such as with lipophilic compounds like dioxins; and (3) the level of contamination and patterns of consumption of foods containing the chemical, which, when aggregated for any individual, determine both acute and chronic exposure to the chemical.

For microbiological hazards, the transmission pathway includes all these factors but is made even more complicated by the biological fact of growth, when conditions permit, and the possibility that pathogens can be killed and rendered harmless during processing or cooking. Thus, whether a microbial pathogen is present in food at the point of consumption at a level that is sufficient to cause illness will be a function not only of the level of initial contamination, but also of all the factors that affect the potentially rapid growth and possible death of the pathogen.

In the case of *E. coli* O157:H7, for example, the complex transmission pathway begins in the bovine gut, where specific ecological factors affect the likelihood of colonization and the presence of the pathogen in the feces, which become the vehicle for contamination of food. The complexity continues in the conditions at the animal production level that affect growth and spread of the pathogen among animals, and at slaughter and initial processing of the beef carcass. The slaughter step is when the initial contamination of meat typically occurs, and the likelihood of contamination and the number of organisms is affected by factors such as the particular carcass dressing practices used, carcass sanitizing interventions, and temperature conditions. The transmission pathway then extends all the way through final processing, such as to produce ground beef; storage; distribution; retail sale; and final preparation and cooking for consumption. At each step, the level of contamination—and ultimately the level at which the consumer is exposed—can increase or decrease depending largely on human-controlled conditions of time and temperature and the application of specific pathogen reduction interventions.

To summarize, an understanding of the *causation* of illness for a particular chemical or pathogen is the first element of an integrated, systems model of foodborne illness; and understanding causation requires understanding both the *transmission pathway* and the specific nature of the *exposure event* that leads to illness.

Prevention

The prevention element of an integrated, systems model of foodborne illness is in part the mirror image of the causation element. At every step along the exposure pathway where a human-controlled condition or a human behavior contributes to increasing the level of a pathogen or chemical contaminant, an opportunity exists for a change in behavior or an intervention to reduce the level of contamination. If the cumulative, net effect of any such measures is to reduce the level of a pathogen or chemical contaminant below the level required to cause infection or trigger a toxic response, the potential illness is prevented.

The prevention element of the model encompasses more, however, than a simple mirroring of the transmission pathway in the causation element. An integrated, systems understanding of foodborne illness requires consideration of any plausible opportunity all across the spectrum from production to consumption to reduce the risk of illness, whether or not directly linked with a step in the transmission pathway. In the *E. coli* O157:H7 example, the prevention element might include vaccination of cattle or other interventions to prevent the initial infection, even though initial infection of cattle with these bacteria often occurs naturally. It could also include better reporting and sharing of data on illness outbreaks so that more effective steps can be taken to contain outbreaks and learn from them to improve future prevention measures. In an integrated, systems model of foodborne illness, the outcomes of concern are the illness and its prevention; and all factors that influence these outcomes—whether contributing to causation or prevention—are important to the model.

To summarize, an understanding of the *prevention* of illness for a particular pathogen is the second element of an integrated, systems model of foodborne illness; and understanding prevention requires understanding all of the possible opportunities to intervene with a measure to reduce the risk of illness, the magnitude of its impact on public health, and associated economic costs.

The Need for New Analytical and Decision Tools

The movement toward a more science- and risk-based food safety system begins with this integrated, systems model of foodborne illness, which permits a more complete understanding of the many factors that explain the likelihood of illness from any foodborne hazard. The goal, however, is not merely to understand foodborne illness but to reduce and prevent it by harnessing the best available scientific data and understanding and, on that basis, deploying effort and resources in ways that bring about the greatest reduction in illness with the resources available.

The effort and resources that are relevant to this approach to food safety reside all across the food, agriculture, and health sectors, in both the public and private sectors, and include:

- Government regulatory interventions at the federal, state, and local levels, including standard-setting, inspection, and enforcement, at any appropriate point on the food system spectrum from farm to table.
- Government investments in the form of research, technology transfer, and education that can make available new knowledge and interventions and contribute to the behavioral changes required to reduce the risk of illness.
- The actions of private sector, commercial participants in the food system, as influenced by the forces and incentives of the marketplace and by government interventions, and that contribute to both causing and reducing the burden of illness.
- National, state, and local public health and health care infrastructures, as they affect surveillance, diagnosis, and treatment of foodborne illness and thus the overall effort to reduce the burden of illness.
- The actions of individuals as purchasers, preparers, and consumers of food and thus as agents in the causation and prevention of illness.

This spectrum of actors and actions comprises the nation's *food safety system,* and the basic assurance of food safety Americans enjoy today rests on the day-to-day activities of these actors. The food safety agencies are implementing food safety laws and regulatory programs that require commercial participants in the system to observe good sanitation practices and guard against the presence of harmful chemicals and bacteria in food. Food producers, processors, and retailers have their own food safety programs that often, in response to market pressures, go beyond what the government requires. In addition, consumers themselves play a significant role in the causation and prevention of illness through their own food handling and preparation practices.

As demonstrated, however, by the persistence of foodborne illness as a significant public health issue,[2] room for improvement exists in how the food safety system is currently working to prevent foodborne illness. The two NAS reports noted earlier describe opportunities to refocus and redeploy the efforts and resources of the food safety system in ways more likely to reduce the risk of illness. Such refocusing and redeployment comprise the essence of the science- and risk-based approach to food safety, to which most participants in the food safety system aspire.

The unresolved question is how best to do it. If we are to shift effort and resources to more productive risk reduction activities, how do we decide what they are? How do we know what are the most important foodborne hazards from a public health perspective? How do we prioritize opportunities to reduce risk? How do we integrate answers to these questions with all the other factors that are properly relevant to allocating both public and private food safety resources?

Policy makers answer these questions every day, sometimes explicitly, based on their judgment and available information about specific problems. At least as often, they answer these questions implicitly, through their decisions and actions, without overt consideration of how particular actions compare with other possible actions in terms of potential contribution to risk reduction. But, across the board, policy makers lack analytical and decision tools that would permit them to harness systematically all relevant and available information and make rigorous, data-driven decisions about how best to deploy their efforts and resources. Such tools are essential if the aspirations for a science- and risk-based food safety system are to be fulfilled.

Constructing the Analytical and Decision Tools

A science- and risk-based food safety system requires tools to help perform at least three functions: (1) ranking the public health impact of foodborne hazards, (2) prioritizing opportunities to reduce the risk of illness, and (3) allocating the efforts and resources of the food safety system.

Ranking Public Health Impacts

The first step in designing and implementing a science- and risk-based food safety system is identifying the most important food safety problems from a public health perspective. This knowledge does not, by itself, answer the question of how best to deploy food safety efforts and resources, but it helps policy

[2]The Centers for Disease Control and Prevention (CDC) estimates that the known bacterial and viral pathogens in food result annually in 5,000 deaths, 325,000 illness, and 76 million cases of illness (Mead et al. 1999).

makers focus their further analytical work and possible data collection on the specific foodborne hazards that are making the greatest contribution to foodborne illness and its adverse health consequences.

As discussed in Chapter 3, the Centers for Disease Control and Prevention (CDC) reports through its FoodNet sentinel site surveillance system on illnesses associated with specific pathogens, and, based on these and other data, CDC estimates the nationwide incidence of illness—reported as the number of cases, hospitalizations, and deaths—associated with a range of bacterial and viral pathogens (Mead et al. 1999). This permits a ranking of pathogens on the basis of their contributions to these categories of health outcomes, but more is needed to rank foodborne hazards for policy-making purposes.

For practical reasons, government food safety regulation is organized around categories of food, not pathogens. Thus, to rank the public health impact of foodborne hazards for policy-making purposes, it is necessary to attribute the illnesses associated with particular pathogens not only to the pathogen but also to the foods bearing the illness-causing pathogens, and thus to be able to rank the health impact of specific pathogen–food combinations. Examples of pathogen–food combinations include *Salmonella* in poultry, *Listeria monocytogenes* in dairy products, and *E. coli* O157:H7 in ground beef.

Finally, rankings of public health impact need to consider and compare the relative health significance of illnesses associated with specific pathogen–food combinations. Some pathogens result mostly in transitory gastrointestinal infection and diarrhea. Others pose a greater risk of hospitalization, long-term health damage, and death. To rank public health impacts of pathogen–food combinations, these diverse health outcomes must be valued in some fashion so that, for example, the public health importance of 1,000 transitory cases of diarrhea can be compared with the public health importance of 10 hospitalizations, or one death. The valuation possibilities include (1) calculations of the cost of illness in terms of medical costs and lost productivity; (2) values derived using tools of economic analysis that measure the individual's willingness to pay (WTP) to avoid the total loss of welfare associated with an illness, including pain and suffering; and (3) measures of loss of health function used in the medical field, such as the quality-adjusted life year (QALY) tool.

The point of these valuations and comparisons is not to suggest that any illness is unimportant or unworthy of preventive efforts. Under current food safety laws, the food industry has a general obligation to prevent harmful contamination of any kind, and even transitory illnesses are of concern to consumers. The point of these comparisons is to inform decisions about how best to deploy available and inevitably scarce resources within the food safety system to do a better job of reducing the public health impact of foodborne illness.

Ranking the public health impact of specific pathogen–food combinations thus requires an analytical tool that can integrate data on: (1) the incidence of adverse health outcomes associated with specific pathogens or chemicals, (2) the attribution of these outcomes to specific food categories, and (3) the relative health importance of these outcomes. FSRC, with funding from The Robert Wood Johnson Foundation, has developed such a tool in the form of an interactive and adaptable computer-based model for ranking the public health impact of specific pathogen–food combinations (FSRC 2003). A number of issues remain to be addressed, however, in further developing tools for ranking the public health impact of foodborne hazards, including:

- *Gaps in data:* The data on incidence of illness are improving through the FoodNet active surveillance system administered by the CDC in collaboration with state health departments.[3] Significant gaps, however, are found in the data that permit the linking of illnesses to specific pathogen–food combinations. Currently, the best available data for making such attributions are derived from investigations and reports of illness outbreaks,[4] but further work is required to learn more about the foods and pathogens causing the sporadic cases that comprise the majority of foodborne illness outcomes.
- *Chemicals:* For policy-making purposes, it will be important to include in the ranking of public health impacts of foodborne hazards the risks posed by chemicals, especially environmental contaminants such as lead, mercury, dioxins, and aflatoxin. These chemicals are not subject to a premarket safety review, such as applied to food additives and pesticide residues, and may pose risks that justify further control efforts.
- *Valuation method:* Active debate is ongoing about how best to measure the value of health outcomes and, in turn, the benefits of preventing illnesses.[5] Moving toward a more common understanding of how best to value health outcomes for food safety purposes, using one or more of the methods outlined earlier or perhaps an integrated valuation index, will be important to the future use of risk ranking in policy making.

Models for Prioritizing Risk Reduction Opportunities and Interventions

Knowing the relative public health impact of key food safety hazards is an important step toward being able to prioritize and plan efforts to reduce illness,

[3]Further information is available on the FoodNet website at http://www.cdc.gov/foodnet/ (accessed November 23, 2003).

[4]The most complete, publicly accessible compilation is maintained by the Centers for Science in the Public Interest. http://www.cspinet.org/reports/outbreak_report.pdf (accessed November 23, 2003).

[5]See materials from a Resources for the Future (RFF) Conference on Valuing Health Outcomes, conducted in February 2003. http://www.rff.org/rff/Events/calendardetail.cfm?eventID=254&eventyear=2003 (accessed November 23, 2003).

because it enables policy makers and risk managers to focus their data collection and analytical efforts on the most important problems. Risk ranking is, however, only a first step.

The central analytical task in a more science- and risk-based food safety system is prioritizing opportunities to reduce risk, focusing on the most significant risks, but taking into account also the feasibility, effectiveness, and cost of risk reduction interventions. This task is central because it provides the basis for answering the question of how efforts and resources can best be deployed to achieve the greatest reduction in risk with the available resources. Such analysis can also help demonstrate the potential benefits of devoting additional resources to food safety.

Prioritizing risk reduction opportunities and interventions requires decision tools and analysis that do not exist today. The starting point is the integrated, systems model of foodborne illness described earlier. Such a model would provide the framework for understanding, with respect to any foodborne hazard, the factors that affect the causation and prevention of illness and how the factors interact. To be useful for priority setting, this model would have to be capable of predicting how alterations in one or more of the causation or prevention factors would affect the risk of illness associated with a particular foodborne hazard. Using the example of *E. coli* O157:H7 in beef, how would the likelihood of illness be affected by changes in the percentage of colonized cows on feedlots? Or by sanitizing interventions of a given effectiveness implemented in slaughter plants? Or by the temperature at which ground beef is stored and cooked? How do these factors and possible changes in them interact to affect the risk of illness?

A model capable of answering such questions would permit analysts for the first time to link possible changes in food production and handling practices with health outcomes and to project the likely effect of possible risk reduction interventions. Just as the risk-ranking model provides the basis for focusing on the most significant hazards in the food supply, the integrated, systems model of foodborne illness, when applied to particular hazards, provides the basis for focusing on the points in the farm-to-table continuum where interventions are likely to have the greatest impact in reducing illness.

Developing this foundational model for a more science- and risk-based food safety system, and making it functional, will be challenging. It will likely require both the integration of existing knowledge and new research on the relationships among the many factors that contribute to causing and preventing foodborne illness. It will require harnessing the tools of mathematics to model and describe these relationships; and it will require the assembly, and possibly new collection, of considerable data on specific foodborne hazards and existing technologies to prevent or mitigate their risk from farm to table. The model's contribution to a more science- and risk-based food safety system will, however, be substantial. In addition to enabling analysts to focus on the most promising points in the system for risk reduction interventions, it provides a framework for the risk management analysis needed to design intervention strategies that make the best use of available efforts and resources to reduce the risk of illness.

The matters discussed so far—ranking the public health impact of specific foodborne hazards and modeling the causation and prevention of illness—are elements of *risk assessment* in the classic risk assessment–risk management paradigm (NAS 1983). Deciding how to prioritize opportunities to reduce risk and allocate food safety efforts and resources is *risk management.* The risk management analysis that would go into prioritizing opportunities to reduce risk includes analysis of the effectiveness and cost of existing interventions and the feasibility, effectiveness, and cost of potential new or modified interventions. In most food safety decision making to date, little has been done to evaluate current or proposed interventions rigorously, especially regarding their relative cost-effectiveness and how they interact with each and the other factors that affect the risk of illness. That is just the kind of analysis that is envisioned in the approach to priority setting outlined here, as described in the following paragraphs.

Evaluating Current Interventions to Reduce Risk. If the goal is to assess how the risk associated with a set of foodborne hazards can be reduced by adopting new intervention strategies, the analytical starting point is an understanding of what current interventions are achieving with respect to those hazards, and at what cost to the food safety system. The choice of hazards to be included in the analysis would be guided by the risk-ranking model described earlier, and the analysis would permit the identification of the most promising opportunities to reduce risk.

The analysis of current interventions requires mapping the points throughout the food chain where contamination and resulting human exposures to the hazards being analyzed can be prevented, minimized, and reduced and identifying the practices and interventions that are currently in place to do so. The mapping of interventions should be as comprehensive as possible, including: (1) actions by commercial participants in the food system through preventive controls and other contamination and exposure reduction strategies; (2) government interventions, including food safety research, regulation, and education; and (3) actions of individuals as purchasers, preparers, and consumers of food.

This stage of analysis then requires asking with respect to the risks being examined such questions as:

- Are generally observed food hygiene practices in the commercial food production sector and among consumers addressing the initial contamination and resulting risk?
- Have targeted interventions to minimize the risks been implemented? If so, At what point in the farm-to-table spectrum?

By whom?

In response to what signal: regulatory? Private tort liability? Market pressure?

- To what extent have current interventions, both general and targeted, been effective in reducing risk?
- What is the nature and value of the risk reduction benefit being achieved?
- What are the costs of current interventions?

  To government?

  To the private sector?

  To consumers?

- What is the impact of current approaches to reporting, diagnosing, and treating foodborne illness?

The answers to these questions permit an appraisal of how well and at what cost current food safety practices and interventions are working to reduce the risk of illness, on an individual basis and in comparison to one another. The next step is to identify and evaluate potential new interventions.

Identifying and Evaluating Potential New Interventions to Reduce Risk. Based on the evaluation of existing interventions outlined earlier, this step involves identifying points along the farm-to-table spectrum where hazards are not being addressed or where opportunities exist to implement new interventions that would improve the prevention or reduction of illness. It then involves asking questions such as:

- Are any practices or technologies known that could prevent or mitigate hazards at these points?
- Why are they not being implemented?
- How might implementation of these interventions be induced?

  Through government regulation?

  Through market-based incentives?

  Through commercial food handler or consumer education?

  Other approaches?

- For any intervention or set of interventions, what degree of effectiveness can reasonably be expected in altering the particular factors in causation or prevention of illness to which the interventions are addressed?
- What are the costs of the interventions?

  To the government?

  To the private sector?

  To consumers?

- Are there key gaps in knowledge that limit the ability to prevent or mitigate the hazard and that could be filled through data collection or other research?

  At what cost?

  Over what time frame?

• Are there possible changes in current practices for reporting, diagnosing, and treating illness that would reduce its public health impact? At what cost?

Constructing Priority-Setting Models. The information obtained through these evaluations of existing and potential new interventions provides the basis for identifying the risk reduction opportunities and intervention strategies—whether in the form of research, regulation, or education—that appear likely to make the greatest contribution to reducing risk. Models for prioritizing risk reduction opportunities and interventions would integrate and analyze the results of these analyses, for two purposes: (1) to project and place a value on the risk reduction benefit that is achievable through one or some combination of new interventions, and (2) to rank the risk reduction opportunities and intervention strategies on the basis of their cost-effectiveness.

The model for accomplishing the first analytical task would draw on both the integrated, systems model for causation and prevention of foodborne illness and elements of the risk-ranking model described earlier. The integrated systems model is a tool for projecting quantitatively the reductions in foodborne illness—in terms of fewer illnesses, hospitalizations, and deaths—that could result from particular intervention strategies. The valuation elements of the risk-ranking model could then be used to value the public health impact of those risk reductions for comparison and ranking purposes.

In a priority-setting system designed to achieve the greatest reductions in the public health burden of foodborne illness with the available resources, the final, critical step is to integrate information on the cost of achieving the reductions. For policy makers responsible for designing the government's food safety program and allocating its efforts and resources, the primary consideration here is the cost to the government of designing and implementing the intervention. Private sector costs are also relevant to the analysis for two public policy reasons. First, under current Executive Orders, the costs and benefits of significant regulatory interventions must be evaluated, with the goal of maximizing benefits in relation to the costs and, ideally, ensuring that the overall social benefits exceed the social costs.[6] Second, in a food safety system that is recognized to encompass both public and private sector efforts and in which all possible intervention strategies should be considered, the feasibility and cost of risk reduction interventions to commercial participants are relevant to devising, through public policy, market-based incentives for reducing the risk of illness.

[6]See Memorandum for the President's Management Council, from John D. Graham, Administrator, Office of Information and Regulatory Affairs (OIRA), Office of Management and Budget, Executive Office of the President, Re: Presidential Review of Agency Rulemaking by OIRA, September 20, 2001. http://www.whitehouse.gov/omb/inforeg/oira_review-process.html (accessed November 23, 2003).

The ultimate task of the priority-setting model is to integrate the information on the public health value of risk reductions achievable through particular intervention strategies with information on the cost of the interventions. The analytical goals are to (1) provide a measure of the cost-effectiveness of particular interventions, in terms of the magnitude of the risk reduction achievable per unit of expenditure; (2) provide a basis for comparing and ranking the cost-effectiveness of interventions; and (3) determine in the aggregate the combination of risk reduction opportunities and interventions that together are likely to achieve the greatest overall reduction in the public health burden of foodborne illness.

This conceptual overview of the models required to prioritize risk reduction opportunities and intervention strategies, even when presented in this simplified form, suggests some of the challenges involved in constructing and applying the models. These include the need for: (1) a better understanding of the physical and biological relationships and interactions among the numerous factors affecting causation and prevention of illness, (2) hazard-specific data to apply this understanding to particular hazards, and (3) information on the cost and effectiveness of interventions.

Over the past two decades, an enormous amount of foodborne illness and food safety research and data collection that is relevant to these issues have been conducted by government, academic, and food industry researchers. Much of the required data for food safety priority setting thus exists. A critical challenge will be to access and assemble existing data in a way that makes them useful to analysts seeking to improve the effectiveness of the food safety system in reducing risk. No doubt, however, important gaps remain in the data available for this purpose. One important benefit of developing the priority-setting models will be to help identify the most critical missing data that need to be produced through future research and data collection.

Resource Allocation Model

In a more science- and risk-based food safety system, policy makers will ground their efforts in risk ranking and prioritization of opportunities and interventions to reduce risk. In allocating their resources prospectively, however, policy makers must also take account of legislative mandates, including the cost and risk reduction effectiveness of pre-market approval systems and mandated inspection activity; other public health and public policy priorities, such as bioterrorism; and necessary contingencies for unplanned and unpredictable events. Thus, risk-ranking and priority-setting models of the kind discussed here ultimately must be supplemented with an overall resource allocation model that takes these factors into account.

Such a model would be unavoidably less empirical and data driven than the risk-ranking or priority-setting models outlined earlier. Moreover, neither government nor private decision making about food safety can or should be reduced to a formula. Nevertheless, a resource allocation model that builds on the risk-ranking and priority-setting models outlined earlier would provide a framework for making resource allocation decisions that more rigorously integrates risk analysis and risk-based priorities into decision making than is the case at present.

Practical Utility of the Models

The models outlined here should be practical tools for policy makers and others interested in how best to solve the problem of foodborne illness. They should be used in an on-going, dynamic process that makes data collection, risk analysis, and program evaluation "built-in" features of how society addresses foodborne illness, with continuous feedback as risk patterns change and progress occurs over time.

The *risk ranking model* provides guidance on where to focus efforts, a framework for targeted collection of data to refine and adjust rankings over time, and an ongoing tool for monitoring changes in the relative importance, and thus possible priority, of foodborne hazards.

The *model for prioritizing opportunities and interventions to reduce risk* is intended to inform priority setting and resource allocation in both the public and private sectors. The data and understanding it will generate about the effectiveness of current and proposed interventions should lead to the development of more effective risk management strategies for food safety.

The *resource allocation model* is primarily a tool for public policy makers to help incorporate the insights gained through risk analysis into a big picture understanding of how best to manage the food safety system.

Conclusion

This chapter provides a conceptual overview of an approach to priority setting and resource allocation in the nation's food safety system. It is an approach that builds on much that has been achieved within the food safety system over the past decade to improve the system's focus on the most significant hazards and on the goal of reducing the public health burden of foodborne illness. It is an approach that is, by design, more quantitative and analytically rigorous than current approaches to food safety policy making and resource allocation. It is intended, however, to be a practical approach that can be useful in the real world of government decision making. Much work remains to be done to develop the tools described here. For the tools to achieve their purpose and make a meaningful contribution to improving food safety in the United States, the work must engage the creativity and effort of scientists, policy makers, and food safety practitioners throughout the food system.

Acknowledgments

This chapter draws substantially on a draft paper prepared by the author as background for a Food Safety Research Consortium project to develop a conceptual framework for prioritizing opportunities to reduce risk. The author acknowledges with gratitude the collective contribution of his FSRC colleagues to the thinking underlying the systems approach to food safety priority setting outlined in the chapter and the important contributions of Julie Caswell, Glenn Morris, Catherine Woteki, and Helen Jensen to the draft paper on which this chapter is based.

References

FNB (Food and Nutrition Board). 2003. *Scientific Criteria to Ensure Safe Food.* Washington, DC: National Academy Press.

FSIS (Food Safety and Inspection Service) U.S. Department of Agriculture. 1998. Salmonella *Enteritidis* Risk Assessment: Shell Eggs and Egg Products. Available at: http://www.fsis.usda.gov/OPHS/risk/index.htm (accessed November 24, 2003).

———. 2001. Draft Risk Assessment of Public Health Impact of *Escherichia coli* 0157:H7 in Ground Beef. Available at: http://www.fsis.usda.gov/oa/topics/o157.htm (accessed November 24, 2003).

IOM (Institute of Medicine). 1998. *Ensuring Safe Food From Production to Consumption.* Washington, DC: National Academy Press.

Mead, P.S., L. Slutsker, V. Dietz, L.F. McCaig, J.S. Breese, C. Shapiro, P.M. Griffin, and R.V. Tauxe. 1999. Food-Related Illness and Death in the United States. *Emerging Infectious Diseases* 5(5): 607–25.

President's Council on Food Safety. 2001 (January 19). *Food Safety Strategic Plan.* Available at http://www.foodsafety.gov/~fsg/cstrpl-4.html (accessed November 23, 2003).

Rodricks, J.V. 1992. *Calculated Risks: Understanding the Toxicity of Chemicals in Our Environment.* Cambridge, UK: Cambridge University Press.

Taylor, M.R. 2002. Reforming Food Safety: A Model for the Future. *Food Technology* 56(5): 190–94.

——— M.O'K. Glavin, J.G. Morris, and C.E. Woteki. 2003. *Food Safety Updated: Developing Tools for a More Science- and Risk-Based Approach.* New York: Milbank Memorial Fund.

U.S. FDA (Food and Drug Administration). 2003. Quantitative Assessment of the Relative Risk to Public Health from Foodborne *Listeria monocytogenes* Among Selected Categories of Ready-to-Eat Foods. http://www.foodsafety.gov/~dms/fs-toc.html (accessed November 24, 2003).

U.S. GAO (General Accounting Office). 2001. *Food Safety and Security – Fundamental Changes Needed to Ensure Safe Food.* GAO-02-47T. Washington, DC.

Appendix A

Responsibilities of Federal Agencies Involved with Food Safety*

The *Agricultural Marketing Service* (AMS), within USDA, is primarily responsible for establishing the standards of quality and condition and for grading the quality of dairy, egg, fruit, meat, poultry, seafood, and vegetable products. As part of this grading process, AMS considers safety factors, such as the cleanliness of the product. AMS carries out its wide array of programs to facilitate marketing under more than 30 statutes—for example, the Agricultural Marketing Agreement Act of 1937, as amended; the Agricultural Marketing Act of 1946, as amended; the Egg Products Inspection Act, as amended; the Export Apple and Pear Act, as amended; and the Export Grape and Plum Act, as amended. AMS is funded largely with user fees.

The *Agricultural Research Service* (ARS), within USDA, is responsible for conducting a wide range of research relating to the Department's mission, including food safety research. ARS carries out its programs under the Department of Agriculture Organic Act of 1862; the Research and Marketing Act of 1946, as amended; and the National Agricultural Research, Extension, and Teaching Policy Act of 1977, as amended.

The *Animal and Plant Health Inspection Service* (APHIS), within USDA, is responsible for ensuring the health and care of animals and plants. APHIS has no statutory authority for public health issues unless the concern to public health is also a concern to the health of animals or plants. APHIS identifies research and data needs and coordinates research programs designed to protect the animal industry against pathogens or diseases that are a risk to humans to improve food safety.

*Source: GAO, *Food Safety: Opportunities to Redirect Federal Resources and Funds Can Enhance Effectiveness*, GAO/RCED-98-224, August 1998.

The *Bureau of Alcohol, Tobacco, and Firearms* (ATF), within the Department of the Treasury, is responsible for administering and enforcing laws covering the production, including safety; use; and distribution of alcoholic beverages under the Federal Alcohol Administration Act and the Internal Revenue Code.

The *Centers for Disease Control and Prevention* (CDC), within HHS, is charged with protecting the nation's public health by providing leadership and direction in preventing and controlling diseases and responding to public health emergencies. The CDC conducts surveillance for foodborne diseases; develops new epidemiological and laboratory tools to enhance the surveillance and detection of outbreaks; and performs other activities to strengthen local, state, and national capacity to identify, characterize, and control foodborne hazards. The CDC engages in public health activities related to food safety under the general authority of the Public Health Service Act, as amended.

The *Food Safety and Inspection Service* (FSIS), within the U.S. Department of Agriculture (USDA), is responsible for ensuring that meat, poultry, and processed egg products moving in interstate and foreign commerce are safe, wholesome, and correctly marked, labeled, and packaged. The FSIS carries out its meat and poultry inspection responsibilities under the Federal Meat Inspection Act, as amended, and the Poultry Products Inspection Act, as amended. Amendments to these acts require that meat inspected by state inspection programs as well as imported meat meet inspection standards "at least equal to" those of the federal program. Furthermore, the Department of Agriculture Reorganization Act of 1994 transferred to FSIS some food safety inspections previously performed by other organizations within USDA.

The *Grain Inspection, Packers and Stockyards Administration* (GIPSA), within USDA, is responsible for establishing quality standards and providing for a national inspection system to facilitate the marketing of grain and other related products. Certain inspection services, such as testing corn for the presence of aflatoxin, enable the market to assess the value of a product on the basis of its compliance with contractual specifications and FDA requirements. Those requesting inspection services, typically the owner of the grain, are responsible for complying with FDA regulations. GIPSA has no regulatory responsibility regarding food safety. Under a memorandum of understanding with FDA, GIPSA reports to FDA certain lots of grain, rice, pulses, or food products, which were officially inspected as part of GIPSA's service functions, that are considered objectionable under the Federal Food, Drug, and Cosmetic Act. GIPSA carries out its responsibilities under the U.S. Grain Standards Act, as amended, and the Agricultural Marketing Act of 1946, as amended.

The *National Marine Fisheries Service* (NMFS), within the Department of Commerce, conducts its voluntary seafood safety and quality inspection programs under the Agricultural Marketing Act of 1946, as amended, and the Fish and Wildlife Act of 1956, as amended. In addition to the inspection and certification services provided for fishery products for human consumption, NMFS provides inspection and certification services for animal feeds and pet foods containing a fish base.

The *U.S. Customs Service,* within the Department of the Treasury, is responsible for collecting revenues and enforcing various customs and related laws. Customs assists FDA and FSIS in carrying out their regulatory roles in food safety.

The *U.S. Environmental Protection Agency* (EPA) is responsible for regulating all pesticide products sold or distributed in the United States and setting maximum allowed residue levels—tolerances—for pesticides on food commodities and animal feed. EPA's activities are conducted under the Federal Insecticide, Fungicide, and Rodenticide Act, as amended, and the Federal Food, Drug, and Cosmetic Act, as amended. The Federal Trade Commission (FTC) enforces the Federal Trade Commission Act, which prohibits unfair or deceptive acts or practices. FTC's food safety objective is to prevent consumer deception through the misrepresentation of food.

The *U.S. Food and Drug Administration* (FDA), within the Department of Health and Human Services (HHS), is responsible for ensuring that domestic and imported food products (except meat, poultry, and processed egg products) are safe, wholesome, and properly labeled. The Federal Food, Drug, and Cosmetic Act, as amended, is the major law governing the FDA's activities to ensure food safety and quality. The Act also authorizes the FDA to maintain a surveillance of all animal drugs, feeds, and veterinary devices to ensure that drugs and feeds used in animals are safe and properly labeled, and produce no human health hazards when used in food-producing animals.

Index